MacArthur and Wainwright

MacArthur and Wainwright

Sacrifice of the Philippines

John Jacob Beck

Foreword by
CLARE BOOTHE LUCE

UNIVERSITY OF NEW MEXICO PRESS
Albuquerque

*To my friend Alma M. Myers, who was
a constant source of common sense,
wisdom, and encouragement*

History . . . is
the tranquil echo
of ugly matters.

—Ben Hecht

Foreword

Knowest thou not there is but one theme for ever-enduring bards?
And that is the theme of War, the fortune of battles,
The making of perfect soldiers.

—Walt Whitman
As I Ponder'd in Silence—1870

Clausewitz called war a continuation of policy by other means. But the course of war is so fraught with incalculable risks, and its fortunes so unpredictable, that its outcome often makes a mockery of the very policy that dictated it.

War is not only the most hazardous, it is the most hideous of all human undertakings. It is the violent disruption of lives, and killing on a massive scale. It ruins in an hour the noblest works of the ages. Its costs in blood and money are often greater than the gains for which it is fought. Its grandest victories are only a little less dreadful than its direst defeats. The passions and the hatreds it engenders seldom evaporate with the smoke of the last battle. The pride of the victor and the vengefulness of the vanquished are the seedbed of the next war. War's greatest legacy is not peace. It is more war, or mayhap revolution.

But the paradox of war, mankind's greatest evil, is that it often inspires men to astounding deeds of courage and self-sacrifice. "Greater love hath no man than this, that a man lay down his life for his friends." In war's fratricidal hell, bonds of brotherly love are often forged which are stronger than death itself.

In all the annals of World War II, there is no more heroic and tragic chapter than the one written by General Douglas MacArthur and General Jonathan M. Wainwright in the Philippines. Theirs is the story of the perfect devotion of two "perfect soldiers" to duty, honor, country, and of that "greater love" which they and their men displayed all during the five agonizing months of bloody combats that ended with the dreadful Bataan Death March.

Mr. Beck foregoes the imaginative or interpretive approach one might expect of the journalist, novelist, or historian. His aim is to be rigorously factual and objective. An assiduous researcher and documentarian, he has exhumed his basic material from the official archives of World War II. He has put together, in chronological order, the once Top Secret and Eyes Only messages that passed between Mac-Arthur's headquarters and the War Department, from December 7, 1941—the day of Pearl Harbor—to May 6, 1942, the day the tattered American flag was hauled down over the Rock of Corregidor, and the white flag was raised by General Wainwright.

These messages form the backbone of the book. But they are well fleshed out with carefully chosen excerpts from the biographies, diaries, memoranda, letters, and accounts of those who actively participated in or influenced MacArthur's desperate struggle to save the Philippine Archipelago from the Japanese invader.

Curiously enough, despite the author's dispassionate approach, the effect that he has achieved is extraordinarily dramatic.

The leading characters in this epic of war are General Douglas MacArthur, Commander of the United States Armed Forces in the Far East (USAFFE); his key staff members and officers; Manuel Quezon, President of the Philippines; Francis B. Sayre, U.S. High Commissioner; and, in Washington, President Franklin D. Roosevelt; Henry L. Stimson, Secretary of War; and Chief of Staff General George C. Marshall.

These characters speak for themselves, and of themselves, in the many messages they send to one another while they are all being inexorably driven to face up to the certainty of MacArthur's utter defeat. And as they speak, it is as though their tragic dialogue were uttered into our own ears.

Hard on the dual shock of Pearl Harbor and the destruction of MacArthur's bombers on the ground at Clark Field, we hear his first imperious demands on Washington for the ships, planes, weapons, and men he will need to hurl back the invaders; then, his incredulity and mounting anger when he is told that, owing to the disaster to the fleet at Pearl Harbor and the more urgent necessities of the war in the Atlantic, his demands cannot be met. We hear him hopelessly argue the highest matters of strategy with his President, as he insists that the war against Hirohito should be given priority over the war against Hitler. We hear him slowly, and bitterly, change his demands for the means of victory to entreaties for the means of mere survival—for medicine and food for the men and women in his beseiged fortress on Corregidor.

We hear the passionate pleas of President Quezon to President Roosevelt for help to his suffering people, and his angry threats to neutralize his country if it is not soon forthcoming. (We seem to hear him spitting out his lungs, as he lies on his bed in the Malinta tunnel on the Rock, dying of tuberculosis.) And again and again we hear the compassionately couched but stern and tightly reasoned refusals of Washington to send any relief to MacArthur's retreating Filo-American armies in Luzon, or to his small, hungry, and sick band of men and women in the bomb-blasted fort, as it threatens to become the tomb of all of them.

Then, as all hope of succor dies, we hear General MacArthur announcing as calmly as though he were saying, "It looks like rain," "The end here will be brutal and bloody." And we weep with the weeping Stimson when he replies, "There are times when men have to die." We hear many men weep in this story. But none for themselves. We hear the sobs of MacArthur's wife and small son, and of Quezon's young daughters. And then we hear Stimson and the President, under the pressure of American public opinion, planning to rescue MacArthur himself. And we hear MacArthur's soldierly refusal to abandon his men.

And when, despite his protests, MacArthur is sternly ordered by the President to effect his escape and that of his family, with the threat of a court-martial if he again refuses, we hear his joyless acceptance of the order.

In the end, we hear the modest and gallant Wainwright, "the soldier's soldier," calmly assume the command of the doomed Rock, knowing that the only alternative to an inglorious surrender is death, and hopeful that the luck of war will permit him the proud alternative to die.

What is, perhaps, most curious about this essentially documentary book, constricted so largely to terse, disciplined official messages, is how vividly the characters and personalities of the *dramatis personae* come through them, and, perhaps even more strangely, how clearly the ever-nearing roar of the battle and the mounting moans of the dying echo through its pages. The last dreadful days of the USAFFE in the Philippines are not described here. But from all that has gone before, we nevertheless seem to see them.

"Every mistake in war is excusable except inactivity and refusal to take risks," wrote that scholar of war, Commander H. H. Frost.

As this book shows, MacArthur, a brilliant strategist and shrewd tactician, a military scholar, and a former Chief of Staff, nevertheless made his share of mistakes in the Philippines. But inactivity and the refusal to take risks were not among them. (The escape of Mac-Arthur and his party from Corregidor is as risky and as suspenseful an episode as military history affords.)

MacArthur's character was flawed by an egotism that demanded consummate obedience not only to his orders, but to his ideas and his person as well. He plainly relished idolatry. But to those who gave it to him, he gave a lambent loyalty in return. He refused to leave his men until he had been given the strongest presidential assurances that his new mission in Australia would be to amass there a force to rescue them. "I shall return," he said. And none doubted him. His soldierly virtues far outshone his human faults. He was a captain of supreme courage and fortitude, with that concern and compassion for his troops and unconcern for his personal safety which deserve the title "hero."

MacArthur's campaign, waged from Australia to reconquer all the Japanese-held islands of the Pacific, including Japan itself, ended in complete victory. But there is no doubt that in the long and triumphant history of the soldier MacArthur, his defense of the Philippines was his finest hour.

The student of American military history will find little in Mr. Beck's book that is new. But the lay reader who has been brought up believing that the Japanese "sneak attack" on Pearl Harbor was a totally unexpected event and the precipitating cause of America's entry into World War II is, perhaps, in for a surprise.

Reading the messages that passed between MacArthur and Washington, he may be startled to learn that, a year before Pearl Harbor, the Roosevelt Administration had reached the decision that it was to the best interests of the U.S. to enter the war against the Axis powers. What was needed was a *casus belli* that would be totally acceptable to the American people. In the isolationist climate of America, Roosevelt was forced to "back into the war" by encouraging an overt Japanese attack on American soil. By embargoing the oil and steel vital to the Japanese war machine in China and the Far East, the Administration knowingly and deliberately took the step which it believed would sooner or later provoke Imperial Japan to war. Roosevelt's mistake, and no doubt Stimson's and Marshall's, was in thinking that if—or rather when—the desired Japanese attack came, it would be made first on the Philippines. Washington war planners, no less than MacArthur, saw the Philippines as the key to the command of all Asian waters. Without securing it, the Japanese could not hope to continue their war against the Chinese, Dutch, and British. The "bottling up" of the U.S. Pacific Fleet in Pearl Harbor was probably ordered partly to convince the American people that the Administration itself had no warlike intentions against Japan (which was not true), and partly to encourage the Japanese to make their move freely against the Philippines. The idea that the Japanese fleet had the capacity—and the daring—to strike at Pearl Harbor does not seem to have occurred to America's war planners. *Bull*

If such was the thinking of the Administration, it proved to be one of the costliest errors ever made in military history. The totally unexpected destruction of a large part of the U.S. Pacific Fleet, idling at anchor in Pearl Harbor, sealed the fate of the Philippines, Hong Kong, Indonesia, and the Malay Peninsula, prolonged the war against Japan for years, and cost thousands upon thousands of American lives. The extent to which the holocaust at Pearl crippled—and traumatized—the Navy in the first year of the war is referred to again and again in MacArthur's Philippine dispatches. (Anyone who wonders why the men of the Navy are something less than enthusiastic about MacArthur will find the answers in these pages.)

On the other hand, "The day that will live in infamy" united the American people as no other conceivable event could have done, and almost in a matter of months turned the United States into the mightiest machine for war that the world had ever so far seen.

The official messages in this book also offer some interesting clues to Roosevelt's pre–Pearl Harbor military strategy. They reveal, though not explicitly, that a firm agreement had been reached between London and Washington that if—or rather when—America got into war "by the Pacific back-door," it would give military priority to the Atlantic "front-door" war. The Roosevelt Administration reasoned, and certainly wisely, that the maintenance of the freedom of the British Isles was more important to the security of the United States than was the salvation of the Philippines. It is hard to believe that General MacArthur was not also aware of this high-level, secret decision. It is clear, however, from the messages in this book, that he could not bring himself to accept it as militarily sound.

There is, perhaps, no greater measure of MacArthur, the soldier, and MacArthur, the man, than this: more than eight thousand miles from Washington, in command of vastly outnumbered, untrained, and retreating troops, bereft of war planes, abandoned by Admiral Thomas Hart's U.S. Asiatic Fleet, and written off by Washington as militarily expendable, he nevertheless undertook to argue the overall grand strategy of the entire World War with his President and Commander in Chief. He insisted that his island of Luzon be given priority over the British Isles, and stoutly maintained that Japan, Enemy No. 1, could be beaten *his* way. "There is no substitute," MacArthur said, "for victory."

The substitute that Roosevelt and Stimson found was General MacArthur himself—MacArthur, landing in Australia, where this book leaves him, became the symbol of the victory that Americans so deeply desired, and which, in the end, he gave them.

CLARE BOOTHE LUCE

Honolulu, Hawaii
December 7, 1973

Preface

This book is the story of General Douglas MacArthur's final days in the Philippine Islands in early 1942 at the start of the war in the Pacific and his subsequent escape via sea and air to Australia. It is also an account of General Jonathan M. Wainwright and the fall of Bataan and Corregidor. The story concerns four other important men—President Franklin D. Roosevelt, Secretary of War Henry L. Stimson, General George C. Marshall, and Philippine President Manuel L. Quezon—whose decisions and actions determined the fate of 90,000 soldiers and sailors in the garrisons of Bataan and Corregidor, and of 16 million Filipinos throughout the Philippine archipelago.

The loyal "lieutenants" of MacArthur and Wainwright are here too: men like Brigadier Generals Richard J. Marshall and Hugh J. Casey, who were instrumental in organizing the defense of the Bataan peninsula; Brigadier General Arnold J. Funk, who epitomized the starved but indomitable soldier on Bataan; Lieutenant John D. Bulkeley, who as commander of PT-boat Squadron Three led the famous "Expendables"; and Lieutenant Colonel John R. Pugh, who was given an opportunity to leave Corregidor three days before its capture but chose to stay and serve General Wainwright until the end.

It is a tale of courage, sacrifice, and patriotism that ranks with Thermopylae, the Alamo, and Dunkirk. As High Commissioner Francis B. Sayre said, "The defense of Bataan and Corregidor will go down in history as one of the great and heroic chapters of human courage and endurance. Those who died there will never be forgotten."

The book had its inception during the summer of 1964 when I was Aquatics Director at Camp Miakonda, the Toledo Area Boy

Scout Camp. That summer I spent part of my leisure time reading Frazier Hunt's biography, *The Untold Story of Douglas MacArthur*. What aroused my interest and curiosity most was Hunt's account of MacArthur's days in the Philippine Islands, the tragedy of his trapped army, and his evacuation to Australia. I knew then if I ever had the opportunity, I also would write a history of General MacArthur and the war in the Philippines, but in greater detail. The opportunity arrived in the fall of 1966 when I was required to write a thesis for a Master's degree in history.

My final thesis was essentially a narrative account revolving around General MacArthur from February 1 to March 17, 1942. Encouraged by my advisers at the University of Toledo to expand the thesis for publication, in early 1968 I requested authorization from the Adjutant General's Office to examine and take notes on all material in the army's classified files concerning Generals Mac-Arthur, George C. Marshall, and Jonathan M. Wainwright. In June 1968 the Adjutant General, Major General Kenneth G. Wickham, notified me that my request had been approved.

The material gleaned from these files made it possible to cover many of the events in greater detail. In particular, numerous previously classified radiograms and memoranda are presented in their entirety. Much valuable information and insight came also from interviews and correspondence with people who took part in the happenings described here.

In 1924 the great American humorist Will Rogers wrote:
Why don't we let people alone and quit trying to hold what they call a protectorate over them? Let people do their own way and have their own form of government. We haven't got any business in the Philippines. We are not such a howling success of running our own government.

Successive administrations of the U.S. government, however, failed to take Will Rogers's advice. On November 29, 1941, Lieutenant Henry G. Lee, a young army officer serving in the Philippines, wrote a letter to his parents. If Japan ever attacked, he told them, "we'll have a hot time in the Philippines." Nine days later the Japanese attack came.

It is my hope that the following pages will give the reader a greater understanding of what actually took place in the Philippines in the early days of the United States' involvement in World War II.

Contents

ILLUSTRATIONS

Following pages 76 and 172

MAPS

Chronology*

1941

December 8   Pearl Harbor bombed by Japanese. Japanese planes destroy half of the U.S. bomber force in the Philippines at Clark Field. Task Force 5, Asiatic Fleet, under Rear Admiral William A. Glassford, heads south toward safer waters.

December 10 Cavite naval base suffers heavily from enemy air attack.

December 14 Admiral Thomas C. Hart withdraws the few remaining patrol bombers of Patrol Wing 10 and three tenders from the Philippines, leaving very little of the Asiatic Fleet to support operations.

December 22 Japanese begin main landings before dawn along coast of Lingayen Gulf on Luzon.

December 23 On Luzon, MacArthur decides to evacuate Manila and withdraw to Bataan to make a delaying stand.

December 24 MacArthur transfers his headquarters from Manila to Corregidor.

December 25 Admiral F. W. Rockwell is put in charge of all naval activities in the Philippines.

December 26 Naval defense forces under Rockwell move to Corregidor. Manila is declared an open city.

December 29 Corregidor heavily bombed for the first time.

December 30 Second inaugural of President Quezon held outside Malinta Tunnel.

1942

January 5   Bataan echelon of headquarters established on Bataan under Brigadier General Richard J. Marshall.

* Dates are based on Philippine time.

January 10   MacArthur inspects Bataan defenses.

January 15   MacArthur issues statement to Filamerican troops on Bataan: "Help is on the way from the U.S. Thousands of troops and hundreds of planes are being dispatched."

January 22   MacArthur orders withdrawal of entire Mauban–Abucay line southward to final defense position on Bataan, behind Pilar–Bagac road; withdrawal started after nightfall on the twenty-third and completed by daylight of the twenty-sixth.

January 30   MacArthur takes control of naval forces in the Philippines.

February 3   Lieutenant Colonel Warren J. Clear departs from Corregidor aboard submarine *Trout*.

February 8   MacArthur has serious difficulties with Quezon, who submits neutralization proposal to Roosevelt.

February 10   Quezon receives Roosevelt's negative reply and threatens to return to Manila and make a deal with the Japanese.

February 12   Quezon decides against returning to Manila.

February 16   MacArthur proposes to Marshall that Quezon and High Commissioner Sayre be evacuated from Corregidor.

February 20   Quezon departs from Corregidor aboard submarine *Swordfish*.

February 23   Sayre leaves Corregidor for Australia aboard the *Swordfish*. MacArthur receives Roosevelt's order to depart for Australia.

March 4   Admiral Rockwell is informed by MacArthur of the departure order. MacArthur tells Rockwell that he wants him and Captain Ray to accompany him.

March 10   Orders issued to Motor Torpedo Boat Squadron 3. Wainwright has conference with MacArthur and learns of impending departure.

March 11   MacArthur, wife, son, and staff depart from Corregidor's North Dock at 7:30 P.M.

March 17   MacArthur and staff arrive in Australia.

March 20   General Beebe informs Wainwright that night at his Bataan headquarters that Wainwright has been promoted to lieutenant general by the War Department.

March 21   Wainwright, Major Pugh, and Captain Dooley leave Bataan for Corregidor.

March 22   General Moore takes Wainwright on an inspection tour of Corregidor's defenses.

April 4   MacArthur radios Wainwright: "Under no conditions should the Bataan command be surrendered."

April 5   Wainwright and Major Dooley return to Bataan for conferences with Generals King and Parker.

April 7   General Funk confers with Wainwright and Beebe on Corregidor concerning the hopeless situation on Bataan.

April 8   Wainwright sends Colonels Galbraith and Irwin to Bataan to confer with General King, and orders Colonel Romulo to leave. That night, tremendous explosions on Bataan; earthquake.

April 9   Wainwright learns at 6:00 A.M. of General King's decision to surrender Bataan forces.

April 10   Wainwright issues proclamation to his besieged forces on Corregidor: "Corregidor can and will be held."

April 13–14 "Royce's raid," twelve bombers stationed in Mindanao attack Japanese targets in the Philippines. Damage negligible.

April 15   Wainwright radios MacArthur: "Assign a Navy seaplane to the mission of ferrying personnel between here and Lake Lanao."

April 29   Two PBYs from Australia arrive at night and evacuate nurses and army and naval personnel from Corregidor.

May 3   Personnel evacuated at night aboard submarine *Spearfish*.

May 5   Japanese from Bataan make amphibious landing on Corregidor's tail.

May 6   Wainwright makes decision to surrender at noon. Conference with Homma at 5:00 P.M. at Cabcaben. Homma refuses to accept Wainwright's surrender unless it includes all forces in the Philippines. Wainwright is forced to return to Corregidor and to surrender all Filamerican forces in the Philippines to the commander of the Japanese invasion force on Corregidor.

Prologue

1

It is the policy of the United States to defend the Philippines.[1]

—Army Chief of Staff
George C. Marshall

The time: early summer of 1939. The place: a luxurious penthouse atop the Manila Hotel in the Philippine Islands. The occasion: a serious discussion between an officer in the United States Philippine Department and the head of the newly created Philippine Army. The discussion concerned the Japanese threat to the Philippine Islands.

Damning "military myopia" in the United States and in Europe, the creator of the Philippine Army emphatically "predicted that, if it were not remedied, the Philippines [would] drop like an overripe plum into the Japanese basket."

"Well, what do you care?" asked the army officer. "Personally, you've done the best you could."

Making a dramatic gesture, Field Marshal Douglas MacArthur, the head of the Philippine Army, replied, "Personally—I must not fail! Too much of the world's future depends upon success here. These Islands may not be the door to the control of the Pacific, they may not even be the lock to the door. But they are surely the key to the lock that opens the door—for America. I dare not allow that key to be lost!"[2]

Regarding the Philippines as an important link between the Eastern and Western worlds, MacArthur believed that it was in the vital interests of the United States to guarantee the security and

1

independence of these islands. If there could be an "uninterrupted development of the Filipino-American culture and economy through the cooperative effort of the two peoples," MacArthur foresaw the time when the Philippines would "flourish as a brilliant product of democracy, contribute to stability and peace in the Far East, and advance the living standards of its people to the full extent attainable under efficient use of its resources."[3]

The United States had passed in 1934 the Tydings-McDuffie Act providing for Philippine independence effective July 4, 1946, to end forty-eight years of U.S. control over the islands. Japan, however, posed a threat to the Philippines. The worldwide economic crisis of the early 1930s and the helplessness of Japan's civilian government in the face of it had caused nationalistic army leaders to take over the government and seek solutions to Japan's problems in their own way: by a policy of military expansion in East Asia. In 1932 the Japanese army on its own initiative moved into Manchuria from Korea and established the puppet state of Manchukuo. When the League of Nations censured Japan, she withdrew from the League. Reneging on the naval disarmament agreements of 1922 and 1930, Japan was fortifying the mandated islands as well as building up her military and naval forces in the western Pacific.[4]

Concerned about the vulnerability of the Philippines, Manuel L. Quezon, the dominant Filipino political figure, visited Washington in 1935. He conferred with General Douglas MacArthur, army chief of staff, who after heading the U.S. Army for five years was on the verge of retiring. Quezon, about to become first president of the Philippine Commonwealth, "bluntly" asked MacArthur if the Philippines could be successfully defended by July 4, 1946. The reply was that "any place could be defended if sufficient men, munitions, and money were available, and above all sufficient time to train the men, to provide the munitions, and to raise the money." Asked by Quezon if he would undertake the task of creating a Philippine Army when his tenure as army chief of staff ended, MacArthur replied that he would; but he "emphasized that it would take a full ten years and much help from the United States if it were to be successful."[5]

By 1935 MacArthur had reached the pinnacle of success in the U.S. Army. In many respects his military career had been unparalleled in army history.

62 years old

The son of a famous Civil War hero, Arthur MacArthur (who later fought in the Philippines and rose to the rank of lieutenant general in the army), Douglas MacArthur was born January 26, 1880. He was graduated from West Point in 1903 at the head of his class. Secretary of War Newton D. Baker called MacArthur "the greatest frontline general" of World War I. In 1919 MacArthur was appointed superintendent of West Point, where he reformed and modernized the academy. He became the youngest active major general in the army in 1925 and in 1930 was appointed army chief of staff by President Herbert Hoover.

Between 1903 and 1930 MacArthur served four tours of duty in the Philippines. He became familiar with the islands, and he developed a close affection for the Filipinos. When he sailed for Manila in the fall of 1935 in answer to Quezon's request, MacArthur was starting his fifth and final tour of duty in the Far East.[6]

In Manila as military adviser to the Philippine government, MacArthur faced the problem of how to defend the Philippines from the leading military power in Asia—Japan. He sought to create a Philippine Army capable of mounting offensive warfare in the Philippines, "patterned after the citizen soldier system of conscription effectively established in Switzerland." His plans called for the division of the country into ten military areas. Every year 4,000 men would be trained in each area. A small professional officer corps made up of Filipino and American officers would be in charge of training carried out in 128 camps to be built throughout the islands. By 1946 the Philippines would have a trained army of forty divisions, comprising 400,000 men. MacArthur's design also included a naval force of about fifty torpedo boats and an air force of about 250 planes.[7]

In order to carry out these ambitious plans, he needed time, money, and support from the Philippine and U.S. governments. The Philippine Army was to be gradually built up over a ten-year period from 1936 to 1946. It would need proper training and equipment.

From the outset, however, MacArthur encountered difficulty in obtaining sufficient funds to meet the needs of his expanding army. His budget was slashed again and again. Some Filipino politicians believed that funds should be used for public works instead of for building an army. At times President Quezon vacillated. In 1939, for example, he had "second thoughts on the large expenditures [needed] for the military establishment he had requested Mac-Arthur to build." Furthermore, owing to strong isolationist sentiment within the United States, and the fact that in 1946 that country was to relinquish control over the Philippines, the extensive help that MacArthur had expected from the U.S. government at the beginning of his assignment did not materialize.[8]

After September 1, 1939, events in the Far East moved rapidly. The State Department was unable to influence Japanese aggression in China, and tension between the United States and Japan mounted. In an attempt to halt militant Japan with economic pressure, on July 26, 1940 Congress cancelled the commercial treaty of 1911 between the two countries. The same day President Franklin D. Roosevelt was granted authority by Congress to control exports to Japan. He acted by drastically curtailing the flow of strategic war materials such as scrap iron, steel, and petroleum.[9]

A year later—on July 26, 1941—with the international situation in the Far East becoming more acute, the War Department recalled MacArthur, who had retired from active duty in 1937, to active duty as Commanding General, United States Army Forces in the Far East (USAFFE). On July 27 MacArthur, whose retired rank was major general, was promoted to temporary lieutenant general. His mission: to establish a headquarters in Manila and to combine U.S. Army forces in the Philippines and his Philippine Army forces into one army capable of repelling any Japanese attempt to conquer the Philippines.[10]

Lying between Japan and the valuable natural resources of the Netherlands East Indies, which Japan coveted, the Philippine Islands posed a serious threat "on the flank of Japan's vital sea lines." Warships or planes stationed in the Philippines would menace commerce moving between Japan and the Netherlands East Indies. American military planners had long realized the extremely vulnerable position of the Philippines with relation to Japan. They believed that if war broke out between Japan and the United States, Japan would move immediately southward and attempt to secure its sea communications with the Netherlands East Indies by conquering the Philippine Islands.

To prevent the islands from being overrun, American plans called for the small American army in the Philippines to retreat into the Bataan peninsula and fight a defensive action in order to gain time.

Corregidor and the other islands in the entrance to Manila Bay were fortified in order to deny the Japanese the use of the port of Manila. The garrisons on Bataan and Corregidor were to hold out against the Japanese onslaught until a major effort could be mounted from the United States. Basically, this was a defensive plan. Its success depended on how long the defenders could hold out and how long it would take a major relief effort to arrive in the Philippines from the United States.[11]

There was no plan for large-scale reinforcement of the Philippines when MacArthur was first recalled to active duty, but "within a few days there was a complete reversal of policy in the War Department." On July 31, 1941, General George C. Marshall, army chief of staff, approved a recommendation by the staff of the War Plans Division to greatly increase the military strength of the Philippine Islands. MacArthur was notified on August 1 that he would soon be receiving substantial reinforcements. In Washington, Marshall told his immediate staff, "It is the policy of the United States to defend the Philippines."[12]

On October 28 MacArthur wrote an optimistic letter to Marshall outlining the military situation in the Philippines. Morale in the Philippine Army was "exceptionally high," he reported, with all ranks showing "a real eagerness to learn," and training as a result had "progressed even beyond expectations." Construction of barracks and other buildings was "making excellent progress," a fleet of fast motor torpedo boats was being constructed, and a number of airfields were being developed.

In the letter, MacArthur also urged a revision of War Department Operations Plan Rainbow–5, providing for the defense of the Philippines. Rainbow–5 had been authorized by the Joint Board of high-ranking naval and army officers and approved by Secretary of War Henry L. Stimson on June 2. MacArthur disagreed with the plan, which was "based upon the old concept of the defense of the entrance of Manila Bay." Considering the growing military strength in the islands, he recommended a new plan that "would contemplate the defense of the archipelago and the Philippine Coastal Frontier." MacArthur closed, "I wish to reiterate my appreciation of the splendid support you and the War Department are giving me. No field commander could ask more. Your attitude has been a marked factor in the building of morale here."[13]

On November 3 Major General Lewis H. Brereton of the Army

Air Corps arrived in Manila with a letter from Marshall for Mac-
Arthur. It authorized MacArthur to enlarge upon the original Rainbow–5 plan. Brereton was ordered to the Philippines by the War
Department to develop an air striking force, mainly of B–17 bombers, capable of controlling the sea lanes on both sides of the islands.
War Department planners, infected by MacArthur's optimism concerning the defense of the islands, believed it might be possible to
hold them by implementing air power and bolstering MacArthur's
Filamerican army.[14]

To broaden the Rainbow–5 plan MacArthur established the North
and South Luzon forces and the Visayan-Mindanao Force. The
mission of the North Luzon Force, commanded by Major General
Jonathan M. Wainwright, was to defend the general area north of
Manila, comprising Lingayen Gulf and the Bataan peninsula; that
of the South Luzon Force, commanded by Brigadier General George
M. Parker, Jr., to defend the general area south of Manila. The
Visayan-Mindanao Force, under the command of Brigadier General
William F. Sharp, was assigned to defend the remainder of the
archipelago.

Since July, when MacArthur had assumed command of USAFFE,
there had been a tremendous increase in the flow of men and supplies
to the Philippines. In November of 1941 the U.S. Army garrison
consisted of 31,095 officers and enlisted men, including 12,000
Philippine Scouts, 5,609 Air Corps personnel, and 1,809 officers and
enlisted men of the 200th Coast Artillery (AA) New Mexico National Guard (the largest single American military organization in
the Philippines). The main force comprised ten reserve divisions of
the Philippine Army, which totaled over 100,000 men. Three Philippine Army divisions (the Eleventh, Twenty-first, and Thirty-first),
the Twenty-sixth Cavalry (PS), and a battalion of the Forty-fifth
Infantry (PS) were among the units that made up the North Luzon
Force. The Seventy-first Division (PA) was assigned to the North
Luzon Force, but it was kept in reserve and controlled by USAFFE.
The South Luzon Force consisted initially of the Forty-first and
Fifty-first Philippine Army divisions and a battery of field artillery.
Three Philippine divisions made up the Visayan-Mindanao Force.
But even though MacArthur's organized forces appeared formidable
on paper, they were not completely mobilized for war.[15]

On November 24 MacArthur received a radiogram from Admiral
Thomas C. Hart, commander in chief of the Asiatic Fleet, who had

originally received it from the chief of Naval Operations, Admiral Harold R. Stark:

> The [army] chief of staff [General Marshall] is in agreement with the estimate presented herewith and requests that you inform the senior army officer in your area: Chances of favorable outcome of United States–Japanese negotiations are very doubtful. This situation together with statements of Japanese government and movement of their naval and military force intimate in our opinion that surprise aggressive movement in any direction including attack on Philippines or Guam is a possibility. This information must be treated with utmost secrecy in order not to complicate an already tense situation or precipitate action.[16]

In Washington on November 26 an important conference was held in General Marshall's office. Present besides Marshall were Brigadier General Leonard T. Gerow, head of the War Plans Division, Major General Henry H. Arnold, head of the Army Air Corps, and Colonels Charles W. Bundy and Thomas T. Handy of the War Plans Division. The minutes of the conference read:

> General Marshall said that the President and the Secretary of State feel the Japanese are dissatisfied with the conferences in Washington and will soon cut loose. While both the President and Mr. Hull anticipate a possible assault on the Philippines, General Marshall said he did not see this as a probability because the hazards would be too great for the Japanese. It is necessary, however, to consider what instructions we will give our people in spite of the fact that a break will not necessarily mean a declaration of war. We know a great deal that the Japanese are not aware we know, and we are familiar with their plans to a certain extent; thus we did not enter the recent conversations with a detached frame of mind. We are not justified in ignoring any Japanese convoy that might be a threat to our interests. Thus far we have talked in terms of the defense of the Philippines, but now the question is what we do beyond that. This is a matter of vital importance affecting all of our military and naval policies.
> General Gerow read from a memorandum figures to indicate that the Asiatic Fleet, less submarines, and certain other vessels, is moving to Balikpapen with the mission of assisting

the British and Dutch in protecting bases in the Dutch East Indies. In the performance of this mission the Fleet will co-operate with the British Eastern Fleet. . . .

General Gerow said he had some hurried notes regarding possible instructions to General MacArthur. He should be told that negotiations have bogged down and that if war cannot be averted, the United States at least does not desire to commit the first overt act; however, General MacArthur should not be required to refrain from acting, particularly as to reconnaissance, if the position of the Philippines or the execution of his mission should be jeopardized. General Marshall asked for a definition of General MacArthur's mission, and General Gerow stated that it is to defend the Philippine Archipelago, to support the Navy and to attack threatening Japanese convoys. In view of this, General Marshall felt that the instructions to General MacArthur should make it clear that General MacArthur is authorized to take such action as might be necessary to carry out that part of his mission which pertains to the defense of the Philippine Archipelago.

One sentence from General Gerow's proposed instructions to General MacArthur was quoted as follows: "Prior to a state of war, it is desired that, in cooperation with the Navy, you take such reconnaissance and other measures as you deem necessary. These measures are left to your judgment." The question was raised whether this granted General MacArthur authority to fly over Japanese mandated and occupied territory. General Marshall thought that this was a matter for General MacArthur to decide, but that the War Department could call for a stop to such action if necessary. General Gerow expressed the opinion that if the Japanese should send planes over the Philippines, General MacArthur would not hesitate to take a shot at them. Since declarations of war have been carefully avoided in recent times, General Marshall said, it might be better to change the words "state of war" to "actual hostilities." There is war in China and there is war in the Atlantic at the present time, but in neither case is it declared war. In addition, General MacArthur should be "directed" to carry out the orders sent him, rather than [be] told "it is desired" that he do so. The word "directed" should appear at the beginning of the communication.

General Gerow's proposed instructions to General Mac-Arthur further directed that in case of hostilities, General MacArthur would carry out the tasks assigned in the revised Rainbow–5, which had been furnished him by General Brereton. General Marshall tentatively approved the instructions to General MacArthur as proposed by General Gerow as a basis of discussion with the Navy.

Colonel Bundy commented that he thought General Mac-Arthur was entitled to very clear instructions as to what he should do both before and after hostilities if they should break out. Colonel Handy added that he thought our action in allowing planes to fly over Formosa constituted an overt act, and we should be aware of this. It might cause the Japanese to fire the first shot, but actually one of our war planes has no legal right over Japanese territory.[17]

On November 27 MacArthur received the following radiogram from the War Department:

> Negotiations with Japan appear to be terminated to all practical purposes with only the barest possibilities that the Japanese government might come back and offer to continue. Japanese future action unpredictable but hostile action possible at any moment. If hostilities cannot, repeat cannot, be avoided the United States desires that Japan commit the first overt act. This policy should not, repeat not, be construed as restricting you to a course of action that might jeopardize the successful defense of the Philippines. Prior to hostile Japanese action you are directed to take such reconnaissance and other measures as you deem necessary. Report measures taken. Should hostilities occur you will carry out the tasks assigned in revised Rainbow Five which was delivered to you by General Brereton. Chief of Naval Operations concurs and request you notify Hart.[18]

The same day MacArthur conferred with Hart and High Commissioner Francis B. Sayre in Sayre's office. Pacing back and forth, smoking a black cigar, MacArthur told Sayre and Hart "in reassuring terms that the existing alignment and movement of Japanese troops convinced him that there would be no Japanese attack before the spring." Admiral Hart, according to Sayre, "felt otherwise."[19]

On November 28 MacArthur radioed Marshall that "everything is in readiness for the conduct of a successful defense," with measures taken for ground security and air reconnaissance extended in cooperation with the Navy.[20]

In response to a warning from General Arnold to guard Philippine airbases against sabotage, MacArthur on December 6 reported:

> All Air Corps stations here on alert status. Airplanes dispersed and each under guard. All airdrome defense stations manned. Guards on installations increased. Counter subversive activities charged air force headquarters by regulations are being organized and have started functioning in limited manner.[21]

2

The Attack on the Philippines

December 8-20, 1941

The resolute and effective fighting of you and your men, air and ground, has made a tremendous impression on the American people and confirms our confidence in your leadership. We are making every effort to reach you with air replacements and reinforcements as well as other troops and supports.[1]

—General George C. Marshall

It was early in the morning of December 8. Major General Richard K. Sutherland, MacArthur's chief of staff, Brigadier General Richard J. Marshall, deputy chief of staff, and Colonel Hugh ("Pat") J. Casey, chief of engineers, were asleep at No. 1 Military Plaza. Shortly after 3:00 A.M. Brigadier General Spencer B. Akin, who headed MacArthur's Signal Corps, entered their sleeping quarters and told Sutherland that Pearl Harbor had been attacked by Japanese aircraft. Seeing that Casey was still fast asleep, Akin went quietly over and whispered, "Pat. Pat. Wake up. The Japanese have just bombed Pearl Harbor."

With Marshall at his side, Sutherland phoned MacArthur on a private line to his penthouse apartment in the Manila Hotel. "Pearl Harbor!" MacArthur repeated incredulously. "It should be our strongest point."

At 3:55 A.M. MacArthur received confirmation of the attack through Admiral Thomas C. Hart, commander in chief of the Asiatic Fleet, who had just received a message from Admiral Husband E.

11

Kimmel, commander in chief of the Pacific Fleet at Pearl Harbor.[2]
About 4:30 A.M. MacArthur was handed the following message:

> Japanese are presenting at 1:00 P.M., Eastern Standard Time
> today, what amounts to an ultimatum. Also they are under orders
> to destroy their code machine immediately. Just what significance
> the hour set may have we do not know but be on alert accordingly.
> Inform naval authorities of this communication.[3]

At 5:00 A.M. MacArthur's staff was "alerted and assembled" at
No. 1 Calle Victoria, a house on the wall of the old walled city of
Manila. After ordering American and Filipino troops to take assembly positions, MacArthur took steps to bring the Philippine Constabulary and Civilian Emergency Administration, made up of
volunteer guards in every city, town, and *barrio*, under military
control. He ordered antisabotage measures, and a "round-up of
Japanese nationals was set in motion." To Jorge B. Vargas, President
Quezon's secretary and chief adviser, MacArthur suggested that the
schools in Manila "not be closed at once, but . . . wait until the end
of the week."[4]

Major General Lewis H. Brereton, commander of the Far East
Air Force, reported to MacArthur's USAFFE headquarters at 5:00
A.M. MacArthur was in conference at the time, so Brereton talked
with Sutherland and requested permission to launch an air attack
using B-17 bombers against Japanese airfields in southern Formosa.
After agreeing to Brereton's plans, Sutherland informed him that
"he would obtain MacArthur's authority for the daylight attacks."
When Brereton left headquarters he was under orders to prepare
for the air strike "but not to undertake any offensive action until
ordered."[5]

At 7:30 A.M. MacArthur received a second radiogram from the
War Department.

> Hostilities between Japan and the United States, British Com-
> monwealth and Dutch have commenced. Japanese made air raid
> on Pearl Harbor this morning December seventh. Carry out tasks
> assigned in Rainbow Five so far as they pertain to Japan. In addi-
> tion cooperate with the British and Dutch to the utmost without
> jeopardizing the accomplishment of your primary mission of de-
> fense of the Philippines. You are authorized to dispatch air units
> to operate temporarily from suitable bases in cooperation with the
> British or Dutch. Report daily major dispositions and all opera-
> tions. You have the complete confidence of the War Department

and we assure you of every possible assistance and support
within our power.[6]

During the morning Casey prepared a memorandum for Sutherland proposing that the military purchase, rent, or seize all civilian-
held stocks of dynamite, sandbags, sugar bags, flour sacks, hand
tools, and heavy engineering equipment. MacArthur picked up the
memorandum from Casey's desk, read it quickly, and marked it
"O.K. MacA." In the coming weeks the explosives would be used by
a group of army and mining engineers hastily organized and directed
by Casey to blow up rail and road bridges, military installations,
and supplies that were in the path of the Japanese advance.[7]

At 7:55 A.M. MacArthur received a transoceanic telephone call
from the head of the War Plans Division, Brigadier General Leonard
T. Gerow, in Washington. MacArthur informed Gerow that he had
received the news of the Pearl Harbor attack. Gerow asked if the
Philippines had been attacked. "No attack at all," MacArthur replied,
although the night before, between 11:30 and 12:00, "a Japanese
bombing squadron was reported by radio detection but turned back
thirty miles from the coast." When Gerow asked if he had "any
other indications of an attack," MacArthur replied, "In the last half
hour our radio detector service picked up planes about thirty miles
off the coast. We have taken off to meet them."

Gerow asked MacArthur to "report immediately any Japanese
operations or any indications," and said twice that he "wouldn't be
surprised if MacArthur got an attack there in the near future." Gerow
also told MacArthur that the first attack on Pearl Harbor had started
at 8:00 A.M. Hawaiian time, and a second attack at 11:00 A.M. "Considerable damage was done to planes and other installations," he
said, by sixty to one hundred dive bombers operating from aircraft
carriers.

"What are the possibilities of a naval engagement off Hawaii?"
MacArthur asked.

"We've got very little information from the Navy as to what the
Japanese have in that vicinity. It is estimated that they have three
or four carriers, protected by cruisers and submarines," Gerow told
him. "General Marshall sends his best to you. He is at home at the
moment," he added in closing.

"Tell General Marshall 'our tails are up in the air,'" MacArthur
replied.[8]

Bombed at dawn in the Philippines were the ports of Davao in

Mindanao and Aparri in Luzon.[9] At 8:30 A.M. high-flying planes were reported north of Clark Field and all of the B-17s at the field were ordered airborne.[10] At 8:50 A.M., Sutherland phoned Brereton and instructed him to "hold off [the] bombing of Formosa for [the] present."[11] Thirteen minutes later Sutherland was notified that contact had been made with the Japanese planes north of Clark Field.[12] Brereton called Sutherland shortly and informed him that if Japanese aircraft succeeded in attacking Clark Field he "would be unable to operate offensively with the bombers." Again he requested authority to carry out offensive action.[13] Just before 10:10 A.M. Sutherland returned Brereton's call and told him "MacArthur had decided that a reconnaissance mission could be sent to Formosa." A coded message was dispatched recalling all of the airborne B-17s to Clark Field for the purpose of refueling the planes and briefing the pilots for the probable raid. Three of the bombers were to be dispatched to Formosa for reconnaissance; later the remainder of the B-17s were to follow on bombing missions.[14]

At 11:00 A.M. Sutherland phoned Brereton "that 'bombing missions' could be executed."[15] Fifty-five minutes later, Sutherland, "at the direction of General MacArthur," again phoned Brereton and requested a report on the air operations that were planned for the following two hours. Brereton replied that the air force would "send out a mission [in the] afternoon."[16]

At 12:35 P.M., while the pilots who were going on the reconnaissance mission were being briefed and the rest of the pilots were at lunch, Japanese bombers and fighters, flying at altitudes of more than 20,000 feet, surprised and attacked Clark Field.[17] When the bombing and strafing stopped at 1:37 P.M., the strength of the Far East Air Force had been reduced by one-half. Of the original thirty-five B-17s, seventeen remained. Also destroyed were fifty-three P-40s and three P-35s, along with twenty-five or thirty miscellaneous aircraft. Extensive damage was inflicted on the airfield and installations; 80 servicemen were killed and 150 wounded.[18]

After the attack on Clark Field, all previous American plans and expectations for defending the Philippine Islands from invasion by using air power were radically altered. One of the reasons for the disaster was the lack of radar to warn of approaching enemy aircraft. Ironically, a radar system was being installed at Clark Field at the time of the Japanese attack. But because of the lack of warning, the attack was virtually unopposed.

Brereton and MacArthur bear dual responsibility for the Clark Field disaster. Brereton failed to provide air cover during the lunch hour, with all of the planes lined up and bunched together on the ground. Some of the planes should certainly have been airborne. Prior to the start of hostilities, MacArthur through Sutherland had ordered Brereton to move all B-17s from Clark Field to Del Monte airfield in Mindanao, but only seventeen B-17s had been moved.

MacArthur, on the other hand, waited too long before ordering Brereton to launch an air strike against Japanese airfields in Formosa. Thus he failed to carry out the task assigned to him in the Rainbow–5 War Plan, which clearly granted him the authority to authorize "air raids against Japanese forces within tactical operating radius of available bases."[19]

At 3:30 P.M. MacArthur conferred with Admiral Hart. Previously Hart had received the following cable from the Navy Department (and presumably handed it to MacArthur):

> Deliver the following to MacArthur from secretary of war: Without diplomatic or other declaration sixty Japanese carrier borne dive bombers attacked airfields and Pearl Harbor Oahu at 8:00 A.M., damaging hangars and planes on ground. Three battleships reported sunk and three others seriously damaged. Second air raid at 11:00 A.M. Six transports were reported in Japanese forces. Reports of attacks on Wake and Guam. All air attacks made with bombs, torpedoes and machine guns. First objectives seem to be air and naval installations and ships. . . . Reports received that Singapore attacked by air. . . . Limit this information to essential officers.[20]

At 3:39 P.M. Brereton phoned Sutherland and announced that he was on his way to the USAFFE headquarters. Eleven minutes later he discussed the strike on Clark Field with MacArthur.[21]

General MacArthur held a conference at 5:30 P.M. with High Commissioner Francis B. Sayre. When Sayre entered MacArthur's office, the general was "pacing the floor" and Sayre could see by the expression on his face that he was deeply troubled. MacArthur read to Sayre a "radio telling of the tragic losses at Pearl Harbor" and informed Sayre of the attack on Clark Field.[22]

During the day the USAFFE headquarters at No. 1 Calle Victoria was equipped for total blackout. MacArthur directed "that Manila be only partially blacked out until the air raid alarm sounded, at which time total blackout would go into effect."[23] Later that night MacArthur reported to the War Department:

> Have sustained continued but light bombing attacks over north and central Luzon during morning and early afternoon. Clark Field only objective of importance. It experienced heavy attack by fifty-two two engined bombers at high altitude coordinated with forty dive bombers. Damage heavy and casualties reported at about twenty-three dead and two hundred wounded. Our air losses were heavy. . . . Now have available seventeen heavy bombers, fifty to fifty-five P-40s and fifteen P-35s. No losses of other types. I am launching a heavy bombardment counter-attack tomorrow morning on enemy airdromes in southern Formosa. Seizure of enemy aliens effected during day without incident. Arrested about forty percent in Manila and ten percent in provinces. No combat except in air.[24]

The following day MacArthur informed the War Department that the Japanese had bombed Nichols Field and Fort McKinley. Casualties at Clark Field were much higher than previously reported, he said, and "further information regarding the damage at Clark Field required the cancellation of the proposed attack on Formosa."[25]

The War Department received word from MacArthur on December 10 that the Japanese had made amphibious landings near the ports of Aparri and Vigan in northern Luzon. He reported that his planes "had sunk one of the six transports, had made direct hits on two others, and had probably damaged the remaining three."[26] Learning of the Japanese landing at Vigan, Casey urged MacArthur in a memorandum not to send major forces north to oppose it. If the Japanese later landed in full force at Lingayen Gulf, Casey reasoned, any Filamerican forces sent north to Vigan would be cut off and trapped. Instead, he recommended the demolition of intervening bridges, ferries, and other installations in order to slow the Japanese advance south. He favored establishing a defensive line generally east of Baguio, covering the principal mountain passes. MacArthur personally approved these recommendations.[27]

Also on December 10 MacArthur received from Admiral Hart the Navy's estimate of the situation: "With the initiative in the hands of the enemy, consideration of his early successes, and the pre-ponderance of forces available to him is the contemplation of a long war, facing the loss of, and ultimate recapture of the Philippines." Even though the mission of the Asiatic Fleet in the event of war had been to support the defense of the Philippines "as long as that defense continues," Hart on December 8 had ordered Task Force Five, the main surface striking force of the Asiatic Fleet, to proceed to Borneo in the Netherlands East Indies. By December 10, the task force had left Philippine waters. Hart undoubtedly reasoned that if his fleet remained in the vicinity of the Philippines, it would suffer the same fate as the Pacific Fleet at Pearl Harbor.[28]

The same day, MacArthur sent a radiogram labeled "extra priority" to General George C. Marshall:

> The mass of enemy air and naval strength committed in the theatre from Singapore to the Philippines and eastward established his weakness in Japan. Proper and definite information available here shows that entry of Russia is Japan's greatest fear. Most favorable opportunity now exists and immediate attack of Japan from north would not only inflict heavy punishment but would at once relieve pressure from objectives of Jap drive to southward. . . . Heavy air attack on Jap objectives would not only pull in much of present widely dispersed air strength but would destroy much of their exposed oil supply. Golden opportunity exists for a master stroke while the enemy is engaged in over extended initial air efforts.[29]

When MacArthur's radiogram arrived, the head of the War Plans Division, Brigadier General Gerow, recommended to Marshall "that every effort be made to bring Russia into the War." Later Marshall discussed MacArthur's proposal with Secretary of War Henry L. Stimson, and Stimson "went over to the State Department and talked it over with Secretary of State Cordell Hull." Both men came to the conclusion that it was very unlikely the Russians could be persuaded to take any military action against Japan.[30]

Stimson, who had been governor general of the Philippines from 1927 to 1929, was deeply worried about their fate. He was "quite proud of his administration of the Islands when he was Governor General" and felt a genuine interest in the Philippine government and "the future role of the Philippines in the Pacific." He had a "real affection" for the Filipino people, and a number of friends in the islands. As governor general he had worked closely with President Quezon, and he knew personally a number of the senior officers, including MacArthur and Major General Jonathan M. Wainwright, who were serving in the Philippines.[31]

At 11:00 A.M. President Roosevelt held an off-the-record conference in the White House. Present were Stimson, Marshall, Hull, Admiral Harold R. Stark, chief of Naval Operations, Admiral Ernest J. King, commander of the Atlantic Fleet, Captain John R. Beardall, Roosevelt's naval aide, and the assistant secretary of the Navy, James Forrestal, since the secretary of the Navy, Frank Knox, was in Hawaii. Among the "important propositions" discussed was "the question of reconsidering the stopping of [the *Pensacola*] convoy headed to the Philippines, which the Joint Board" the day before had decided to order back to Hawaii.[32]

The *Pensacola* convoy, made up of ships carrying warplanes, army personnel, war materials, and ammunition, had been en route to the Philippines at the time of the attack on Pearl Harbor. The Joint Board of high-ranking army and naval officers had decided that the preponderance of Japanese naval forces in the vicinity of the Philippines made the risk of the convoy's destruction unacceptable.[33] President Roosevelt, however, in reconsidering the Joint Board's decision, believed "that it was better not to stop [the convoy] but [to] take the chance of getting it to Australia where the men and the material it carried could probably be gotten by air or otherwise to the Philippines." Stimson "sympathized with [Roosevelt's] view very strongly" and urged the same course of action, even though he recognized that "it was a serious proposition." General Marshall also supported the President's decision, although the day before at the Joint Board meeting he had "unwillingly consented" to the recall of the convoy.[34]

During the morning of December 11 in the Philippines, Brereton received a distraught transoceanic telephone call from the chief of the Army Air Forces, Major General Henry H. Arnold, in Washington. Arnold wanted to know "how in the hell" an experienced airman like Brereton had been caught with all his planes on the ground at Clark Field. Brereton explained that he had tried to do everything in his power "to get authority to attack Formosa on December 8 but had been relegated to a 'strictly defensive attitude' by higher authority."[35]

Troubled by Arnold's phone call, Brereton related the incident the same day to MacArthur, who had received the following radiogram from Arnold:

> Reports of Japanese attacks all show that numbers of our planes have been destroyed on the ground. Take all possib'e steps at once to avoid such losses in your area, including dispersion to maximum possible extent, construction of parapets and prompt take off on warning noise.

Brereton requested MacArthur's "assistance in setting the facts straight." Becoming "furious," MacArthur told him "to go back and fight the war." As Brereton walked out of MacArthur's office, MacArthur ordered Sutherland "to get General Marshall on the phone." Later MacArthur sent the following cable to Arnold:

> Every possible precaution within the limited means and time available was taken by the Far East Air Force. Their losses were due entirely to the overwhelming superiority of enemy force. They have been hopelessly outnumbered from the start but no unit could have done better. Their gallantry has been conspicuous; their efficiency good. No item of loss can properly be attributed to neglect or lack of care. They fought from fields not yet developed and under improvised conditions of every sort which placed them under the severest handicap as regards to any enemy fully prepared in every way. You may take pride in their conduct.[36]

The sky above Manila was overcast on December 12. In the forenoon the Japanese launched an air attack with more than 113 airplanes, hitting Batangas, Clark Field, and Olongapo. American and Filipino pilots shot down 13 of the attacking planes. MacArthur reported to the War Department that he had only 27 operational P-40s, and "in order to make [a] show of strength and to have air reconnaissance," it was necessary for him "to conserve them." Consequently, he had issued orders for the pilots of the remaining P-40s "to avoid direct combat."[37]

Strong Japanese naval forces were "reported off [the] Zambales coast on the West, and at Legaspi on the East." The Japanese landed forces at Legaspi from four transports and "augmented" their forces at Aparri and Vigan. MacArthur believed that one purpose of these "concentric thrusts" was to "confuse and demoralize" him. Reasoning that the Japanese had "an additional objective of securing airdromes for the operation of land based aircraft" at each of the coastal landing points, MacArthur also believed that the Japanese wanted him to make a "premature commitment of his forces."[38]

MacArthur received notice from the War Department on December 13 that the *Pensacola* convoy would arrive at Brisbane about December 19. Desperately needing the personnel, aircraft, and other war material that the ships in the convoy carried, he conferred with Admiral Hart and later sent the following radiogram to the War Department.

Immediately conferred with Hart as to possibility of reasonably safe arrival of convoy from Brisbane here. I emphasized imperative necessity of supplies and reinforcements arriving here explaining fully the very limited resources now at my disposal. Stated that army estimate was: If Philippines were to be saved, forces should be built up here at least as rapidly as the enemy could concentrate against us; that action versus his supply lines from north would delay his operations but that if our supply lines to the south were not guaranteed by our naval forces it would only be a question of time until the enemy could transport a sufficient preponderance of force to crush our garrison. I suggested he should endeavor with his own surface forces and with assistance of Australian and Dutch naval and air forces to bring in the present convoy and to keep my line open.

He gave as his estimate that before the ships could reach here a complete blockade would be established. He said the use of Torres Strait was forbidden him necessitating a voyage completely around Australia. In effect he seemed to be of the opinion that the islands were ultimately doomed. He thought it possible that before the final phase of an attack might be made versus the Netherlands East Indies because of the necessity for oil supply, the Philippine Islands being merely contained until this had been accomplished, a complete blockade being maintained.

As he is charged with the security of army supply lines, his estimate causes me the gravest concern. If such a condition exists and cannot be remedied with Allied resources, the time this position can be held under severe attack is definitely limited. It would represent abandonment of Philippine Islands and if the suspicion of such action ever materialized the entire structure will collapse over my head. If Japan ever seizes these islands the difficulty of recapture is impossible of conception. If the Western Pacific is to be saved it will have to be saved here and now. If the Philippines and Netherlands East Indies go, so will Singapore and the entire Asiatic continent.

The enemy here is isolated from his allies; the winter season precludes any real effort on other major fronts; he is completely susceptible to concentrated action. Every resource of the Allies should be converged here immediately. The Philippine theatre is the locus of victory or defeat and I urge a strategic review of the entire situation lest a fatal mistake be made.

The immediate necessity is to delay the hostile advance. This can be effectively accomplished by providing air support: (1) pursuit, to prevent continuation of enemy day bombardment and to allow continued development and maintenance of airfields: (2) bombardment, to operate against his air bases, communications and other installations. The presence of air forces here would delay the enemy advance and permit the completion of the projected organization that will insure the retention of these islands and the protection of the Netherlands East Indies and Singapore, thus insuring the comparatively rapid defeat of the enemy. It justifies the diversion here of the entire output of air and other resources. Please advise me on the broadest lines possible.[39]

On December 14 MacArthur notified the War Department that he needed ten squadrons of pursuit aircraft, pointing out that "the immediate situation could be met with 250 dive bombers" flown to airfields in the Philippines from two aircraft carriers.

Dive bombers adequately supported by pursuit would offer a powerful threat to a hostile main force landing and their bomb capacity is effective threat versus capital ships. . . . Attrition will be great but reinforcement of both types should be forthcoming from Australia. Supply of 50 caliber ammunition is critical. Dive bombers [from aircraft carriers] could bring ashore approximately two [deliveries]. Other means of delivery must be formed. Use of Pan American Airways clippers is suggested. They could shuttle to Australia ferrying pilots south and bringing ammo north.

The ultimate requirement of 300 pursuit fighter planes, including replacements, and the necessary interceptor equipment and personnel are a vital requisite preliminary to the reinforcing of the heavy bombers command. The bomber reinforcements, if adequate, can prevent successful Jap operation versus the Philippines, versus the Netherlands East Indies, versus Malaya.[40]

In Washington on December 14, Brigadier General Dwight D. Eisenhower, who had served as the senior active U.S. Army officer on MacArthur's staff in the Philippines from 1935 to December 1939, reported to Army Chief of Staff Marshall in the War Department. For twenty minutes Marshall outlined "the general situation, naval and military in the western Pacific," then "abruptly" asked

Eisenhower, "What should be our general line of action?" After thinking a second, Eisenhower replied, "Give me a few hours." Marshall agreed.[41]

Eisenhower was determined to formulate an answer "short, emphatic and based on reasoning." Since the Navy lacked the capability for any offensive action and "dared not venture with surface vessels into the Philippine waters," Eisenhower believed "that the Philippines could not, at that time, be reinforced directly by land and sea forces." He concluded that the surest way to prolong the duration of the defense, and in turn allow the Navy time to recuperate, was to build up a large base in Australia. From Australia, vitally needed supplies could be shipped northward to the Philippines by submarines, blockade-runners, and, if the line of communications could be kept open, airplanes.

"With these bleak conclusions" Eisenhower returned to Marshall's office. "General," Eisenhower said, "it will be a long time before major reinforcements can go to the Philippines, longer than the garrison can hold out with any driblet of assistance, if the enemy commits major forces to their reduction. But we must do everything for them that is humanly possible. The people of China, of the Philippines, of the Dutch East Indies will be watching us. They may excuse failure but they will not excuse abandonment. Their trust and friendship are important to us. Our base must be Australia, and we must start at once to expand it and to secure our communications to it. In this last we dare not fail. We must take great risks and spend any amount of money required."

In a tone of voice implying that he had only "given the problem as a check to an answer he had already reached," Marshall replied, "I agree with you." He added, "Do your best to save them." Eisenhower was given the assignment of prolonging the defense in the Philippines by providing limited assistance.[42]

About 12:00 noon Stimson returned to his office and discovered "a new crisis." In his diary he wrote, "General MacArthur had sent two urgent telegrams calling for help. He was instigated to do so by a conference he had had with Admiral Hart who took the usual Navy defeatist position and had virtually told MacArthur that the Philippines were doomed, instead of doing his best to keep MacArthur's lifeline open. I found that Marshall agreed fully with me that we could not give up the Philippines in that way; that we must make every effort at whatever risk to keep MacArthur's line open and that otherwise we would paralyze the activities of everybody in the Far East. . . ."

Stimson received a phone call shortly from Roosevelt requesting his presence at a 3:00 P.M. meeting in the White House. The purpose of the meeting was to consider the president's plan of initiating a series of conferences at Chungking, Singapore, Washington, and Moscow, to be attended by representatives from China, Great Britain, the Netherlands, Russia, and the United States, "prior to December 17 to exchange information and to consider the military and naval action particularly in Eastern Asia which [would] most effectively be employed to accomplish the defeat of Japan and her allies."

Presidential adviser Harry L. Hopkins was also at the White House meeting. When Roosevelt finished reading the telegrams he had written to the Allies concerning the proposed military conferences, Stimson, saying that he "had something very germane" to the conferences, showed MacArthur's radiograms of December 13 and 14 to Roosevelt. Roosevelt read them "most carefully with tremendous interest, if not excitement," and sided with Stimson and Marshall "against the Navy." Stimson then read to Roosevelt a memorandum he had drawn up in the War Department, with the aid of Marshall, containing "the full facts and figures" of what the War Department could do to reinforce MacArthur in the Philippines. It also contained information on what the War Department was doing to strengthen the defenses of Hawaii and Panama, and related "what the chances were in the future." By the time Stimson had finished, Roosevelt "had fully made up his mind to side with [Stimson and Marshall] against the Navy." Sending for Assistant Secretary of the Navy James Forrestal, Roosevelt "told him . . . that he was bound to help the Philippines" and that the Navy had to make a positive contribution in this effort.[43]

Stimson made the following entry in his diary on December 14.

I have been in constant conference with Marshall as to what we could send to the Philippines by air or before the Japanese had actually blockaded the island. We have met with many obstacles, particularly because the Navy has been rather shaken and panic-stricken after the catastrophe at Hawaii and the complete upset of their naval strategy which depended upon that fortress. They have been willing to think of nothing except Hawaii and the restoration of the defense of that island. They have opposed all our efforts for a counter-attack, taking the defeatist attitude that it was impossible before we even tried.[44]

On December 16 MacArthur was informed by the War Department of Roosevelt's plan to initiate military conferences at Singapore, Moscow, Chungking, and Washington. Also, he was told:

> Your messages of December thirteenth and fourteenth have been studied by the president. The strategic importance of the Philippines is fully recognized and there has been and will be no, repeat no, wavering in the determination to support you. The problem of supply is complicated by naval losses in the Pacific but as recommended in yours of December fourteenth bomber and pursuit reinforcements are to be rushed to you. Keep us advised of the situation as you see it.[45]

In Washington Stimson received a telephone call from Roosevelt, who asked him to attend a White House conference at 4:40 P.M. with Marshall, Knox, and Stark to discuss "the question of the carrier convoys to the Far East." Admiral Stark, opposing MacArthur's suggestion of using aircraft carriers to supply airplanes to the Philippines, claimed that it would be "cutting down the striking power of the Fleet." General Marshall "suggested . . . a possible compromise," which would provide "quicker service" in getting aircraft to the Philippines without the use of aircraft carriers. The conference ended at 6:00 P.M., and Marshall and Knox departed "to see whether they could work this out."[46]

On December 17 MacArthur sent his aide, Lieutenant Colonel Sidney L. Huff, on a mission to convince President Quezon that he should make plans to transfer on four hours' notice the seat of the Philippine government from Manila to Corregidor if the Japanese seemed on the verge of capturing the city. MacArthur's evacuation plan shocked Quezon. It would be his duty to remain with his people in Manila, he said, but he told Huff he would see MacArthur that night at the Manila Hotel.

About 9:00 P.M. Quezon and Huff arrived at the hotel's rear entrance to avoid attention and speculation. They entered an air conditioned hall leading to the "Winter Garden," from which they could hear the soft music of a dance orchestra and people dancing and talking. Huff telephoned MacArthur that Quezon was downstairs and wanted to talk with him.

The two met in the dark hall. MacArthur explained that he was only preparing Quezon for the worst in case the Japanese should land in great force. If such an eventuality occurred, he pointed out, it would be unwise to keep the North and South Luzon forces "scattered all over Luzon." In such a situation, his plan was "to concentrate his army in the Bataan Peninsula and on Corregidor where he was determined to fight until the end."

"But, General," Quezon remonstrated, "why would I have to go to Corregidor in that case? The military defense of the Philippines is primarily America's responsibility and not mine. I have already placed every Filipino soldier under your command. My own first duty is to take care of the civilian population and to maintain public order while you are fighting the enemy. Were I to go to Corregidor, my people would think I had abandoned them to seek safety under your protection. This I shall never do. I shall stay among my people and suffer the same fate that may befall them."

"Mr. President," said MacArthur, "I expected that answer from such a gallant man as I know you to be." He tried to convince Quezon that it was not merely a "question of running away." Reminding Quezon of an earlier agreement to declare Manila an open city to avoid the destruction of the city and save the lives of its populace, MacArthur pointed out that once Manila was declared an open city there would be no need for his presence.

Quezon asked MacArthur if he intended to declare Manila an open city and move to Corregidor the following day. The reply was a "most emphatic 'no.'" Quezon still hesitated. The general reminded him that it was MacArthur's duty to prevent the head of the Philippine government from being captured by the Japanese. As long as Quezon was free, MacArthur stressed, the occupation of Manila, or even the Philippines, by the Japanese army would not have the same significance under international law as it would if the government had been captured or had surrendered.

Quezon concluded the interview by saying, "General, I shall convene tomorrow the Council of State and hear their views; then I will let you know my decision."[47]

On December 17 Chief of Naval Operations Stark radioed Admiral Hart that he recognized Hart's inability to guarantee the safe passage of the *Pensacola* convoy to the Philippines. Hart was told to try to ship supplies through to the Philippines, especially crucial items like airplanes, which the army particularly needed, when it became "practical" to do so, with one further instruction:

> When in your judgment you can from elsewhere more effectively direct the operations of your fleet the chief of Naval Operations approves your departure from Manila and the prior transfer southward of advance base personnel and material. Assure MacArthur you will continue your full support of the defense of the Philippines and upon your departure place all remaining naval and marine personnel under MacArthur's command and make available to him naval munitions, stores and equipment.[48]

The same day MacArthur and Hart sent a radiogram to Lieutenant Colonel Francis G. Brink, representing the War Department at the military and naval conferences in Singapore.

> Enemy has secured three positions at distant undefended points on Luzon each with a small airfield and each behind a difficult defile. He can support a ground attack or assist in attempt at blockade of Balintang Channel and San Bernardino Strait. Enemy has command of the air and our remaining air forces are weak. Our land forces are intact. Marked diminution of enemy air pressure last forty-eight hours. No local indications of major attack here. Naval basing facilities badly damaged and remainder are vulnerable. Therefore wholly impractical to operate surface forces from here. Powerful submarine force will continue operations from here as long as sufficient basing facilities remain. Enemy can now dispose sufficient naval forces to blockade islands effectively unless driven out by forces superior to those now available to us. Therefore the maintenance of sea communications into this area cannot be assured by forces here. No blockade yet known to be established. Reiterate strategic policy enunciated by President Roosevelt that Far East area is now dominant locus of war and most rapid and concentrated effort should be made by convergent action of Allies.[49]

In Washington at the War Department, Stimson conferred with his closest assistants, John J. McCloy, Robert A. Lovett, and Harvey H. Bundy. Stimson laid before them the important issue of whether the War Department should make every possible effort in the Far

East by attempting to defend the "Southwestern Pacific as a whole," or whether it should adopt the Navy Department's position and "treat the area as doomed."

Stimson reasoned that if Allied forces were driven out of Singapore and the Philippines, they still could "fall back on the Netherlands East Indies and Australia." He believed that if the Allies could continue to fight from the Netherlands East Indies and Australia and maintain the cooperation of China, it would still be possible to "strike good counter blows at Japan." If the "Navy's defeatist theory" was adopted and Japan was allowed to swallow up the southwestern Pacific, he believed the results would be disastrous. Not only would Japan be strongly ensconced in the southwestern Pacific, making it extremely difficult to drive her out, but "it would psychologically do even more in the discouragement of China and in fact all of the four powers. . . . Also, it would have a very bad effect on Russia."[50]

When Stimson arrived at the War Department on the morning of December 18, he learned that the *Pensacola* convoy was still 500 miles out of Brisbane. "A new group of warships" was going out to rendezvous with the convoy and escort it into port. To Stimson it meant "two days more of uncertainty."[51]

At 3:30 P.M. Stimson attended a White House conference with the president, Marshall, Knox, Stark, King, Hopkins, and the new commander of the Pacific Fleet, Admiral Chester W. Nimitz. Roosevelt opened by informing them of a very important conference scheduled for December 23 with Prime Minister Winston S. Churchill and the British chiefs of staff, who would be arriving in Washington on December 22. Roosevelt appointed Stimson, Marshall, Knox, Stark, King, and Hopkins to act as his advisers at the conference. A memorandum was distributed "containing a suggested agenda which had been drawn up by the British." Roosevelt asked his advisers to formulate an American agenda and to be able to discuss the British agenda. Marshall replied that the War Department had been working on the matter for several days. According to Stimson, the War Plans Division had been "working hard in getting together its views as to the world strategy necessary to meet the present situation."

Following his return to the War Department, Stimson held a "preliminary conference" with Lovett, McCloy, and Bundy. He showed them the agenda and divided among them the responsibility for investigating certain factors, then discussed the first item on the British agenda: "Fundamental Basis of Joint Strategy."

Concerning the forthcoming conferences with the British, Stimson wrote in his diary:

> Knowing as I do the President's unmethodical habits, I felt that somebody in whom he has confidence must be prepared to keep him straight so far as possible in the discussions that are coming up because there are a number of things on which there will be sure to be sharp divergence— some between the British and us, some between the Navy and us, and some individually. So that I see before me at least a week of very unremitting work and strain before this thing is over, and the trouble is that it is mixed in between with the constant necessity of pushing the progress of the war which has now become intense in the Philippines and Malaya. The Japanese, aided by their naval victories, are pushing hard on the Malayan peninsula toward Singapore. They have bunched their forces there and seem to be pushing with their major strength at that place and at Hong Kong. In the Philippines they are not pushing so hard and I am inclined to think they are just containing the Philippines until they get through with the other places when they will probably try to bunch us off and fight. So enough strength must be conserved to be ready to push, push, push on the question of the reserves coming up which move slowly "and so slowly."[52]

On December 19 MacArthur received notice from General Marshall that the *Pensacola* convoy was due to arrive at Brisbane the following day and that a fast ship containing fifty-five pursuit planes and crews had left the West Coast, with two other ships scheduled to leave in about eight days. Clippers and armored flying boats carring 50-caliber ammunition were leaving the United States via Africa for Australia and the Philippines, and fifteen heavy bombers were being dispatched to the Philippines.[53]

After receiving this information, MacArthur notified the head of the *Pensacola* convoy in Australia, Brigadier General Julian F. Barnes, that he wanted the convoy to proceed to the Philippines by the "most expeditious route." Although MacArthur had "no evidence to show that any route was blocked," he recognized that the

movement of the convoy would "undoubtedly require the cooperative assistance of the United States and Allied sea and air" power.
Admitting that he was not in possession of sufficient information to
order the movement of the convoy, which had to be coordinated and
executed by the Navy, he said he was requesting the War Department to arrange with the Navy for the movement of the convoy to
the Philippines. MacArthur also told Barnes that he wanted the Air
Corps elements to remain in Australia.[54]

Later MacArthur repeated this message to the War Department.

> Request you coordinate with navy so that orders may be issued
> from Washington to bring convoy through. I will furnish all avail-
> able information on situation here with particular emphasis on
> air.[55]

MacArthur also wrote a lengthy memorandum to Admiral Hart
reviewing the question of the movement of the *Pensacola* convoy
to the Philippines. Pointing out that President Roosevelt recognized
the "strategic importance of the Philippines" and that the War
Department recognized the importance of reestablishing limited
sea travel from Australia to the Philippines, MacArthur informed
him that, since the control of the convoy at Brisbane had been
turned over to Hart, it was his "urgent desire, in accordance with
the policy of President Roosevelt, that reinforcements and supplies
be pushed forward to the Philippines."[56]

For Stimson in Washington December 19 had been "a day of hard
work, trying to find a way out of the mess, and many disappointments." At 9:30 A.M. he met with Richard G. Casey, the Australian
minister. Assuring Casey that the United States would defend
Australia "no matter what happened," Stimson said that if the
Japanese succeeded in conquering the Philippines and Singapore,
the Allies "would fall back on the Netherlands East Indies and on
Australia . . . and fight it out there."[57]

On December 20 Stimson completed a memorandum, "A Suggested Analysis of the Basic Topics and Their Attendant Problems,"
for use by Roosevelt at the forthcoming conferences with the British.
The basic premise of the memorandum was set out in Stimson's
opening statement: "Our joint war plans have recognized the North
Atlantic as our principal theatre of operations should America become involved in the war. Therefore it should now be given primary

consideration and carefully reviewed in order to see whether our position there is safe. Its safety must underlie all our other efforts in the war."

The memorandum also covered secondary theaters: Egypt and Libya, Western Africa, Syria and Iran, and the southwestern Pacific. Of these, Stimson considered the last as having the greatest priority:

1. The Southwestern Pacific
   A. This is of first importance because it has been forced upon us by a new combatant power which is challenging our entire position in the Pacific and our troops are already fighting desperately to carry out our legal and moral obligation to protect the Philippines.
   B. It is also of vital importance:
      (1) To assist the British in defending Singapore, the fall of which would be an almost vital blow to the British Empire as well as to our own future commercial interests in the Pacific.
      (2) To protect the Netherlands East Indies and their sources of oil from falling into the hands of the Japanese and thus aiding Japan in her contest for the control of the Pacific against us.
      (3) For protecting the great dominion of Australia and New Zealand from domination by Japan.
      (4) To encourage and keep China fighting—who has and is still carrying the main effort of holding Japan in check.
      (5) To encourage Russia in staying in the war against the Axis powers.[58]

Even though Stimson recognized the great importance of the southwestern Pacific theater, he believed that the Atlantic theater was more important. In his view the most essential problem confronting the United States was the preservation of sea communication across the North Atlantic to the British Isles. Regardless of the consequences in the Philippine Islands, it was decided that the primary theater must be across the Atlantic Ocean, while the Pacific Ocean would be only a secondary theater.[59]

3

The Moves to Bataan and Corregidor

December 21–31, 1941

The Philippine Islands bear the same strategic relationship to the Southern Asian coast as the Japanese Islands do to the Northern. . . . Without the Philippines, Japan's dominion of Asian seas will be no more than tentative, and her eventual dominion or destruction will depend upon who holds these Islands.[1]

—Homer Lea

From Manila on December 21 General MacArthur radioed the War Department:

Aggressive attempts at infiltration increasing both north and south. Enemy air raiding over Luzon, Cebu and Mindanao. Indications point to progressive building up of forces. His naval units move with complete freedom which makes it possible for him to concentrate in force at one or at many points. If possible some naval threat should be made so as to curtail such complete freedom of movement in all sea lanes.[2]

In Washington, Stimson took a copy of the radiogram to a conference with Roosevelt. He called the president's attention "to the fact that the Japanese were enjoying apparently complete freedom of naval action in the sea route through the Islands," and impressed this fact upon the commander in chief of the United States Fleet, Admiral King, who was also present. The three discussed the ques-

31

tion of Japanese naval supremacy in Philippine waters, and King said "he would take it up with Admiral Stark and they would discuss it with General Marshall."[3]

On December 22 MacArthur had the following radiogram relayed to the War Department:

> Initial concentration of seventy to eighty transports in Lingayen Gulf on the front Aringay-Agoo-San Fabian indicate major enemy effort in strength estimated at eighty thousand to one hundred thousand men of four to six divisions. I have available on Luzon about forty thousand men in units partially equipped. I anticipate that this enormous tactical discrepancy will compel me to operate in delaying action on successive lines through central Luzon plain to final defensive position on Bataan to cover Corregidor. When forced to do so I shall release Manila and the metropolitan area by suitable proclamation in order to save civilian population. I will evacuate the high commissioner and the government to Corregidor. I intend to hold Corregidor.[4]

Japanese troops landed on Lingayen's beaches at dawn and started to advance south, their objective Manila. For a time, reports indicated that Wainwright's North Luzon Force of Filipino and American troops "had more than held their own." But later reports flowing into MacArthur's Victoria Street headquarters showed that the tide was turning in favor of the Japanese. After studying the discouraging intelligence reports, MacArthur looked at a map showing Lingayen Gulf and remarked to his chief of staff, Sutherland, "What a target this would have been for the submarines." There had been virtually no American naval opposition to the landings.[5]

After announcing that Manila might be declared an open city, MacArthur discussed in his office the topic of propaganda with the correspondent of North American Newspaper Alliance, Arch Royal Gunnison. Manila was being continually bombed, and the population was becoming jittery.

"Why tell them this discouraging news and then say that you are considering declaring Manila an open city?" Gunnison asked. "Don't you think that will create a feeling of great helplessness?"

Taking a long draw at his cigar, MacArthur replied, "I want to be perfectly honest with these people. I want them to know nearly everything I know. I'm confident they can take it and come back for more. They realize I'll fight to the last. They realize I'll not take a run-out powder on them. If I give them the bad news along with the good when it comes, then they'll know I've never tried to trick them."

He paused in thought for a moment, then continued: "I don't believe in feeding the population of any country false information. If you build false confidence and you are not successful, you lose their trust forever. If you give the average civilian the truth, he can take a lot more than these propaganda artists tell you is possible. And then when you tell the public you are holding or you are doing better it gives them something to hang on to."[6]

In spite of the grave threat to the Philippines posed by the new Japanese landings, MacArthur found time that day to present the Distinguished Service Cross to Captain Jesus A. Villamor of the Philippine Army Air Corps and Second Lieutenant Jack Dale of the American Army Air Corps. At the ceremony, held at No. 1 Military Plaza, MacArthur spoke:

> It gives me great pleasure to pin these decorations on your breasts where for all time and for all eyes they will be the outward symbol of the devotion, the fortitude and the courage with which you have fought for your country. It is my profound sorrow that Captain Colin Kelley is not here. I do not know the dignity of Captain Kelley's birth but I do know the glory of his death. He died unquestioning, uncomplaining with fortitude in his heart and victory his end. God has taken unto himself a gallant soldier who did his duty.[7]

That morning in Washington, Stimson reviewed MacArthur's radiogram concerning the landings at Lingayen Gulf. He found it "extremely conservative—not to say gloomy." Because of his previous experiences with MacArthur, as governor general of the Philippines and as secretary of state during the Hoover administration, Stimson believed that the general "was apt to do more than he prophesied for himself." He recalled that MacArthur, "in 1932 at least, had been inclined to overestimate the power and skill of the Japanese."[8]

For Stimson there was "one bright spot" that day—a report that the *Pensacola* convoy had arrived safely in Brisbane. He wrote in his diary:

> If it had not been for the delay in turning the convoy back by the Navy, we should not have lost at least two days and

the convoy afterwards moved very slowly; so that the precious guns and planes which we have been so anxious to rush up to MacArthur may be too late to affect the great battle which is now going on. But thank heaven, the Navy is now reorganized and under Admiral King is now putting some punch into decisions, and Admiral Hart has been ordered to take a more active and courageous part in the Philippine matters.[9]

Later on December 22 Marshall replied to MacArthur's radiogram:

> Your proposed lines of action approved. We are doing our utmost to organize in Australia to rush air support to you. The convoy arrived there last night with seventy planes aboard. Our number thirty-four outlined instructions to Hart and also to Brett via military attaché Australia. Three B-24 planes departed yesterday. Three B-17s leave today via same route and three B-17s and B-24s alternate each day thereafter to total of eighty heavy bombers. Fifty-five pursuit planes four days at sea and fifty-five more sail in three days. . . . President has seen all of your messages and directs navy to give you every possible support in your splendid fight.[10]

Another dispatch came on December 22 from MacArthur, desperate for air reinforcements.

> One of the main features of our attempt at air reinforcement here was the recommendation contained in my radios of December 13 and 14 regarding pursuit and dive bomber reinforcement by means of aircraft carrier. Present enemy air encirclement permits interruption of ferry route to south due to day bombardment [of] Mindanao fields. Early reinforcement by carrier would solve problem. Your radios make no reference to this feature. Can I expect anything along that line? In this general connection can you give me any inkling of strategic plans Pacific Fleet?[11]

Brigadier General Gerow, in charge of the War Plans Division, submitted a copy of MacArthur's message to Admiral Stark, chief of Naval Operations. In a memorandum to Marshall on December 23, Stark wrote that owing to the "existing strategic situation, delivery of aircraft to the Philippines over the direct route from the Hawaiian area [is] not practicable in any type of ship." Aircraft carriers should not be diverted "from their necessary functions as fighting ships," Stark emphasized, and the movement of planes via aircraft carriers was likewise impractical. The "best way to move army pursuit and dive bombers to the Far East," he said, was "by shipment in cargo vessels." Stark recommended there be no change in plans to move aircraft to the Far East by cargo vessels.[12]

The gist of Admiral Stark's negative memorandum was shortly dispatched by Marshall to MacArthur.

> The routes and methods already adopted and described to you for supporting you with air strength are the only practicable ones under the existing strategic situation. This refers to your [radiogram of] December 22. It is expected that the fighter and dive bomber planes now in Australia will quickly determine feasibility of route from Darwin to Luzon for transiting small fighter planes which are being rushed to that base by fast ships. The heavy bombers beginning to flow from this country via Africa to your theater should be able to support you materially even if compelled initially to operate from distant bases. They will be valuable also in cooperating with naval forces and smaller aircraft in protecting your line of communications. The great range, speed and power of these bombers should permit, under your direction, effective surprise against particularly favorable targets anywhere in the theatre. So far as possible critical items listed in your recent messages are being shipped to Australia for delivery as quickly as circumstances will permit.[13]

In Washington during the morning of December 23, Stimson, Marshall, Gerow, and General Henry H. Arnold had a long conference with Field Marshal Sir John Dill, the former chief of the British Imperial General Staff, and Air Marshal Sir Charles Portal concerning "the general features of the [military] situation." Both of these British officers had arrived in Washington the night before with Prime Minister Churchill for the Arcadia Conference.

At 4:15 P.M. Stimson attended a military conference in the cabinet room of the White House. Present were Roosevelt, Churchill, Marshall, Arnold, Stark, Secretary of the Navy Frank Knox, Harry Hopkins, Lord Beaverbrook, Sir Dudley Pound, the First Sea Lord, and Portal and Dill. Roosevelt began the conference "with a statement as to the talks which he already had during the day with Churchill." Then, to Stimson's "utter surprise," he picked up Stimson's memorandum of December 20 and "made it the basis of the entire conference." Carefully considering the memorandum "point by point," Roosevelt had the members of the conference relate their views "on each point and then asked Churchill to follow and comment on it, which he did."

Concerning the conclusion of the White House conference, Stimson entered in his diary:

> There was then a little general discussion participated in by the American military and naval members and the British military and naval members, and it became very evident that there was a pretty general agreement upon the views of the grand strategy which we had held in the War Department and which were outlined in my paper. Churchill commented feelingly on the sentence of my summary where I described our first main principle as "the preservation of our communications across the North Atlantic with our fortress in the British Isles covering the British fleet."[14]

The same day the Australian minister, Richard G. Casey, submitted to Roosevelt and Churchill a diplomatic cable from Prime Minister John Curtin. In it, concerned about the Japanese threat to Singapore, Curtin urged Roosevelt and Churchill to bolster Allied defenses in Malaya by reinforcing Singapore. Further, he said, "Should the Government of the United States desire, we would gladly accept an American Commander in the Pacific area."[15]

On December 24 MacArthur sent a radiogram on the continually deteriorating situation to Marshall:

> On north front bitter fighting continues. The pier area of Manila has just been bombed by the enemy. Four enemy transports now unloading at Atimonan, one at Mauban and one are [sic] standing off west coast near Nasugbu. Tonight I plan to disengage my forces under cover of darkness, concentrating center of gravity of my movement toward Bataan. I am evacuating this afternoon the high commissioner and the commonwealth government. I will subsequently issue the following proclamation:
>
> > In order to spare the metropolitan area from the possible ravages of attack either by air or ground, Manila is hereby declared an open city without the characteristics of a military objective. In order that no excuse may be given for possible mistake, the American high commissioner, the commonwealth government and all combatant military installations will be withdrawn from its environs as rapidly as possible. The municipal government will continue to function with its police

power, reinforced by constabulary troops, so that normal protection for life and property may be preserved. Citizens are
requested to maintain obedience to the constituted authorities
and to continue to use normal process of business.

My bombing attacks yesterday were only partially successful.
My bombing potentialities operating from this area are exhausted.
I shall continue operating my pursuit to provide observation. In
anticipation of severed communications I am instructing the
Visayan-Mindanao commanding general Sharp repeat Sharp to
continue resistance operations by guerrilla methods to the end that
he may obtain indisputable loci of American resistance. For the
present I am remaining in Manila establishing an advanced headquarters on Corregidor. The behavior of our troops has been de-
sirable in every respect in spite of the overwhelming odds against
them.[16]

MacArthur spent most of December 24 in his headquarters at No.
1 Calle Victoria. Throughout the day he "was constantly reviewing
intelligence reports and talking to commanders and his staff officers."
While his chief of staff, Sutherland, was mainly concerned with
operational problems, his deputy chief of staff, Brigadier General
Richard Marshall, busied himself with logistic problems. Marshall
was concerned with transferring some supplies to Bataan and de-
stroying others before the advancing Japanese could capture them.
MacArthur's chief engineer, Casey, was at the front preparing
additional reserve positions and supervising the destruction of
bridges, power facilities, and all nonremovable military supplies.
At 11:00 A.M. Sutherland announced to members of the USAFFE
staff in the Victoria headquarters that they would be leaving that
night to establish a headquarters on Corregidor.[17]

At 12:30 P.M. Major General Brereton of the Far East Air Force
entered MacArthur's office. Expressing "his extreme gratification
over the part the Far East Air Force had taken in the battle of
Luzon," MacArthur informed Brereton that he and his headquarters
were being ordered to proceed south to Australia. When Brereton
offered to remain on MacArthur's staff in any useful capacity,
MacArthur replied, "No, Lewis, you go on south. You can do me
more good with the bombers you have left and those you should be
receiving soon than you can here. Since communications over that
distance are practically impossible now, I must depend to the
greatest extent upon your initiative to support our forces here."

As Brereton rose to leave, MacArthur said, "I hope that you will tell the people outside what we have done and protect my reputation as a fighter."

"General, your reputation will never need any protection," Brereton replied, shaking MacArthur's hand.[18]

Early in the afternoon Sutherland told Marshall that MacArthur had decided to make the transfer to Corregidor that night with his principal staff officers. Marshall was to be left in charge of an echelon at the Victoria headquarters made up of representatives of all General Staff and Special Staff sections, for the purpose of maintaining contact with field forces and coordinating the withdrawal of the North and South Luzon forces to Bataan. Marshall was also ordered to expedite the movement of supplies to Bataan and to destroy supplies that could not be moved.

Shortly afterward, MacArthur called Marshall into his office and outlined the mission. Marshall was to turn over to the Manila chief of police the bank of flags in MacArthur's office, and to remain in Manila as long as necessary to complete his mission. Under no circumstances was he to allow the Victoria headquarters to be captured by the Japanese beforehand. MacArthur, his family, and his staff would leave for Corregidor aboard the *Don Esteban*, which would later be on call to transfer the remaining staff members to Corregidor. Because High Commissioner Sayre and President Quezon would also be going to Corregidor, MacArthur told Marshall to keep him informed of events in Manila and of the positions of the South and North Luzon forces by using the one telephone cable to Corregidor.[19]

That afternoon Major Carlos P. Romulo watched MacArthur in his office through the open door. The general was reading reports scattered on his desk, studying the large maps on the walls, and talking with Sutherland. Now and then he would get up from the chair and pace the room in deep thought, his head bowed and his hands clasped behind his back. To Romulo, the expression on his "hawkish face" seemed "cast in bitter lines."

At exactly 6:00 P.M. MacArthur stopped pacing, put on his garrison cap, glanced quickly around at his flags, and strode out of the room as if leaving for the day. He stopped at Romulo's desk. Romulo was one of the few officers who knew that he was leaving for Corregidor that night, and they talked in low voices. MacArthur told him he was to stay behind with Marshall's rear echelon in order to keep in touch with newspaper correspondents in Manila. "I'll be back, Carlos!" MacArthur said, extending his hand.[20]

At 6:00 P.M. the USAFFE staff started to board the interisland steamer *Don Esteban*. At 8:00 MacArthur and Sutherland came on board and the ship pulled away from the deserted pier. It was a beautiful moonlit night. The blacked-out *Don Esteban* headed out into Manila Bay toward the island of Corregidor. On deck the officers talked quietly against the steady background thunder of exploding demolitions. The night sky flared with great fires along the Cavite shore—the Navy's fuel dump of more than a million gallons of oil had been ignited during the day.

The officers could see the receding lights of the Army and Navy Club and the Manila Hotel. Lieutenant Commander Thomas C. Parker's heart sank as he thought of friends left behind in Manila. Colonel Arnold J. Funk remembered other times in the beautiful city, called the "Pearl of the Orient" before the war. One of the staff officers, Colonel William P. Morse, noticed MacArthur. He was sitting, holding his head in his hands. It was a joyless Christmas Eve.[21]

The fortress of Corregidor loomed ahead. "The Rock," as it was called, guarded the entrance to Manila Bay with the fifty-six coastal guns and mortars of Fort Mills, ranging in caliber from 3 to 12 inches. Corregidor, shaped like a tadpole, was 3½ miles long and 1¼ miles across at its widest point. Its bulbous head, "Topside," rising 500 feet above the sea, held most of the large coastal artillery, which pointed west toward the South China Sea. North of the island across 2 miles of water was the Bataan peninsula; south were the smaller fortified islands of Forts Drum, Hughes, and Frank, extending intermittently across 13 miles of water to the mainland.[22]

At the junction of the head and tail of Corregidor, the island narrowed to 600 yards across and its elevation dropped to just above sea level. In this low area, "Bottomside," were North and South docks, the *barrio* of San José, shops, warehouses, a power plant, and cold-storage units. To the east of Bottomside stood Malinta Hill. Bored through the hill to the tail of the island was Malinta Tunnel, a passageway 1,400 feet long and 30 feet wide with a labyrinth of smaller offshoots. The bombproof tunnel housed a hospital, headquarters, and a vast storage-shop area.[23]

At about 11:00 the *Don Esteban* tied up at Corregidor's North Dock after the 26-mile voyage. Brigadier General George F. Moore,

[handwritten margin note: Fort Mills ARMY Name for Corregidor]

who commanded the Harbor Defenses at Corregidor, boarded and explained to MacArthur the arrangements he had made. The staff and their equipment were to be temporarily housed in Malinta Tunnel. "The Quezons and Sayres and you will be in the hospital section of the tunnel tonight," Moore closed, "and we've partitioned off another section for women. We have never had women around here and things may be a little crude. I want you and Mrs. Mac-Arthur to take my house tomorrow, it's Topside—up on the rock."

"That's fine, George. Thank you very much," MacArthur replied.[24]

In Washington on the morning of December 24, Stimson learned that Churchill was "anxious" to discuss "the subject of the Philippines." He spent the first part of the morning preparing for the conference. Later, when he went to the White House, Stimson took Brigadier General Dwight Eisenhower of the War Plans Division to back him up in case Churchill asked questions Stimson "could not answer." The conference was held upstairs in a map room that Churchill had established next to his bedroom. "Wearing a sort of zipper pajama suit and slippers," Churchill greeted Stimson and Eisenhower. From maps of the Philippines, Stimson "explained the location of the different troops on both sides, the course of the campaign, and its probable outcome in a retreat on Corregidor." Eisenhower departed early and Stimson "had a further talk with [Churchill] about other matters in the various parts of the [Philippine] terrain."[25]

Later Stimson wrote out a short message that was subsequently dispatched to President Quezon:

> Your gallant defense is thrilling the American people. As soon as our power is organized we shall come in force and drive the invader from your soil. My heartfelt good wishes to you and your family and people.[26]

Another radiogram went from Marshall to MacArthur:

> . . . Plans for reaching you quickly with pursuit plane support are jeopardized. Your day to day situation and that of Borneo will determine what can be done at any moment but the War Department will press in every way for the development of a strong United States air power in the Far East based in Australia. Every effort permitted by the situation in the Pacific is being devoted to this purpose and our fighter and bomber strength will soon begin

to increase rapidly. Your plans and orders are fully approved by
the secretary of war.[27]

On December 25 MacArthur divided his forward staff echelon
into two divisions. One representative each from the Personnel,
Intelligence, Operations, Supply, and Adjutant General sections,
along with MacArthur, Sutherland, and some of the aides, moved
into the west-wing first floor of the three-story Coast Artillery
Barracks located on Topside. The balance of the forward staff
echelon on Corregidor moved into Malinta Tunnel.[28]

In the afternoon, MacArthur notified the War Department of
the successful movement of his forward staff echelon to Fort Mills.
He set forth his intention of establishing a command post on Bataan,
while leaving an administrative echelon at Fort Mills. He also told
the War Department that heavy bombardment operations were no
longer possible from Philippine bases, but that pursuit operations
providing reconnaissance would be maintained under the command
of Colonel Harold H. George. Explaining that all remaining B-17s
had departed for bases in the Netherlands East Indies and Australia,
MacArthur said Major General Brereton and a small staff had left
the previous day with the following instructions:

> You will proceed to the south with the Headquarters of
> the Far East Air Force. Your mission is to organize advance
> operating bases from which, with the Far East Air Force,
> you can protect the lines of communications, secure bases
> in Mindanao, and support the defense of the Philippines by
> the USAFFE. You will cooperate with the United States
> Navy and with the Air and Naval Forces of Australia and the
> Netherlands East Indies. You will establish liaison with the
> Commanding General United States Forces in Australia.
> You will direct the operation of the Far East Air Force from
> those bases and the disposition of air corps troops in ad-
> vance thereof. . . . You will make a request upon the Com-
> manding General United States Forces in Australia for such
> movement and disposition of the ground elements of your
> command as may be required in the execution of your mis-
> sion.[29]

On Christmas morning in Washington, Stimson learned of Japanese successes in the Philippines and of the Japanese capture of
Hong Kong. It was not the only disturbing news. Later on, Eisen-

hower, Arnold, and Marshall came to Stimson's office with "a rather astonishing memorandum which they had received from the White House concerning a meeting between Churchill and the President and recorded by one of Churchill's assistants." According to the memorandum, President Roosevelt proposed "to discuss the turning over to the British, [American] proposed reinforcements for Mac-Arthur." The "astonishing" memorandum made Stimson "extremely angry."

At noon Stimson went home to Woodley for lunch. The more he thought about the memorandum, the more angry he became. Finally he telephoned Harry Hopkins at the White House and told him about the memorandum. If Roosevelt intended to carry out these plans he would have to accept his resignation as secretary of war, Stimson said; and "it was very improper to discuss such matters while . . . fighting was going on [in the Philippines] and to do it with another nation." Hopkins, "surprised and shocked," told Stimson that he would take the matter up with Roosevelt.

Hopkins called back in a short while. He told Stimson that he had relayed Stimson's words to Roosevelt "in the presence of Churchill," and that both men "had denied that any such proposition had been actually made." Stimson read Hopkins excerpts from the memorandum. Hopkins agreed "that they certainly bore out [Stimson's original] view."

The president called a meeting of his military and naval advisers for 5:30 P.M. Stimson joined Marshall, Arnold, Knox, King, Stark, and Hopkins at the White House. In the meeting Roosevelt discussed current reports and "various things which were happening and the ways and means of carrying out the campaign in the Far East." Then, "incidentally and as if by aside, Roosevelt flung out the remark that a paper had been going around which was nonsense and which entirely misrepresented a conference between him and Churchill." Since Roosevelt had given up any "idea of discussing the surrender of MacArthur's reinforcements," Stimson did not reply. But for him this unfortunate incident helped to cause "a strange and distressful Christmas."[30]

On December 26 MacArthur reported to the War Department that Admiral Thomas C. Hart had "left Manila to join naval forces in the south," his "destination to be reported later." Rear Admiral Francis W. Rockwell, with headquarters on Corregidor, was given command of all remaining naval forces. The preceding day Mac-Arthur had received this information from Hart.[31]

The withdrawing North Luzon Force was along the Agno River, MacArthur reported, in heavy artillery dueling. In the southeast, Brigadier General Albert M. Jones's Fifty-first Division of the South Luzon Force was "very heavily engaged with the enemy making full use of superiority in the air and on the ground." The Japanese were "steadily bringing up reinforcements from fleets of transports at Lingayen and Atimonan."[32]

Later that day MacArthur and his aide-de-camp, Lieutenant Colonel Sidney Huff, walked for exercise up and down Malinta Tunnel. MacArthur told Huff to return to Manila that night "for some documents that had been left behind and to carry some messages for President Quezon." In closing MacArthur added, "While you're in my apartment look in the bedside table, where you'll find my Colt .45—the one I carried in the First World War. Bring that. And if you look in the cupboard, you'll see my old campaign hat. I'd like to have that." Then, pausing "thoughtfully," he said, "I think if you look in the dining room you may see a bottle of Scotch. Just as well bring that too. It may be a long, cold winter over here."[33]

On the morning of December 26 in Washington, Stimson received "a fine cable" from Quezon:

> Your message [of December 24] is most encouraging. We are doing all we can to uphold the honor, rights and interests of America in the Philippines. My whole family appreciate your greetings and join with me in wishing you and Mrs. Stimson a happy New Year.[34]

Later Stimson talked with Marshall and Assistant Secretary of War John J. McCloy concerning the establishment of a united command for the Netherlands East Indies. Commenting that Marshall had come out "finely and bravely for a united command, if necessary, under British Lieutenant General Sir Archibald P. Wavell," Stimson "pointed out, by way of caution or limitation," that the principles of command should be made clear enough and finalized so that an "overwhelming air force" would be built up in the Netherlands East Indies. Stimson feared that under a British commander planes would be wasted "in small detachments" without any noticeable effect on the enemy, and wanted assurances that this would not happen. He believed it was necessary to wait until the Allies had accumulated a superior air force in the south that would enable them to "control the air and then go in and clean up the country again, even if it has been overrun by the Japanese."[35]

On December 27 the message center at Fort Mills received a radiogram from Marshall to MacArthur:

> Your reports and those of press indicate splendid conduct of your command and troops through trials of Christmas Day. The president and secretary of war and quite evidently entire American people have been profoundly impressed with your resistance to Japanese endeavors. Your reports on arrangement of your command setup and disposition of your air forces are acknowledged and approved.
>
> General Brett should now be in Australia prepared with his immediate staff together with General Clagett and General Barnes to further your interests to utmost. Yesterday the president again personally directed the navy to make every effort to support you. You can rest assured [the] War Department will do all in its power in Far East to completely dominate that region. It would be helpful to us to have a statement of [your] plans, and experienced air staff with General Brereton, and strength of your remaining [air] pursuit in Luzon.[36]

MacArthur radioed back the same day.

> The following is my present strategic concept of the situation: Enemy penetration in the Philippines resulted from our weakness on the sea and in the air. Surface elements of the Asiatic Fleet were withdrawn and the effect of submarines has been negligible. Lack of airfields for modern planes prevented defensive dispersion and lack of pursuit planes permitted unhindered Jap bombardment. The enemy has had utter freedom of naval and air movements. This has resulted in the loss of Luzon as an operating base for air. It can be anticipated that similar methods will be used in the Netherlands East Indies, utilizing Mindanao as a base if secured. If enemy is successful it will be necessary for United States forces to undertake task of advancing from Australia, retaking Netherlands East Indies. Bases are still available and must be retained; they can be given pursuit protection, permitting bomber operation from them. The Netherlands East Indies can be protected and hostile development on Mindanao can be prevented.
>
> I deem it essential to rush air forces to operate from Netherlands East Indies' advanced airdromes and Australian and Nether-

lands East Indies' bases, preventing Jap air development in the Davao region and in Borneo. Strong naval forces must seek combat with the enemy. With support of the fleet, communication with Mindanao can be maintained and airdromes there can be occupied, Jap air driven out. Ground forces should be landed in Mindanao. Such line of action will permit immediate check to the hostile southward drive and speedy recovery in the Philippines regardless of the outcome here. Utmost rapidity of action by air, navy, and ground forces is essential.

I have initiated skeleton staff and all bombers to Netherlands East Indies and Australia. I am moving from here to Mindanao all air corps personnel possible. They will remain in Del Monte, Lake Lanao–Malabalog area—prepared [to] assist in forward movement. I am supporting Mindanao with reinforcements and ammunition to extent possible. I wish to emphasize the necessity for naval action and for rapid execution by land, sea and air.[37]

On December 28 MacArthur informed the War Department that Japanese pressure against the South Luzon Force on the southeastern front was "very heavy," with Filamerican casualties estimated at "fifteen percent"; Japanese pressure against the North Luzon Force on the northern front was "not so great nor casualties so heavy":

Local commanders estimate enemy forces already committed as two divisions in the south, three in the north. Caliber of troops seems to be excellent, equipment modern and extensive. Enemy is undoubtedly setting up a powerful attack both north and south simultaneously designed to pin me down in places and crush me. Under such conditions I can no longer safely attempt to cover Manila from the south and east. I am accordingly breaking contact there tonight and shifting towards Bataan. Enemy air activity continues heavy with violation of the open city of Manila. Successfully broke contact with southern forces last night. Losses slight. Am endeavoring to temporarily hold hard in north until [the] two forces make contact in San Fernando area. Will then pivot on my left in case of necessity to covering position in Bataan. Troops are tired but well in hand.[38]

A second December 28 radiogram to the War Department described a new problem:

There has appeared a crescendo of enemy propaganda throughout all elements of society claiming inactivity of United States in support of Filipino effort especially with reference to apparent inactive American naval force. I am not in position here to combat this theme which is now being used with deadly effectiveness. Suggest the employment of counter propaganda from Washington especially with reference to naval activity.[39]

On the night of December 28 President Roosevelt responded with a message, accompanied by a statement from the Navy Department, to the people of the Philippine Islands. The message was broadcast by short-wave radio direct to Manila and rebroadcast and given to the press.

The people of the Philippines:
News of your gallant struggle against the Japanese aggressor has elicited the profound admiration of every American. As President of the United States, I know that I speak for all our people on this solemn occasion.

The resources of the United States, of the British Empire, of the Netherlands East Indies and of the Chinese Republic have been dedicated by their people to the utter and complete defeat of the Japanese war lords. In this great struggle of the Pacific, the loyal Americans of the Philippine Islands are called upon to play a crucial role.

They have played, and they are playing tonight, their part with the greatest gallantry.

As President I wish to express to them my feeling of sincere admiration for the fight they are now making.

The people of the United States will never forget what the people of the Philippine Islands are doing this day and will do in the days to come. I give to the people of the Philippines my solemn pledge that their freedom will be redeemed and their independence established and protected.

The entire resources, in men and in materials, of the United States stand behind that pledge.

It is not for me or for the people of this country to tell you where your duty lies. We are engaged in a great and common cause. I count on every Philippine man, woman and child to do his duty. We will do ours.

The Navy Department announced the Japanese Government is circulating rumors for the obvious purpose of persuading the United States to disclose the location and intentions of the American Pacific Fleet.

It is obvious that these rumors are intended and directed at the Philippine Islands.

The Philippines may rest assured that, while the United States Navy will not be tricked into disclosing vital information, the fleet is not idle.

The United States Navy is following an intensive and well-planned campaign against the Japanese forces which will result in positive assistance to the defense of the Philippine Islands.[40]

An air raid alarm sounded on Corregidor at 11:45 A.M. on December 29. Coming over were eighty-one Japanese medium bombers and ten dive bombers. Part of MacArthur's forward staff echelon was working in the Coast Artillery Barracks on Topside. The officers hurriedly left their desks to check the type and number of planes. As the bombers passed overhead, the men, hearing the sound of falling bombs, hit the floor. "Well, I guess this is it," Sutherland said. Several waves of planes tried to hit the command post, but miraculously only a storeroom attached to the post exchange was struck. Shortly afterward, MacArthur sent the enlisted men to Malinta Tunnel and the officers to the old Station Headquarters (later the officers also moved into Malinta Tunnel).[41]

MacArthur was caught in the open within view of his deserted bungalow. With Corporal Benny and Sergeant Domingo Adversario, his Filipino orderly, he "crouched up against a building," counting the bombers. Just before a bomb crashed through the roof of the bungalow, Adversario covered MacArthur's body with his own and used his helmet to shield MacArthur's head. Steel fragments from exploding bombs hit Adversario's hand and dented the helmet, but MacArthur was unhurt. He dressed his orderly's injured hand and later awarded him the Purple Heart.[42]

About an hour after the beginning of the raid, Captain John K. Wallace of the Medical Corps, assigned to the First Battalion of the Thirty-first Infantry Regiment, was on his way back to the Coast Artillery Barracks. He had been out picking up casualties. Covered with dirt and blood, Wallace was stopped by MacArthur, who was walking around without a helmet, wearing his garrison cap. The Japanese were bombing and strafing the area heavily. Wallace was anxious to return to the barracks' protective cover, but MacArthur was unconcerned. He questioned Wallace about the number of casualties—how many dead, how many seriously wounded, how many slightly wounded. He asked Wallace's name, his unit, and the number of years he had been in the army. They talked for only two or three minutes, but to Wallace it seemed they had been out in the open for three or four hours.[43]

The air raid lasted approximately two and one-half hours. During it twenty-two men were killed and about eighty wounded. Although the Japanese failed to inflict any vital damage, they hit the Station Hospital, Middleside Barracks, the officers' clubs, numerous wooden buildings, and several water tanks. Power, water, and communication lines were disrupted. A Navy gasoline storage dump burned profusely at the tail of the island. The raid cost the Japanese nine medium bombers and several dive bombers.[44]

After the all-clear signal had been sounded and some lights had come on in Malinta Tunnel, President Quezon was handed a radiogram containing President Roosevelt's proclamation of December 28 to the people of the Philippines. Quezon was so "electrified and thrilled" by the message that he walked out of the tunnel into the bright sunlight. Later he held a cabinet meeting and read Roosevelt's message to the members. He told his colleagues that "the sacrifices [the Filipinos] were making were not in vain."[45]

On December 30 General MacArthur moved his family to a cottage on Bottomside about one mile east of Malinta Tunnel. Although beds were reserved in the tunnel for him and his family, MacArthur refused to sleep there.[46]

At 4:30 that afternoon, President Quezon and Vice President Sergio Osmena were inaugurated for their second terms of office. For the occasion a platform was constructed outside the east portal of Malinta Tunnel at the officers' mess. Directly behind the speakers' platform, which faced the sea, a screen had been erected. The flags of the United States and the Commonwealth of the Philippines stood between the screen and the officials. In a wheel chair before the Philippine flag sat President Quezon. To his right were High Commissioner Francis B. Sayre and Vice President Osmena; to his left, MacArthur and the Filipino chief supreme court justice, José Abad Santos. A small audience assembled in front of the platform: Quezon's war cabinet, Brigadier General Moore, Major General Edward P. King (the USAFFE artillery officer), Brigadier General Charles C. Drake (the quartermaster general), Quezon's family, high-ranking

Filipino and American army officers, Quezon's staff, doctors and nurses, and a few civilians.

The solemn ceremony began with "Hail to the Chief" played on the chaplain's organ, followed by a prayer from the army chaplain, Major Albert Braun. After being sworn in by Chief Justice Santos, Quezon delivered an address in which he repeated in its entirety Roosevelt's December 28 pledge to the people of the Philippines. Next Sayre read a short, congratulatory message from Roosevelt, sent prior to the outbreak of hostilities, and remarks of his own that praised the Filipinos' loyalty to the United States. Then, after the swearing in of Vice President Osmena by the chief justice, General MacArthur rose from his chair. He spoke slowly in a voice charged with emotion.

> "Never before in all history has there been a more solemn and significant inauguration. An act, symbolical of democratic processes, is placed against the background of a sudden, merciless war.
>
> "The thunder of death and destruction, dropped from the skies, can be heard in the distance. Our ears almost catch the roar of battle as our soldiers close on the firing line. The horizon is blackened by the smoke of destructive fire. The air reverberates to the roar of exploding bombs.
>
> "Such is the bed of birth of this new government, of this new nation. For four hundred years the Philippines have struggled upward towards self-government. Just at the end of its tuitionary period, just on the threshold of independence, came the great hour of decision. There was no hesitation, no vacillation, no moment of doubt. The whole country followed its great leader in choosing the side of freedom against the side of slavery.
>
> "We have just inaugurated him, we have just thereby confirmed his momentous decision. Hand in hand with the United States and the other free nations of the world, this basic and fundamental issue will be fought through to victory. Come what may, ultimate triumph will be its reward.
>
> "Through this its gasping agony of travail, through what Winston Churchill called 'blood and sweat and tears,' from the grim shadow of the Valley of Death—"

MacArthur's voice faltered and tears streamed down his face. Then, looking at the silent group of soldiers in front of him and the bowed heads of Quezon's family, he "raised his eyes to the heavens and his voice broke as he concluded, 'O merciful God, preserve this noble race.' "[47]

To Moore, sitting in the front row, MacArthur had spoken "briefly but impressively." President Quezon believed that these remarks "were deeply felt by all present." The national anthems of both nations closed the inauguration. Afterwards, many of those present shook Quezon's hand with "strong, expressive, significant, hand-clasps"; yet no one "dared utter the word 'congratulations.' " To one army officer present, it had been "truly a historic inauguration."[48]

Air raid alarms continued throughout the day, but Corregidor was not bombed. Incendiaries were dropped on the small port of Mariveles at the tip of the Bataan peninsula, and fires and smoke from the burning town were visible from Corregidor.[49]

MacArthur remembered the Army chief of staff's birthday with a radiogram to General Marshall:

> We have not forgotten your birthday. I send heartiest felicitations and reiterate the complete confidence I feel in your professional leadership of the army.[50]

In response to this greeting, Marshall replied:

> I am touched by your remembrance of my birthday in the midst of the trials of desperate fighting. You have given me further evidence of the gallant defense you and your people are making against great odds. We are leaving no stone unturned to provide you with assistance and the president is giving your affairs his direct and personal attention. The hopes of the entire nation are centered on your struggle.[51]

In Washington, Churchill, Roosevelt, and their military staffs had been engaged in a series of conferences and discussions regarding global war strategy. Marshall advocated a unified command in the Southwest Pacific of American, British, Australian, and Dutch military forces under Lieutenant General Sir Archibald Wavell. On December 27 Marshall had "dictated a proposed agreement between the various countries of the Southwest Pacific," later approved by the president. Although Churchill had some serious reservations concerning Marshall's plan, on December 29 he notified his war cabinet in London that with their approval he was prepared to accept the proposal. Churchill had feared that "British forces might be diverted from the defense of Singapore and 'wasted' on the Philippines or Borneo." Even though Wavell's sphere of command would include the Philippine Islands, MacArthur, who was designated commander in chief of the Philippines under Wavell, would continue to receive all significant instructions pertaining to the defense of the Philippines from the War Department in Washington.[52]

At a conference on December 28 Roosevelt severely criticized American naval officers for "the lack of initiative and enterprise of the Navy." He "specifically" criticized "some of their recent movements in the Pacific." On December 30 Roosevelt, aware of the fact that the United States had a moral and political commitment to defend the Philippines, wrote in a memorandum to the secretary of war and the secretary of the Navy, "I wish that War Plans would explore every possible means of relieving the Philippines. I realize great risks are involved but the object is important."[53]

December 31 was a critical day for MacArthur's forces in Luzon. The North Luzon Force under the command of Major General Jonathan M. Wainwright had withdrawn to the Bamban-Arayat line in front of San Fernando and the road leading into Bataan. Launching southward from Cabanatuan a major thrust east of the Bamban-Arayat line, the Japanese army threatened to drive a wedge between the North and South Luzon forces. Aside from splitting these forces, the main objective of the attack was the capture of Manila.

MacArthur notified Brigadier General Richard Marshall in Manila to order immediately the complete withdrawal of the South Luzon Force into Bataan and to take measures that would block the Japanese advance threatening to cut off this movement. At 3:00 P.M. the South Luzon Force evacuated the Parananique line and started moving west through Manila toward Bataan. The South Luzon Force was ordered to clear San Fernando by 6:00 A.M. on January 1, but the time was later changed to 4:00 A.M.[54]

MacArthur's staff remained "tense" during the day on Corregidor. Toward evening, however, they learned that the North and South Luzon forces would be able to join in Bataan, and the tension eased. Some officers even enjoyed "a few nips in honor of New Year's Eve."[55]

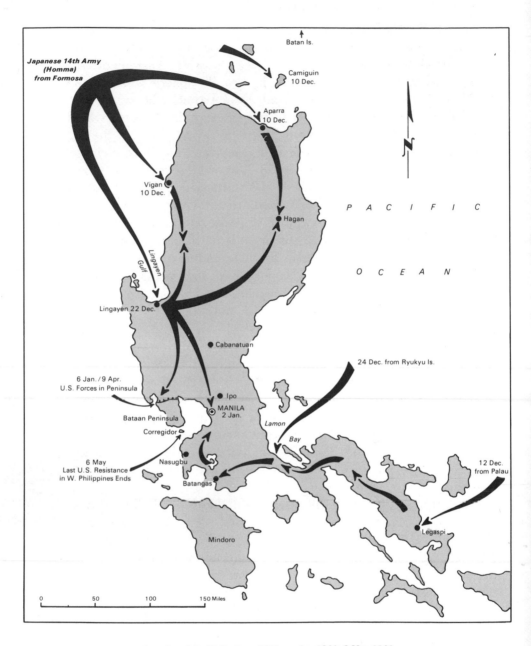

Invasion of the Philippines, 10 December 1941–6 May 1942

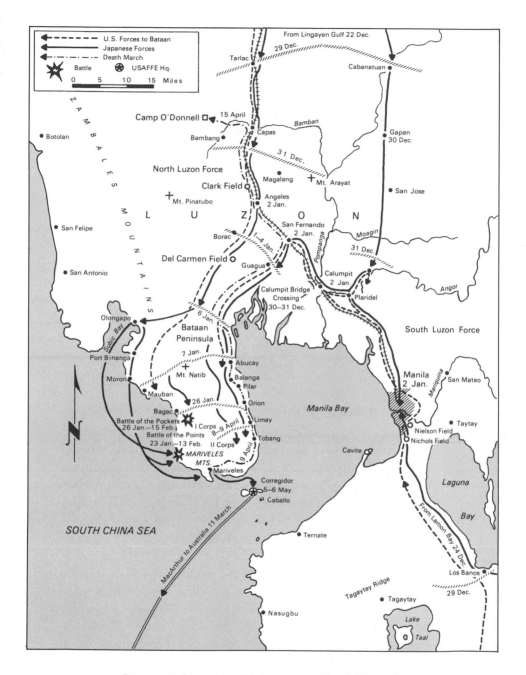

Bataan and Corregidor, 29 December 1941–6 May 1942

53

In Washington on the last day of the year, Stimson's diary reflected the mood of the events:

The last day of the old year and a pretty gloomy one, for the Japanese are encircling Manila and the fall of the city is very imminent. MacArthur seems to be making a successful and skillful retreat to the peninsula of Bataan and Corregidor. But the psychological effect on the Filipinos is very bad and, coming after the defeat at Hawaii, the effect here in this country is also very bad. It has been easy to foresee this situation for in 1921 the Washington Conference gave up our naval power and decided to rely on the covenants of the Nine Power Treaty. It was a highminded endeavor but it was built upon moral qualities which the Japanese Government did not possess and now we have to sit helpless while our thirty years' successful experiment in laying the foundation of free government in the Philippine nation goes down in fragments under the military autocracy of Japan. I think and trust that our people will have enough steadfastness to carry through the work of driving the invaders out and reestablishing our effort in the Philippines, but I foresee many difficulties . . . and a long strain.

To emphasize this, I had a visit here today from Joaquin M. Elizalde, the Resident Commissioner of the Philippines in the United States. I knew him and his family well when I was in the Philippines. It is an old Spanish family which has built up a fortune in the Islands and for many years has been an honored group. In those days Elizalde and his brother were two of the foremost young polo players at the Manila Polo Club. The family estate was estimated as worth some twelve millions of dollars. Today he came to tell me that everything was gone and he was greatly worried for the safety of his mother and his family and he himself had nothing left but his official salary. The specific purpose of his visit was to suggest that Quezon, the President of the Commonwealth, must be rescued from Corregidor and brought to the United States to serve as a rallying post for the continuance of the Philippine loyalty and stimulating their resolution to stand fast until the invader is driven out. I agreed with him fully that Quezon is the only man in the Islands

who had the resolution and the fighting power to do this.
Unfortunately his health is very fragile. But I sent a telegram to MacArthur saying that it was the opinion of the
President, Elizalde, and myself that this was the thing to do.
I left to MacArthur the discretion of finding the means by
which Quezon could be rescued—whether by air or submarine or otherwise.[56]

Farther north on a train bound for Washington, Prime Minister
Winston Churchill was returning from a two-day visit to Ottawa,
Canada. Just before midnight he entered a Pullman car filled with
American newspaper reporters. Wishing them all "a glorious New
Year," Churchill said, "Here's to 1942. Here's to a year of toil—a
year of struggle and peril, and a long step forward towards victory.
May we all come through safe and with honor!"[57]

4

Confrontation on Bataan

January 1–31, 1942

Here I should like to express, in the name of the House, my admiration of the splendid courage and quality with which the small American army, under General MacArthur, has resisted brilliantly for so long, at desperate odds, the hordes of Japanese who have been hurled against it by superior air power and superior sea power. Amid our own troubles, we send out to General MacArthur and his soldiers, and also to the Filipinos, who are defending their native soil with vigour and courage, our salute across the wide spaces which we and the United States will presently rule again together.[1]

—Winston S. Churchill

On January 1 General MacArthur had further information for the War Department:

The South Luzon Force has made firm contact with the North Luzon Force in the San Fernando area. I am occupying the Bataan position as follows: Covering forces on the Porac-Guagua line and vicinity [of] Olongapo. First defensive position Abucay-Mauban, second position generally along Pilar-Bagac road, rear boundary Limay-Paysawan. In this position I intend to accept decisive battle.[2]

At about 3:00 A.M. Colonel Casey left Manila aboard a launch bound for Corregidor. He was the last USAFFE staff officer to leave. Before departing he had led small demolition squads that blew up the gigantic Pandacan oil installations, blasted facilities at

Fort McKinley and Nichols Field, burned warehouses along the Manila waterfront, destroyed bridges, power plants, and radio stations, and dynamited the boilers of two dozen locomotives in the yards of the Manila Railroad. Casey and his "dynamiters" had taken every precaution to prevent military stores and usable material from falling into the hands of the Japanese.

On Corregidor, Casey learned that the South Luzon Force had safely crossed the Calumpit bridge and was moving into the Bataan peninsula. One of his demolition engineers, Lieutenant Colonel Harry A. Sherry, had blown the bridge at 6:15 A.M. to prevent the Japanese from capturing it. "Sir, we've run clean out of bridges," Casey reported to MacArthur later; "now it's up to the infantry."[3]

Early in the morning of January 1 Brigadier General Richard Marshall arrived at Corregidor's North Dock aboard the *Don Esteban*. With the Japanese at the outskirts of Manila, his mission as head of the rear echelon in the city had come to an end. He and his small staff had left Manila at 1:30 A.M. Extremely tired from the long ordeal, Marshall was assigned a bunk in one of the Malinta Tunnel laterals for "a good long sleep into the late morning," after which he was to report to MacArthur in the General Headquarters lateral.[4]

MacArthur's General Headquarters lateral in Malinta Tunnel was a semicircle about 35 feet wide, 100 feet long, and 12 feet high. A portion in the rear was uncompleted tunnel construction. The walls and ceilings were natural limestone, the floor rough cement. Bulbs in simple sockets hung from the ceiling. Viewed from the entrance, on the right side of the lateral were desks parallel to the wall; on the left were desks placed at right angles to the wall.

About thirty officers and enlisted men worked here. The first third of the lateral was occupied by the air officer and the adjutant general, with modest staff groups. The second third was occupied by the section heads of personnel, intelligence, operations, and supply and their deputy assistants. In the far end of the lateral Chief of Staff Sutherland and his secretary-stenographer, Sergeant Paul P. Rogers, had desks, as did MacArthur's two aides, Lieutenant Colonel Sidney Huff and Lieutenant Colonel LeGrande A. Diller, who acted as the press relations officer. The last antiquated desk in the back of the lateral was MacArthur's.[5]

Accompanied by Sutherland, Marshall reported to MacArthur in the lateral. MacArthur congratulated him on the successful conduct and closeout of the rear echelon in Manila. Marshall wished Mac-Arthur a Happy New Year. Saying "he had decided that he could best handle" the military defense of Bataan by establishing a head-quarters behind the front lines on the Bataan peninsula, MacArthur assigned Marshall to establish the advanced headquarters echelon on Bataan in order to maintain personal contact with senior frontline commanders and their staffs.

Along with representatives from Personnel, Intelligence, Opera-tions, and Supply, Marshall was to leave Corregidor for Bataan five days later and establish the headquarters echelon on Signal Hill, part of Mariveles Mountain. From this Bataan headquarters, he would have frequent telephone contacts with Sutherland concern-ing the military situation and would also send him periodic reports.[6]

In Malinta Tunnel on his way to see President Quezon that morning, MacArthur met Major Carlos Romulo, who had been visiting with the Philippine president. Romulo had come from Manila aboard the old steamer *Hyde*. Gripping Romulo by the shoulders, MacArthur exclaimed, "I'm glad to see you! You boys did a swell job in Manila. You're a soldier, Carlos." The greeting pleased Romulo deeply, but he thought MacArthur, in unpressed uniform and with shaggy hair, looked tired.

Romulo was assigned the task of making anti-Japanese radio-broadcasts from Corregidor to the occupied and unoccupied areas in the Philippine Archipelago. Earlier MacArthur had told Marshall in Manila to dismantle the equipment for a radiobroadcasting sta-tion and send it to Corregidor. "Get it going, Carlos. I want the radio working in forty-eight hours," MacArthur instructed Romulo concerning the dismantled radio equipment. He even had a name for it: "The Voice of Freedom."[7]

It was a quiet New Year's Day on Corregidor. Although there were a few air raid alarms, only one plane attacked, and it was shot down. The staff members of Marshall's rear echelon "were settled in the tunnel and most of them rested during the day." Colonel Casey "was the object of much joshing on his New Year's Eve celebration. He estimated that at least 15,000,000 dollars' worth of property was destroyed."[8]

Late in the afternoon a radiogram arrived from the War De-partment concerning the desirability of evacuating President Que-zon from Corregidor. Before consulting Quezon, MacArthur held a conference in his small cottage with Sutherland, Marshall, Huff, and Colonel Charles A. Willoughby, assistant chief of staff for intelligence. They decided that the best course of action was for Quezon to remain on Corregidor, and the staff officers started to draft a reply to that effect. MacArthur sent Huff to ask Quezon to meet with the officers in his cottage.

Quezon arrived, followed shortly by High Commissioner Sayre, and MacArthur read the radiogram from General George Marshall.

> Philippine commissioner here and Secretary Stimson in consultation with the president feel that evacuation of Manuel Quezon from Luzon to United States where he could carry on as head of a Philippine government in exile and as the symbol of the redemption of the islands is highly desirable if it can be accomplished. Please give this matter your consideration and if it is practicable under the circumstances and Quezon agrees, effect the evacuation according to the best means available to you. If you wish us to seek cooperation of navy from this end please advise.

MacArthur then read the draft reply. A profound silence followed, broken finally by Quezon. Before he could consent to the sending of the reply, he said, he would have to confer with his War Cabinet.

Quezon discussed this question with Vice President Sergio Osmena, Chief Justice and Acting Secretary of Finance José Abad Santos, Acting Secretary of National Defense General Basilio Valdes, and his unofficial adviser, Major Manuel Roxas. Then he wrote a short message to Marshall, which was delivered to MacArthur and enclosed within the general's reply:

> The evacuation of President Quezon is deemed by me to be too hazardous to attempt. This garrison is now beleaguered in Bataan and Corregidor. The only means of egress is by air or submarine, both fraught with great danger in view of complete control of sea and air by the enemy. The government of the commonwealth is now in exile here on Corregidor. Quezon is here accompanied by his wife and children, the vice president, chief justice, secretary of national defense and secretary of finance. The appointments of the remainder of the cabinet expired on December 30 and were not renewed upon the president's inauguration that day. I have here also the high commissioner, his wife and minor son, and several members of his staff and their wives.
>
> I referred your telegram to President Quezon. He states:
>
>> I have come to the conclusion that insofar as the suggested trip is concerned I have no preference. I am willing

to do what the government of the United States may think
will be more helpful for the successful prosecution of the
war. My immediate concern, however, is to secure prompt
and adequate help from the United States because our
soldiers at the front and the Filipino people in general have
placed their trust in this indispensable help coming from
America, especially after the proclamation of the president
and the announcement made by the navy which gave them
the impression that help is forthcoming.

President Quezon's departure would undoubtedly be followed
by the collapse of the will to fight on the part of the Filipinos. It
will be recalled that there are only about seven thousand American
combat troops here exclusive of air corps which has no planes, the
balance of the force being Filipino.

I wish to reiterate my strategic concept that contemplated the
immediate combined effort of all resources of the United States
and her allies by land, sea, and air, beginning with the securing
of air supremacy in the Netherlands East Indies and Mindanao,
the landing of an expeditionary force on that island to secure bases
and the reopening of the line of communications, followed by a
drive to the north. Mindanao has been invaded by probably only
one enemy division at Davao, with a small force at Jolo; the
Visayan Islands are as yet untouched.

I wish to reemphasize my firm belief that loss of the Philippines
will be followed by the fall of the Netherlands East Indies and
Singapore. Even if this were not true, the yielding of the Philippines
by default and without a major effort would mark the end of white
prestige and influence in the East. In view of the Filipinos effort the
United States must move strongly to their support and promptly or
withdraw in shame from the Orient.

The question of time is paramount. It is estimated that this
garrison unsupported can survive serious attack for possibly
three months at most although it is not possible to predict the
date of such attack. Munitions and food are limited; there are only
thirty thousand rounds of anti-aircraft ammunition; water supply
is critical and might curtail the defense. The first bombing attack
disrupted water pipes which are laid close to the surface and are
not supplied with alternate mains. The power supply is very vulnerable. Continuous bombing from nearby airdromes can quickly
reduce the garrison of Fort Mills to a serious condition.

I have no resources except as provided from the United States
and lines of communication will remain broken until restored by
aggressive air and naval action. This immediately raises the question of the intention to effect relief and the rapidity of action. I

believe there is time if the resources of Great Britain and the United States are exerted. England is safe from attack during the winter and should lend material aid in view of the threat to Singapore, Australia, India and her trade routes. It is vital to me in the conduct of this defense to be informed in the broadest terms of United States plans. I realize the danger of trusting codes, but a general statement from which I can derive a basic concept with a definite time factor is now essential. I have conferred with Mr. Sayre on the foregoing exclusive of military points and he concurs.[9]

Stimson read MacArthur's radiogram early on the morning of January 2. He described it as being "of a most harassing and agonizing character" to all of the officials in the War Department, who understood MacArthur's "difficulties without being able to help them speedily." Stimson sent a copy of the message to Roosevelt. At a cabinet meeting during which the contents of the radiogram were discussed, Stimson thought that Roosevelt "might show some sign of being stampeded by the tone of the [radiogram]." To Stimson's surprise, Roosevelt remained undisturbed.[10] Stimson also talked with Marshall concerning the Philippine dilemma. Even though "every possible line was being tried" in attempting to aid MacArthur, Stimson realized that he and the other members of the War Department would "probably all have to go through the agonizing experience of seeing the doomed garrison gradually pulled down" as a result of uncompleted preparations.[11]

On January 3 Marshall had the following radiogram dispatched to MacArthur.

There is here a keen appreciation of your situation. The president and prime minister, Colonel Stimson and Colonel Knox, the British chiefs of staff and our corresponding officials have been surveying every possibility looking toward the quick development of strength in the Far East so as to break the enemy's hold on the Philippines.

Previous losses in capital ships seriously reduce the capacity of the navy to carry on indispensable tasks including convoys for heavy reinforcements for the Far East and protection of vital supplies for six hundred thousand men in the Near East and to the British Isles. The net result is a marked insufficiency of forces for any powerful naval concentration in the Western Pacific at this time. Our great hope is that the rapid development of an overwhelming air power on the Malay barrier will cut the Japanese communications south of Borneo and permit an assault in the southern Philippines.

A stream of four engine bombers, previously delayed by foul weather, is enroute with the head of the column having crossed Africa. Another stream of similar bombers started today from, repeat from, Hawaii staging at new island fields. Two groups of powerful medium bombers of long range and heavy bomb load capacity leave next week. Pursuit planes are coming on every ship we can use. Our definitely allocated air reinforcements together with British should give us an early superiority in the Southwestern Pacific. Our strength is to be concentrated and it should exert a decisive effect on Japanese shipping and force a withdrawal northward. These measures provide the only speedy intervention now possible unless naval carrier raids may be managed.

We are searching our resources to develop means to disrupt the present Japanese operations. Every day of time you gain is vital to the concentration of the overwhelming power necessary for our purpose. Furthermore the current conferences in Washington between all anti-Axis nations are developing a unity of purpose, plans and execution which are extremely encouraging in respect to accelerating speed of ultimate success.[12]

Later on January 3 in Washington, Brigadier General Gerow completed an important memorandum for the Army chief of staff. It answered Roosevelt's directive of December 30 concerning the possibility of a major effort to relieve the Philippine garrison. Gerow recognized that the Philippine Islands were "the key to the Far East position of the Associated Powers," since "heavy bombers established in strength on Luzon [could] interrupt Japanese communications along the Asiatic coast." He also pointed out to Marshall that if Japan succeeded in capturing the Philippines, the Netherlands East Indies and Singapore would soon fall, "Australia then would be seriously threatened and vital British trade routes might be severed," China would soon be isolated, and "Japan would be greatly strengthened by gaining the raw materials of the Netherlands East Indies."[13]

In order to prevent Japan from completely conquering the Philippines, and to restore the position of the United States there, Gerow believed that it would be necessary to execute the following "general strategic concept of operations," which "would require the immediate combined effort of the available land, sea, and air resources of the United States, the British and the Netherlands East Indies."

(1) First gain naval and air superiority south of the line Malaya-Borneo-Celebes, and prepare to extend this control northward.

(2) Gain air supremacy in the Netherlands East Indies and operate for Netherlands East Indies bases to gain air supremacy over Mindanao.

(3) Covered and supported by strong naval and air forces, land a force on Mindanao to secure bases there.

(4) Operating from bases on Mindanao, reopen the line of communications and launch a drive to the north.

Estimating "that a large Allied land force—several hundred thousand men—would be required to regain control of the Philippine Islands in the face of the opposition Japan [could] interpose," Gerow concluded:

(1) That the forces required for the relief of the Philippines cannot be placed in the Far East area within the time available.

(2) That allocation to the Far East area of forces necessary to regain control of the Philippines would necessitate an entirely unjustifiable diversion of forces from the principal theater—the Atlantic.

(3) That the greatest effort in the Far East which can be sustained on strategic grounds is that contemplated by the Chiefs of Staff in their directive ABC–4/3 (hold Malay Barrier, Burma and Australia, projecting operations to the northward to provide maximum defense in depth).

His final recommendation was "that operations for the relief of the Philippines be not undertaken."[14]

It was Sunday, January 4. Colonel Paul D. Bunker, who commanded the large batteries of Corregidor's Seaward Defenses, wrote in his diary:

The Filipinos are most cowardly and jittery—seemingly not the same breed who fought us in 1898. Reports from the

North are unanimous in saying that they will not stand, but will run without firing a shot. If, in camp, a man accidentally fires a rifle, they all grab their rifles and start shooting wildly and into the air—anywhere so long as they can fire! And those are the "heroes who are fighting so gloriously" that President Quezon raves about in his eulogies.[15]

On Corregidor on January 4, Brigadier General Charles C. Drake had a conference with General MacArthur in the USAFFE headquarters lateral of Malinta Tunnel concerning the serious shortage of food on Bataan and Corregidor. Drake, the quartermaster general, gave MacArthur an inventory of the food supplies on Bataan, showing an appalling lack of many components of the field ration. "As things stood," Drake said, the army on Bataan could hold out "for possibly two months on a most unbalanced one-half ration unless [it received] help from some outside source." The following day, on Drake's recommendation, MacArthur ordered all troops on Bataan, Corregidor, and the other fortified islands in Manila Bay to be placed on half rations (30 ounces a day).[16]

Gerow's memorandum of January 3 reached Stimson's desk on January 5. To Stimson it was a "very gloomy study" that was "worked out with ruthless severity and some over statement that it would be impossible . . . to relieve MacArthur." It was a "bad kind of paper to be lying around the War Department," Stimson thought, since officials already knew that chances of getting aid to MacArthur were slim. It seemed unnecessary to him to take such a pessimistic position until everything possible had been tried.[17]

On January 6 MacArthur was driven to the "Chicago" antiaircraft battery, west of Malinta Tunnel on Topside. Wearing a plain suntan uniform and field glasses around his neck, he was escorted by Captain Godfrey R. Ames to the command post, where Ames ran the battery. Suddenly the air raid alert sounded. The men of the Chicago battery scurried to their positions. Japanese bombers were coming dead in on course. MacArthur was standing in the pit of battery number three when the 3-inch antiaircraft guns started firing. Through his binoculars he watched the enemy bombers unload. When the gun barrels pointed straight up the men fired the customary six rounds and hit the ground. MacArthur, standing tall and never taking the field glasses from his eyes, calmly remarked that "the bombs would fall close." Captain Ames urged "the Old

Man" to take cover, but he refused. The bombs hit and exploded about 100 yards away.[18]

Two days before, MacArthur had dispatched a message to the War Department reporting that the antiaircraft ammunition supply on Corregidor was "critical." The lack of ammunition was forcing a "curtailment of fire during attacks," and MacArthur urged that a "general plan of blockade running should be at once initiated for anti-aircraft ammunition and other critical items." He suggested "the use of submarine transportation, especially of [the] mine laying type."[19]

On January 7 MacArthur informed the War Department that he was increasing the strength of Mindanao by bolstering its defenses. He urged "that blockade running ships be forced through to Mindanao with ground and air operating supplies."

> Have several airdromes in operation on Bataan subject to intermittent interruption but only very limited gasoline. Will keep air force advised thereon. An army corps should be landed in Mindanao at the earliest possible date. Essential that blockade runners bring vital items. Numerous small vessels should be used and though losses may be high a certain percentage will get through and a few will relieve the situation. Enemy appears to have tendency to become over confident and time is ripe for brilliant thrust with aircraft carriers.[20]

In Washington on January 8, Brigadier General Eisenhower notified the Navy Department of MacArthur's need for antiaircraft ammunition, requesting the dispatch of a submarine carrying ammunition to Corregidor. Later Eisenhower wrote in his private notebook, "Admiral King has issued orders—but I'm still not sure we'll get it done. May merely lose another sub."[21]

MacArthur dispatched the following radiogram to the War Department on January 9:

> An order to commander-in-chief, Asiatic Fleet, was quoted in your [recent radiogram]. Brett reports [from Australia] as follows: "Admiral Hart states no submarines now available for transporting of anti-aircraft ammunition and considering small amount that could be carried in submarines does not believe diversion from other mission is justifiable. Regrets no means now appear available to comply with your request."
> As previously reported [in] my radiogram [of] December 13,

Hart maintains defeatist attitude regarding the Philippines. He accepts complete blockade which probably does not exist with effort to penetrate. Two destroyers and a merchant vessel have successfully made their way to the south from this harbor within the last ten days. I urge steps be taken to obtain more aggressive and resourceful handling of naval forces in this area.

A copy of this message was delivered personally by Eisenhower to Admiral King, chief of Naval Operations.[22]

At 6:45 A.M. on January 10 a PT-boat carrying MacArthur, Sutherland, Brigadier General William F. Marquat (an antiaircraft officer), and Huff, MacArthur's aide-de-camp, departed from Corregidor's North Dock and headed for Cabcaben on the Bataan peninsula. Several days before, MacArthur had received a memorandum from Casey, who was maintaining a headquarters on Bataan. Casey had informed MacArthur that there was a "need for his . . . presence on Bataan to stimulate sagging morale."[23]

On January 9 Sutherland had telephoned Brigadier General Arnold J. Funk, operations officer of Brigadier General Richard Marshall's advance headquarters on Bataan, and told him that MacArthur would make an inspection of the Bataan forces the following day. He explained in detail the route of the inspection and the commanders MacArthur desired to see, and ordered Funk to meet the inspection party at Cabcaben the following morning to accompany them on the inspection. Major General Wainwright, commander of the I Corps, and Major General Parker, commander of the II Corps, were also told to have their staffs assembled at specific locations, where they would be receiving a very important visitor.[24]

At Cabcaben MacArthur and his staff were greeted by Brigadier General Funk. MacArthur conferred there with several of the division commanders, including Brigadier General Maxon S. Lough, Philippine Division commander, and his chief of staff, Colonel Harrison C. Browne. When General MacArthur asked Lough if there were anything that he could do for him, Lough said, "Yes. You can make Colonel Browne a Brigadier General and assign him to the Philippine Division as my chief of staff." MacArthur replied, "Take it up with my chief of staff." Although Lough immediately wrote a letter to Sutherland about the matter, nothing ever came of it.[35]

The inspection party left Cabcaben in a four-car convoy and

proceeded north along the East Road to Parker's II Corps headquarters. MacArthur stopped and gave the staff a "brief pep talk
about help being on the way."[26]

The party then motored to the junction with the Pilar-Bagac
Road. There MacArthur met the commanding officers of the Fifty-
seventh Infantry Combat Team and the Fifty-seventh Infantry
Division. Major Royal Reynolds, a battalion commander of the
Fifty-seventh Infantry, watched MacArthur as he inspected the
positions. Noting that MacArthur was not wearing a helmet, Reynolds was impressed by his "calmness and confidence in a difficult
situation."[27]

The inspection party proceeded west along the Pilar-Bagac Road,
300 to 1,000 yards behind the front line, to meet Wainwright and
the staff officers of the I Corps. Shortly after leaving the junction the
convoy was stopped by heavy Japanese artillery fire. Ordering the
officers to get out of the cars and seek shelter, MacArthur remained
in the center of the road. Urged by Generals Sutherland and Funk
to seek cover from the exploding artillery shells, he replied, "There
is no Jap shell with MacArthur's name on it." At a letup in the shelling the convoy continued across the peninsula toward Bagac. In a
clearing several miles east of Bagac, Wainwright and his officers
were waiting.[28]

To Wainwright, MacArthur looked exceedingly "fit" when his car
pulled up before the line of assembled officers. Greeting Wainwright
warmly, MacArthur said, "Jonathan, I'm glad to see you back from
the north. The execution of your withdrawal and of your mission in
covering the withdrawal of the South Luzon Force were as fine as
anything in history. And for that I'm going to see that you are made
a permanent major general of the Regular Army." After greeting
some of the other officers, MacArthur turned back to Wainwright
and asked, "Where are your 155-mm. guns?" Explaining the location
of six of the guns, Wainwright suggested that they walk over and
take a look at two of them that were near.

"Jonathan," MacArthur replied, "I don't want to see them. I want
to hear them."[29]

In an optimistic and enthusiastic manner, MacArthur addressed
the assembled staff officers of the I Corps. He told them that "the
enemy's temporary superiority of the air would soon be a thing of
the past. And if events proceeded as he expected, a counterattack
was in the offing." The defense of the Philippines had "caught the

imagination of the American people," MacArthur said, and "plans of immediate help by way of Australia are in the mill."[30]

Leaving Wainwright's I Corps, the officers moved south along the West Road toward Marshall's command post on Signal Hill on the south slope of Mariveles Mountain. To Marshall, waiting impatiently for MacArthur and his party, it seemed hours before they arrived. The troops on Bataan were on half rations, and normally Marshall and his staff ate only twice daily, at 8:00 A.M. and 4:00 P.M. On this day, because of the general's visit, they would eat their second meal several hours earlier.

When MacArthur and his staff arrived, a meager lunch was served in a wooded area filled with canvas cots. Besides talking with Mac-Arthur, Marshall discussed with Sutherland administrative details concerning the Bataan echelon and the USAFFE headquarters on Corregidor. Shortly, the officers left Marshall's command post and returned to Mariveles, where they boarded a PT-boat and departed for Corregidor, arriving about 3:40 P.M.[31]

The discussions General MacArthur had with the frontline commanders were detailed and thorough: combat situation, positions, condition of troops, defensive plans. Knowing that his visit had been good for morale, MacArthur later told members of his headquarters staff that he had been very pleased and encouraged by what he had observed on Bataan. "Our 155's were music to my ears," he remarked. Unfortunately, it was his only visit to the Bataan front.[32]

On January 12 General George Marshall informed MacArthur that the governments of Australia, the Netherlands, the United Kingdom, and the United States were establishing "a theatre of operations to be known as the ABDA Area" in the Southwestern Pacific, under the Supreme Command of British General Sir Archibald P. Wavell.

> You will be under General Wavell's command . . . but because of your present isolation this will have only nominal effect upon your command of all United States and Filipino forces in the Philippines. . . . While, provided secret communication is possible, such reports as General Wavell may request should be sent to him direct, it is intended that because of your special situation you will continue direct reports to and communication with the War Department on same basis as heretofore. The main purpose of the associated powers is to concentrate American and Allied naval and

air forces under unified direction for operations against critical points. The arrangement offers the only feasible method for the eventual relief of the Philippines. . . .[33]

On January 15 Major General George F. Moore ordered Colonel Bunker to prepare an inventory of all foods that had been salvaged, largely by the soldiers of Bunker's Seaward Defense Command, from sunken and breached barges in the sea off Corregidor. Concerning the order Bunker wrote in his diary:

> MacArthur has ordered us, through General Moore, to do this, possibly with the idea of making all hands turn their stores in; and yet his damn staff had days in which to salvage this stuff and did nothing! Our troops saved it from utter loss and are now to be punished! How to raise morale! Colonel Crews furnished me with this order—and I was thunderstruck to see him on Topside, outside of Malinta Tunnel.[34]

The same day MacArthur had the following general order issued:

SUBJECT: MESSAGE FROM GENERAL MACARTHUR
TO: ALL UNIT COMMANDERS

The following message from General MacArthur will be read and explained to all troops. . . .

Help is on the way from the United States, thousands of troops and hundreds of planes are being dispatched. The exact time of arrival of reinforcements is unknown as they will have to fight their way through Japanese attempts against them. It is imperative that our troops hold until these reinforcements arrive.

No further retreat is possible. We have more troops in Bataan than the Japanese have thrown against us; our supplies are ample; a determined defense will defeat the enemy's attacks.

It is a question now of courage and determination. Men who run will merely be destroyed but men who fight will save themselves and their country.

I call upon every soldier in Bataan to fight in his assigned position resisting every attack. This is the only road to salvation. If we fight we will win; if we retreat we will be destroyed.[35]

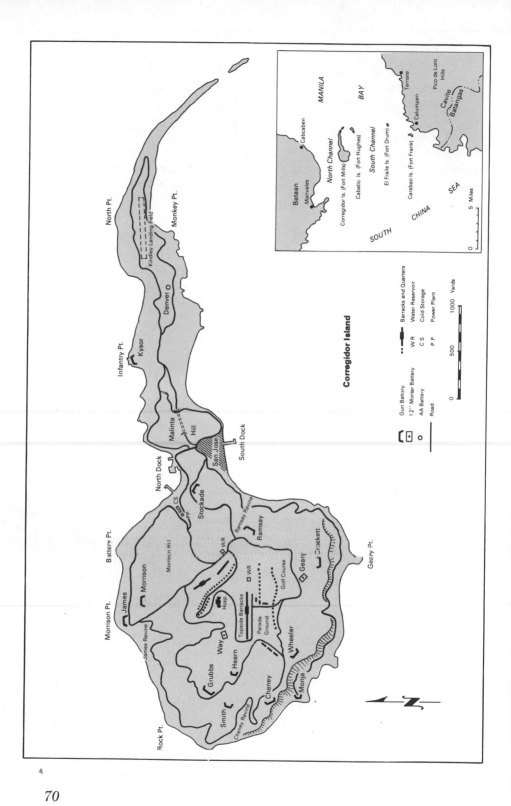

Corregidor Island

Barracks and Quarters
Gun Battery
12'' Mortar Battery   W R   Water Reservoir
AA Battery   C S   Cold Storage
Road   P P   Power Plant

0   500   1000   Yards

North Pt.

Monkey Pt.

Kindley Landing Field

Denver

Infantry Pt.

Kysor

Malinta
Hill

San Jose

South Dock

North Dock

Battery Pt.

CS
PP
Stockade

Ramsay Ravine

Ramsay

Morrison Hill

W R

Crockett

Morrison Pt.

Morrison

W R

Golf Course

Geary

James

James Ravine

Way

Hosp

Topside Barracks

Parade
Ground

Wheeler

Grubbs

Hearn

Cheney

Monja

Smith

Cheney Ravine

Rock Pt.

Geary Pt.

N

MANILA

BAY

Bataan

Mariveles

Cabcaben

North Channel

Corregidor Is. (Fort Mills)

Caballo Is. (Fort Hughes)

South Channel

El Fraile Is. (Fort Drum)

Carabao Is. (Fort Frank)

Ternate

Calumpan

Pico de Loro
Hills

Cavite
Batangas

SOUTH

CHINA

SEA

5 Miles

0

The message prompted the January 16 entry in Bunker's diary:

MacArthur issues exhortation to troops:—No further retreat! Thousands of men and hundreds of planes are enroute
to help, but must fight their way, and so will be delayed—
etc. (If the Navy is responsible, they'll never get here!)

Rumors are persistent that, instead of a six months reserve of food, we have only three months! Brass hats in
Malinta Tunnel have a rotten mess and are complaining that
our enlisted men are too well fed—even though they are on
half-rations. So perhaps that is one reason for the stink they
are raising because we salvaged the food from those
grounded and sunken barges.

Another owlish remark was that of Admiral Yarnell, as
published in our USAFFE *Bulletin:* "The result in the
Pacific will be determined by the preponderance of power
there." Nothing less than a mighty intellect could evolve
such a gem of brilliant cogitation and deduction.[36]

On January 17 MacArthur sent to the War Department a radiogram that emphasized the gravity of the situation in the Philippines.

The food situation here is becoming serious. For some time I
have been on half rations and the result will soon become evident
in the exhausted condition of the men. The limited geographical
area which I occupy offers no food resources. I am entirely dependent upon a line of sea communications, the responsibility for
which has not been under my control. In my radio of January 4 I
asked for blockade running ships. No reply has been received
except to that feature dealing with a submarine carrying anti-aircraft ammunition. The strategic problem involving an advance
from the south will not relieve the food situation here in time. The
rations necessary to supply this command measured in ships
capacity are small indeed. Many medium sized or small ships
should be loaded with rations and dispatched along various routes.
The enemy bomber formations are no longer here but have moved
south. Unquestionably, ships can get through but no attempt yet
seems to have been made along this line. This seems incredible
to me and I am having increasing difficulty in appeasing Philippine
thought along this line. They cannot understand the apparent lack
of effort to bring something in. I cannot over emphasize the psychological reaction that will take place here unless something
tangible is done in this direction. A revulsion of feeling of tre-

mendous proportions against America can be expected. They can understand failure but cannot understand why no attempt is being made at relief through the forwarding of supplies. They contrast the lack of efforts against a stronger blockade line in the Atlantic. This reaction may eventually appear among the troops. Hungry men are hard to handle.

Recommend that the question be immediately taken up with General Wavell and that simultaneous efforts be made from the Netherlands East Indies and the United States to get in the small amount of food that would see me through. The repeated statements from the United States that Hitler is to be destroyed before an effort is made here is causing dismay. The Japanese forces— air, land, and ground—are much overextended. His success to date does not measure his own strength but the weakness of his opposition. A blow or even a threatened blow against him will almost certainly be attended with some success. I am professionally certain that his so called blockade can easily be pierced. The only thing that can make it really effective is our own passive acceptance of it as a fact.

I repeat that if something is not done to meet the general situation which is developing the disastrous results will be monumental. The problems involved cannot be measured or solved by mere army and navy strategic formulas. They involve the comprehensiveness of the entire oriental problem.[37]

On January 17 in Washington, Patrick J. Hurley, former secretary of war during Hoover's administration, reported to Army Chief of Staff Marshall and asked if he could be of service.

"If I could only help Doug," Hurley said.

"All right, you can help him," Marshall replied. In a note to the chief of the Operations Division, Eisenhower, Marshall said, "Show Col. Hurley McArthur's [sic] cable re rations, and tell him what we have done and are doing. I am thinking of sending him out on a special mission on this matter. His former relation with McA would mean much encouragement."

Hurley reported to Eisenhower with the note. After reading it, Eisenhower looked at Hurley and asked, "When can you be ready to report for duty?"

"Now!" exclaimed Hurley.

"Be back at midnight," Eisenhower said, "prepared for extended duty." Hurley "seemed to change color slightly; he never batted an eye but replied, 'That will give me time to see my lawyer and change my will.' "[38]

Hurley called Stimson, his former colleague in the Hoover cabinet, "to say good-bye." In his diary Stimson wrote:

We are promoting [Hurley] in the Reserve Corps to Brigadier General and he is going to be given the post of Minister to New Zealand. But before he goes there we have asked him to go to Australia to speed up the work in getting food supplies to MacArthur through small surface vessels. Pat is a hustler and I think it was a very happy thought of Marshall to use him in this way on a matter which is sure to be delayed in the present congestion of other duties imposed upon the American members of Wavell's staff.[39]

At midnight Hurley reported to Eisenhower. Knowing that Hurley would be officially promoted to the rank of brigadier general by the time he reached Australia, both Eisenhower and Gerow removed one star from their uniforms and pinned it on his shoulders. At 1:00 A.M. he boarded a plane for Australia. On his memorandum pad Eisenhower noted that Hurley "was equal to the quick transition and I'm hopeful he can do something in organizing blockade running for MacArthur. The whole Far East situation is critical."[40]

Marshall notified MacArthur of Hurley's mission to Australia in the following radiogram:

Two officers from the War Department have arrived in Australia with instructions . . . to organize blockade running measures on a broad front for your supply of food and critical munitions. We have placed practically unlimited funds at their disposal to pay bonuses for such services. We have sent additional instructions to Australia regarding the urgency of this matter and the commanding general there has been advised of availability of funds and directed to procure vessels and crews necessary for repeated efforts to carry out this mission. The substance of your cable [of January 17] has been transmitted to General Wavell. Your reports indicate that you have occasional sea communication with Cebu and Iloilo. Is there any possibility of getting in foodstuffs from that region? I now place a million dollars at your disposal to offer in rewards for successful local efforts to penetrate the blockade and reach you with supplies. I am repeating the substance of this to General Brereton in Australia because he is familiar with conditions in the Philippines and may be able to provide valuable assistance in solving the problem. Colonel Patrick Hurley is starting for Australia by air tomorrow to lend his energetic support to efforts to reach you with supplies.[41]

On January 18 General MacArthur replied.

Your radiogram has relieved me greatly. I have already initiated all possible local steps to relieve the situation here. Inter-island shipping however has been greatly depleted leaving scant resources.[42]

On January 19 President Quezon gave MacArthur a letter and requested that its contents be relayed to President Roosevelt.

I have just received the following telegram from the Chief of Constabulary of Negros Oriental "Civilian military situation Negros Oriental excellent. About fifty thousand civilians of military age ready for induction into the army. Civil activities being carried on as usual; morale of people very high. Entire population very happy to receive the news that the President is well and safe." That is the picture of the situation in the unoccupied territory of the Philippines. On the other hand where the enemy has landed and especially in Luzon and parts of Mindanao the people are beginning to wonder why no help is being received from or even attempted by the United States. Thousands of the flower of the youth of the land are being killed and wounded and with the complete mastery of the air on the part of the enemy these boys will continue to be slaughtered. I myself although suffering from tuberculosis am living under the most unfavorable conditions. The Vice President and Chief Justice and the Secretary of National Defense are with me. Also my wife, two young daughters and one very young boy are sharing with me not only the hardships of this war but the danger of being bombed.

The Filipinos are doing their full part in the defense of their country which for the present is as much an American Territory as any State of the Union. I feel that with everything at stake we have the right to know if America's plan is to let the Philippines be conquered and not attempt to defend it except with the present American and Filipino forces leaving for a much later date the reconquest of the Philippines.[43]

By January 22 the Japanese had succeeded in breaking through the left flank of the II Corps on the Abucay–Mount Natib position. Inspecting the front that day on MacArthur's orders, Sutherland realized after a talk with the II Corps commander, Major General Parker, that a major withdrawal to defensive positions behind the Pilar-Bagac Road would be necessary. That night orders were issued to the headquarters of the I and II Corps for the withdrawal, which was to begin the following night. MacArthur notified the War Department of the move:

> In Luzon: Heavy fighting has been raging all day. The enemy has been repulsed everywhere. He seems to have finally adopted a policy of attrition as his unopposed command of the sea enables him to replace at will. My losses during the campaign have been very heavy and are mounting. They now approximate thirty-five percent. My diminishing strength will soon force me to a shortened line on which I shall make my final stand. I have personally selected and prepared this position and it is strong. With its occupation all maneuvering possibilities will cease. I intend to fight it to complete destruction. This will leave Corregidor.
>
> I wish to take this opportunity while the army still exists and I am in command to pay my tribute to the magnificent service it has rendered. No troops have ever done so much with so little. I bequeath to you the charge that their fame and glory be duly recorded by their countrymen. In case of my death I recommend that my chief of staff, General Sutherland, be designated as my successor. Of all my general officers, he has the most comprehensive grasp of the situation.[44]

On January 26 the withdrawal was successfully completed, and MacArthur informed the War Department:

> In Luzon: Under cover of darkness I broke contact with the enemy and without the loss of a man or an ounce of material am now firmly established on my main battle position. The execution of the movement would have done credit to the best troops in the world.[45]

In Malinta Tunnel on January 26 High Commissioner Sayre wrote out a letter in longhand. Two days later the submarine *Seawolf*, having been replenished at night with sixteen torpedoes from Corregidor, submerged in the South China Sea. On board was Sayre's letter to Roosevelt:

My dear Mr. President,

I am taking the opportunity of sending this personal word to you by submarine which I hope will succeed in breaking through the Japanese blockade.

We are holding the fort here and keeping our colors flying. Our men are keeping their chins up, and the casualties coming in the hospital invariably ask: "When will American planes arrive?" and "How soon can I get back onto the firing line?"

Our supreme confidence is in you. I know that you will not allow red tape or hesitation to slow the aid which we must have soon. If we wait so as to gather an attacking force of sure superiority and allow Corregidor or Singapore to fall in the interim, the winning of the war against Japan will be delayed immeasurably. Although I am no military strategist I am convinced that a smashing attack NOW, while the Japanese lines are overextended and while Corregidor and Singapore are still in our hands, will be worth more than ten victories later on.

We are hoping that President Quezon's health will not break under the rigors of our underground life. The kind of life we have to live here is a strain upon all but the morale is good. The sight of American planes overhead will put new fight into everyone.

I have not been able to secure reliable reports of the Japanese treatment of Americans in Manila. Such reports as I have had have not been reassuring.

With affection and confidence,

Ever sincerely yours,

Frank[46]

On January 27 MacArthur received the subsequent radiogram from President Roosevelt:

General MacArthur, standing in foreground, participates in a ceremony honoring his arrival in Manila on October 23, 1935. Given the title "Military Adviser to the Commonwealth Government," MacArthur was to create a system of national defense for the Philippines. Standing behind MacArthur in a white civilian suit is his principal assistant, Colonel Dwight D. Eisenhower. *U.S. Army photograph*

General MacArthur and Manuel Quezon, president of the Philippines. Although Quezon was one of the first to come to the Manila Hotel to congratulate MacArthur when he was recalled to active duty in July 1941 and named commanding general of the U.S. Army Forces in the Far East, a strain developed later in their personal relationship. No longer was it a relationship between the president and commander in chief of the Philippine Armed Forces and his adviser. As commanding general of USAFFE, MacArthur was an important representative of the sovereign power of the United States. *U.S. Army photograph*

Secretary of War Henry L. Stimson presenting commissions to Assistant Secretaries of War John J. McCloy *(center)* and Robert A. Lovett, after taking the oath of office in the munitions Building on April 22, 1941. *U.S. Army photograph*

Lieutenant General MacArthur, commanding general USAFFE, accepting command of the Philippine Army troops in the induction ceremony of the Philippine Army Air Corps at Zabalan Field, Camp Murphy, August 15, 1941. *U.S. Army photograph*

Army Chief of Staff George C. Marshall approved a proposal by the War Plans Division on July 31, 1941 to strengthen the defense of the Philippine Islands. Marshall told his staff, "It is the policy of the United States to defend the Philippines." *Copyright, Karsh of Ottawa*

On October 10, 1941, MacArthur conferred with Major General Jonathan M. Wainwright, commander of the North Luzon Force. Wainwright's mission was to defend the central plains of Luzon, Lingayen Gulf, the Zambales coast, and the Bataan peninsula. *U. S. Army photograph*

Burned and gutted, the Manila Hotel shows the scars of war. Before the war it was beautiful and luxurious. MacArthur was living with his family on the top floor of the hotel when he learned of the Japanese attack on Pearl Harbor. *Courtesy of Edward Fromme*

On December 8, 1941, President Franklin D. Roosevelt signed the Declaration of War. *U.S. Office of War Information*

A meeting of the Joint Board, composed of high-ranking naval and army officers, during November 1941. *Left to right:* Brigadier General Harold F. Loomis, Major General Henry H. Arnold, Major General William Bryden, General Marshall, Admiral Stark, Rear Admiral Royal E. Ingersoll, Rear Admiral John H. Towers, and Rear Admiral Richmond K. Turner. On December 9 the Joint Board decided to recall the *Pensacola* convoy, which was bound for the Philippines, to Hawaii. President Roosevelt, however, disagreed with the decision. *U.S. Army photograph*

The Cavite Navy Yard after it was bombed by the Japanese on December 10. Setting the entire yard ablaze, bombs directly hit the power plant, warehouses, barracks, repair shops, dispensary, and radio station. The main U.S. Navy base in the Philippines became untenable, forcing the small Asiatic Fleet to sail to the Netherlands East Indies. *U.S. Army photograph*

During the morning of December 11, Major General Lewis H. Brereton, commander of the Far East Air Force, received a distraught transoceanic call from the chief of the Army Air Forces, Major General Henry H. Arnold, in Washington. "How in the hell," Arnold wanted to know, had an experienced airman like Brereton got caught with all his planes on the ground at Clark Field? *U.S. Army photograph*

Admiral Thomas C. Hart, commander in chief of the Asiatic Fleet, disagreed with MacArthur concerning naval strategy. On January 9, 1942, MacArthur reported to Marshall, "Hart maintains defeatist attitude regarding the Philippines." *Official U.S. Navy photograph*

Admiral Harold R. Stark, chief of Naval Operations, refused to authorize the delivery of fighter planes to the Philippines from aircraft carriers during December 1941. *Official U.S. Navy photograph*

Brigadier General Richard J. Marshall, MacArthur's deputy chief of staff, was left in charge of the USAFFE Headquarters in Manila following MacArthur's departure for Corregidor on December 24, 1941. *U.S. Army photograph*

Major General Hugh J. Casey was MacArthur's chief of engineers. When Manila was declared an open city, Casey supervised the destruction of bridges, power facilities, warehouses, and the gigantic Pandacan oil installations. *U.S. Army photograph*

Corregidor controlled the entrance to Manila Bay with its fifty-six coastal guns and mortars. The island is shaped like a tadpole, its bulbous head pointing west toward the South China Sea. *U.S. Army photograph*

A Japanese aerial reconnaissance photograph of Corregidor showing North Dock, Malinta Hill, and the tail of the island. The Japanese lettering and arrow indicate the west entrance to Malinta Tunnel. *Courtesy of the Japanese Defense Agency*

マリンタトンネル入口

Malinta Tunnel was bored through Malinta Hill to the tail of the island. A passageway 1,400 feet long and 35 feet wide, it contained a labyrinth of smaller tunnels housing the USAFFE Headquarters, a hospital, and a vast storage-shop area. *U.S. Army photograph*

The lateral tunnel containing the USAFFE Headquarters staff. The ventilation was poor and the air was fetid, but it was a bombproof shelter. *Melville Jacoby, LIFE Magazine, © 1947/73 by Time Inc.*

The general and his wife, Jean, leaving the officers' mess on Corregidor. Mrs. MacArthur, who had just waved her hair, is protesting having her picture taken. *Melville Jacoby, LIFE Magazine, © 1942 / 70 by Time Inc.*

Japanese Mitshubish "Betty" bombers over Corregidor. The island was bombed extensively for two and one-half hours on December 29. Kindley airfield is visible on the tail of the island. *Courtesy of the Japanese Defense Agency*

Arthur MacArthur III, the general's four-year-old son, standing in front of the main entrance to Malinta Tunnel. *Courtesy of the MacArthur Memorial Bureau of Archives*

Prime Minister Winston S. Churchill arrived in Washington on the night of December 22. His mission was to reach an agreement with Roosevelt concerning global war strategy. *Copyright, Karsh of Ottawa*

The leaders of the War Plans Division. *Left to right:* Brigadier General Robert W. Crawford, Brigadier General Dwight D. Eisenhower, and Brigadier General Leonard T. Gerow, chief of the War Plans Division. Eisenhower wrote most of the radiograms that were dispatched to MacArthur over General Marshall's signature. *U. S. Army photograph*

The two most prominent shapers of global war strategy for the United States: General Marshall and Secretary of War Henry L. Stimson. They are conferring in the War Department's Munitions Building during January 1942. *U.S. Army photograph*

General MacArthur walking with Brigadier General Albert M. Jones, the fighting commander of the 51st Division (PA) on Bataan. Taking a PT-boat to the peninsula early in the morning of January 10, MacArthur inspected units of his trapped army. *U. S. Army photograph*

Admiral Ernest J. King replaced Stark as chief of Naval Operations in December. In January he issued orders for a small number of submarines to be dispatched periodically to Corregidor with antiaircraft ammunition and other vital supplies. *Official U.S. Navy photograph*

Colonel Charles A. Willoughby, MacArthur's chief of intelligence, spoke with President Quezon on Corregidor. ''I cannot stand this constant reference to England, to Europe,'' said Quezon. ''How typically American to writhe in anguish at the fate of a distant cousin while a daughter is being raped in the back room.'' *U.S. Army photograph*

On February 6 General Emilio Aguinaldo, President Quezon's principal political antagonist in the Philippines, made an impassioned plea to General MacArthur in a radiobroadcast from Manila. He urged MacArthur to end the resistance and surrender in order to spare the Filipino people further death and the Philippine Islands further destruction. *Courtesy of the MacArthur Memorial Bureau of Archives*

Congratulations on the magnificent stand that you and your
men are making. We are watching with pride and understanding,
and are thinking of you on your birthday.[47]

At 4:30 P.M. at his headquarters on Bataan, Major General Wainwright dictated to his assistant operations officer, Lieutenant Colonel Jesse T. Traywick, the following memorandum for MacArthur:

I asked General Sutherland to send a representative of G-3
here or send General Marshall as I had definite suggestions
to make to USAFFE, which I did not care to make over the
phone and felt it would be better to handle the matter ver-
bally by conference than send it by the radio which also
might be broken down. I am making no recommendation
whatever but I am suggesting the USAFFE consider withdrawing the front of both Corps to such position as they may
select so as to shorten the front and very greatly shorten the
Coastal Flank, neither of which can, in my opinion be adequately held by this Corps with the number and quality of
troops available. My coastal flank is very lightly held, so
lightly that the Japs appear to infiltrate through it at night
at points selected by them. If I take troops off my front to
thicken the Coast Defense, they will certainly crash through
the front. They already attacked there today with infantry
and artillery and have tanks in position. Another consideration is the 11th Division on my right with no roads and only
foot trails to move on. Should the enemy drive down the
Mariveles-Bagac Road, they will surely cut off the 11th Division and the 2nd Philippines Constabulary. The landings on
the West Coast, so far accomplished, can and probably will
be handled. Our experience however, indicates such landings to be only a prelude to landings of much greater force.
With reliable troops, the situation would not be particular
serious but with the majority of troops available, it becomes
distinctly serious. One battalion of the Philippine Army ran
away last night from the front lines without having had a
shot fired at it. It probably heard a little firing at its left and
pulled out. I repeat I am making no definite recommendation for a withdrawal. Unless ordered to withdraw, I will
hold here to the last. I am merely suggesting that USAFFE

consider this matter in order that our troops may hold out longer. Shorten and therefore strengthen the front and seaward flank.[48]

On January 28 at 12:15 P.M. MacArthur finished dictating to Sutherland a reply to Wainwright:

There is no position that we can take that will shorten your line except the mere beach-head. Were we to withdraw to such a line now it would not only invite immediate overwhelming enemy attack but would completely collapse the morale of our own force. Sooner or later we must fight to the finish. Heretofore we have been maneuvering, falling back from position to position until we have now reached our last ditch. Our only safety is to fight the enemy off. He is not in great strength and if you can once really repulse him you will obtain relief from his pressure. He will continue to apply pressure, however, just as long as we continue to yield to it. If you clear him out on the coast his threats there will always be small. You must, however, hold on your front and there is no better place we can find than the one you are now on. Strengthen your position constantly. Organize your defensive groups in depth and prepare each one then to attack either to the right or to the left. Cover each beach and trail and do not let the enemy penetrate your main line of resistance. Call for volunteers from each unit to compose a sniper company such as was ordered some time ago and such as that which fought so successfully in the II Corps under Funk. Explain constantly to your officers and men if they run they will be doomed but that if they fight they will save themselves. The few days which we will have now before the enemy can make a serious attack, if vigorously employed by all officers, may spell the difference between victory and defeat. Drive everything hard in this period of lull. Make the maximum use of artillery; it is your most reliable arm and its efficient use saved the II Corps on the original battle position. Every available resource at the disposition of the Headquarters has been committed and you must depend largely upon what you have.

Once again I repeat, I am aware of the enormous difficulties that face you. Am proud, indeed, of the magnificent efforts you have made. There is nothing finer in history. Let's continue and preserve the fair name that we have so fairly won.[49]

At 3:35 P.M. Sutherland handed MacArthur's memorandum to the adjutant general, Brigadier General Carl H. Seals, and it was then delivered by an officer courier to Wainwright. At 7:35 P.M. Wainwright telephoned Sutherland regarding the tactical situation. Sutherland suggested that more infantry be shifted to the center and right of the front held by the I Corps.[50]

Also on January 28 MacArthur received a lengthy letter from President Quezon, which he relayed to the War Department:

> I have been mortified by the radio broadcast from Tokyo asserting that a new government has been established in the Philippines [and] . . . has pledged its conformity with Japan's new East Asia policy.
>
> I know what the real sentiments of my people are and I am certain that their stand has not changed despite the military reverses of our forces. I am likewise convinced of the loyalty of the men who have accepted positions in the so-called new government.
>
> I want you, therefore, to give publicity to the following statement:
>> The determination of the Filipino people to continue fighting side by side with the United States until victory is won has in no way been weakened by the temporary reverses suffered by our arms. We are convinced that our sacrifices will be crowned with victory in the end and In that conviction we shall continue to resist the enemy with all our might.
>
> Japanese military forces are occupying sections of the Philippines comprising only one third of our territory. In the remaining areas constitutional government is still in operation under my authority.
>
> I have no direct information concerning the veracity of the news broadcast from Tokyo that a commission composed of some well known Filipinos has been recently organized in Manila to take charge of certain functions of civil government. The organization of such a commission, if true, can have no political significance not only because it is charged merely with purely administrative functions but also because the acquiescence by its members to

serve in the commission was evidently for the purpose of safe-guarding the welfare of the civilian population and can, in no way, reflect the sentiments of the Filipino toward the enemy. Such sentiments are still those I have repeatedly pressed in the first: Loyalty to America and resolute resistance against the invasion of our territory and liberties.

At the same time I am going to open my mind and my heart to you without attempting to hide anything. We are before the bar of history and God only knows if this is the last time that my voice will be heard before going to my grave.

My loyalty and the loyalty of the Filipino people to America have been proven beyond question. Now we are fighting by her side under your command, despite overwhelming odds. But, it seems to me questionable whether any government has the right to demand loyalty from its citizens beyond its willingness or ability to render actual protection.

This war is not of our making. Those that had dictated the policies of the United States could not have failed to see that this is the weakest point in American territory. From the beginning, they should have tried to build up our defenses. As soon as the prospects looked bad to me, I telegraphed President Roosevelt requesting him to include the Philippines in the American defense program. I was given no satisfactory answer.

When I tried to do something to accelerate our defense preparations, I was stopped from doing it.

Despite all this we never hesitated for a moment in our stand. We decided to fight by your side and we have done the best we could and we are still doing as much as could be expected from us under the circumstances. But how long are we going to be left alone? Has it already been decided in Washington that the Philippine front is of no importance as far as the final result of the war is concerned and that, therefore, no help can be expected here in the immediate future, or at least before our power of resistance is exhausted? If so, I want to know it, because I have my own responsibility to my countrymen whom, as president of the commonwealth, I have led into a complete war effort. I am greatly concerned as well regarding the soldiers I have called to the colors and who are now manning the firing line. I want to decide in my own mind whether there is justification in allowing all these men to be killed, when for the final outcome of the war the shedding of their blood may be wholly unnecessary. It seems that Washington does not fully realize our situation nor the feelings

which the apparent neglect of our safety and welfare have en-
gendered in the hearts of the people here. . . .

I am confident that you will understand my anxiety about the
long awaited reinforcements and trust you will again urge Washington to insure their early arrival.[51]

Secretary of War Stimson spent a large part of January 29 "in trying to frame an answer" to Quezon's letter. He wrote in his diary,
"Eisenhower made a very good draft which Marshall and I worked
over and finally got one which is the best we can do. We sent it
over to the White House and later in the evening McCloy, who had
been in New York all day, called me up to say that he went to the
Department on his arrival and found the draft telegram returned
from the White House with the President's approval, and I directed
him to send it at once."[52]

At 11:49 P.M. the answer to President Quezon was dispatched to
MacArthur.

I have read with complete understanding your letter to General
MacArthur. I realize the depth and sincerity of your sentiments
with respect to your inescapable duties to your own people and I
assure you that I would be the last to demand of you and them
any sacrifice which I considered hopeless in the furtherance of
the cause for which we are all striving. I want, however, to state
with all possible emphasis that the magnificent resistance of the
defenders of Bataan is contributing definitely toward assuring the
completeness of our final victory in the Far East. The gaps existing in our offensive armaments are those that are to be expected
when peace-loving countries such as the United States and the
Philippines suddenly find themselves attacked by autocratic power
which has spent years in preparation for armed conflict. Initial
defeats, privations and suffering are the inevitable consequences
to democracy in such circumstances. But I have pledged to the
attainment of ultimate victory the full man power, finances and
material resources of this country; and this pledge of victory includes as an essential objective the restoration of peace and
tranquility in the Philippines and its return to the control of a
goverment of its own choosing. While I cannot now indicate the
time at which succor and assistance can reach the Philippines, I
do know that every ship at our disposal is bringing to the South
West Pacific the forces that will ultimately smash the invader and
free your country. Ships in that region have been loaded and

dispatched to Manila with various supplies for the garrison. Already our forces, with those of our allies, have inflicted severe losses upon enemy convoys and naval shipping and are definitely slowing his southward advance. Our four engine bombers are daily reporting to General Wavell from the trans-African route and more recently via the Pacific. Ten squadrons of pursuit and fighter planes have already been made available in that theater and a steady flow of such planes is crossing the Pacific. Our navy is heavily engaged in escorting to the same region large troop convoys. Every day gained for building up our forces is of incalculable value and it is in the gaining of time that the defenders of Bataan are assisting us so effectively.

I have no words in which to express to you my admiration and gratitude for the complete demonstration of loyalty, courage and readiness to sacrifice that your people, under your inspired leadership, have displayed. They are upholding the most magnificent traditions of free democracy.

Those portions of your letter to General MacArthur on which you asked publicity are being broadcast to the world from Washington. Your words and your example will rally to renewed effort not only the people of your own country but all those that in every section of the globe are enlisting in the fight for democratic principles and freedom of government.[53]

During the morning of January 29, three Japanese bombers had appeared over Corregidor. Instead of dropping bombs they dropped propaganda leaflets labeled "Ticket to Armistice." The leaflets urged the Filipino soldiers to surrender. Similar leaflets by the thousands were dropped over the front lines in Bataan. To combat the Japanese propaganda offensive, "President Quezon issued a proclamation by radio from Corregidor designed to reassure the Filipino people and warn them against Japanese propaganda designed to lead them to believe a large group of Filipino leaders were disloyal to America."[54]

The Japanese propaganda offensive chagrined and troubled General MacArthur, who dispatched to the War Department the following radiogram:

The following public statement is reported in the *Tribune Manila,* January 24, as having been made by General Aguinaldo:

"Independence with honor!"—this is the reassuring announcement of policy made by Prime Minister Hideki Tojo regarding the Philippines in the course of his speech at the opening of the seventy ninth session of the Japanese Imperial Diet. It is a formal and official commitment which all Filipinos should hark and welcome. The only condition imposed is that we should "recognize and cooperate with Japan's program of establishing a greater East Asia co-prosperity sphere."

This is a laudable objective from viewpoint of Japan. It is an objective that deserves the support of our nation, because geographically we are located in a region embraced within the sphere of co-prosperity.

Inspired by its loyalty to the ideal of independence, our country, although not a belligerent, has sacrificed and is still sacrificing side by side with American troops, thousands of Filipino soldiers. The Japanese command cannot but recognize the valor and heroism displayed by our soldiers in the fields of battle. Without modern armament, submarines, airplanes, and anti-aircraft guns in sufficient numbers and range, without receiving the help that has repeatedly been promised, our valiant countrymen have done their duty. We should realize by now that further resistance would not have any practical advantage and would only mean unnecessary sacrifice in lives and properties, inasmuch as Japan "does not regard us her enemies" and that Japan would "gladly grant the Philippines its independence"—the same ideals which impelled us revolutionaries, to fight in the past, and which our soldiers have been made to believe they are fighting for in the present.

In view of this official assurance given by the prime minister of the empire of Japan, let us invite our countrymen to return to their towns and homes, to cultivate their farms and to harvest their crops in order to prevent starvation and further misery, and let us place our confidence in the promise of the commander-in-chief of the imperial Japanese force in the Philippines that the lives, and properties and individual rights of our countrymen shall be protected.

I believe, therefore, we should lend our wholehearted cooperation to Japan, especially in the immediate task confronting us of reconstructing and alleviating the suffering of our people from the ravages of war.

The psychological situation here is becoming critical. If something is not done shortly to bring reassurance to these people there is grave danger of the success of the enemy's propaganda campaign. Silence will defeat us.[55]

In reply, General Marshall sent the following radiogram to Mac-Arthur:

> It appears to the War Department that the only way to combat statements such as that issued by Aguinaldo is to have our propaganda agencies here contrast against the Aguinaldo attitude the position, examples, and statements of President Quezon with the purpose of exciting admiration for the latter and contempt for the former. This effort will be undertaken immediately all over the world and in appropriate languages. Coupled with this will be a program of contrasting the proved record of the United States in the Philippines with that of Japan in China and Manchoukuo. The purpose will be to show that if Aguinaldo is sincere in his statement he is merely being deceived by insincere and worthless promises. An important part of our publicity will be the glorification of Filipino loyalty and heroism under the inspiring leadership of Quezon and a continuous effort to show that he represents the true feelings of the great masses of Filipino population and that Aguinaldo and others like him are mere opportunists seeking immediate power and publicity. If you have any suggestions for making more effective this propaganda effort please send them to me at your earliest opportunity.[56]

From Corregidor MacArthur radioed to President Roosevelt:

> Today, January 30, your birth anniversary smoke begrimed men covered with the murk of battle, rise from the foxholes of Bataan and the batteries of Corregidor, to pray reverently that God may bless immeasurably the President of the United States.[57]

MacArthur's birthday greeting to Roosevelt received wide publicity in the nation's newspapers. So impressed with the message was Senator Lee O'Daniel of Texas that he sent Roosevelt a telegeram:

> In view of the daring, heroic and almost miraculous defense of Luzon Island by our national hero, General MacArthur, and his brave men and further moved as the people of our nation are by the inspired birthday greetings you have just received from him, permit me to suggest that if practical and possible . . . you advise him on this your birthday that hereafter all American citizens will refer to the island he and his brave patriotic men are defending as "MacArthur Island." This action will typify our American way of life by tossing flowers to the living both ways across the Pacific in this tragic hour.

Later Major General Edwin M. ("Pa") Watson, the Presidential secretary in charge of appointments, acknowledged O'Daniel's wire: "The President wished me to thank you for your telegram and to say that the subject matter will receive very careful consideration."[58]

On January 31 the message center on Corregidor dispatched a radiogram from MacArthur to Marshall:

> The President's message to Quezon was most effective. Quezon sends following reply for President Roosevelt: "Your letter has moved me deeply. I wish to assure you that we shall do our part to the end. Signed Quezon."

In reality, however, Quezon was far from placated, and his anxiety and discontent continued to grow.[59]

5

Quezon's Neutralization Proposal

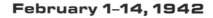

February 1–14, 1942

There are times when men have to die.[1]

—Secretary of War Henry L. Stimson

On February 1 MacArthur dispatched the following radiogram concerning guerrilla warfare in the Philippines to General George C. Marshall:

> Guerrilla activity in Mindanao . . . is now organized and directed by this headquarters using various agencies both Filipino and American. It is not deemed feasible nor practical to introduce any outside agents for use in this type of work. Supplies are vital not only there but to the main fighting forces and if not forthcoming will result in the ultimate collapse of all resistance in the Philippines. This country produces absolutely no direct war material and when scant supply we have is gone there is no source of replacement except the United States.
>
> Guerrilla operations in occupied portions of Luzon present a picture entirely different from Mindanao. Until the military forces are built up to a strength warranting such activity it would be most inadvisable to attempt anything along that line except with organized troops. It could only result in wholesale massacres of the civilian population by the enemy in reprisal. I have a force of approximately six hundred organized troops operating in the Cagayan Valley on the enemy's lines of communications and am in constant touch with this force by radio. I believe that extensive guerrilla efforts prior to the arrival of reinforcements from the

United States will be abortive and destructive. I have complete plans to launch the guerrilla movement to support the main effort upon arrival of reinforcements.[2]

General MacArthur was extremely anxious about the sagging morale of the Filipinos. Through the radio and press media, the Japanese continued to emphasize to them that no help had reached them from the United States, that no help was forthcoming, and that they were foolishly fighting and dying for the white Americans. MacArthur had asked Marshall to have propaganda leaflets printed in the United States and shipped to the Philippines to counteract Japanese propaganda. Approving the request, Marshall suggested sending Brigadier General Theodore Roosevelt to Mindanao with the leaflets to take charge of a propaganda campaign and to supervise the distribution of the leaflets throughout the Islands. Roosevelt, the eldest son of President Theodore Roosevelt, had been governor general of the Philippines in 1932 and 1933.[3]

MacArthur replied to Marshall:

The local distribution of handbills and propaganda in the Philippines should be through native elements. I have innumerable contacts of this sort which enable me to reach all sections of the country and distribute through tribal means which are impossible of direct accomplishment by an American officer. I have the greatest admiration and respect for General Roosevelt but I doubt whether these sentiments are shared by the Filipino people. Speaking frankly I do not believe he possesses their confidence or that they would welcome him here.

The dissemination of propaganda in the Visayas and Mindanao is a simple matter. We control all the islands and the means of communications although the latter have been very greatly curtailed. The problem in Luzon is difficult since our means are limited to one broadcasting station operating from Corregidor, airplanes without landing fields except those under control here, and secret agents who make their way very slowly through adjacent provinces. We have also in the Visayas a broadcasting station KZRC Cebu which is operating without interference. The War Department could assist materially by transmitting propaganda material to the radio station at Cebu. Moreover, printed matter can be prepared in that city for distribution throughout the Philippines. The greatest assistance in this respect would be the dispatch of a few airplanes which could provide communications throughout the archipelago.[4]

On February 2 Lieutenant Colonel Allison W. Ind of Brigadier General Harold H. George's staff walked into the USAFFE Headquarters lateral. He delivered an oral report to MacArthur and Sutherland concerning the activities and logistic requirements of George's small Air Corps on Bataan. MacArthur instructed Ind to convey to George "his personal congratulations for outstanding leadership." When Ind handed Sutherland an appeal from George for additional airplanes, Sutherland pulled out and handed Ind a bulky file of radiograms. "Just in case you have some idea that we are not trying," Sutherland said in clipped phrases, "look at this— and this—and this!"[5]

The same day MacArthur dispatched to Marshall a radiogram dealing with the possible evacuation of President Quezon from Corregidor.

> In case of ultimate loss of Bataan and consequent siege of Corregidor, the question arises as to the ultimate preservation of President Quezon and his family, Vice President Osmena and the immediate members of the commonwealth cabinet. By that time the usefulness of his presence here due to the changed conditions will have been greatly dissipated. I have no means of evacuating him and his physical condition precludes use of air transportation. It is possible he could sustain a submarine trip. Can any plans be arranged from Washington for his possible evacuation thereto? Under the contingency I have described, he wishes to take advantage of the previous suggestion that he be evacuated to the United States.[6]

In his reply to MacArthur, Marshall stated:

> The President and his advisers feel that if and when military considerations no longer call for continued presence of President Quezon and other Philippine officials, the evacuation of Quezon and family, of Osmena and of other such officials will become desirable.
>
> The question whether any of those persons and whether any other persons including Mr. Sayre and family, Mrs. MacArthur and son, and other Americans, shall at any time be evacuated will be for your decision in the light of the military situation, the feasibility and hazard of operation of evacuation and wishes of individuals concerned.
>
> Opportunities for such evacuation should occur shortly with arrival of a submarine from the south carrying three inch AA

ammunition to you and another from Hawaii also carrying three inch ammunition.

Steps will be taken to provide for reception of those evacuated at whatever places they may be taken while enroute to this country and upon their arrival in the United States.[7]

General MacArthur held a conference with Major General George F. Moore, in command of the Harbor Defenses, during the night of February 3. If the Filamerican army on Bataan collapsed, Mac-Arthur told Moore, he intended to evacuate the Philippine Division from Bataan to Corregidor. The division would be assigned to Moore's command and would be used to strengthen the beach defenses. Moore was directed "to make plans for their employment, to select bivouac areas, and to plan for an extension of hospital facilities." When the division would be ordered to Corregidor, Mac-Arthur said, "would depend on the development of the situation on Bataan." He directed that food for 20,000 men, based on half rations then in effect, be held by Moore at Corregidor to last until June 30, 1942. MacArthur explained that supplying the Bataan Force from Corregidor's stores should not be permitted to reduce the food supply below that amount. At that time Moore's ration strength on Corregidor was for 11,000 men.[8]

During the night of February 4 the submarine *Trout*, after unloading 2,750 rounds of 3-inch antiaircraft mechanical fuze ammunition, departed from Corregidor with nearly $10 million in gold and silver bullion from the Philippine Treasury vault on Corregidor. Also aboard was Lieutenant Colonel Warren J. Clear, who had been sent to the Far East in July 1941 on a confidential military assignment by the Intelligence Division of the War Department. After working with British authorities in Singapore for some months, Clear had arrived in the Philippines two days prior to the outbreak of hostilities.

Before boarding the *Trout*, out of Honolulu and bound for Java, Clear had been asked "pointed questions" by MacArthur about how seriously government and army officials in Washington had originally intended to support his Filamerican Army. Clear told Mac-Arthur that before he left Washington he had received several letters from Brigadier General Albert M. Jones, who was serving in the Philippines and had been Clear's former commander, pleading with him to see if he could obtain additional troops and more and better modern weapons for the defense of the Philippines. Jones's letters had made him "extremely anxious," Clear said, and he had personally taken the subject up with Stimson, presidential press secretary Stephen T. Early, and high-ranking army and naval officers, who had in turn discussed the matter with President Roosevelt. Roosevelt had stated "very emphatically that England and Russia had priority in all things and would continue to receive such priority."

Becoming "flushed," MacArthur replied, "Never before in history was so large and gallant an army 'written off' so callously."

Nearby, listening to the conversation, was President Quezon.[9]

On February 4 the following radiogram from Marshall to Mac-Arthur raised for the first time the possibility that MacArthur would be ordered to leave Corregidor.

The following personal message from General Marshall is to be seen by no one except the individual decoding it and General MacArthur:

Your [message of February 2] refers to a subject to which we have given continuous consideration. The possibility that there will develop a situation such as you describe raises questions for which carefully considered advance planning is advisable.

One of these relates to the disposition of such portion of your Filipino forces as should or could not repeat not, in your judgment, be transferred to Corregidor. Should these elements be authorized under the senior Filipino officer to capitulate with assurance that such action would not imply unsoldierly action?

The question of the evacuation of President Quezon and associates and others was covered in a message already sent and the possible use of one of the submarines scheduled to reach you at an early date with ammunition was suggested though it is not anticipated that there will be a noticeable deterioration of your defenses by the time of the arrival of the first of these.

The most important question concerns your possible movements should your forces be unable longer to sustain themselves in Bataan and there should remain nothing but the fortress defense of Corregidor. Under these conditions the need for your services there might be less pressing than at other points in the Far East.

There seem to be but two possible courses of action: the first is that you, at least initially, proceed to Mindanao. How long you would remain there would depend on the good you might do toward stimulating guerrilla operations in the Visayas and Min-danao, especially if our blockade running operations now under way meet with fair success and the Japanese threats at the Malay barrier are checked. From there you could later proceed south to resume command of the United States forces in the Far East. The alternative would be for you to proceed south direct without pause in Mindanao.

Measures now progressing should soon provide, unless seri-ously interrupted, a comprehensive service of supply in Australia and an active U.S. air force of five bomber and four pursuit groups in the Netherlands East Indies. The entire task of directing opera-tions and maintaining the force in that area is a most difficult one.

The purpose of this message is to secure from you a highly confidential statement of your own views. It is to be understood that in case your withdrawal from immediate leadership of your beleaguered forces is to be carried out it will be by direct order of the president to you. What I want are your views in advance of a decision. No record is being made of this message within the War Department and I have arranged that your reply labeled personal to General Marshall for his eyes only will come directly from the decoding clerk to me with no copy retained and no other individual involved.[10]

The following day MacArthur answered the inquiry by urging a concept of strategy diametrically opposed to that outlined by Mar-shall.

In compliance with your previous directive that from time to time I present my strategic conception of the situation, I take this opportunity of presenting what I believe is a fatal mistake on the part of the democratic Allies.

The Japanese are sweeping southward in a great offensive and the Allies are attempting merely to stop them by building up forces in their front. This method, as has almost universally been the case in war, will fail. Such movements can only be negatived by thrusts not at the enemy's strength but at his weakness. The lines of weakness from time immemorial have been the lines of com-munication. In this case they are stretched out over two thousand miles of sea with the whole line subject to American sea thrust. This line is not defended by enemy bombers but is held by scattered naval elements. A sea threat would immediately relieve the pressure on the south and is the only way that pressure can be relieved. A great naval victory on our part is not necessary to ac-complish this mission; the threat alone would go far toward the desired end. The enemy would probably not engage his entire fleet in actual combat. If he did and lost, the war would be over. If he did and won, the losses he would sustain would still cripple his advance and take from him the initiative. You must be prepared to take heavy losses, just so heavy losses are inflicted in return.

I wish to reiterate that his bomber strength is practically entirely engaged on his southern front and represents little menace to such a naval thrust. With only minor threats from the fleets of Germany and Italy, the American and British navies can assemble without serious jeopardy the force to make this thrust. I unhesitatingly predict that if this is not done the plan upon which we are now working, based upon the building up of air supremacy in the Southwest Pacific, will fail, the war will be indefinitely prolonged and its final outcome will be jeopardized. Counsels of timidity based upon theories of safety first will not win against such an aggressive and audacious adversary as Japan. No building program, no matter of what proportions, will be able to overtake the initial advantages the enemy with every chance of success is trying to gain. The only way to beat him is to fight him incessantly. Combat must not be avoided but must be sought so that the ultimate policy of attrition can at once become effective. No matter what the theoretical odds may be against us, if we fight him we will beat him. We have shown that here.

In submitting these views I may be exceeding the proper scope of my office and therefore do so with great hesitancy. My excuse, if excuse is necessary, is that from my present point of vantage I can see the whole strategy of the Pacific perhaps clearer than anyone else. If agreeable to you I would appreciate greatly the presentation of this view to the highest authority.[11]

On February 6 General Emilio Aguinaldo, President Quezon's principal political antagonist in the Philippines, made an impassioned plea to General MacArthur in a radiobroadcast from Manila. He urged MacArthur to end the resistance and to surrender in order to spare the Filipino people further death and the Philippine Islands further destruction.

The broadcast disturbed MacArthur greatly, as it did President Quezon. Although Quezon looked upon the struggle of the Filamerican army as heroic, like Aguinaldo he believed it was futile. He was especially embittered at the United States government because of its reluctance to authorize a major military effort to break through the Japanese naval blockade of the Philippines and bring in supplies and reinforcements.[12]

One recent day Quezon, who suffered from tuberculosis, had been sitting in a wheel chair inside his tent near the entrance of Malinta Tunnel, listening to a radiobroadcast from the United States. The broadcast spoke of the tremendous production potential of the United States and the great amounts of war material that soon would go to Europe. Hearing the broadcast and understanding Quezon's frustration, MacArthur "quietly motioned" his chief of intelligence, Colonel Charles A. Willoughby, who spoke fluent Spanish, to go to Quezon.

Upon entering the tent, Willoughby could see that Quezon was enraged. His Swiss physician, Dr. Trepp, and his wife, Doña Aurora, were trying unsuccessfully to quiet him. "You arrived at a good time!" shouted Quezon in Spanish to Willoughby. "Listen to what the shameless ones are saying in Washington." Quezon denounced the American government in a stream of bitter Spanish, gesturing toward Manila, or toward Cavite and the south. Although it was a beautiful day with deep blue skies and glorious sunshine, "far to the south, probably in Ternate, black columns of smoke rose high in the skies above a burning hamlet, where the Japanese had been."

"For thirty years I have worked and hoped for my people," Quezon said, pointing to the ominous black column of smoke. "Now they burn and die for a flag that could not protect them. By God and all the Saints, I cannot stand this constant reference to England, to Europe. . . . I am here and my people are here under the heels of a conqueror. Where are the planes that this shameless one is boasting of? What a demon—how typically American to writhe in anguish at the fate of a distant cousin while a daughter is being raped in the back room. . . ."[13]

Quezon believed that General Aguinaldo's radiobroadcast would have a great effect on the "less educated classes" of Filipinos. He thought they would be swayed by the Japanese promise to grant independence to the Philippines, reiterated by Aguinaldo in his broadcast. Fearing that the Filipinos might side with Aguinaldo, Quezon told MacArthur that he was seriously considering turning himself over to the Japanese. He believed that he would then be in a position to defy the Japanese and to "solidify the opposition of the Filipinos to any Japanese influence."

MacArthur argued that this would be a mistake. He did not believe the Japanese would make a martyr of Quezon, he said, for fear of turning the Filipino people completely against them. But he did believe that the Japanese would probably keep Quezon in residence in Malacanan Palace, isolated from other Filipinos. Then they could issue statements in his name without his consent, "telling the Filipinos that they should cooperate with Japan and advising the Filipino soldiers at the front to surrender and abandon the American forces." Furthermore, MacArthur told Quezon, if he turned himself over to the Japanese, his "action might be misinterpreted abroad." Quezon was incensed at this. He retorted that he "was not interested in the judgment of outsiders." Impressed, however, with MacArthur's projection of what the Japanese might do, Quezon said he would "think more about the matter."[14]

Although Quezon gave up the idea of placing himself at the mercy of the Japanese, he formulated out of desperation a second plan, just as serious in its implications, which he believed would end the war in the Philippines. It called for the neutralization of the Philippines by the United States and Japan. After writing out his plan, along with an introductory letter which severly criticized the conduct of the war on the part of the U.S. government, Quezon called a meeting of his skeleton cabinet on Corregidor. At the meeting he read the message he proposed to send to Roosevelt. Vice President Sergio Osmena and Manuel A. Roxas immediately "questioned the wisdom" of his plan. Quezon, unmoved, threatened to resign "unless the others agreed with him." Osmena, Roxas, and the remaining officials reluctantly assented.[15]

On February 8 a very important message from Marshall was dispatched to MacArthur in reply to MacArthur's radiogram of February 5. The message explained why the strategy MacArthur had proposed could not be carried out. It definitely ruled out any possibility that a major naval effort might be expended in an attempt to reduce the Japanese pressure against the Philippines.

> The fundamental strategy outlined in your [radiogram of February 5] has been under most careful study. From the moment the enemy began his southward drive the decisive effect of a successful flank attack against his communications has been recognized. Two factors have stood in the way of initiating such operations. The first is that, as a feature of his opening operations, in early December the enemy provided for naval flank security by seizing Guam and Wake and establishing there as well as in the Marshall and Gilbert islands heavy protective forces principally air. The second factor has been naval weakness due to the initial elimina-

tion at Pearl Harbor of virtually the entire heavy striking elements of the Pacific Fleet. This weakness is now rapidly being corrected by repairs and transfers but very heavy convoy duties to Hawaii and Australia and the submarining of one of our few Pacific air carriers has seriously limited aggressive naval operations. From now on aggressive tactics are becoming possible. It has been necessary to convoy and set up garrisons on Canton Christmas Palmyra islands, Bori Bori and Samoa and Fiji and a garrison for New Caledonia now enroute—all to cover communications with Far East. On January 30 the navy carried out an offensive against the hostile flank, striking the Gilbert and Marshall islands. A great deal of damage was inflicted upon Japanese shipping and local installations; but the reaction, particularly by air, was such as to preclude deeper penetration with the limited forces available.

More recently United States and Dutch naval forces in the Netherlands East Indies, conducting an offensive against an isolated portion of the enemy's extended position, were met by formations of land based bombers. All cruisers participating in this attack were heavily damaged and were compelled to proceed to naval bases for repair. Similar results have been experienced in the Mediterranean, in the North Sea and in the South China Sea. It is obvious that surface vessels cannot operate in regions where they are subjected to heavy attack by hostile land based aircraft. Nevertheless a second offensive is now under way to strike at the flank of the hostile advance on New Britain. But army heavy bombers from Hawaii have to be moved into position to support this distant action. These facts and considerations have forced us to oppose the Japanese aggression in the only areas in which the required air bases and fields remain in our possession; namely, northern Australia and the Netherlands East Indies. It is clearly recognized that the decisive effects that would follow successful flanking operations as suggested in your radio cannot be accomplished through the methods we are now employing. However, these methods were adopted simply because there appeared to be no alternative except complete inaction.

Due to unannounced losses the number of aircraft carriers presently available to the Allies is not sufficient to permit the substitution of this type of air power for land based craft in a general offensive westward from Hawaii. Similarly, the number of capital ships that could conceivably be made available in the Pacific is not sufficient to permit an advance toward Japan, northward of the mandated islands, in an effort either to destroy his communications at their base or to force his main fleet into action on the high seas. The basis of all current effort is to accumulate through every possible means sufficient strength to initiate operations along the lines you suggest, building up behind the effort the forces required to push home a deep attack. More is under way than I dare risk reference to in this communication. In the meanwhile we are endeavoring to limit the hostile advance so as to deny him free access to land and sea areas that will immeasurably strengthen his war making powers or which will be valuable to us as jump off positions when we can start a general counteroffensive. There is always the possibility, as the Russians complete their highly successful winter campaign of tremendous counter attacks along the entire front, which are having a serious effect on German arms and morale, that Stalin will feel more free to consider action in his Pacific theater. He has stated his expectation on an eventual Japanese attack on Siberia. He realizes the enemy's great advantage if that attack should follow rather than coincide with their present tremendous thrust southward. If we have an early success in checking Japanese progression and secure air superiority there is the strong probability that at that moment Stalin will strike against Japan. His eastern submarine force and bomber force should permit devastating action against Japanese shipping and industry.

I welcome and appreciate your strategical views and invariably submit them to the President.[16]

During the afternoon of February 8 in Washington, Secretary of War Stimson was notified that a long radiogram was coming in to the War Department Message Center from Fort Mills. Reaching the War Department, Stimson learned that the message was from President Quezon and had been sent by General MacArthur.

The following message has just been received by me from President Quezon for President Roosevelt.

The situation of my country has become so desperate that I feel that positive action is demanded. Militarily it is evident that no help will reach us from the United States in time either to rescue the beleaguered garrison now fighting so gallantly or to prevent the complete overrunning of the entire Philippine archipelago.

My people entered the war with the confidence that the United States would bring such assistance to us as would make it possible to sustain the conflict with some chance of success. All our soldiers in the field were animated by the belief that help would be forthcoming. This help has not and evidently will not be realized. Our people have suffered death, misery, devastation. After two months of war not the slightest assistance has been forthcoming from the United States. Aid and succor have been dispatched to other warring nations such as England, Ireland, Australia, the Netherlands East Indies and perhaps others, but not only has nothing come here, but apparently no effort has been made to bring anything here. The American fleet and the British fleet, the two most powerful navies in the world, have apparently adopted an attitude which precludes any effort to reach these islands with assistance.

As a result, while enjoying security itself, the United States has in effect condemned the sixteen millions of Filipinos to practical destruction in order to effect a certain delay. You have promised redemption, but what we need is immediate assistance and protection. We are concerned with what is to transpire during the next few months and years as well as with our ultimate destiny. There is not the slightest doubt in our minds that victory will rest with the United States, but the question before us now is: Shall we further sacrifice our country and our people in a hopeless fight? I voice the unanimous opinion of my war cabinet and I am sure the unanimous opinion of all Filipinos that under the circumstances we should take steps to preserve the Philippines and the Filipinos from further destruction.

Thanks to wise generalship two thirds of my country is as yet untouched. We do not propose to do this by a betrayal of the United States. It appears to us that our mission is only to fight as a sacrifice force here as long as possible in order to help the defense of the Dutch and British in this area of the world. But you do not need to sacrifice the people of the Philippines to win this war. Members of your government have repeatedly said that the action against Hitler would determine the outcome of the entire war.

I feel at this moment that our military resistance here can no longer hold the enemy when he sees fit to launch a serious attack. I feel that the elements of the situation here can be composed into a solution that will not reduce the delaying effect of our resistance here but which will save my country from further devastation as the battle ground of two great powers.

I deem it my duty to propose my solution. . . .

Note: Remainder of message will be forwarded by code room as soon as possible.[17]

Although it was only the first part of Quezon's message, Stimson correctly surmised after reading it that Quezon wanted ultimately to "surrender for his people in order to avoid useless sacrifice." Stimson sympathized with Quezon, but he believed that "his radiogram brought forward a number of alleged instances of failure" on the part of the War Department "which were not true."

For an hour and a half Stimson deliberated with Marshall, who had been shocked by the radiogram, concerning the implications of the message. They talked about President Quezon and the future of the Philippines; the future of the gallant American army on Bataan and Corregidor; and the fate of General MacArthur. At the conclusion of the talk Stimson believed that he and Marshall were thinking along similar lines, but he knew that the situation raised by President Quezon "was ghastly in its responsibility and significance."[18]

The following morning when Stimson arrived at the War Department, he learned that the remainder of Quezon's message, transmitted through MacArthur, had been decoded, along with messages from MacArthur and High Commissioner Sayre. First was Quezon's proposal of neutralization.

> The government of the United States under the McDuffie-Tydings Law is committed to grant independence to the Philippines in 1946, and the same law authorized the president to open negotiations for the neutralization of the Philippines. On the other hand, the Japanese government has publicly announced its willingness to grant the Philippines her independence. In view of the foregoing I propose the following: that the United States immediately grant the Philippines complete and absolute independence; that the Philippines be at once neutralized; that all occupying troops, both American and Japanese, be withdrawn by mutual agreement with the Philippine government within a reasonable length of time; that neither country maintain bases in the Philippines; that the Philippine army be immediately disbanded, the only armed forces being maintained here to be a constabulary of modest size; that immediately upon granting independence the trade relations of the Philippines with foreign countries be a matter to be determined entirely by the Philippines and the foreign countries concerned; that American and Japanese civilians who so desire be withdrawn with their respective troops under mutual and

proper safeguards. It is my proposal to make this suggestion publicly to you and to the Japanese authorities without delay and upon its acceptance in general principle by those two countries that an immediate armistice be entered into here pending the withdrawal of their respective garrisons. Signed Manuel L. Quezon.

I took the liberty of presenting this message to High Commissioner Sayre for a general expression of his views. States as follows: "If the premise of President Quezon is correct that American help cannot or will not arrive here in time to be availing I believe his proposal for immediate independence and neutralization of the Philippines is the sound course to follow."

My estimate of the military situation here is as follows: The troops have sustained practically fifty percent casualties from their original strength. Divisions are reduced to the size of regiments, regiments to battalions, battalions to companies. Some units have entirely disappeared. The men have been in constant action and are badly battle worn. They are desperately in need of rest and refitting. Their spirit is good but they are capable now of nothing but fighting in place on a fixed position. All our supplies are scant and the command has been on half rations for the past month.

It is possible for the time being that the present enemy forces might temporarily be held, but any addition to his present strength will insure the destruction of our whole force. We have pulled through a number of menacing situations but there is no denying the fact that we are near done. Corregidor itself is extremely vulnerable. This type of fortress, built prior to the days of air power, when isolated is impossible of prolonged defense. Any heavy air bombardment or the location of siege guns on Bataan or even on the Cavite side would definitely limit the life of the fortress. My water supply is extremely vulnerable and may go at any time. Every other vital installation can be readily taken out.

Since I have no air or sea protection you must be prepared at any time to figure on the complete destruction of this command. You must determine whether the mission of delay would be better furthered by the temporizing plan of Quezon or by my continued battle effort. The temper of the Filipinos is one of almost violent resentment against the United States. Every one of them expected help and when it has not been forthcoming they believe they have been betrayed in favor of others. It must be remembered they are hostile to Great Britain on account of the latter's colonial policy. In spite of my great prestige with them, I have had the utmost difficulty during the last few days in keeping them in line. If help does not arrive shortly nothing, in my opinion, can prevent their utter collapse and their complete absorption by the enemy. The Japanese made a powerful impression upon Philippine public imagination in promising independence.

So far as the military angle is concerned, the problem presents itself as to whether the plan of President Quezon might offer the best possible solution of what is about to be a disastrous debacle. It would not affect the ultimate situation in the Philippines for that would be determined by the results in other theatres. If the Japanese government rejects President Quezon's proposition it would psychologically strengthen our hold because of their prime minister's public statement offering independence. If it accepts it, we lose no military advantage because we would still secure at least equal delay. Please instruct me.[19]

Stimson's reaction to the messages was "disappointment." Quezon's proposal was "wholly unreal," Stimson thought, since it ignored "what the war was for or what the well-known characteristics of Japan towards conquered people were." He considered MacArthur's estimate of the situation to be "worse" than Quezon's message; it "went more than half way towards supporting Quezon's position."

Stimson walked into General Marshall's office, where Marshall and Eisenhower were working on replies to the messages, and gave his views concerning the messages and the necessary responses. "There are times," he said at one point, "when men have to die." Marshall agreed with him; the messages they had been working on, he said, "arrived at the same conclusions."

By telephone Stimson informed the president of Quezon's proposal. Roosevelt suggested that Stimson and Marshall meet him in the White House at 10:30 A.M. They held their conference in the president's study, with Assistant Secretary of State Sumner Welles also present. After Roosevelt had read Quezon's and MacArthur's messages, he asked Marshall what line of action was being proposed. Marshall replied that Stimson could state his views better than he could.

Desiring no interruption, Stimson rose and spoke as if addressing a jury in a courtroom. He wanted to state his position "in full," he said, and he spoke very deliberately. When he had concluded, Roosevelt, who had listened "very attentively," said that he was in complete agreement. Welles complimented Stimson on his presentation and said he too agreed. They decided to meet again at 2:30

P.M. after Stimson had drafted a message to Quezon and Marshall one to MacArthur.

At the White House meeting that afternoon Welles was again present, along with Admirals Ernest J. King and Harold R. Stark. Roosevelt read Stimson's reply to Quezon, using his pen to correct some facts and make deletions. Where Stimson had referred to the Filipino people as "a dependent people," Roosevelt crossed out "a dependent" and substituted "another." He deleted two whole sentences: "The United States has become involved in this war because of its defense of the rights of small nations," and "We have not hitherto nor do we now impose any compulsion upon your soldiers who have been cooperating with us in this endeavor." It took more than an hour to go over Stimson's draft to Quezon and Marshall's draft to MacArthur.

By 4:00 P.M. the messages had been corrected and the White House conference ended. Stimson and Marshall returned to the War Department to have the messages readied for sending. For Stimson it had been a long day. The decision reached had been "a difficult one" since it ordered a "brave garrison to a fight to the finish." But aside from that aspect, it put the "attitude" of the United States government toward the Philippines "upon a correct and elevated basis."[20]

Late in the afternoon of February 9, the two long messages from Roosevelt were given to the radio operator in the War Department Message Center to be dispatched to General MacArthur and President Quezon. Late into the night a continuous stream of code went out to the message center at Fort Mills on Corregidor.

> In the second section of this message I am making, through you, an immediate reply to President Quezon's proposals of February eight. My reply must emphatically deny the possibility of this government's agreement to the political aspects of President Quezon's proposal. I authorize you to arrange for the capitulation of the Filipino elements of the defending forces, when and if in your opinion that course appears necessary and always having in mind that the Filipino troops are in the service of the United States. Details of all necessary arrangements will be left in your hands, including plans for segregation of forces and the withdrawal, if your judgment so dictates, of American elements to Fort Mills. The timing also will be left to you.
>
> American forces will continue to keep our flag flying in the

Philippines so long as there remains any possibility of resistance. I have made these decisions in complete understanding of your military estimate that accompanied President Quezon's message to me. The duty and the necessity of resisting Japanese aggression to the last transcends in importance any other obligation now facing us in the Philippines.

There has been gradually welded into a common front a globe encircling opposition to the predatory powers that are seeking the destruction of individual liberty and freedom of government. We cannot afford to have this line broken in any particular theatre. As the most powerful member of this coalition we cannot display weakness in fact or in spirit anywhere. It is mandatory that there be established once and for all in the minds of all peoples complete evidence that the American determination and indomitable will to win carries on down to the last unit.

I therefore give you this most difficult mission in full understanding of the desperate situation to which you may shortly be reduced. The service that you and the American members of your command can render to your country in the titanic struggle now developing is beyond all possibility of appraisement. I particularly request that you proceed rapidly to the organization of your forces and your defenses so as to make your resistance as effective as circumstances will permit and as prolonged as humanly possible.

If the evacuation of President Quezon and his cabinet appears reasonably safe they would be honored and greatly welcomed in the United States. This applies also to the high commissioner. Mrs. Sayre and your family should be given this opportunity if you consider it advisable. You yourself, however, must determine action to be taken in view of circumstances.

Please inform Sayre of this message to you and to Quezon.

Submit by radio the essentials of your plans in accordance with these instructions.

Please convey the following message to President Quezon:

I have just received your message sent through General MacArthur. From my message to you of January 30, you must realize that I am not lacking in understanding of or sympathy with the situation of yourself and the commonwealth government today. The immediate crisis certainly seems desperate but such crises and their treatment must be judged by a more accurate measure than the anxieties and sufferings of the present, however acute. For over forty years the American government has been carrying out to the people of the Philippines a pledge to help them successfully, however long it might take, in their aspirations to become a self-governing and independent people with individual freedom and economic strength which that lofty aim makes requisite. You yourself have participated in and are familiar with the many carefully planned steps by which that pledge of self-government has been carried out and also the steps by which the economic independence of your islands is to be made effective. May I remind you now that in the loftiness of its aim and the fidelity with which it has been executed, this program of the United States towards another people has been unique in the history of the family of nations. In the Tydings-McDuffie Act of 1934, to which you refer, the Congress of the United States finally fixed the year 1946 as the date in which the Philippine Islands established by that act should finally reach the goal of its hopes for political and economic independence.

By a malign conspiracy of a few depraved but powerful governments this hope is now being frustrated and delayed. An organized attack upon individual freedom and governmental independence throughout the entire world, beginning in Europe, has now spread and been carried to the Southwestern Pacific by Japan. The basic principles which have guided the United States in its conduct toward the Philippines have been violated in the rape of Czechoslovakia, Poland, Holland, Belgium, Luxembourg, Denmark, Norway, Albania, Greece, Yugoslavia, Manchukuo, Indo-China, China, Thailand and finally the Philippines. Could the people of any of these nations honestly look forward to true restoration of their independent sovereignty under the dominance of Germany, Italy, or Japan? You refer in your telegram to the announcement by the Japanese prime minister of Japan's willingness to grant to the Philippines her independence. I only have to refer you to the present condition of Korea, Manchukuo, North China, Indo-China, and all other countries which have fallen under the brutal sway of the Japanese government, to point out the hollow duplicity of such an announcement. The present sufferings of the Filipino people, cruel as they may be, are infinitely less than the sufferings and permanent enslavement which will inevitably follow acceptance of Japanese promises. In any event is it longer possible for any reasonable person to rely upon Japanese offer or promise?

The United States today is engaged with all its resources and in company with the governments of twenty-six other nations in an effort to defeat the aggression of Japan and its Axis partners. This effort will never be abandoned until the complete and thorough overthrow of the entire Axis system and the governments which maintain it. We are engaged now in laying the foundations in the Southwest Pacific of a development in air, naval, and military power which shall become sufficient to meet and overthrow the widely extended and arrogant attempts of the Japanese. Military and naval operations call for recognition of realities. What we are doing there constitutes the best and surest help that we can render to the Philippines at this time.

By the terms of our pledge to the Philippines implicit in our forty years of conduct towards your people and expressly recognized in the terms of the Tydings-McDuffie Act, we have undertaken to protect you to the uttermost of our power until the time of your ultimate independence had arrived. Our soldiers in the Philippines are now engaged in fulfilling that purpose. The honor of the United States is pledged to its fulfillment. We propose that it be carried out regardless of its cost. Those Americans who are fighting now will continue to fight until the bitter end. Filipino soldiers have been rendering voluntary and gallant service in defense of their own homeland.

So long as the flag of the United States flies on Filipino soil as a pledge of our duty to your people, it will be defended by our own men to the death. Whatever happens to the present American garrison we shall not relax our efforts until the forces which we are now marshaling outside the Philippine Islands return to the Philippines and drive the last remnant of the invaders from our soil.[21]

At 7:00 A.M. on February 10 President Roosevelt's message was received by the code section of the Army's Signal Corps on Corregidor. At 10:00 A.M. the decoded message was handed to General MacArthur.

Before Roosevelt's message could be given to President Quezon, it had to be paraphrased—a precaution taken in order to protect the secret code and the usual procedure before a Top Secret message could be taken from the USAFFE Headquarters. This message was paraphrased by Lieutenant Colonel Francis H. Wilson, an aide-de-camp to MacArthur and Sutherland. It was vital that the original meaning be retained. Wilson's paraphrase was approved by Sutherland and delivered to Quezon.[22]

Quezon was resting in his tent outside Malinta Tunnel when he received Roosevelt's message. He read it hurriedly and flew into a "violent rage." Deriving strength from his anger, he rose from his wheel chair and paced the narrow tent. Talking as if addressing an audience, he attacked Roosevelt's concept of global war strategy. He "had been misled into believing that reinforcements would arrive in time to save the Philippines," Quezon stormed; "Who is in a better position, Roosevelt or myself, to judge what is best for my people?" His energy dissipated, he sank into his wheel chair, called for his secretary, and "dictated a brief statement in which he resigned as President of the Commonwealth."

About an hour later, Quezon read his resignation to his cabinet. He and his family would return to Manila, Quezon said; "he wanted no further responsibility for the continued participation of the Filipinos in the war." Quezon told the cabinet members, listening in a state of near-shock, that they could either return to Manila with him or remain on Corregidor.

In an emotional voice Vice President Osmena urged Quezon to reconsider. If Quezon entered Japanese-controlled territory, he pointed out, he would in all probability bring dishonor to himself and to his country as well. Osmena "emphasized that, however adverse the circumstances, the Filipino people could not even think of diminishing their determination to defend their homeland against the invading enemies." Manuel Roxas supported Osmena's stand with feeling. But Quezon was unmoved. The discussion continued, with Quezon adamantly reiterating, "Because of Roosevelt's insulting message, it is no longer possible for me to serve as President of the Commonwealth. I have been deceived and I intend to return to Manila." Later that day he requested one of his staff members to procure a small boat for the trip.[23]

At 6:00 P.M. on February 10 a second message from Quezon was handed to the Signal Corps officer for President Roosevelt. At 7:25 P.M. the signal officer reported to Sutherland that it had been encoded and sending was about to start.

> The following is the letter I propose to address to you and to the emperor of Japan if my recent proposal meets with your approval:

> Two great Nations are now at war in the Western Pacific. The Commonwealth of the Philippines is still a possession of one of those nations, although through legislative processes it was about to attain complete independence which would have insured its neutrality in any conflict. The Philippines has therefore become a battleground between the warring powers and it is being visited with death, famine and destruction, despite the fact that occupation of the country will not influence in any way the final outcome of the war, nor have a bearing upon the conflicting principles over which the war is being waged.

Under the Tydings-McDuffie Law the United States has promised
to recognize the independence of the Philippines in 1946 and the
same law gave authority to the President of the United States to
begin parleys for the neutralization of the Philippines. On the other
hand, the premier of imperial government of Japan, addressing the
Diet, stated that the imperial government of Japan was ready to
offer the Filipino people independence with honor. On the strength
of these commitments and impelled by a sincere desire to put
an end to the sufferings and sacrifices of our people, and to
safeguard their liberty and welfare, I propose the following program of action:

> That the government of the United States and the imperial
> government of Japan recognize the independence of the
> Philippines; that within a reasonable period of time both
> armies, American and Japanese, be withdrawn, previous
> arrangements having been negotiated with the Philippine
> government; that neither nation maintain bases in the Philip-
> pines; that the Philippine army be at once demobilized, the
> remaining force to be a constabulary of moderate size; that
> at once upon the granting of freedom trade agreements with
> other countries become solely a matter to be settled by the
> Philippines and the nation concerned; that American and
> Japanese noncombatants who so desire be evacuated with
> their own armies under reciprocal and appropriate stipula-
> tions.

It is my earnest hope that, made by the highest considerations
of justice and humanity, the two great powers which now exercise
control over the Philippines will give their approval in general
principle to my proposal. If this is done I further propose, in order
to accomplish the details thereof, that an armistice be declared
in the Philippines and that I proceed to Manila at once for necessary consultations with the two governments concerned.[24]

Vice President Osmena made no attempt after the cabinet meeting to dissuade Quezon. He believed that such an attempt would
only increase his chief's obstinacy. Still Osmena felt that Quezon,
"if given a face-saving opportunity, might wish to talk with him as
he had done in the past."

Early in the morning of February 11, in a lateral of Malinta
Tunnel where Quezon and his cabinet members were sleeping,
Osmena rose from his cot and slowly made his way toward the
latrine. As he walked past the alcove where Quezon slept, he heard
the president coughing. Quezon saw Osmena and called to him.

Osmena entered the alcove and sat down beside the sick man. To his long-time colleague, Quezon seemed very depressed as he reminisced about the experiences they had shared through the years.

Osmena listened to Quezon for a few minutes. Then, sensing that he was in a "receptive mood," Osmena brought up Quezon's resignation and his plan to return to Manila. He reviewed in detail the reasons why Quezon should reconsider. Osmena did not want his life-long friend "to make a mistake so serious in character that history might record him as a gross coward and a traitor," he said. Knowing Quezon's great love for his wife and nearly grown daughters, Osmena "concluded his remarks by referring to the personal safety of the other's family." There were confirmed reports that Japanese soldiers had raped Filipino girls and women, and Osmena mentioned the possibility that the Japanese would force their will on Quezon by seizing his daughters. After listening attentively without interrupting, Quezon said quietly, "Compadre, perhaps you are right. I shall think it over."[25]

On February 11 General MacArthur had the subsequent radiogram dispatched to President Roosevelt:

> I have delivered your message to President Quezon and have shown your [message to me] to High Commissioner Sayre. If opportunity presents and can be done with reasonable safety, and, of course, with their consent, I will evacuate the members of the commonwealth government, the high commissioner, Mrs. Sayre and their son. I am deeply appreciative of the inclusion of my own family in this list but they and I have decided that they will share the fate of the garrison.
>
> My plans have already been outlined in previous radios; they consist in fighting my present battle position in Bataan to destruction and then holding Corregidor in a similar manner. I have not the slightest intention in the world of surrendering or capitulating the Filipino elements of my command. Apparently my message gave a false impression or was garbled with reference to Filipinos. My statements regarding collapse applied only to the civilian population, including commonwealth officials, the puppet government and the general populace. There has never been the slightest wavering among the troops. I count upon them equally with the Americans to hold steadfast to the end.[26]

MacArthur dispatched a second radiogram to Roosevelt:

After witnessing our burying of about four hundred dead Japs whom we had just mopped up, the governor of Bataan has reported: "I am having a little difficulty collecting the taxes because of some trouble in my province." I assured him that you were broad-minded and would understand.[27]

The same day MacArthur and Sutherland read a radiogram from General Marshall:

Confidential for General MacArthur only. Referring further to the message from President Quezon in your [message of February 8] to the President of the United States. Please note that portion which states: "It is my proposal to make this suggestion publicly to you and to the Japanese authorities without delay." This proposal was, of course, made contingent upon acceptance by President Roosevelt of the basic suggestion and since the president's answer did not repeat not so accept, it is assumed that further action along the line indicated is not repeat not intended. However, to insure that no misunderstanding or misapprehension may be created, the president has additionally directed me to inform you as follows: The president desires that no, repeat no, public statement of any kind bearing directly or indirectly on this subject be permitted to go out from any station or source under your control, unless and until the president of the United States has had prior and specific notification and you have received his reply and further instructions. Please exercise particular care with respect to this matter.

As stated in the president's radiogram, President Quezon can be certain, because of the gallant struggle the Filipino soldiers have made under your command, that he would receive in the United States an extraordinary welcome and honors. As quickly as any plans for his evacuation by submarine may even partially materialize, I should like to be advised so as to arrange so far as possible for a safe and speedy trip to the United States.[28]

In Washington on the morning of February 11 no reply had yet come in to President Roosevelt's message of February 9 from either MacArthur or Quezon. Quezon's radiogram of February 10 had been received, however. An afternoon conference was held in the White House to consider a course of action concerning this message. Roosevelt felt that it deserved "a special answer." He asked Stimson and Marshall "to draft a sharp answer" to Quezon and outlined what he particularly wanted this message to contain: "first, that the President had no constitutional right to cede or transfer American land or property to any other nation; second, that the United States had entered into a pact with twenty-six nations in which they were going to take care of Japan and her efforts in the East and in which the United States had pledged itself with the other nations not to make a separate peace or to stop fighting; third, that Quezon had no powers in such matters as he was suggesting."

Marshall drafted the following reply to Quezon:

> From the President to General MacArthur. Transmit the following message from me to President Quezon: "Your message of February tenth evidently crossed mine to you of February ninth. Under our constitutional limitations the President of the United States is not empowered to cede or alienate any territory to another nation. Furthermore, the United States has just bound itself in agreement with twenty-six other nations to united action in dealing with the Axis powers and has specifically engaged itself not to enter into any negotiations for a separate peace.
>
> "You have no authority to communicate with the Japanese government without the express permission of the United States government.
>
> "I will make no further comments regarding your last message dated February tenth pending your acknowledgment of mine to you of February ninth through General MacArthur."—Franklin D. Roosevelt.

Stimson thought it was "a very good draft," and approved it "with gratitude." The draft was submitted to Roosevelt, who changed "limitation" to "authority" and "twenty-six other nations" to "twenty-four other nations." It was then dispatched to General MacArthur at Fort Mills.[29]

During the early afternoon of February 12, MacArthur had the subsequent radiogram dispatched to Marshall.

> President Quezon's suggested proposal was entirely contingent upon prior approval by President Roosevelt. . . . He has no intention whatsoever so far as I know to do anything which does not meet with President Roosevelt's complete acquiescence. I will, however, take every possible precaution that nothing of this nature goes out. President Quezon has several times declined to accept a trip by submarine. His physical condition is such that his medical advisers do not believe he could survive it.[30]

At 4:20 P.M. MacArthur instructed Sutherland to deliver Roosevelt's February 11 message to Quezon. After reading it, Quezon told Vice President Osmena, "I have decided against going to Manila. At this point I shall make other plans."

The crisis was over. MacArthur dispatched to the War Department the following message from Quezon:

> To the President of the United States: I wish to thank you for your prompt answer to the proposal which I submitted to you with the unanimous approval of my war cabinet. We fully appreciate the reasons upon which your decision is based and we are abiding by it.[31]

In Washington shortly before noon on February 12, General Benedict Crowell walked into Secretary of War Stimson's office. His purpose in seeing Stimson was to urge the appointment of a "Commander in Chief of all the armies of the United States." Stimson disagreed. He had "just come from a series of discussions . . . with . . . draftsmen engaged in drawing the reorganization of the [War] Department," where he "had strongly maintained just the opposite position." Stimson told Crowell "there should be nobody between the President and the commander of different task forces, and that the Chief of Staff should be the Chief of Staff."[32]

That night in honor of Abraham Lincoln's birthday, Thomas E. Dewey, a candidate for the Republican nomination for President in 1940 and a prospective nominee for governor of New York, spoke at the annual dinner of the National Republican Club at the Waldorf Astoria Hotel in New York City. Speaking on the subject of "appeasement," Dewey said, in part:

> I am informed that there is already an American Cliveden set in Washington and other cities. They are scheming to end the war short of military victory. They are waiting for the time to come out in the open with plans for a negotiated peace.
>
> The issue of appeasement and compromise will surely rise. While today its advocates are present in both parties, history teaches that they all may attempt to sneak into the party of the opposition. They may even attempt to use it to achieve their cowardly end.
>
> Our first Quisling, however unimportant, has already appeared in the person of the Filipino Aguinaldo. If history teaches correctly, he will not be the last. . . .[33]

The same night another Republican-sponsored Lincoln birthday dinner was held at the Middlesex Club in Boston. The main speaker was the defeated Republican candidate for the presidency in 1940, Wendell L. Willkie. He urged that in order to remove "deadwood, redtape, jealousies and prejudices," and "to bring about effective co-operation," one man was needed to "direct the military services." Acknowledging that "ordinarily it might be hard, it might be almost impossible to find such a man," Willkie named the man he had in mind:

> The last two months have proved we have the man— the one man in all our forces who has learned from first-hand, contemporary experience the value and the proper use of Army, Navy and Air Forces fighting together toward one end; the man who on the Bataan Peninsula has accomplished what was regarded as the impossible by his brilliant tactical sense; the man who also alone has given his fellow-countrymen confidence and hope in the conduct of this war—General Douglas MacArthur.
>
> Bring Douglas MacArthur home. Place him at the very top. Keep bureaucratic and political hands off him. Give him the responsibility and the power of coordinating all the armed forces of the nation to their effective use. Put him in supreme command of our armed forces under the President.
>
> Then the people of the United States will have reason to hope that skill, not bungling and confusion, directs their efforts.[34]

The following morning Stimson "picked up the newspapers and read that Willkie had come out for making MacArthur General-in-Chief of all forces of the United States under the President." Remembering his conversation of the day before with General Crowell, Stimson "wondered whether Benedict Crowell had been hearing some of the same Republican talk."[35]

Stimson had been thinking the night before about "the people locked up in Corregidor." When he arrived at the War Department he wrote out a short message to Quezon and MacArthur because "they deserved a response to their firm acceptance of the President's rather severe" message of February 9. Stimson had come to know "Quezon's dramatic volatile character" during his tenure as governor general of the Philippines, and he believed "that [Quezon's] earlier message suggesting the appeal to the Japanese was the result of his illness and the strain of battle." Stimson "felt that a strong pat on the back would go a long way towards restoring the morale of everybody."

Stimson showed the message to Marshall, who agreed that it was a good idea, and then had it dispatched in his own name:

> Your messages of February 11 and February 12 received. The superb courage and fidelity of you and Quezon are fully recognized by the president and every one of us.[36]

Roosevelt was told about the message later that day and also endorsed it fully.

On February 13 Colonel Paul Bunker, commanding the batteries of Corregidor's Seaward Defenses, wrote in his dairy:

> General Moore says that Quezon is in mighty bad physical shape. Somebody said they saw him hobble to his car the other day and he looked bad. Somebody else said they saw him in a wheel chair. But he has been in bad health for years.[37]

On February 14 Stimson received an answering radiogram from Quezon:

> I appreciate deeply your message. Never shall I forget our association when you were governor general and I president of the Senate.[38]

That Saturday afternoon at his weekend residence at Highhold, Long Island, Stimson talked with his law partner and friend, Bronson Winthrop. Stimson told Winthrop about the exchange of communications during the week. "Thrilled" by the episode, Winthrop thought "it was a wonderful performance on all sides." He "only wished that the whole thing could be given to the public."[39]

6

Isolation and the Order to Depart

February 14–28, 1942

The president directs that you make arrangements to leave Fort Mills and proceed to Mindanao. . . . From Mindanao you will proceed to Australia where you will assume command of all United States troops.[1]

—General George C. Marshall

Concerned about the safety of MacArthur's wife and son, General George C. Marshall on February 14 sent the following radiogram to General MacArthur:

> . . . Regarding decision that your family will not be evacuated, I think it very important that you have in mind the possibility that some later situation might require duty from you that would compel separation from them under circumstances of greatly increased peril. While I intend no, repeat no, interference in your freedom of action and decision in this matter, I am anxious that you do not overlook this particular possibility of poignant embarrassment to you personally.
>
> You have never specifically notified us of receipt of anti-aircraft ammunition from submarine. Was such received? Have you direct notice of further submarines with three inch anti-aircraft ammunition due to reach you?[2]

On February 14 the *New York Times* carried an article by military analyst Hanson W. Baldwin entitled "Unity of Command Needed." Referring to Wendell L. Willkie's suggestion that Mac-

Arthur be brought home and placed in supreme command of all the armed forces under the president, Baldwin called the idea "sound in principle but difficult in application." Not sure in any case that MacArthur would be the man for this assignment, Baldwin discussed the difficulties involved merely in removing MacArthur from his Philippine command.

MacArthur had managed to "knit together . . . a fighting team" from a "heterogeneous collection of troops" by the "sheer force of his personality." Because he was "a good soldier . . . it would be difficult, if not impossible, to persuade [him] to leave his command." Although MacArthur might be ordered by the president for the good of the country to turn over his command," according to Baldwin "it would probably take at least a direct Presidential command to persuade General MacArthur to leave his troops."

Baldwin admitted that MacArthur's evacuation "before the safety of his troops was assured would be a psychological blow to the enlisted man's morale and to the morale of the Filipino and would shatter a basic tradition upon which much of the structure of military élan has been reared—the tradition that a commander shares the fate of his men." Considering the danger in running the Japanese blockade and the fact that the general's wife and young son would be with him, Baldwin wrote that the timing "would have to be precise or disaster might result." If MacArthur were "ordered to turn over his command too soon, the Bataan defense —still useful in a delaying and attrition sense . . . might be weakened prematurely . . . General MacArthur—while he remains on [Corregidor]—may be able to spin out a heroic tragedy to new and epic chapters. He may be able to lengthen American resistance in the area he holds by additional weeks or months."[3]

On February 15 MacArthur replied to Marshall's February 14 radiogram. The antiaircraft ammunition had been received, he said; he did not have any knowledge of further shipments via submarine en route to Corregidor. He did not mention his family.[4]

MacArthur proposed to Marshall on February 16 that Quezon and High Commissioner Sayre be evacuated from Corregidor:

> President Quezon and his war cabinet desire to establish the seat of the commonwealth government in the unoccupied portions of the Philippine Islands initially in the Visayas. They feel certain that their usefulness will be greatly enhanced by contact with the

Filipino public which is now impossible to them because of siege conditions existing here. Their purpose, in accordance with President Roosevelt's desires as expressed in his recent directive, is to maintain the cohesion morale of the populace in the unoccupied communities in order to prolong and make more effective resistance to the Japanese. Their usefulness here is over and it is advantageous from every point of view that they do not share the destruction which now faces this garrison.

I propose to evacuate them by water, travelling only by night, proceeding first to Mindoro and thence south to Capiz or Antique or Panay. If pressed they will continue to Mindanao where they could safely exist in the interior indefinitely. I am heartily in favor of the plan and propose to execute it promptly unless you order otherwise.

In order to assist in the movement, I request authority to utilize the submarine which will be here within the next three or four days to evacuate them as far as Capiz and then to return to the far south. Under present plans the high commissioner's party is scheduled to leave here in this submarine immediately upon its arrival. My plan would involve the postponement of his departure for four days. The available capacity is not sufficient to accommodate both groups at the same time and hence they must be evacuated separately. The Quezon trip being the short one, I place it first.

If this authority is given the proper instructions should be radioed to the commander in chief Asiatic Fleet, who controls not only the submarine but the allocation of the passengers who are to be transported. If the submarine is not made available to me then Quezon will attempt the trip in a small surface vessel. The use of the submarine, however, would increase the factor of safety. Request immediate action.[5]

Learning of the British surrender of Singapore, which occurred on February 15, MacArthur sent a second radiogram to Marshall on February 16, again calling for an audacious naval thrust at Japan's extended lines of communication:

The unexpected early capitulation of Singapore emphasizes the fact that the opportunity for a successful attack upon the hostile lines of communication is rapidly vanishing. If this enemy victory is followed by further success in the Netherlands East Indies the sensitiveness of his lines of communication will largely disappear due to consolidation of his positions in the south. A determined effort in force made now would probably attract the assistance of

Russia, who will unquestionably not move in this area until some evidence is given of concrete effort by the Allies. The opportunities still exist for a complete reversal of the situation. It will soon, however, be too late for such a movement.[6]

Although Marshall did not concur with MacArthur's latter proposal, he did agree with the former. It was deemed advantageous, not only by Marshall but by Roosevelt and Stimson as well, that Quezon, Sayre, and other important Philippine officials leave Corregidor. MacArthur was notified to carry out his plan.[7]

At sunset on the evening of February 20, Malinta Tunnel was closed to vehicles for the first time. Quezon, his family, and other Philippine government officials were preparing to leave Corregidor for Panay, which was not occupied by the Japanese.

At about 11:00 p.m. an automobile stopped at North Dock. President and Mrs. Quezon, MacArthur, and Sutherland got out. The dock was not at the moment being shelled. In the moonlight, watching both generals assist the gravely ill Quezon on the dock, Major Carlos P. Romulo thought that Quezon "looked like a ghost" of his former self.

Before Quezon boarded the tender *Perry*, the small boat that would take him to the submarine waiting in the deeper waters of Manila Bay, MacArthur took Quezon in his arms. "Manuel," he said, "you will see it through. You are the Father of your country and God will preserve you." Slipping from his bony finger a signet ring that he used to stamp his official documents, Quezon placed it on MacArthur's finger. "When they find your body," Quezon said brokenly, "I want them to know that you fought for my country." MacArthur, Sayre, Sutherland, Romulo, and Manuel Roxas, whom Quezon had designated to represent him on Corregidor, where among those who stood quietly on the dock and watched while the small boat moved toward the submarine *Swordfish*. At 11:40 p.m. the *Swordfish* cleared Manila Bay's swept channel and moved out into the South China Sea.[8]

In Washington on February 20, Secretary of War Stimson had a long discussion with Marshall and Eisenhower, in charge of the War Plans Division, concerning "what should be done in respect to MacArthur" and "the question of further defense of the Philippines after the fall of Corregidor." They thought that even after the surrender of Corregidor resistance could be continued on the southernmost Philippine island, Mindanao. They hoped that Mindanao could be held at least until sufficient forces could be moved into the Southwest Pacific and a counteroffensive launched.[9]

During the morning of February 21, Stimson met again with Marshall. The main topic under discussion was the Australian-British-Dutch-American (ABDA) region. The Japanese were on the verge of capturing Java and the battle for the Netherlands East Indies was almost over. Lieutenant General Wavell had reported that the end was near and that he had already started evacuating his headquarters from Java to India and Burma. Marshall decided to order Wavell's deputy chief of staff, Major General George H. Brett, to Australia.[10]

Stimson and Marshall also learned of a successful Japanese air attack on Port Darwin in northern Australia, in which "a destroyer, an Army transport, and four or five merchant vessels, besides a number of airplanes on the ground" were lost.

At lunch Stimson talked with Colonel William J. Donovan about the prospects of initiating "guerrilla fighting in the Philippines." Although Stimson thought Donovan's plans were "mostly wind" and lacked "substantial practical value," he told Donovan to go ahead. Stimson realized that if MacArthur were ordered out of the Philippines, "some vigorous guerrilla work under American leadership in Mindanao" could give the Japanese trouble. Also it would save valuable time.[11]

Marshall radioed MacArthur later on February 21 that President Roosevelt was seriously considering ordering him from Corregidor to Mindanao:

> From Marshall to be seen only by decoding clerk and General MacArthur: The president is considering advisability of ordering you to Mindanao to continue your command of the Philippines from that locality. There is the immediate factor of the importance, as indicated by the president in [his radiogram] to you of February 9, which has to do with the Battle of Bataan and the eventual defense of Corregidor Island. There is the problem of the continuance of resistance in the southern islands and especially in Mindanao as outlined in your message of December 24 and your [message] of February 16. There is now the further consideration of the effect of the transfer of the Philippine government in the person of President Quezon to the southern islands and the fact that it is the opinion here that the future of the Philippines would

be greatly influenced by the continuance of American resistance in Mindanao. Also the probability that from Mindanao your personal influence could be exercised over a large area of the southern Philippines and that physical communication with other theatres in the Far East would be possible to a degree not practicable from Fort Mills. The blockade runners have been given Gingoog, Mindanao as their initial port of call.

The foregoing considerations underlie the tentative decision of the president but we are not sufficiently informed as to the situation and circumstances to be certain that the proposal meets the actual situation.

The secretary of war and I desire your views on the above. Address same manner I have followed above.[12]

Early in the morning of February 22 General MacArthur authorized the transmission of two optimistic radiograms to the War Department. The first message concerned the apparent apathy of the Japanese Army on Bataan:

There are indications that the enemy has been so badly mauled during the Bataan fighting that he is unable to set up with his present forces the attack necessary to destroy me. Practically every regiment has consolidated by eliminating one battalion, and a number of regiments themselves have totally disappeared. His artillery groupment may be from weakness rather than strength. I may have gained the respite I so desperately need. Do not publicize in any way any of the above.[13]

In his second radiogram, MacArthur urged that greater emphasis be placed on logistics:

The *Coast Farmer,* first surface vessel dispatched to run blockade from Australia, arrived safely in Mindanao February 19. Cargo twenty-five hundred tons balanced rations, two thousand rounds eighty-one mm mortar ammunition, eight hundred thousand rounds caliber thirty and thirty thousand rounds caliber fifty. She had no difficulty in getting through. The thinness of the enemy's coverage is such that it can readily be pierced along many routes including direct westward passage from Honolulu. I have secure bases for reception in Mindanao and the Visayas. I suggest that the problem of supplying me should be revised in the above circumstances. This revised effort should center in Washington and not in Australia or the Netherlands East Indies. The commanders there, however able they may be, have neither the resources nor the means at their disposal properly to accomplish this mission. Many categories of supply that are required are not available in that area. Moreover, they are so engaged in the actual zone of immediate or threatened conflict that it is impossible for them to concentrate upon my needs.

The size of the problem is greater than the means now being used to solve it. The prime requisite is the making available in the United States of the necessary ships and material, especially the former, and their continuous dispatch to destination. Nowhere is the situation more desperate and dangerous than here. The War Department has complete knowledge of our needs which is not true in Australia. The quantities involved are not great, but it is imperative that they may be instantly available in the United States and that the entire impulse and organization be reenergized and controlled directly by you. If it is left as a subsidiary effort, it will never be accomplished. Careful consideration should also be given as to troop replacement by this means; even if losses occur they will be small compared to the loss out here if we do not have success.[14]

Clark Lee, a representative of the Associated Press, caught a glimpse of MacArthur during the morning of February 22. Lee was shocked at the change in MacArthur's appearance. Looking years older and ill, he seemed "drained of the confidence he had always shown." Staff officers would only tell Lee that the general had received an important message from Washington.

Shortly after noon, Lee and Melville Jacoby, a reporter and photographer for Life and Time Publications, walked into the USAFFE Headquarters lateral to see General MacArthur. They had an opportunity to leave Corregidor that night on a small freighter, the *Princesa de Cebu*, bound for Cebu. However, they needed MacArthur's permission and were still undecided as to whether they should leave.

Receiving them at his desk, MacArthur asked, "Do you want to go?"

They told him it depended on whether they "could do more good by staying than by going." Although MacArthur refused to make the decision for them, he talked for more than an hour in an eloquent and stirring manner. Discussing his own desperate situation in the Philippines as well as the "whole strategy of the world struggle," MacArthur said he "felt that there was not sufficient understanding in Allied councils of the time element in the Pacific," and believed that the Allies "did not have unlimited time to defeat Japan." It was futile to try to defeat Japan by blockade and attrition, he said; because Japan had captured Singapore and was on the verge of taking Java, she would have sufficient raw materials and the essential bases to withstand a "war of blockade and attrition."

Lee and Jacoby, after listening closely to MacArthur, decided to leave Corregidor. "Go ahead," MacArthur authorized them. "Go armed while you are in the Philippines. When you board a ship to leave the islands, if you are fortunate enough to make connections, throw away your khaki, your guns, passports, and all diaries and identification papers. When you get to Cebu look up the names of some businessmen and learn about them so as to enable you to assume their identity, if you are captured."

The general closed on a somber note. "Even if you don't make it, even if you are drowning at sea or being machine-gunned in a lifeboat, or starving on a raft, don't regret having tried, for if we don't get reinforcements, the end here will be brutal and bloody." Shaking hands with the men, he said, "I hope you'll make it."[15]

At 8:55 P.M. on the twenty-second, Sutherland phoned Brigadier General Richard J. Marshall at his command post on Bataan and received a report on the military situation in the peninsula. He ordered Marshall to proceed to Corregidor that evening for the purpose of receiving a decoration from President Quezon.

In darkness Marshall came in by launch from Mariveles and reported to Malinta Tunnel. MacArthur and Sutherland greeted him and Sutherland asked him to come to his room in the tunnel. There Sutherland disclosed the fact that the decoration, although real enough, was also a subterfuge to bring him in for additional orders. Briefing Marshall on the exchange of radiograms between MacArthur and the War Department, Sutherland told him that Quezon had already left Corregidor, on a submarine bound for Panay, and that High Commissioner Sayre, his family, and his staff would soon take the same submarine to Australia.

Sutherland also told Marshall about the chief of staff's February 21 radiogram to MacArthur. On February 4, Sutherland said, when MacArthur had received a message indicating the possibility of his evacuation, MacArthur had remarked to several of his staff that he would never leave Corregidor. MacArthur wanted to remain on Corregidor until he believed he had done all he could to prolong its defense, Sutherland explained, but preparations for leaving were to be made soon because MacArthur might get a peremptory order to depart at any time.

Marshall was ordered to return to Bataan the next evening and arrange to turn over his Bataan echelon to Brigadier General Arnold J. Funk, then to return to Corregidor no later than March 1.[16]

On February 21, Brigadier General Patrick J. Hurley in Melbourne, Australia, completed a lengthy memorandum for General George C. Marshall in Washington. Hurley had just returned from the Netherlands East Indies after endeavoring "to get badly needed supplies to MacArthur." He said that, "in spite of almost insuperable difficulties," he had managed to "put some supplies through including approximately eight thousand tons of much needed four and three inch AA, 50 calibre and 30 calibre ammunition."

Hurley believed that Australia "was extremely vulnerable" to the Japanese threat because of "the present state of preparations for the defense of Australia." The Australian people did not "appear to be aware of the critical situation confronting them," and the newspapers, the day after a major Japanese air raid on Darwin, "had much more news concerning horse-racing than they did concerning the raid on Darwin." The Australians "give about as much space in their newspapers to racing as we do to glamor, sex appeal and the figures of almost naked beautiful women," according to Hurley, and "the military establishments seem . . . too complacent.

"The United States' contributions to the defense of the Southwest Pacific [will] enormously exceed the total output and resources of the combined British Dominions in ships, tanks, planes, equipment and manpower," Hurley continued. "For the safe conduct of great reinforcements and material to the Southwest Pacific Area, it is logical and essential that the supreme command in the Southwest Pacific should be given to an American. To this all parties agree. This should be done as promptly as possible so that plans for present defensive and offensive operations may be coordinated by supreme American authority."

Claiming the Allies "must fight aggressively, not always defensively," Hurley went on:

The Japanese have been forging ahead because they have

out-fought their opposition. On the Bataan Peninsula they have been stopped because they were confronted by a greater fighter.

I have talked at length with General Wavell regarding MacArthur and he frankly stated that he would like to have MacArthur with him. He went beyond that and generously offered to relinquish command to MacArthur if it appeared to be the best thing to do. He recognized that recent publicity had made a pre-eminent personality and hero of MacArthur and that the latter had captured the public imagination. He inquired closely as to MacArthur's ability and character, and I assured him that I knew MacArthur well and that his ability and character were both of the first order.

He further asked me as to why MacArthur could not be taken out of the Philippines and given a more important command. I replied that I did not believe that MacArthur would leave his command for his own aggrandizement unless and until one of his general officers had been established in the public confidence and estimation, and both the public and the troops were assured that command had passed to competent leadership. I also stated that it would be necessary for the President to definitely order MacArthur to relinquish command and proceed elsewhere and that even if such orders were issued, MacArthur might feel that he had destroyed himself by leaving his beleaguered command—that I knew MacArthur well enough to realize that his most treasured possession is his honor as a soldier.

If MacArthur is to be made available for greater responsibilities and achievements in this theatre of operations, his transfer from Corregidor will have to be effected in a way that cannot possibly compromise his honor or his record as a soldier. I hope it can be done.[17]

Present at a White House conference on the afternoon of February 22 were Roosevelt, Secretary of State Cordell Hull, Marshall, Admiral Ernest J. King, and presidential adviser Harry L. Hopkins. Churchill had notified Roosevelt that Prime Minister Curtin of Australia, concerned about the military threat to his country from

Japan, was demanding that all Australian soldiers in the Middle East be returned to Australia.

Roosevelt recognized the Japanese military threat to Australia's security in view of the breakup of the ABDA command and the southward movement of the Japanese army and navy. Even more important to him was the threat of reversing the basic strategic concept of the war—defeating Hitler's Germany in Europe before concentrating for the final blow against Japan in Asia—which was posed by Curtin's demand for the recall of Australian forces from the Middle East. To forestall this, Roosevelt now authorized the order for General MacArthur to leave Corregidor and proceed to Australia.

Roosevelt knew that MacArthur in command of Allied forces in Australia could be depended on to bolster and strengthen Australian defenses, and that his presence would "bolster the morale of the people of Australia and New Zealand." These were the primary considerations that caused the president to order MacArthur's departure from Corregidor, but not the only ones.

Knowing that Corregidor would soon be captured by the Japanese, Roosevelt realized that MacArthur's death or capture would be a propaganda victory for Japan and a psychological blow to the American people. Not only had the president received numerous appeals from American citizens to save the popular military hero, but also this course of action had been urged on him by Hull, Stimson, and Marshall.

It was still an "indescribably difficult decision." According to presidential adviser Robert E. Sherwood, "Roosevelt knew full well that the departure of MacArthur from Corregidor would be a grievous blow to the heroic men of his command and thus to the whole United States. It was ordering the captain to be the first to leave the sinking ship." Considering the underlying circumstances, however, Roosevelt's decision was the logical one.[18]

The same day the order for MacArthur's departure was drawn up, approved by Marshall, Stimson, and Roosevelt, and dispatched to MacArthur.

At 11:23 A.M. on February 23 the radiogram was received and decoded at Fort Mills. The order was handed to MacArthur at 12:30 P.M.

From General Marshall to General MacArthur. To be seen by decoding clerk only:

With reference to the rapidly approaching reorganization of the ABDA area and also to the rather favorable report on the situation in Bataan in your [first message of February 22] as well as your [second message of February 22] regarding the build up of resources in Mindanao: The president directs that you make arrangements to leave Fort Mills and proceed to Mindanao. You are directed to make this change as quickly as possible.

The president desires that in Mindanao you take such measures as will insure a prolonged defense of that region—this especially in view of the transfer of President Quezon and his government to the southern Philippines and the great importance the president attaches to the future of the Philippines by prolonging in every way possible the continuance of defense by United States troops and the continuance of the active support of the Philippine government and people. From Mindanao you will proceed to Australia where you will assume command of all United States troops.

It is the intention of the president to arrange with the Australian and British governments for their acceptance of you as commander of the reconstituted ABDA area. Because of the vital importance of your assuming command in Australia at an early date your delay in Mindanao will not be prolonged beyond one week and you will leave sooner if transportation becomes available earlier.

Instructions will be given from here at your request for the movement of submarine or plane or both to enable you to carry out the foregoing instructions. You are authorized to take your chief of staff General Sutherland.[19]

As the general read the radiogram in the USAFFE Headquarters lateral, his aide-de-camp, Lieutenant Colonel Sidney Huff, was packing some of MacArthur's records in a locker. The locker was to be placed aboard the submarine *Swordfish* that night for transport to the United States. Huff had paid no attention when the radiogram was first handed to MacArthur, but when he saw the general's face he "knew that something had happened."

MacArthur was silent for a few minutes after reading the message. Then, in a "harsh" manner, he asked where Mrs. MacArthur was. Huff replied that she was in another lateral of the tunnel. Hurriedly, MacArthur and Sutherland walked out of headquarters.

MacArthur, Mrs. MacArthur, and Sutherland left Malinta Tunnel and walked toward MacArthur's small cottage. They stayed inside for quite some time.[20]

That evening just after sunset, there was a lull in the Japanese shelling of Corregidor. High Commissioner Sayre, his family, and a small staff were leaving Corregidor. Major Romulo bid Sayre good-bye regretfully: "I am sorry, Mr. High Commissioner, that you have to go this way." The Sayres were driven rapidly down the hill to North Dock in MacArthur's car. A few men were loading the small tender *Maryanne*. Shelling of North Dock might resume at any moment, and the Sayres had to take their leave without delay. MacArthur reassured them, "You will have a hard trip, but when you come up at the end, you will be in a different world." As Rear Admiral Francis W. Rockwell, commandant of the Sixteenth Naval District, shook their hands in parting, he said, "Good luck. You are going out with our ace submarine skipper. He'll get you through." Sayre and his family departed at 8:00 P.M. on the *Maryanne* and rendezvoused with the *Swordfish*, waiting in the darkness.

That night Romulo wrote in his diary, "They are leaving us, one by one."[21]

MacArthur returned to the dilemma that President Roosevelt's order presented. If he disregarded it, he would undoubtedly be subject to a court-martial; if he complied, it might be said that he had run out on his doomed but gallant army. Failure to comply would probably mean death for himself and his family; compliance would mean a risky trip but at least an opportunity for eventual safety.

MacArthur said his "first reaction was to try and avoid the latter part of the order, even to the extent of resigning [his] commission and joining the Bataan force as a simple volunteer." He started to write a refusal and told several of his staff officers that he had received an order to leave Corregidor from the president but that he had decided to disobey it.

Sutherland and the other staff officers were vehemently opposed to this action. A large American army was undoubtedly being amassed in Australia, they said, and MacArthur was the logical one to lead it back to the Philippines and relieve the besieged Corregidor and Bataan garrisons. MacArthur finally agreed.[22]

During the evening of February 24 the signal officer at Fort Mills started relaying an answering message from MacArthur to Marshall:

> To be seen by the decoding clerk only. I am deeply appreciative of the confidence in me that is implied in your [radiogram of February 22].
>
> As my communications have shown, I am completely in accord with the strategical importance of the continued active support of the government and the people and of the consequent prolonged defense in the Philippines. It is my studied opinion, however, that the immediate movement directed is too sudden and abrupt in that it may result at this time in collapse in the Philippine area with ensuing adverse effect on the entire theatre before the means are available for counter offensive action from Australia.
>
> The lack of visible support for the Philippines has created here a very difficult situation which I have been able to meet only through the peculiar confidence placed in me by the Filipino people and army on the one hand and President Quezon on the other.
>
> The intent of the enemy in this area is not yet clear. We may be approaching the stalemate of positional warfare, but it is possible that a major effort may soon be made to break my Bataan front; his plans will shortly become evident. I am of the opinion that I can throw back an attack if made with the troops now available locally and can then restabilize the situation.
>
> I am not in possession of information regarding your developments in Australia. But it is apparent that there must be a great deal of organizational work accomplished in the accumulation of forces and in the building of a service of supply repeat service of supply before offensive action will be possible. I am of the opinion that during the initial stages of that organizational effort, I can better accomplish the aims of the president as set forth in your radio by temporary delay in my departure. This would not prevent any immediate reorganization that you may have in mind nor my reassumption of command of the troops in the Far East at this time; it would merely permit me temporarily to maintain my headquarters here until the psychological time to leave.
>
> I earnestly hope that you accept my advice as to the timing of this movement. I know the situation here in the Philippines and unless the right moment is chosen for this delicate operation, a sudden collapse might occur which would carry with it not only the people but the government. Rightly or wrongly these people are depending upon me now not only militarily but civically and any

idea that might develop in their minds that I was being withdrawn for any other purpose than to bring them immediate relief could not be explained to their simple intelligence. At the right time I believe they will understand it, but if done too soon and too abruptly, it may result in a sudden major collapse. Please be guided by me in this matter.

With regard to the actual movement, I deem it advisable to go to Mindanao by combined use of surface craft and submarine and thence to destination by air, further movement by submarine being too time consuming. A flight of three B-24s or B-17s will be able to fight through if intercepted. To set up the transportation will require a period of time that will probably suffice to make essential psychological and physical adjustments here. Advise the navy that no repeat no fuel is available here for a submarine.[23]

MacArthur's message was received at the War Department Message Center at 9:07 A.M. on February 24 and delivered to General Marshall. Marshall read the message, reached for his memorandum pad and wrote "secret" at the top of the slip of paper: "My dear Mr. President: Herewith is McArthur's [sic] reply. I would like to discuss this with you tonight."[24]

At 4:10 P.M. President Roosevelt held a news conference. He was asked whether military censorship was due to the fact that Mac-Arthur was "at odds with the high command" in Washington concerning their inability to "reinforce him." Roosevelt's reply was ambiguous: "I wouldn't do any—well, I wouldn't—I am trying to take a leaf out of my notebook. I think it would be well for others to do it. I—not knowing enough about it—I try not to speculate myself." On February 17 at another press conference, Roosevelt had been asked, "Mr. President, would you care to comment on the agitation to have General MacArthur ordered out of the Philippines and given over-all command?" Roosevelt replied, "No. I don't think so. I think that is just one of 'them' things that people talk about without very much knowledge of the situation. A very polite statement."[25]

On February 23 Marshall had conferred with Stimson concerning the eventualities of MacArthur's evacuation to Australia. Marshall had told Stimson that he knew sending MacArthur to Australia would "involve close relations between MacArthur and [the American] naval command in the ANZAC area"; yet he thought that MacArthur's "dominating character" would be of use in Australia since it would "make the Navy keep up to their job." Marshall also foresaw the possibility of "rows" developing between MacArthur and the Navy since MacArthur had "bitterly complained of the Navy during the last two months."[26]

The night of February 24, Marshall and Roosevelt decided to agree to MacArthur's request for a delay but not to his plan for assuming and exercising command of all forces in the Far East and Australia while he was still on Corregidor.[27] On February 25 Marshall answered MacArthur.

Your [message of February 24] has been carefully considered by the President. He has directed that full decision as to timing of your departure and details of method be left in your hands since it is imperative that the Luzon defense be firmly sustained.

Because of conditions now existing in the Netherlands East Indies and Australia, no repeat no change in your command status will be made at this time.

Your message indicates that the duration of your stay in Luzon will necessarily be indefinite and the date of your departure can not repeat not be predicted. It is therefore not repeat not possible at this time to make exact plans for necessary transportation. It appears to us that arrangements made from here should consist of a request to the Navy Department to direct the U.S. naval headquarters at Freemantle, Australia to dispatch, on call from you, a submarine to such point as you may designate, with fuel for round trip. Also that the War Department give timely instructions to Brett, at Melbourne, to dispatch a flight of heavy bombers to Mindanao at such time as you may designate.

If you have no means of direct communication with the U.S. naval commander at Freemantle, you can reach him through Brett, now commanding U.S. forces in Australia. Please inform me at once whether these proposed arrangements appear satisfactory to you. Meanwhile you should not repeat not communicate on this subject with army and navy commanders in Australia, until after receipt of message from me that general arrangements from this end have been completed.[28]

On February 26 MacArthur replied.

The proposed arrangements entirely satisfactory. Suggest you request Navy Department order submarine immediately to Corregidor. If navy has doubt as to probability of arrival here, suggest that two be sent to insure arrival. Also suggest directive to Brett to dispatch planes on call. Anticipate possibility of execution of plan about March 15.[29]

After Marshall read MacArthur's radiogram, he wrote in long-hand a note for President Roosevelt: "McArthur [*sic*] has just radioed that he anticipates March 15—as about the date he would feel free to leave Fort Mills, and requests certain preliminary arrangements—submarine and plane."[30]

The same day Marshall sent the following radiogram to Major General Brett in Australia:

> For the execution of a special task General MacArthur will call upon you in the near future, probably shortly before March 15, to dispatch in a single flight three long range bombers to Mindanao. You are to be prepared to respond promptly to his request, and he has been authorized to communicate with you directly for arranging details. Planes will be prepared to transport a small number of passengers from Luzon to Australia. This matter is highly secret.[31]

To Brett it meant "only one thing. MacArthur had been ordered out."[32]

Marshall requested the Navy Department to authorize the naval commander at Freemantle, Australia to place a submarine at the disposal of MacArthur. Admiral King dispatched the implementing message to Vice Admiral William A. Glassford: "ALLOCATE SUBMARINES SO THAT ONE IS ALWAYS AT THE DISPOSAL OF GENERAL MACARTHUR."[33]

On February 26 an article by syndicated columnist Hugh S. Johnson, a former classmate of MacArthur at West Point, appeared in the newspaper:

> Will MacArthur and his army hold out like the Greeks at Marathon and have to be killed like caged animals in a trap?
>
> There is little prospect of their relief in sufficient force to evacuate them, and knowing Douglas MacArthur well, I have little doubt that he will not surrender as long as there is a man left to serve a gun.
>
> There is a very considerable opinion that he should be ordered out of there alone leaving the troops that have fought for him so well to surrender. That would put up to him a terrible choice and ordeal.
>
> I think the President has too much humanity and affec-

tion for him to place such a burden upon him. He would be torn between his duty to obey orders and his flawless loyalty to his men. Such a decision would have to be made in his heart.

I don't know for certain what it would be, but I would give odds that he would stay by his men—regardless of his soldierly respect for superior authority. I only know that I would hate to be the man who transmitted such an order. Mac knows how to swear as well as General Pershing.

These are MacArthur's own men, who have shown their willingness to die for him. They have lifted him to a pinnacle of glory. Would he desert them? I think not.

Few generals have done that and gotten away with it. Napoleon deserted his army in Egypt. It might have ruined him, but he came home in time to seize the government, which with what else he proceeded to do, over shadowed his soldier's shame. He never ceased to regret it until the last moment of his life.

There are very few instances and they invariably ruined the reputation of the man who did it. Such a thought could not find lodgment in MacArthur's heart.

No matter what happens to MacArthur, he has set an example that will be a military asset worth a whole army corps to his country as long as the flag continues to fly. Let no one do anything to impair that glory.[34]

On February 28 MacArthur received the following radiogram from Marshall:

> Under date of February 26 Vice Admiral Glassford, commanding Southwest Pacific U.S. naval force, was directed to allocate submarines so that one is always at your disposal. . . . at the same time General Brett, in Australia, was directed to be prepared on notice from you to dispatch a flight of three heavy bombers to Mindanao. He was further instructed that this matter is highly secret and that you would probably call on him for these airplanes about March 15.[35]

MacArthur had dispatched a radiogram to the War Department the same day:

> President Quezon today issued a proclamation in which he cited the valiant defense of Philippine territory and the steadfast

loyalty of the civilian population. He announced the allocation of funds for civilian relief and urged every Filipino to trust America. The proclamation closed with the following: "The United Nations will win this war. America is too great and too powerful to be vanquished in this conflict. I know she will not fail us."[36]

7

Evacuation via Sea and Air

March 1–17, 1942

Departed from Corregidor at dark on twelfth [*sic*] with party of twenty including my family, Rear Admiral Rockwell and his chief of staff, traveling on four U.S. Navy Motor Torpedo Boats. . . . This hazardous trip by a commanding general and key members of his staff through enemy controlled territory undoubtedly is unique in military annals.[1]

—MacArthur to Marshall

On March 1 at dusk Lieutenant James H. Baldwin, an operations officer in the Army Transport Service, was having supper on the afterdeck of a converted motor yacht, the *Jem*, moored to one side of the "Lorcha" (barge) dock. This dock was the most easterly of the three piers at Corregidor's North Harbor. Unexpectedly a Patrol-Torpedo Boat, with Lieutenant John D. Bulkeley in command, moored on the opposite side of the pier. In a few minutes General and Mrs. MacArthur and Lieutenant Colonel Sidney L. Huff arrived and boarded.

Bulkeley took the party for a ride of about thirty minutes in the waters adjacent to Corregidor, as General MacArthur wanted his wife to have some idea of what a PT-boat would be like on the open sea. During the ride Bulkeley suggested to MacArthur that Captain H. James Ray, Rear Admiral Rockwell's chief of staff, be included in the group of officers designated to go to Australia, because of his familiarity with the Philippines, his experience with Motor Patrol Torpedo boats, and his knowledge of navigation.[2]

132

During the evening Sutherland called Captain Joseph R. McMicking aside near the entrance to Malinta Tunnel and told him of MacArthur's planned departure. McMicking was to be one of the officers who would leave with the general, Sutherland told him, but he did not reveal the names of the others. McMicking, a fighter pilot in the Philippine Air Corps based at a satellite airfield near Clark Field when the war began, had been transferred later to MacArthur's staff as an assistant intelligence officer.[3]

That night MacArthur sent a radiogram to Major General Brett, commander of the United States Army Air Corps in Australia.

> To be seen only by decoding clerk and General Brett. You have probably surmised purpose of mission. Request detail best pilots and that best available planes be placed in top condition for trip. B-24s if available otherwise B-17s. Ferry mission only. Desire if possible initial landing on return to be south of combat zone. Anticipate call for arrival Mindanao about March 15.[4]

Although MacArthur had been authorized by Marshall on February 22 to take with him only his family and Sutherland, he had Sutherland prepare a list of thirteen army officers, one enlisted man, and two naval officers who would also leave Corregidor. The officers were largely selected, according to MacArthur, "because of their anticipated contribution to the liberation of the Philippines." The group included Brigadier General Richard J. Marshall, deputy chief of staff; Brigadier General Hugh J. Casey, chief engineer officer; Brigadier General Spencer B. Akin, chief Signal Corps officer; Brigadier General William F. Marquat, chief antiaircraft officer; Brigadier General Harold H. George, Air Force officer; Colonel Charles P. Stivers, operations officer; Colonel Charles A. Willoughby, chief intelligence officer; Lieutenant Colonel LeGrande A. Diller, aide-de-camp to General MacArthur and head of press relations; Lieutenant Colonel Francis H. Wilson, aide to General MacArthur and acting secretary of the General Staff; Lieutenant Colonel Sidney L. Huff, aide-de-camp to General MacArthur; Lieutenant Colonel Joseph R. Sherr, assistant Signal Corps officer; Major Charles H. Morhouse, Medical Corps officer; Captain Joseph R. McMicking, assistant intelligence officer; and Master Sergeant Paul P. Rogers, a stenographer and typist.[5]

On March 4 MacArthur and Sutherland held a conference with Rear Admiral Rockwell. MacArthur informed Rockwell "that he had received instructions to proceed south with certain members of his staff" and that "he would be pleased" if Rockwell and several members of his staff went with him. A submarine had been placed at his disposal to be used in the evacuation, MacArthur told Rockwell, and he intended to use it "for the first leg of the trip in coordination with the four remaining boats of Motor Torpedo Boat Squadron Three to assist in escort and disembarkation." Rockwell radioed Naval Operations "a brief estimate of the situation" and received permission for himself and "senior members of his staff to proceed south with General MacArthur." Rockwell authorized his chief of staff, Captain H. James Ray, to accompany him.[6]

Six Motor Torpedo Boats had arrived in Manila in September 1941. They had been based initially at the Manila Yacht Club and later transferred to the Cavite Navy Yard, where they came under the command of Captain Ray, the acting commandant of the Sixteenth Naval District. Before the outbreak of war, the PT-boats had participated in a night war game against units of the Asiatic Fleet. From that time, Lieutenant Bulkeley, commander of Motor Boat Squadron Three, and Captain Ray had been close friends.

After the war had started, Ray and Bulkeley had discussed the worsening situation every time Bulkeley reported to Rear Admiral Rockwell on Corregidor. With the fall of Sandakan and Tarakan in North Borneo late in January, it became apparent to them that the distances were too great to fly fighter planes into the Philippines. Without air capability, Ray and Bulkeley believed, the fall of Bataan and Corregidor was only a matter of time.

Two of the original six PT-boats—PT-33 on December 15 and PT-31 on January 29—had run aground and been destroyed, but the remaining four were operational, with torpedoes and trained crews. Bulkeley and Ray discussed the possibility of using them against Japanese shipping in the Formosa Channel near Swatow if Bataan fell.

Bulkeley talked about this possibility first with Colonel Chih Wang, Generalissimo Chiang Kai-shek's liaison officer on Corregidor. Would the crews of the four PT-boats be able to land in a coastal area of China still controlled by Chiang's guerrilla forces, and make their way inland after their torpedoes had been expended and their PT-boats destroyed? Colonel Wang communicated with his government in Chungking and then assured Bulkeley that arrangements would be made. As a result, Ray suggested to Bulkeley that he run a measured mile on the southern tip of Bataan to establish his RPM-MPII curve and fuel consumption and check his compasses on the range.

Because this had been done, preparations for the trip to Mindanao required only reorienting the axis from the northwest to southeast— the distance to be covered was approximately the same, a little more than 500 miles.[7] Bulkeley was directed "to prepare his squadron for a trip over 500 miles to an undisclosed destination." He made "fuel consumption and speed runs with a fully loaded boat" and swung the compasses of the PT-boats for deviations. He procured a dinghy and a deckload of gasoline for each boat, and provided each boat with emergency provisions.[8]

A graduate of the United States Naval Academy, class of 1933, Lieutenant John Bulkeley was audacious and courageous. He reminded one naval officer "of a swashbuckling pirate in modern dress. He wore a long, unruly beard and carried two ominous looking pistols at his side. His eyes were bloodshot and red-rimmed from staring his eyes out on his nightly missions and from lack of sleep. His nervous energy was tremendous and the supply of it never seemed to give out. He walked with a cocksure gate and one could always count on him to raise particular hell with any Jap who crossed his path. Highstrung, temperamental and gallant, Bulkeley was one of the most colorful figures in the Philippine campaign."[9]

In Washington on March 6, General George C. Marshall authorized the following radiogram to be dispatched to General MacArthur:

> To be seen only by decoding clerk and General MacArthur.
> Reference to my radiogram of February 25. Air Corps anxious to profit by experience of General George. Include him if practicable. Australian situation developments indicate desirability of your early arrival there. Acknowledge.[10]

The following day MacArthur replied:

> I had already planned to take George for his outstanding value to me in future air operations in this theatre. Plan to arrive there in about ten days.[11]

On March 8 MacArthur sent the following radiogram to Marshall concerning his command reorganization on Corregidor and Bataan.

The immediate temporary promotion of the following officers is recommended: To be major general, Brigadier General Albert M. Jones; to be brigadier general, Colonel Lewis C. Beebe. These officers have been outstanding during the last three months. Jones is to be assigned to the command of the First Philippine Corps and Beebe is to be assigned as deputy chief of staff at this headquarters. These assignments are essential in the reorganization which you will understand. I request favorable action and radio information without delay.[12]

On March 9 Brigadier General George, who commanded the Army Air Corps on Bataan, returned to Bataan from Corregidor and informed two members of his staff, Majors Allison W. Ind and Harold E. Eads, that they should be prepared to leave Bataan at 3:00 on the morning of March 11. They would be flown to Mindanao by Lieutenant William R. Bradford in his Bellanca aircraft. George would not accompany them to Mindanao, but, he added mischievously, "I can't tell you just how at this moment, but I'll be there." He told them to prepare an objective folder of bombing targets, complete with photographs, sketches, and logistics data, for the entire area, including Cavite, Manila, Pampanga, Subic Bay, and adjacent districts. The folder was to be in his hands by the afternoon of March 11.[13]

On March 9 there was a very marked increase in the activities of enemy surface craft on Subic Bay, north of Corregidor. A surface patrol was reported off Corregidor, and a destroyer division was sighted in the southern Philippines, steaming north at high speed. The conclusion drawn was that the Japanese High Command had issued orders to prevent MacArthur from leaving Corregidor. The Japanese were aware of the possibility that the general would try to leave because the radio-press had been "repeatedly broadcasting to the world an insistent and growing demand that General MacArthur be placed in command of all Allied Forces in Australia." In light of these factors MacArthur decided not to wait for the submarine *Permit*, scheduled to arrive some time after March 13, but to take the four PT-boats "as soon as preparations could be completed."[14]

On March 10 Lieutenant Bulkeley was handed an operation order:

1. Motor Torpedo Boat Squadron Three is to be used for the transportation of a party of twenty-one passengers to a

southern port which will be designated later. Enemy air and surface activity is to be expected along the route.

2. The party will embark . . . on March 11, in time to rendezvous at Turning Buoy at 8:00 P.M. Proceed to sea via swept channel and arrive TAGAUAYAN ISLAND about 7:30 A.M. March 12. Anchor close to lee shore (West side) and disembark party for the day. Re-embark at 5:00 P.M. and proceed to designated port, arriving not later than 7:00 A.M. March 13. . . . If any boat breaks down she will transfer passengers and proceed independently or transfer all personnel and scuttle ship if necessary.

3. Take fuel for five hundred and ten miles, and food for five days.[15]

Bulkeley, in PT-41, was to pick up at North Dock General MacArthur, his wife and son, their servant, Ah Cheu, Sutherland, Ray, Huff, and Major Morhouse at 7:30 P.M. on March 11. The rest of the officers would be taken aboard PT-32, PT-34, or PT-35 at other locations. If en route Japanese warships or planes were sighted, "evasion tactics" were to be used. If the boats were attacked, the senior boat carrying MacArthur was to turn away and attempt to escape while the others engaged the enemy. Provisions were also made for unforeseen emergencies such as damage inflicted by enemy warships or planes.[16]

The captain of the *Permit* was instructed to investigate Tagauayan Island at daylight on March 13. Should one of the PT-boats be hit by enemy fire, the captain of the *Permit* would be signalled at Tagauayan to prepare to take passengers aboard. The *Permit* might also pick up MacArthur and his family at Mindanao if plane transportation failed at the Del Monte Pineapple Plantation airfield.[17]

On the morning of March 10, Sutherland went to see Brigadier General Richard Marshall, recovering since March 1 from a bad case of dysentery, in the hospital lateral in Malinta Tunnel. He asked Marshall, who had lost about 25 pounds since December, if he would be able to stand a PT-boat trip to Mindanao. Marshall replied in the affirmative. Sutherland told him to report to the USAFFE Headquarters lateral the following morning.[18]

At about noon a fast Elco cabin cruiser, the J-230, pulled up at a Mariveles dock on the tip of Bataan. The cruiser, skippered by Lieutenant James Baldwin, had been dispatched from Corregidor on a special ferry mission. Three officers stepped aboard and the cruiser pulled quickly away from the pier and headed for Corregidor. The passengers were Major General Wainwright and his two aides, Major John R. Pugh and Captain Thomas Dooley. Wainwright had known Baldwin's family before the war, so he recognized Baldwin, and they exchanged a few words while crossing the strait.

"Wonder what he wants, General?" Pugh remarked as the cruiser neared the island.

"Wish to God I knew," Wainwright replied, his eyes on Corregidor. "All I know is that Sutherland phoned last night and told me to come over, the General wanted to see me."[19]

Wainwright arrived at North Dock and went to MacArthur's USAFFE Headquarters in Malinta Tunnel. MacArthur was absent, and Sutherland took Wainwright aside:

> General MacArthur is going to leave here and go to Australia. He's up at the house now and wants to see you. . . .
>
> The President has been trying to get him to leave Corregidor for days, but until yesterday the General kept refusing. He plans to leave tomorrow evening around six-thirty by motor torpedo boat for Mindanao. A plane will pick him and his party up there and fly us the rest of the way. Tell no one—no one—of this until the morning after next, the morning of the twelfth.
>
> The General plans a number of changes. He's going to divide his Philippine forces into four sub-commands, himself retaining over-all command while in Australia.
>
> You will be placed in command of all troops on Luzon. If it's agreeable to you, General Jones will get another star and take over your I Corps. Your new command will include Jones's corps and General Parker's II Corps, all service troops on Bataan, and the men up in the Cagayan Valley and in the mountain province.
>
> General Moore will remain in command of the harbor defenses and the fortified islands in the bay. General Chynoweth will command the troops in the Visayan Islands, and General Sharp will have charge of Mindanao.
>
> He's going to leave Colonel Beebe here, give him a star,

and make him his Deputy Chief of Staff, to carry out his
commands from Australia.

Sutherland and Wainwright walked from the tunnel to Mac-
Arthur's small slate-gray cottage, a quarter of a mile away. As
they approached, MacArthur came out on the porch. Obviously
tired, he grinned and shook hands with Wainwright.

"Jonathan, I want you to understand my position very plainly,"
he began. "I'm leaving for Australia pursuant to repeated orders of
the President. Things have gotten to such a point that I must comply with these orders or get out of the Army. I want you to make it
known throughout all elements of your command that I'm leaving
over my repeated protests." Wainwright assured him that this
would be done.

MacArthur repeated substantially the same things Sutherland had
told Wainwright concerning changes in the command setup. "We're
alone, Jonathan," he went on, turning to the tactical situation on
Bataan. "You know that as well as I. If I get through to Australia
you know I'll come back as soon as I can with as much as I can. In
the meantime you've got to hold."

Wainwright replied that "holding Bataan was their one aim
in life."

"Yes, yes, I know," said MacArthur. "But I want to be sure that
you're defending in as great depth as you can. You're an old
cavalryman, Jonathan, and your training has been along thin, light,
quick-hitting lines. The defense of Bataan must be deep. For any
prolonged defense you must have depth."

"I know that," Wainwright said. "I'm deploying my troops in as
great depth as the terrain and the number of troops permit."

"Good!" replied MacArthur. "And be sure to give them everything
you've got with your artillery. That's the best arm you have."

Thinking of the small amount of ammunition that remained, "and
of the malaria and dysentery, the one-half rations, the wounded in
their vulnerable hospital tents, [an] Air Corps of two P-40s, and of
many other things," Wainwright finally said, "You'll get through."

"And back," replied MacArthur with determination. MacArthur
explained briefly "why he was taking certain officers and men with
him and why he was leaving others behind." Wainwright told him
again that he understood.

Sensing that it was time to leave, Wainwright stood up. Mac-Arthur rose and they walked down the porch steps. MacArthur gave Wainwright a box of his cigars and two large jars of shaving cream.

"Good-bye, Jonathan," MacArthur said, shaking Wainwright's hand. "When I get back, if you're still on Bataan I'll make you a lieutenant general."

"I'll be on Bataan if I'm alive," Wainwright replied. He walked slowly back to Malinta Tunnel, where he joined his two aides and went on to the boat that was waiting to take them back to Bataan.[20]

On Bataan Brigadier General George handed Majors Ind and Eads secret orders to be delivered to Lieutenant Colonel Raymond T. Elsmore, in charge of the airfield at Del Monte, Mindanao. To the two officers, who would be leaving late that night for Del Monte, George explained, "I'll leave here about 7:30 P.M. tomorrow evening. There will be some others. Important others. Besides getting yourselves south without losing your airplane or your lives, you will keep sharp eyes for Japanese naval concentrations. If you see anything more than an occasional destroyer, you must radio us without delay from Iloilo [Panay], stating strength, disposition, and direction. In other words, accomplish a 'recon' sweep of the waters you pass over between here and Mindanao. Got it?"[21]

During the evening of March 10, Major Charles Morhouse, an Army Air Corps regimental surgeon, left Bataan for Corregidor. He had received a message to report to General MacArthur's headquarters. He arrived on Corregidor without a pass and was immediately thrown into the guard house. After repeated protests by Morhouse, the provost marshal phoned MacArthur's headquarters.

Sutherland's car arrived shortly with a staff officer and Morhouse was released. He was told to report to MacArthur's headquarters the following morning after breakfast, and in the meantime to find some food, shave, shower, and get a haircut.[22]

In Washington President Roosevelt was given a long radiogram for his approval, from Army Chief of Staff Marshall to Brett, commanding general of U.S. Army forces in Australia. Roosevelt read it and penned "O.K.—F.D.R." at the top. It was dispatched to Brett in Melbourne:

. . . It appears probable that General MacArthur will land in

Australia on March 17. Until that time you are to keep this entire matter one of profound secrecy.

The following instructions to you from the president: General MacArthur has been instructed to telegraph you at Melbourne immediately upon landing in Australia. Within the hour you will call upon the prime minister or other appropriate governmental official of Australia, stating that your call is made by direction of the president. You are to notify the prime minister that General MacArthur has landed in Australia and has assumed command of all U.S. Army forces therein. You will propose that the Australian government nominate General MacArthur as the supreme commander of the Southwest Pacific area, and will recommend that the nomination be submitted as soon as possible to London and Washington simultaneously. You will inform the prime minister that the president is in general agreement with the proposals regarding organization and command of the Australian area as recently submitted by the Australian government except as to some details concerning relationship to combined chiefs of staff and as to boundaries. These matters will be adjusted with the interested governments as quickly as practicable. Upon completion of your visit to the prime minister you will inform the War Department by urgent radio that this mission has been completed. End of president's instructions.

You will arrange to turn command of American army forces in Australia over to General MacArthur as soon after his landing as practicable and will report to him as his deputy for command of air forces, the U.S. immediately and all air forces if arrangeable.

Inform General MacArthur fully concerning above instructions and of all steps heretofore taken reference this and other matters. Request him to inform the War Department immediately as to the name of each individual accompanying him to Australia.[23]

On the morning of March 11 Major Morhouse reported to the USAFFE Headquarters lateral. General MacArthur escorted him outside Malinta Tunnel for their conversation. He had been ordered to Australia, MacArthur said, and he had selected Morhouse to accompany him as attending physician. He asked if Morhouse could be ready to leave that night.

"Hell! I *am* ready!" Morhouse replied. MacArthur authorized him to tell his medical friends on Bataan that he would soon be in a position to send messages to their families, but cautioned him not to disclose his destination. Morhouse eventually sent nineteen messages to families in the United States.[24]

After his discharge from the hospital Brigadier General Richard Marshall reported to the USAFFE Headquarters lateral. Sutherland handed him a list of names and told him to assign the officers to the four PT-boats. The departure, Marshall learned, was set for that night.[25]

The same morning Sutherland asked Major Carlos Romulo to meet him in President Quezon's old tent outside Malinta Tunnel. Sutherland explained that what he was about to say had to be kept "strictly confidential."

"General MacArthur has been ordered out by the first available transportation. He is leaving Corregidor tonight. The General hopes to be of better service to us in Australia. His usefulness is limited here. He can send help to us from Australia."

"I'm afraid this means a slump in morale," Romulo said, wondering how he was going to explain it to the soldiers in the foxholes on Bataan.

"It shouldn't," Sutherland answered crisply. "No one knows our needs better than General MacArthur." As they left the tent, Romulo wished that he could share Sutherland's assurance; but to him "Corregidor had never seemed more helpless and hopeless." He followed Sutherland back into the headquarters lateral and slumped down at his desk. Someone tapped him on the shoulder, and he looked up into the "worn and smiling face" of MacArthur.

"Carlos," MacArthur said, "I want to talk with you." They walked along the long main tunnel. His hand on Romulo's shoulder, MacArthur told him that he believed Bataan could hold out; but that if any serious crisis developed he would return to Corregidor. Romulo could proceed to Australia with him, he said, or could remain on Corregidor and continue his broadcasts over the "Voice of Freedom." Romulo wanted to go with MacArthur, but he realized it was important that the Voice of Freedom continue to make "liars out of the Japanese propagandists."

"I'll stay," he said simply.

"I knew you'd say that, Carlos," MacArthur smiled. "The Voice of Freedom can't be stilled. It must go on. It's our voice." A plane would be sent for Romulo, MacArthur assured him, if Bataan fell and Corregidor became "untenable." "You will join me in my headquarters," he told Romulo, "wherever that may be." He ended the conversation on a personal note: "I have just given the orders to promote you to lieutenant colonel. You've done a fine job, Carlos.

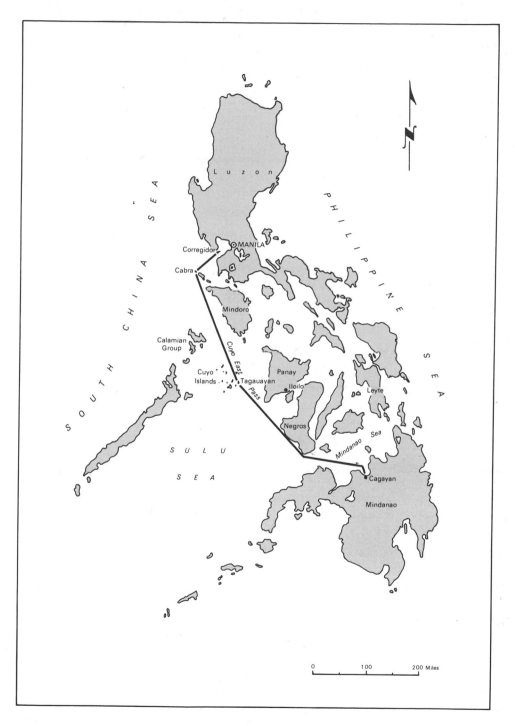

MacArthur's Evacuation Route, 11 March 1942

Keep it up, and God bless you!" Then, adjusting his cane under his arm, MacArthur walked out of the tunnel.[26]

During the afternoon Captain William E. Dyess of the Twenty-first Pursuit Squadron set his P-40 fighter down on a Bataan airfield after a reconnaissance flight. Waiting for Dyess was Brigadier General George. "I guess this is good-by for a while, Ed," said George. He told Dyess that he had been ordered to accompany General MacArthur to Australia. "Tell the boys that if I'm not back pretty soon it will not be because I don't want to come back." At 7:15 P.M. Brigadier Generals George, Akin, Casey, and Marquat boarded PT-32 at Quarantine Dock in Mariveles.[27]

At the same time on Corregidor MacArthur stepped onto the porch of his cottage and said gently to his wife, "Jean, it is time to go." General MacArthur, Mrs. MacArthur, their four-year old son, Arthur, their Cantonese amah, Ah Cheu, Huff, and Morhouse entered two cars in Malinta Tunnel and were driven to North Dock.[28]

At the dock the party walked slowly along a wide concrete pier to the waiting PT-41. Along the way they shook the hands of a few spectators. Each of them carried a bag or a suitcase. MacArthur had his cane, a suitcase, and a musette bag. Lieutenant Bulkeley greeted the MacArthurs and carried their two suitcases aboard PT-41.[29]

While Mrs. MacArthur, Ah Cheu, and Arthur boarded, General MacArthur talked with Major General George F. Moore, who commanded the Harbor Defenses. Previously, MacArthur had cautioned Moore "that in case of the ultimate fall of Corregidor [he] was to make sure that the armament was destroyed to such an extent that it could not be used against an American effort to recapture the Philippines." Now, telling Moore "to hold Corregidor until he returned," MacArthur said, "George, keep the flag flying. I'm coming back."[30]

Lieutenant Commander Melvyn H. McCoy, the radio material officer for the Sixteenth Naval District, gave MacArthur a hand as he stepped aboard PT-41. He was followed by Morhouse, Sutherland, Ray, and Huff. Seeing Colonel Frederick A. Ward, who commanded the Army Transport Service, among the spectators, Huff waved and yelled, "We're coming back up here, Freddy."[31]

With all passengers aboard, MacArthur turned to Bulkeley and said, "You may cast off, Buck, when you are ready." As PT-41 left the dock, MacArthur looked back at the people on the pier and raised his cap in a farewell salute.[32]

From North Dock, Bulkeley headed PT-41 northwest toward the Turning Buoy, in front of the outer mine channel to Manila Bay. By 8:00 P.M. PT-41, PT-32, PT-34, and PT-35 had reached the Turning Buoy and rendezvoused on schedule. In the dark the four boats moved in single file through the minefield channel out of Manila Bay. Led by PT-41, they headed into the South China Sea toward Cabra Island, southwest of Corregidor.[33]

The course from Corregidor channel was set to keep the boats at least five miles offshore of the western end of Cabra Island, but strong currents and a possible compass error brought them within two miles. As they approached the island they sighted many white lights, and a wider detour than originally planned was necessary. The lights came from bonfires set by farmers who mistook the noise of the PT-boats for planes; these fires were used as guides for night flights between Mindanao and Bataan.[34]

Before the four boats left Manila Bay, Philippine Q-boats had staged a diversion to the north off Subic Bay and a last-minute air reconnaissance had been flown as far south as Verde Island Passage. The air reconnaissance had reported a destroyer in Apo East Pass and a cruiser off the southwest end of Mindoro. The PT-boats therefore set a course westward of Apo Island, in spite of bad weather there. The Apo West Pass was only three miles wide between Apo Island and the shoals to the westward, so that it was unlikely any enemy patrol vessel would be stationed there at night.[35]

After the sweep around Cabra Island, the four PT-boats proceeded on a southeastward course through the Mindoro Strait and into the Sulu Sea. The sea was moderate, with one- to two-foot waves, but even in a light chop the PT-boats gave a rough ride. Because of their hull configuration and speed, the spray kicked up over the bows, and the topsides of the boats were throughly drenched. On PT-41 young Arthur and Ah Cheu, seasick, occupied the officers' bunks. MacArthur and his wife sat on a mattress on the floor of the lower cockpit.[36]

By 3:30 A.M. the four boats had scattered, although the convoy had tried to stay together in an echelon formation. Gas strainer stoppages and engine breakdowns resulted in their being separated by several miles in the dark. Bulkeley looked for the other boats, but there was no moon and visibility was essentially zero.[37]

Just before dawn on March 12, near a small island of the Cuyo

Group, Ensign Vincent E. Schumacher in command of PT-32 scanned the horizon with a pair of binoculars. Idling on one engine, PT-32 rolled from side to side in the rough sea. After a sleepless night with extended stops to repair the fuel and ignition systems, Schumacher was wet, cold, and tired. Wind and spray blew against his face. Suddenly he sighted a "strange, unidentified craft," dim in the distance. Believing he was miles behind the other three PT-boats because of the delays throughout the night, Schumacher thought the unknown craft must be a Japanese patrol boat or destroyer.

Brigadier Generals Casey and Akin were on deck with him. Exclaiming that he had sighted an approaching Japanese craft, Schumacher asked them if he should open fire—although such resistance would risk the destruction of the boat and the lives of the men. He was told to prepare to open fire; Akin added that he should wait until the ship was in range.

Schumacher shouted commands to his crew to man the 50-mm. machine guns and get ready to launch torpedoes. Akin prepared to drop overboard a barracks bag filled with code devices. Schumacher proposed they "make a run for it," and Akin agreed. Immediately Schumacher cut the lines and jettisoned the four tons of fuel in barrel drums lashed to the deck, to improve maneuverability and reduce the risks in being hit by enemy fire.

Only one of PT-32's three engines was running. The other two engines, their magnetoes grounded out by water leaking through vent holes in the deck, refused to start. The deck was starting to come apart from the rough seas and the weight of the fuel drums.

Focusing his binoculars again on the oncoming ship, as it took shape more clearly out of the rough sea and dawn light, Schumacher realized it was a PT-boat. "That's not a Jap destroyer," he exclaimed, "it's one of our boats!" Asking Schumacher for his binoculars, Akin identified the craft as PT-41, carrying MacArthur and his party. In a moment Bulkeley's PT-boat pulled alongside Schumacher's PT-32. On the deck of the "Japanese destroyer" that had narrowly missed being fired on was MacArthur, wearing his familiar cap and field jacket, splattered with salt water.[38]

Schumacher later explained how he had mistaken PT-41 for an enemy destroyer:

Ensign George E. Cox, Jr., skipper of PT-41, had posted a lookout standing high on each side of the flying bridge. I wondered then, and still do, how those men managed to maintain their positions in that sea. My concern that night had been to keep people down and inboard, to prevent anyone falling over the side. Those high lookouts added a "superstructure" that was uncharacteristic of the low, smooth silhouettes of the early PT-boats. Although the size and distance of PT-41 as it came up astern were next to impossible to determine in those conditions of light and sea, I do recall that it was my impression that it was larger than a PT-boat, and that it appeared to be further away than it actually turned out to be. . . . I mistook two men for substantial parts of the ship's superstructure.[39]

MacArthur asked Brigadier General Casey to join him on PT-41 and they talked about what should be done next. The two boats were anchored in a cove of an island in the Cuyo Group, several hours away from Tagauayan Island, where the four boats originally had intended to rendezvous and spend the day in hiding. Rather than risk traveling in daylight, they decided to remain in the cove.

Bulkeley allowed no one except a lookout to go ashore; if the PT-boats were spotted by Japanese planes, they would have to make a fast run, leaving the lookout. Since Schumacher had jettisoned four tons of fuel needed for the remainder of the journey to Mindanao, Bulkeley transferred some of PT-41's precious fuel to PT-32.

Everyone waited for darkness. Soon, however, MacArthur became restless. If they missed the rendezvous at Tagauayan by waiting too long, he believed, they would jeopardize the entire mission. He conferred with Sutherland, Bulkeley, and Ray. Ray and Bulkeley pointed out the chance of running into Japanese ships in daylight; with faulty engines, the two PT-boats might not be able to outrun them. On the other hand, if they remained in the cove, they might be sighted by enemy planes. It was finally decided that 2:30 P.M. would be the optimal time to leave the anchorage—offering the best chance to avoid aerial detection and still allow sufficient time to arrive at Tagauayan before the scheduled departure for Cagayan.[40]

Early in the afternoon Bulkeley and Schumacher set their course for Tagauayan Island. It was a trip of only several hours, but it was a miserable ride owing to the rough sea. Salt-water spray washed over the deck, soaking everyone to the skin. Bulkeley and Ray had hammerlocks on the stub mast to keep from being swept overboard.

Looking aft at the bodies stretched out on the deck, Bulkeley turned
to Ray with a large grin: "That's the wettest bunch of generals I
have ever seen." Most of the time MacArthur stayed in the lower
cockpit of PT-41 with his wife. In the heavy sea he began to think
it might be a good idea to wait at Tagauayan for the scheduled
arrival of the *Permit*.[41]

At approximately 4:00 P.M. PT-32 arrived on the lee side of
Tagauayan Island and moored alongside PT-34. PT-41 arrived a
few minutes later. Sweltering in the sun aboard PT-34, Rear Admiral
Rockwell had been waiting since 9:30 A.M. There was still no sign
of the fourth boat, PT-35.[42]

The three boats anchored in a cove overlooked by a low cliff.
MacArthur asked Casey and Akin to join him on PT-41. They discussed what should be done next: wait for the *Permit*, scheduled
to arrive at daylight the following day, or continue that night by
PT-boat to Mindanao as planned. MacArthur was especially concerned for the safety of his family.

Pointing out how quickly secret information had leaked through
the front lines to the Japanese in the past, Akin said he believed the
Japanese knew of MacArthur's departure from Corregidor and were
probably looking for him. Casey advised MacArthur to carry out
the original plan and go by PT-boat to Mindanao and then by plane
to Australia. He stressed that they had already successfully completed the most difficult and dangerous part of the journey.[43]

Rockwell also wanted to proceed according to the original plan.
"We'd better get the hell out of here fast," he advised, pointing out
that there was also the possibility that the *Permit* would not appear.
Sutherland agreed. Bulkeley warned them that the next lap would
be even rougher than the first, but Rockwell, anxious to get moving,
assured MacArthur that the weather would be good and the sea
calm. Turning to Sutherland, MacArthur said, "Dick, I can't do
anything to Rockwell. But if it's rough tonight, I'll boil you in oil."[44]

The passengers aboard PT-32 were divided between PT-41 and
PT-34. Ensign Schumacher was to remain behind and deliver a
message to the captain of the *Permit*, then proceed to Iloilo City,
Panay, to refuel, and on to Cagayan, Mindanao. Additional fuel was
transferred to PT-32 for the trip. Bulkeley's final instructions were
"make out as best you can."[45]

Under cover of approaching darkness, PT-34 and PT-41 departed

at 6:00 P.M. from Tagauayan Island. For the second leg of the trip
PT-34, commanded by Lieutenant Robert B. Kelly, took the lead,
with PT-41 following. In heavy weather PT-34 would bear the brunt
of the seas and PT-41, in the relative calm of its wake, would provide
a smoother ride for MacArthur's party. The sea was rough, with
high waves, and spray soon drenched everyone in the two
boats.[46]

At 7:00 P.M. a Japanese cruiser on an easterly course was sighted
in the twilight to the south. Bulkeley issued orders for the PT-boats
to turn at maximum speed due west into the setting sun. MacArthur,
lying on a mattress in the cockpit of PT-41, overheard the crew's
conversation regarding the sighting but said nothing. Major Morhouse held little Arthur on his lap. After about twenty minutes of
anxious waiting the danger passed. In the glare of the setting sun
the Japanese lookouts had failed to see the two small boats. With
tropical suddenness it was pitch dark.[47]

Once again on a southeastward course, the PT-boats crossed the
traffic lane between Tagauayan and Panay and slipped past the long
coastline of Negros Island as close inshore as was thought safe. In
spite of navigation difficulties, both entered Mindanao Sea.[48] In
its open waters they fought extremely heavy seas from 1:00 A.M.
until daylight, with severe buffeting from waves up to fifteen feet
high. Rain squalls blinded anyone who was topside. At 2:00 A.M.
Silino Island, lying in the Mindanao Sea between Mindanao and
Negros, was sighted. The PT-boats headed for the pass between
Silino Island and the shoals off Mindanao's Tagolo Point because
of the narrowness of the channel and the small likelihood of en-
countering patrol vessels.[49]

During the night MacArthur awakened his aide, Sidney Huff. In
a "voice slow and deliberate and barely distinguishable above the
high whine of the engines," he talked about what had happened in
the Philippines since 1935. He recalled how he had tried to obtain
funds to create and build the Philippine Army, and the difficulties
and obstacles he had encountered. He had had differences with
officials in Washington before the war started, MacArthur said;
"orders had been prepared for his recall and . . . he had, more or
less, been forced into retirement in 1937." He touched on his chagrin
at being ordered to leave Corregidor. After a time he "stopped thinking out loud and was silent for a few moments." Then he told Huff
that if they ever reached Australia the first thing he would do would

be to raise Huff's rank to full colonel. Huff thanked him and, thinking about what he had said, tried to go back to sleep.[50]

Past Silino Island, the PT-boats continued southeastward through the heavily patrolled Mindanao Sea without interruption toward their objective, Cagayan. Their only navigational aid was a small magnetic boat compass. In the heavy seas PT-34 yawed violently and the compass oscillated wildly, 30 to 40 degrees on each side of the course, making it impossible to do more than estimate the effective course made good. The night's trip was made solely on dead reckoning (estimated course and speed made good), which fortunately proved accurate.[51]

Early in the morning of March 13, Father Edward Haggerty, rector of a small college in Cagayan, received a telephone call from Major Joseph R. Webb, commander of the 103d Infantry Regiment at Cagayan.

"Padre, want to be in on a good show?" Webb asked.

"Sure!" Haggerty said. "Where?"

"Come down to the wharf in fifteen minutes," Webb told him.

"Sorry, I am just vesting for Mass," said Haggerty.

"Well, you're going to miss the chance of a lifetime," Webb said. "No, no danger—just a thrill—something big."

Later Father Haggerty heard a sound like many planes flying low over the bay. Although the engines died out suddenly, he saw no planes.[52]

At approximately 7:00 A.M. PT-41 and PT-34 came alongside the pier near Cagayan. MacArthur was greeted by Major General William F. Sharp, commander of the Visayan-Mindanao force, who was waiting on the dock with a guard of U.S. soldiers.

Before leaving for Sharp's headquarters at the Del Monte Pineapple Plantation, high up on the Mindanao Plateau, MacArthur called together the officers and crews of the two PT-boats to thank them for their efforts in the successful completion of the mission. "It was done in true naval style," he said. "It gives me great pleasure and honor to award the boats' crews the Silver Star for gallantry [and] for fortitude in the face of heavy odds."[53]

The fourth boat, PT-35, with Colonel Willoughby, Lieutenant Colonels Wilson and Diller, and Master Sergeant Rogers aboard, would arrive at Cagayan about noon. It had missed the assembly point at Tagauayan by several miles and had laid up in the lee of an uninhabited island during the day. When it arrived at Tagauayan the skipper, Ensign Anthony Akers, joined PT-32 and learned that MacArthur and party had departed for Mindanao.[54]

Why did MacArthur use Motor Torpedo Boats for the arduous trip from Corregidor? Lieutenant Robert B. Kelly, commander of PT-34, provided an explanation.

It has often been questioned why General MacArthur elected to be evacuated from Corregidor to Mindanao by PT-boat rather than by submarine since the submarine *Permit* was available. The ability of submarines to enter Manila Bay and depart safely had already been clearly demonstrated. Only a short while earlier, the submarine *Seawolf* had entered the bay, docked at Corregidor while it unloaded supplies and ammunition and loaded a supply of gold for evacuation. During daylight hours it had rested on the bottom of Manila Bay.

Certain personal characteristics of General MacArthur strongly influenced this decision. He was a brilliant but somewhat vain individual with a flair for the dramatic. He had a high regard for those subordinates whom he personally knew and whose judgment and ability he respected and trusted. In times of difficulty he felt more comfortable with such persons in positions of responsibility under his immediate command. For this reason several members of his staff, for example, had served with him for many years in various assignments.

When General MacArthur had served as Chief of Staff of the Army during the 1930s, he had recommended to the Navy Department that small craft such as the PT-boats would be a valuable adjunct to the Fleet as defensive weapons. The Navy had derided and turned down this recommendation. MacArthur never forgot nor forgave this rebuff.

After the start of the war, when he was assigned the responsibility for the defense of the Philippines, he took a personal interest in the operations of the PT-boats and had Lieutenant John D. Bulkeley, their squadron commander, report to him daily in person. In this way, over a three month period he became not only familiar with their capabilities and accomplishments but he had an excellent opportunity to get to know and evaluate their commander, Lieutenant Bulkeley. It was on the basis of this personal exaluation that he seriously considered the use of the PT-boats for his evacuation from Corregidor.

Lieutenant Bulkeley was an outstandingly dynamic and competent young officer. His sincerity and resoluteness to duty were unquestioned. General MacArthur recognized and respected these characteristics. When he queried Bulkeley concerning the feasibility of the PT-boats accomplishing such a mission, he received an unqualified affirmative. There was no question in Bulkeley's mind that he could successfully complete this mission despite the long odds. This fortified General MacArthur's tentative decision.

Having served with Lieutenant Bulkeley as his second in command on this and a prior assignment, I was privy to much of what transpired during his conferences with General MacArthur during the decision making process. MacArthur's decision to use the PT-boats for the evacuation of his party dramatically emphasized to the American public the overwhelming odds against which the United States forces were fighting in the Philippines. It evened an old score with the United States Navy. And since he had a tendency toward claustrophobia and did not relish making the trip on a submerged submarine with a commander whom he did not personally know, it provided an acceptable alternative which he elected to exercise.[55]

About 10:00 A.M. on the morning of MacArthur's arrival, Father Haggerty drove to the Del Monte Plantation on business with Major General Sharp. Haggerty noticed that the headquarters guard seemed unusually alert. In the reception room he saw a number of unfamiliar high-ranking officers. Intent on his interview with Sharp, though, he paid little attention.

While discussing with Sharp the possibility of preparing an evacuation place for American civilians, Father Haggerty noticed that he was nervous and preoccupied. Sharp granted his requests, but Haggerty could sense that he was anxious for him to go.

The priest was about to leave when an air-raid warning sounded. Two Japanese planes had been sighted circling at high altitude.

Suddenly a handsome four-star general appeared from a bedroom and calmly inquired about the alert. MacArthur was unshaven and his eyes looked tired. He was wearing worn, unpressed khaki. Seeing Father Haggerty, he walked across the wide room and, without an introduction, shook his hand and called him "Father." Taken completely by surprise, Haggerty complimented MacArthur on the gallant stand of his army on Bataan.

While Sharp was anxiously telephoning, MacArthur excused himself and went back to his room. Bringing out his wife, his son, and Ah Cheu, MacArthur placed them in the safety of a dugout. He then returned to Haggerty. "Would you like to go to a shelter, Father? There are only two planes; I never bother about so few."

"No," Haggerty replied. "Your calmness makes me feel brave."

Sitting down, MacArthur began to talk. "Bataan cannot be taken if food holds out. We have food for less than two months. . . . The men on Bataan are splendid. . . . They have proven their valor far beyond my expectations—beyond the expection of friend and, especially, of the enemy. . . . I have been ordered by President Roosevelt to Australia to begin the offensive. . . . If the Jap does not take Mindanao by Easter, all he will receive is bullets. . . ."

Within five minutes an all clear sounded. When Major General Sharp returned, MacArthur left to get his family, without saying a word to the priest about secrecy. As Sharp escorted Father Haggerty to the door, however, he said with a smile, "Padre, I think you've scooped a few of us. Please consider everything secret—even his presence here."[56]

Greeting Major Ind, who had flown from Bataan to Del Monte with Major Eads during the early morning of March 11, Brigadier General George exclaimed, "I'll take mine in the air! But I'd like to take Bulkeley. He's good!" George was going to Australia with MacArthur and his staff, he told Ind; B-17 bombers were being dispatched from Australia to pick up the party. "I will speak to the Chief of Staff about your coming down with me," George added. "I don't want to take a chance on leaving you here. You must come with me, and together we will turn every effort to the relief of those we left up there. It will be an unhappy day for Tojo when he discovers that General MacArthur and his staff are no longer bottled up, but free again to organize for the day when we strike north with a force that will shake him to his knees."[57]

Four B-17 bombers should have been waiting to take the Mac-Arthur party on to Australia. Major General Brett in Australia had authorized a flight of four B-17s from Australia to Del Monte, but only one had arrived. Two of the bombers had developed engine trouble and returned to Australia, and the third had crash-landed in a heavy rainstorm in Cagayan Bay.[58]

In setting up the mission Brett had tried to borrow four new Flying Fortresses assigned to the naval command in Australia. To the highest naval authority in Australia, Vice Admiral Herbert F. Leary, he had explained that he was authorized to send four bombers to Del Monte to evacuate MacArthur, his family, and staff officers from Mindanao. All the B-17 bombers under his command were in decrepit condition, Brett explained, having been through extensive operations in Java.

"I'd like to help you, Brett," replied Leary, "but it is quite impossible. We need those planes here, and can't spare them for a ferry job, no matter how important it is. You'll have to do the best you can with what you have."[59]

When MacArthur saw the one battered B-17 and its young pilot, Lieutenant Harl Pease, Jr., he sent the following message to Brett:

> Arrived Del Monte today with Admiral Rockwell, his chief of staff, fourteen army officers, and my own wife and child. Upon arrival here discovered that only one of the four planes dispatched here had arrived; and that with an inexperienced pilot, no brakes and superchargers not repeat not functioning. This plane was returned to you by General Sharp since it was not repeat not suitable for the purpose intended. It is necessary that only the best planes and most experienced pilots of adequate service be employed for the transportation of such a party. This trip is most important and desperate and must be set up with absolutely the greatest of care lest it end in disaster. Properly functioning B-17s must be obtained from Hawaii or the United States if they are not otherwise available. As my presence at Del Monte must be kept secret, radio me full information addressed as usual to Fort Mills. Be careful not repeat not to send clear text addresses or text signatures which would disclose my presence here.[60]

A second message was dispatched to General Marshall in Washington:

> I have made hazardous trip successfully by naval Motor Torpedo Boat to Del Monte Mindanao. In order to expedite move-

ment I did not await submarine. Upon arrival discovered that Brett had sent four old B-17s of which only one arrived and that not repeat not fit to carry passengers due to inoperative super-charger. Failure of three planes to arrive not repeat not due to enemy action. The other plane took off for return trip before my arrival. I am informing Brett but request you inform him of group to be transported and order him to dispatch suitable planes if on hand, otherwise that you make such planes available to him. I am accompanied by my wife and child and fourteen officers, Admiral Rockwell and his chief of staff. The best three planes in the United States or Hawaii should be made available with completely adequate and experienced crews. To attempt such a desperate and important trip with inadequate equipment would amount to consigning the whole party to death and I could not accept such a responsibility. I am in constant communication with Corregidor and request reply to that station in usual manner. I am continuing to function in command of all forces in the Philippines. My presence in Del Monte should be kept completely secret and every means taken to create belief that I am still in Luzon. Pursuant your order I did not inform Brett of mission and it would appear that he was ignorant of importance.[61]

When Brett received MacArthur's "sharp" radiogram, he made a second visit to Vice Admiral Leary. Expecting another "no," he was prepared to be adamant. But this time, to his surprise, Leary agreed to lend him three new B-17s. Evidently in the meantime Leary had received instructions from Washington.[62]

Upon his return to headquarters Brett immediately composed the following reply to MacArthur:

Regarding your radiogram of March 13. Not understood. Every effort made for successful accomplishment and have personally supervised preparation this trip appreciating full importance. Pilots specially selected for their experience in operating in and out of Del Monte. Godman and Adams decorated with distinguished Flying Crosses for operations during Philippine campaign and work in Java. Every effort made to ensure equipment in perfect operational condition. Planes have been in service but considered prefectly suitable for purpose. No other planes available nor could they be secured from Hawaii in time to perform mission as specified in War Department orders. Crews specially selected. B-17 Es selected due to necessity for maximum protection during flight. I am preparing three additional B-17 Es which can be dis-

patched within twenty-four hours. These planes will be taken
from tactical units now conducting important operations with
navy towards Rabaul.[63]

Brett had second thoughts, however, and dispatched the following
radiogram instead.

Regarding your radiogram of March 13. This mission arranged under my personal supervision fully appreciating importance thereof. Will dispatch three additional planes as soon
as possible.[64]

On March 14, from the War Department in Washington, General
Marshall replied to MacArthur:

Information contained in your radiogram has been repeated to
General Brett. He has been instructed to dispatch at once the
three best B-17s under his control. He has been informed of the
size of your party which is probably too large to permit simultaneous movement on three B-17s. However this is the maximum
number of planes that we are justified in dispatching at this time
because of needs in Australia. If necessary, therefore, you should
reduce the size of your staff to a number that can be transported
without preventing the proper functioning of the operating crews,
including gunners. Such officers as are left behind can be evacuated later under your authority and at your convenience.[65]

On March 15 Brett was able to radio MacArthur the following:

Three B-17s leave Australia early sixteenth repeat sixteenth.
Will arrive Del Monte dark same day.[66]

During the afternoon of March 16, Brigadier General Richard
Marshall was notified by Sutherland to be ready to depart from Del
Monte at nightfall. Rear Admiral Rockwell learned that three B-17
bombers were scheduled to arrive at 8:00 P.M. That evening Mac-
Arthur's staff went in jeeps to the airfield at about 8:00 P.M. At
approximately 10:00, two hours behind schedule, two B-17s, piloted
by Captains Frank P. Bostrom and William Lewis, landed. Because
there was the threat of a Japanese air attack, lights were not allowed
on the ground or in the planes. The third B-17 failed to arrive; it had
developed an oil leak and had not left Australia. MacArthur and one
of the pilots decided that if all of the baggage were left behind the
two B-17s could carry the entire party. After the B-17 that would

carry MacArthur had been refueled, Major Victor C. Huffsmith, the base ordnance officer at Del Monte, assisted in providing mattresses and bedding in the navigator's compartment for the comfort of the general and his family. A delay resulted from engine trouble in one of the planes, and it was shortly after midnight when the heavily overloaded B-17s left the airfield at Del Monte.[67]

The planes headed due east until they were well clear of the Mindanao coast, then due south for Darwin. Aboard the B-17 that carried MacArthur, Marshall and Huff rode in the bombardier's compartment in the nose of the plane. Huff sat in the bombardier's seat, and Marshall, his feet reaching into the aisle, stretched out on the floor and tried to sleep. The second B-17, carrying Rear Admiral Rockwell, Generals Casey, George, and Marquat, and Captain McMicking, was also crowded. Looking at his fellow passengers lying head to foot, squeezed together, Rockwell could only think of tightly packed "sardines in a can."[68]

As daylight approached from the east, the B-17 carrying Rockwell and the other officers passed over the island of Ceram in the Netherlands East Indies. The bomber cruised at 800 feet, and Rockwell sighted two or three surface vessels. From the bombardier's compartment on MacArthur's bomber, Marshall witnessed a spectacular sunrise.[69]

On approaching Darwin they learned that the designated airfield was under attack by Japanese planes. The planes were rerouted to Batchelor Field, 45 miles south of Darwin. The B-17 carrying MacArthur arrived at about 9:00 A.M., the other about 40 minutes later. After disembarking from his plane, MacArthur asked an American officer about the number of military personnel being assembled in Australia for the purpose of rescuing the Philippine garrison. The officer replied in bewilderment, "So far as I know, sir, there are very few troops here." MacArthur turned to Sutherland and commented, "Surely he is wrong."[70]

While the weary travelers were guided to a mess hall for a breakfast of canned peaches and baked beans, MacArthur was greeted by Brigadier General Ralph Royce. Sent by Brett, Royce had arrived earlier with two DC-3s borrowed from a commercial airline to fly MacArthur and his party to Melbourne. MacArthur refused, however, to fly any farther.[71]

When Major Morhouse walked into the office of the base commander, he found MacArthur, Royce, and several other officers.

MacArthur was agitated, pacing up and down in his long underwear and shouting.

"What is the matter?" asked Morhouse.

"They're just too damned lazy to do what I want," said MacArthur angrily. "I want to take a train to Daly Waters and drive overland to Alice Springs. Mrs. MacArthur is tired of flying."

Morhouse listened and then explained that he "could not guarantee little Arthur would make 600 miles of desert without shelter, food, etc." Arthur had been ill since the arrival at Del Monte, so sick that Morhouse had had to give him intravenous fluids.

MacArthur stopped pacing and said, "Doc, do you mean that?" Morhouse replied that he meant every word, and MacArthur ordered the plane made ready.[72]

Sutherland called Huff aside and told him that Japanese planes were headed for Batchelor Field. He ordered Huff to get Mrs. MacArthur, Arthur, and Ah Cheu on the plane immediately. In the meantime he started General MacArthur moving toward the plane. Neither Sutherland nor Huff mentioned the approaching planes. Instead the MacArthur's were hurried aboard a B-17. Just as the bomber's side door was slammed, the pilot, Major Richard H. Carmichael, heard the air-raid sirens go off. Releasing the brakes and pushing in the throttle, Carmichael quickly started the B-17 rolling down the runway. The occupants, still in the aisle, were "thrown violently toward the rear of the plane." Regaining his balance, MacArthur yelled angrily at Huff, "Sid, get that pilot's name!" Later Huff explained the reason for Carmichael's abrupt takeoff. Shortly after MacArthur's departure, Japanese planes bombed the field.[73]

The flight from Batchelor Field to Alice Springs was extremely rough. Most of the passengers were airsick. As the B-17 flew south over the wasteland of northern Australia, Morhouse noticed MacArthur looking out the bomber's window at the desolate landscape. After they landed at Alice Springs, MacArthur put his arm on Morhouse's shoulder and said, "We would not have made it. Thank you."[74]

As the passengers deplaned they were "almost smothered by the intense heat and swarms of cattle flies." Realizing that he had narrowly escaped from the Japanese planes approaching Batchelor Field, MacArthur remarked to Sutherland, "It was close, but that's the way it is in war. You win or lose, live or die—and the difference is just an eyelash."[75]

At his headquarters in Melbourne, Brett had learned of Mac-Arthur's arrival in Australia when his deputy chief of staff, Brigadier General Ralph Royce, telephoned him. "General MacArthur," Royce had said, "won't fly another mile. At least, that's what he said at the start. When I pointed out that he would have to ride three hundred miles over dusty, rutted roads to get to Alice Springs, where the rail line ends, he agreed to fly to Alice Springs, but that's as far as he will go by plane."

"Anything wrong with the DC-3s?" Brett asked.

"Not a thing. They're perfect. He's just sick and tired of airplanes, I guess."

"All right," Brett said. "I'll see what can be done about getting a private car for him and Mrs. MacArthur and his aides. The rest of the staff, of course, will fly?" Royce replied that the remainder of the staff would fly on to Melbourne.[76]

In accordance with General George Marshall's instructions of March 10, Brett phoned Prime Minister John Curtin and relayed the following message:

> The President of the United States has directed that I present his compliments to you and inform you that General Douglas MacArthur, United States Army, has today arrived in Australia from the Philippine Islands. In accordance with his directions General MacArthur has now assumed command of all United States Army Forces here.
>
> Should it be in accord with your wishes and those of the Australian people, the President suggests that it would be highly acceptable to him and pleasing to the American people for the Australian Government to nominate General MacArthur as the Supreme Commander of all Allied Forces in the Southwest Pacific. Such nomination should be submitted simultaneously to London and Washington.
>
> The President further has directed that I inform you that he is in general agreement with the proposals regarding organization and command of the Australian Area, except as to some details concerning relationship to the Combined Chiefs of Staff and as to boundaries. These exceptions he

wishes to assure you, however, will be adjusted with the interested Governments as quickly as possible.

The President regrets that he has been unable to inform you in advance of General MacArthur's pending arrival but feels certain that you will appreciate that his safety during the voyage from the Philippine Islands required the highest order of secrecy.[77]

Brett also dispatched a radiogram to General Marshall in Washington:

General MacArthur and party arrived Australia today expected arrival Melbourne Sunday via rail from Alice Springs. Have read to prime minister and confirmed by letter authorized statement regarding arrival General MacArthur and his assumption of command United States Army forces here and president's suggestion his nomination to supreme allied command. Prime minister enthusiastically concurred with suggestions and approved. Will act promptly and agrees make simultaneous announcement with Washington and with this headquarters. Danger of leakage is serious if announcement delayed. Request urgent cable GMT for simultaneous release from Washington, Canberra and this headquarters, Melbourne. Also any specific recommendations form of announcement. It is arranged that we will notify prime minister as to time and suggested form of announcement.[78]

At 4:15 P.M. Brett telephoned an army officer at Alice Springs. He asked the officer if he had received any information concerning planes arriving from Batchelor Field and received a negative answer. Informing the officer that an important person was due to arrive, Brett told him to contact the plane immediately and ask General MacArthur to call General Brett.

At about 5:00 P.M. Sutherland phoned Brett's headquarters and talked to Brigadier General Patrick J. Hurley. They discussed at length whether MacArthur would proceed to Melbourne by rail or air, and Hurley read over the phone the message that had been relayed to Prime Minister Curtin. Sutherland also talked with Brigadier General Stephen J. Chamberlin about the possibility of obtaining better rail accommodations. It was finally arranged to send Hurley as Brett's representative to Alice Springs that night by plane.[79]

Brigadier General Chamberlin arranged with Brigadier Norman

of the Australian army for the return of a sleeping car, which had left Alice Springs that morning, to Alice Springs by 12:30 A.M. the following day. He also made arrangements for a special nurse and for cooking accommodations on the car, and for a special car on the *Adelaide Express* which ran from Terowie to Melbourne. At 6:30 P.M. Chamberlin tried to phone Sutherland and explain the train arrangements. Although he was unable to speak to Sutherland, he talked with an Australian officer who informed him that Sutherland and MacArthur understood the new arrangements. Afterward, Chamberlin phoned the manager of the Menzies Hotel and reserved rooms for the staff officers arriving that night.[80]

At 6:30 P.M. Brigadier General Ralph Royce's B-17 with about ten officers aboard took off from the airfield at Alice Springs and headed for Melbourne. Among the officers were Rear Admiral Rockwell, Captain Ray, Brigadier Generals Marshall, Casey, Marquat, and George, and Captain McMicking. Before leaving Alice Springs, Marshall had been instructed by MacArthur "to rejoin him as quickly as possible with data on forces that would be available to him [in Australia] and their disposition." At 1:00 A.M. the B-17 landed at Laverton Field. The officers were met by Brigadier General Chamberlin who saw that they were accommodated in the Menzies Hotel.[81]

On March 17, on the other side of the world, President Roosevelt had dispatched the following cable to the "Former Naval Person," Prime Minister Winston S. Churchill:

> General MacArthur and a small staff arrived in Australia by air today. Since the prime minister of Australia as well as New Zealand had proposed a United States supreme commander in that region, suggesting Brett, I had instructed Brett immediately on MacArthur's arrival to propose the latter officer to Mr. Curtin as supreme commander in Australia. Brett in cabling MacArthur's arrival reports that Mr. Curtin enthusiastically accepts MacArthur. They urge immediate joint press release to avoid leak. This I think highly important if Axis propaganda attacking MacArthur's departure from Philippines is to be forestalled. Therefore I authorized a press release at ten thirty A.M. Washington time announcing MacArthur's appointment as supreme commander in that region. This action will in no way interfere with procedure of determining strategic areas and spheres of responsibility through established channels.[82]

At 4:15 P.M. Roosevelt held a press conference. He began by giving the reporters the following statement concerning MacArthur's evacuation from Corregidor:

> There will be, of course, immediately—we all know that —because we are accustomed to that sort of thing—there is going to be Axis propaganda that will appear this afternoon on their short-wave, and tomorrow morning, about how this is the abandonment of the Philippines, and that General MacArthur's leaving the Philippines is nothing more than another Van Mook having to get out of Java, etcetera. And of course we know what they will say. On the other side of the picture, put it this way:
>
> [Reading] "I know that every man and woman in the United States admires with me General MacArthur's determination to fight to the finish with his men in the Philippines. But I also know that every man and woman is in agreement with all important decisions that must be made with a view toward the successful termination of the war. Knowing this, I am sure that every American, if faced individually with the question as to where General MacArthur could best serve his country, could come to only one answer."
>
> In other words, he will be more useful in Supreme Command of the whole Southwest Pacific than if he had stayed in Bataan, where of course the fighting is going on.[83]

Commenting on the true significance of MacArthur's recall from Corregidor to Australia, Secretary of War Stimson, using a dictaphone, recorded the following, which was typed later by his secretary and became part of the March 17 entry of his diary:

> This morning came the bright news of General MacArthur and his party having safely arrived in Australia. . . . The announcement of his arrival has had a great effect in the United States and all over the world. It is the first good news we have had for so long that people are inclined to exaggerate it and make the most of it. But its morale effect is very good and the papers have treated it not only enthusiastically but intelligently. It may mean some difficulties to us

in the strategic control of events. MacArthur will make great demands upon us and he will not always be easy to manage in respect to other theatres of action which may become more important than his. But he is a great asset and skillful fighter and I am very glad that I have throughout taken the action that he must be saved. Even when five or six weeks ago we had to order him and Quezon to stay and fight it out, both Marshall and I were planning to get him out eventually before he was lost.[84]

8

Jubilation and Disappointment

March 18–21, 1942

> Wars are not won by evacuations. But there was a victory inside this deliverance, which should be noted.[1]
>
> —Winston S. Churchill

It was Wednesday, March 18, 1942. The *New York Times* headline proclaimed: "MacArthur In Australia As Allied Commander; Move Hailed As Foreshadowing Turn of Tide." MacArthur's arrival in Australia was stupendous news. Well known, respected, and admired by most Americans, MacArthur was the hero of the Philippines, the man of the hour who had become a living legend. Even though his army in the Philippines might be forced to surrender, he would still be able to continue the fight. MacArthur symbolized America's determination to defeat Japan.[2]

Many Americans sent telegrams to President Roosevelt congratulating and commending him for having ordered MacArthur to Australia:

> Your recent action in the appointment of General MacArthur as commander in chief of the Allied forces in the Pacific is the greatest inspirational force the Allied nations have received since our entry into the war and has been generally received with the greatest of encouragement for future successes of the United Nations. May I humbly congratulate you upon this great decision. . . .
>
> People seem to take a new lease on life. . . . Now let's give him the equipment for war necessary to get the job done promptly.

> We enthusiastically commend you on the appointment of General MacArthur. The American people will support you whole-heartedly on such decisions. With such inefficient apprentices as Ickes, Hopkins, Perkins and Jesse Jones replaced by some more MacArthurs we can win this war in forty-two. We have the resources. We are giving you our money and our boys. What more can we do? It's up to you Mr. President.[3]

Prominent Washington officials also voiced their approval. Hearing the news, Wendell L. Willkie, the Republican presidental candidate in 1940, exclaimed, "That's wonderful!" On February 14 Willkie had suggested that the President order MacArthur out of the Philippines and make him commander of all armies of the United States. Representative Joseph J. Mansfield of Texas said, "If we can keep him supplied with men and materials, he will sure raise hell with the Japs." "Delighted" with the news, Representative Joseph W. Martin, Jr., of Massachusetts, the House Republican leader, said: "His appointment will give great confidence to the American people." Senator Thomas Connelly, chairman of the Senate Foreign Relations Committee, asserted, "General MacArthur will give great leadership to the United Nations forces in Australia. It is fortunate for the entire civilized world that he is there. The democracies are thrilled and will respond gloriously to his generalship."[4]

At a press conference on March 20 President Roosevelt was asked the following question:

> Mr. President, there have been two stories from Australia, I believe, about General MacArthur's general plans for an offensive, or offensive action, and relief of the Philippines perhaps. Is there anything you could say that would not transgress the strategic bounds on that problem?

Roosevelt responded:

> No, except to say that of course we are doing everything that we possibly can. . . . Once more it's the little old lesson in geography. In getting anything from the United States out there it takes an awfully long time. And as you all know, in the whole world there is a very great shortage of shipping. Every effort is being made.
>
> I thought you were going to ask me about how he got out. Well, we had a few people in for supper the other night, and

one charming lady—this was the day that it had been announced that Douglas MacArthur had got there—and she said, "Oh, Mr. President, tell me how he got there." So I told her just how he got there, and she really believed it! [Laughter]

I told her that he had taken a rowboat, which was the only safe way, had disguised himself as a Filipino fisherman, and had passed right by—almost right alongside a lot of Jap warships, and destroyers, and submarines and everything else, and they had not suspected that it was Douglas MacArthur at all. He had rowed all the way down there [laughter]—right past the Japs. Perfectly simple. It was only a matter of 2,500 miles. And I think that several people at the table believed it. [Laughter]

Stephen T. Early, the President's press secretary, remarked audibly, "That's the 'rumor factory' for you!" "Rumor factory" was the appellation that Roosevelt had given the city of Washington when he was criticizing its residents for spreading false rumors about the war.[5]

But not everyone was happy about MacArthur's evacuation:

> We the parents of boys who fought so valiantly under General MacArthur protest his removal with all the sorrow and bitterness at our command, since he and his brave little army are the only Allied forces who have made a commendable showing in this war.
>
> We believe this to be a political move to bolster the morale of some of our Allied nations, and possibly intended to bolster the morale of our own people. In this we believe you have miserably failed.
>
> We believe our boys and those loyal Filipinos are entitled to some consideration. Nothing you could have done would have broken their morale and that of their parents at home so thoroughly as removal of General MacArthur from their direct command.[6]

In Australia at noon on March 18, after spending the night in a dilapidated hotel, the MacArthurs, Ah Cheu, Sutherland, Huff, and Morhouse boarded a small train at Alice Springs. The train moved south through the middle of the continent toward Adelaide on the southern coast.[7]

After MacArthur's train had departed from Alice Springs, Brigadier General Hurley climbed aboard a plane and returned to Brett's headquarters in Melbourne. Hurley was in a disturbed frame of mind when he talked with Brett about his recent conversations with MacArthur and Sutherland at Alice Springs. He told Brett that he sensed MacArthur was "antagonistic" toward him.

"Why?" Brett asked.

"I don't know," replied Hurley. "I couldn't put my finger on any particular reason, but the feeling is there all right."

"It couldn't be just the trouble we had getting him out of the Philippines," Brett commented.

Hurley shrugged. "You'll probably find out soon enough after MacArthur gets here. But there are other things to worry about. There has been too much publicity about General MacArthur. That may be all right in the States, where the people don't know anything more about war than what they read in the papers, but it's different here. After all, there are thousands of soldiers in Australia, who lived through Tobruk and the Western Desert, Singapore and Java. They won't look on the men who came out of the Philippines as supermen."

"It will be too bad if the publicity backfires" Brett agreed. "We'll need all we can get in the way of cooperation from the Australians."

In a moody fashion, Hurley replied, "MacArthur's staff won't help. To hear them tell it, they're the greatest heroes and finest soldiers the world ever saw. That won't sit well with a lot of people."[8]

On March 20 at the town of Burra, about fifty miles north of Adelaide, the train stopped. MacArthur's deputy chief of staff, Brigadier General Richard Marshall, who had just come from Melbourne, boarded with information: There were not sufficient forces in Australia to offer any hope of saving the beleaguered Philippine Islands. Marshall handed MacArthur a radiogram from General George C. Marshall in Washington that more than confirmed this tragic fact. At the same time MacArthur learned from his deputy chief of staff that Australia herself was in grave peril. He realized at last that the Philippines were doomed. It was a terrible blow.[9]

In Adelaide, MacArthur was asked by several reporters for a statement. After writing on the back of a used envelope, he spoke:

The President of the United States ordered me to break

through the Japanese lines and proceed from Corregidor to Australia for the purpose, as I understand it, of organizing the American offensive against Japan, a primary object of which is the relief of the Philippines. I came through and I shall return.[10]

On March 21 General MacArthur arrived in Melbourne at 9:57 A.M. aboard the *Adelaide Express*. It was a beautiful, sunny Saturday morning. MacArthur received a tumultuous welcome from a crowd of about 30,000 in the vicinity of Melbourne's Spencer Street Railroad Station. Fifty Victoria State constables with high black helmets held back the excited spectators from the station platform; 360 U.S. soldiers formed an honor guard. On hand to welcome MacArthur was a group of Australian military and civilian leaders headed by Lieutenant General A. H. Sturdee, Vice Admiral Sir Guy C. Royle, Air Chief Marshal Sir Charles Burnett, and Francis M. Forde, Australian deputy prime minister. Vice Admiral Herbert F. Leary and Lieutenant General George Brett were also waiting to greet the general.[11]

When MacArthur emerged from the train, wearing a khaki uniform and his famous gold-embroidered garrison cap, the crowd shouted and applauded. MacArthur shook hands and spoke to the assembled dignitaries. On behalf of Prime Minister John Curtin, Francis M. Forde told MacArthur that "he had the complete confidence of the Australian government and the people in the stern task ahead." Shaking hands with Air Chief Marshal Burnett, MacArthur recalled that they had met previously in Manila. While MacArthur was greeting the American general officers, he spotted Lieutenant Colonel Lloyd Lehrbas, a former war correspondent who was serving as a press liaison officer, and shouted, "Larry, you old rogue! I'll see you later."[12]

The hand-shaking over, MacArthur was escorted to a microphone fifteen feet from the train. Taking a paper from his pocket, he slowly read the following statement:

I am glad indeed to be in immediate cooperation with the Australian soldier. I know him well from World War days and admire him greatly. I have every confidence in the ultimate success of our joint cause; but success in modern war requires something more than courage and a willingness to die: it requires careful preparation. This means the furnishing of sufficient troops and sufficient material to meet the known strength of a potential enemy. No general can make something out of nothing. My success or failure will depend primarily upon the resources which the respective governments place at my disposal. My faith in them is complete. In any event I shall do my best. I shall keep the soldier's faith.[13]

MacArthur and Sutherland then strode toward a waiting limousine. Approaching them, Brett asked, "Would you care to have me accompany you, sir."

"No," replied MacArthur, entering the limousine.[14]

Brigadier General Stephen J. Chamberlin rode with MacArthur and Sutherland in near silence to the Menzies Hotel. Although arrangements had been made for a motorcycle escort to accompany MacArthur's limousine, the plans had miscarried and the escort had followed the car that took Mrs. MacArthur, Arthur, Ah Cheu, and Huff to the hotel before the general gave his prepared statement. Chamberlin apologized to MacArthur for the departure of the motorcycle escort with Mrs. MacArthur, but he replied, "That is as it should be."[15]

Later in the day Brett and Brigadier General Royce went to the Menzies Hotel to pay their respects to MacArthur. They waited rather uncomfortably for quite a while, then, irked and disappointed, departed when it became apparent that he did not wish to receive them. On the way out, Royce growled disgustedly, "What's the idea? You'd think we were orderlies. Or don't we belong to the right fraternity?"[16]

The same day MacArthur sent to the Army chief of staff in Washington the following radiogram:

In Australia I have found the Air Corps in a most disorganized condition and it is most essential as a fundamental and primary step that General Brett be relieved of his other duties in order properly to command and direct our air effort. His headquarters in Melbourne is too far from the scene of air activity to perform most effectively the functions of organization, training and combat. I propose to relieve him immediately of all duties pertaining to ground forces and to have him establish his headquarters in the forward area in some locality he may select. I propose to assign General Barnes to command U.S. Army ground forces.

Coordination with Australian forces for the present in accordance with your radio will be secured through cooperation. Task forces will be created to meet tactical requirements. Request immediate approval of this organization as a fundamental step in order to bring some order in to what is at present a most uncoordinated and ineffective system which is a menace to the safety of this country. I will later and in more detail inform you of glaring deficiencies and make recommendations for their rectification.[17]

9

The End of Resistance on Bataan

March 11–April 9, 1942

In this critical hour I have nothing but praise and admiration for the conduct of yourself and your troops in handling a desperate situation.[1]

—Stimson to Wainwright
April 8, 1942

On the night of March 11, Lieutenant Colonel Arnold D. Amoroso, who commanded the guns of antiaircraft Batteries B, C, D, E, and F of the Sixtieth Coast Artillery, sat on a bank overlooking Corregidor's South Channel with several of his officers. They listened to distant sounds from PT-boats passing through the channel into the South China Sea. Gradually the sounds grew faint and faded away. Since it was dark and hazy, the officers were unable to see the PT-boats or their wakes.[2]

Also on Corregidor was Staff Sergeant Robert K. Branch, who served in General Moore's Harbor Defense Headquarters. Branch had known for about a week that General MacArthur and other selected personnel would be leaving the fortress that night, but he could divulge the information to no one. Gratified that President Roosevelt had not allowed a great military leader to perish, thus further diminishing the prestige of the United States, Branch still felt despondent and envious of those who were leaving. With MacArthur's departure, he knew, "the eventual capitulation of the Philippines was inevitable."[3]

North of Corregidor on the embattled Bataan peninsula, Major John R. Pugh, Wainwright's senior aide, had learned from Wainwright of MacArthur's departure. In his diary, Pugh wrote:

History is in the making tonight as General MacArthur and his staff leave secretly for Australia where he will carry on in command of the Allied effort in the Southwest Pacific. General Wainwright is left in command of all forces in Luzon. The latter is not a command to be envied surrounded as we are. If we can just hold out until our troops can work from Australia to us our place in the hearts of all loyal Americans will be secure. . . .

Communications between the different Islands have become more difficult. Six of our eight blockade runners have been sunk by enemy action in the last ten days. The enemy on our front became more aggressive today launching an attack on the II Corps front. Estimated number of enemy include two companies and a battery of light artillery. There is no doubt it is preliminary testing of our strength. Numerous feelers will be made all along the line before they try any large-scale operation.

As I write from this dugout to the light of a Coleman lantern, I can't but believe our cause will win in the end. I don't know how we will hold, but know we will. I refer, of course, to the Philippine Island stand. There is no doubt in the mind of anyone here that the heathen Jap, whether he takes the Philippine Islands or not, is in for the licking of his life.[4]

Brigadier General Bradford G. Chynoweth was on the island of Cebu, about 350 miles southeast of Corregidor. In accordance with MacArthur's instructions, Chynoweth had arrived several days before from Panay to assume command of the Filipino and American troops on Cebu. He and his staff had serious problems with untrained troops, insufficient ammunition, no artillery or air force, and chaotic plans. They were desperately trying to prepare for guerrilla hit-and-run raids against the Japanese in the hills. Almost overwhelmed in their attempts to master the situation in Cebu, they simply did not have time to think about MacArthur's departure.[5]

On Bataan the following morning at nine o'clock, General Wainwright had the general officers of his I Corps assemble at his

"There are times when men have to die," said Secretary of War Henry L. Stimson in response to President Quezon's neutralization proposal. A highly respected former governor general of the Philippines, Stimson was deeply concerned with the future and integrity of the islands. *Copyright, Karsh of Ottawa.*

MacArthur conferring with Quezon outside his tent on Corregidor. Colorful and a clever politician, but highly emotional and suffering from tuberculosis, Quezon could not understand why the United States was unable to send help to his besieged Philippines. On February 8 he urged Roosevelt to reach an agreement with Japan for the neutralization of the Philippines. *Melville Jacoby, LIFE Magazine,* © *1942 by Time Inc.*

Vice President Sergio Osmena urged Quezon to withdraw his neutralization proposal. He told Quezon that if his neutralization plan was carried out, he would bring dishonor not only to himself but to the Philippines as well. *Courtesy of the MacArthur Memorial Bureau of Archives*

General MacArthur and his chief of staff, Major General Richard K. Sutherland, leaving the main entrance to Malinta Tunnel. Sutherland, sharp-tongued and ambitious, was MacArthur's chief confidant and alter ego. *Melville Jacoby, LIFE Magazine, © 1942 by Time Inc.*

MacArthur and Sutherland seated at their desks in the USAFFE Headquarters lateral of Malinta Tunnel. Ten days later, they left Corregidor for Australia. *U.S. Army photograph*

Rear Admiral Francis W. Rockwell became commander of U.S. Naval Forces in the Philippines following Admiral Hart's departure. In a conference on March 4, MacArthur told Rockwell that he had been ordered to proceed to Australia. *Official U.S. Navy photograph*

During the evening of March 11, MacArthur, his family, and part of his staff boarded PT-41 from Corregidor's North Dock. *U.S. Army photograph*

Major General George F. Moore, commander of the Harbor Defense of Manila Bay. Before leaving Corregidor, MacArthur told Moore "to hold Corregidor" until he returned. *U.S. Army photograph*

As commander of Motor Torpedo Boat Squadron Three, Lieutenant John D. Bulkeley led the famous "Expendables." Because of his faith in Bulkeley, MacArthur decided to use PT-boats for the first leg of his trip to Australia. *U.S. Army photograph*

Major General George H. Brett commanded the air force in Australia at the time of MacArthur's arrival. Blaming Brett for the delays in arranging air transportation from Mindanao to Australia, MacArthur was extremely cool to him when they met on March 21 at Melbourne's Spencer Street Railroad Station. *U.S. Army photograph*

Vice Admiral Herbert F. Leary, the senior naval authority in Australia, refused at first to lend Major General Brett four new B-17s in order to evacuate MacArthur, his family, and his staff from Mindanao to Australia. "I'd like to help you, Brett," said Leary, "but it is quite impossible. We need those planes, and can't spare them for a ferry job. . . ." Later, Leary changed his mind. *Official U. S. Navy photograph*

Brigadier General Patrick J. Hurley and MacArthur, followed by Sutherland, leaving Spencer Street Station. *United Press International*

MacArthur inspecting the small honor guard of American soldiers at Melbourne's Spencer Street Railroad Station. *United Press International*

MacArthur with Brigadier General Stephen J. Chamberlin. When MacArthur arrived in Melbourne, Chamberlin accompanied him and Sutherland to the Menzies Hotel. *U.S. Army photograph*

Mrs. MacArthur, young Arthur, and Ah Cheu, his Cantonese amah, following their arrival in Melbourne. *Courtesy of the MacArthur Memorial Bureau of Archives*

John J. McCloy, assistant secretary of war, recalled the meetings Stimson often had with his immediate staff at his home, Woodley, at the close of the day. The fate of the Philippines and the Filamerican Army was usually discussed. Stimson ''used to say like Queen Mary in respect of Calais, his heart was involved in the plight of the Philippines.'' *U.S. Army photograph*

After yielding to overwhelming force on April 9, the survivors of the Bataan army, undernourished and wracked with malaria and dysentery, began the long and terrible ''death march'' as prisoners of war. *Courtesy of the Japanese Defense Agency*

Lieutenant Colonel John R. Pugh, Wainwright's senior aide, was given an opportunity by Wainwright to leave Corregidor on May 3 aboard the submarine *Spearfish*. Refusing to leave, Pugh told Wainwright that it was his duty as an army officer to remain on Corregidor. *U. S. Army photograph*

Japanese assault boats from Bataan heading for Corregidor. *Courtesy of the Japanese Defense Agency*

San José Point and South Dock on Corregidor. In the afternoon of May 6, Lieutenant Colonel Pugh, Brigadier General Beebe, Major Lawrence, and Sergeant Carroll walked from Malinta Tunnel to South Dock, boarded Lieutenant William H. Baldwin's cabin cruiser—dispatch boat, and departed for Bataan and a conference with General Homma. *U.S. Army photograph*

On May 6 Wainwright confronted Homma on the porch of a cottage near Cabcaben on Bataan. *Left to right:* Lieutenant Colonel John R. Pugh, Lieutenant General Wainwright, Brigadier General Lewis L. Beebe, and Major Thomas Dooley. Across the table from Wainwright sat Homma. Although Wainwright wanted to surrender Corregidor and the fortified islands, Homma refused to accept because Wainwright would not order the surrender of the remaining American and Filipino forces in the Philippines. From K. Uno, *Corregidor: Isle of Delusion,* published in China in 1943

General Wainwright broadcasting the announcement of the surrender of Corregidor. From K. Uno, *Corregidor: Isle of Delusion,* published in China in 1943. *U.S. Army photograph*

Brigadier General Charles C. Drake, the quartermaster on Corregidor, took charge of surrendering Malinta Tunnel to the Japanese. When a Japanese Officer demanded that everyone leave the tunnel within ten minutes, Drake flared at the interpreter: "You tell him there are two thousand men in this tunnel alone. It will be imposible to get them out in that time." *U.S. Army photograph*

Grim, gaunt, and exhausted after a long ordeal, the occupants of Malinta Tunnel held up their hands and surrendered during the afternoon of May 6. *World Wide Photos*

MacArthur on Corregidor during February 1945, upon returning to the Philippines, with members of his staff who had gone by PT-boat with him from Corregidor to Mindanao in March 1942. *Left to right:* Brigadier General LeGrande A. Diller, Lieutenant Colonel Joseph R. McMicking, Major General Charles A. Willoughby, Major General Spencer B. Akin, Lieutenant General Richard K. Sutherland, General MacArthur, Major General Richard J. Marshall, Major General Hugh J. Casey, Colonel Sidney L. Huff, and Major General William F. Marquat. At the far right is an unidentified GI. *Courtesy of the MacArthur Memorial Bureau of Archives*

headquarters. Informing them of MacArthur's departure, Wainwright cautioned them to keep the information confidential. He then told them about the various changes in the command structure. In accordance with MacArthur's instructions, Wainwright was assuming command of all Army forces in Luzon. General Albert M. Jones, in command of the Fifty-first Division, would take command of the I Corps and would turn over the command of the Fifty-first to his chief of staff, Colonel Stuart C. MacDonald.[6]

On Corregidor at 11:00 A.M. Major General George F. Moore called a conference of his regimental commanders and told them of General MacArthur's departure. MacArthur had first been ordered to leave three weeks before without his family or staff, Moore said, and had "fought against leaving at all, but finally had to go or disobey orders." Among the officers present was Colonel Paul D. Bunker. Knowing that MacArthur had embarked on a "dangerous trip," Bunker wrote in his diary, "I hope he makes it. . . . Now to convince our men that he has not deserted, but has gone into a job where he can do something real toward helping us! It would be bad for our men's morale if they put the wrong interpretation on his leaving."[7]

During March 12 the knowledge of MacArthur's evacuation, supposedly restricted to the higher command echelons, gradually filtered down to the troops on Bataan and Corregidor. Their reactions were mixed. When Brigadier General Clyde A. Selleck heard the news from his close friend, Brigadier General Allan C. McBride, they discussed MacArthur's chances of reaching Australia. Damning MacArthur for leaving them in such a "mess," Selleck believed that MacArthur was recklessly risking his life and the life of his wife and son "ostensibly to comply with orders."[8] When Lieutenant Colonel Roscoe Bonham, who commanded the Engineering Supply Service for the entire USAFFE command, and Chief Petty Officer Forrest G. Hogg first learned about it on Corregidor they could only think of a man abandoning a sinking ship.[9] Brigadier General Arnold J. Funk and Major Charles E. N. Howard, however, felt that MacArthur could do more good in Australia than sitting in Corregidor's Malinta Tunnel.[10]

Most of the officers and men serving in the Philippines accepted MacArthur's departure stoically, knowing that the services of a brilliant military leader would be preserved and used to further the Allied global war effort. But most of them also realized that they

were now definitely out on a limb, and that no significant help would
be coming from the United States. The general's evacuation, a
definite blow to their morale, also strengthened their resolve to
keep the flag flying on Corregidor and Bataan to the end.[11]

On March 14 Lieutenant Malcolm M. Champlin, who had been
acting as Wainwright's naval liaison aide, received a phone call at
Wainwright's Bataan headquarters from Captain Kenneth M. Hoeffel. Telling Champlin to pack his bags, Hoeffel ordered him to report
to Corregidor by six o'clock. Bewildered about being ordered to
Corregidor, Champlin asked to speak with Captain Ray. "He is not
available," replied Hoeffel. "You are to come down at once."

Champlin packed his few belongings into a musette bag, his mind
full of questions. Was he going to be relieved? Had he been deficient
in his work? Finally he walked over to Wainwright's trailer and told
Wainwright that he had just received instructions from Captain
Hoeffel to report to Corregidor. Champlin asked Wainwright if this
was in accord with his desires.

"Yes, it is, Champ," Wainwright said. "I might as well tell you
something now which Admiral Rockwell told me . . . when I went
to Corregidor to see General MacArthur. You are to leave for
Australia tonight. General MacArthur has been ordered out and so
has Admiral Rockwell. They planned to leave by Motor Torpedo
Boat and I assume that, by now, that plan has been successfully
carried out.

"Champ," Wainwright continued, "You are still Admiral Rockwell's aide and I only borrowed you for a short period. You are to
carry out your orders and I wish you luck." He paused, then added,
"Please take a letter which I have here and mail it for me in Australia." They shook hands in parting and Champlin, through tears,
could see a slow, half-amused smile appear on Wainwright's face.[12]

The bony horses of the Twenty-sixth Cavalry had to be shot and
butchered for food. One afternoon, a captain of the Twenty-sixth had
approached Wainwright and informed him that the supply of fodder
for the horses was almost gone. Among the sixty or seventy cavalry
horses and pack animals on Bataan was Wainwright's mount, a prize
jumper named Little Boy. The winner of a series of ribbons in com-
petition in the United States, he had been given to Wainwright by
Major Pugh's wife. Wainwright loved horses, and occasionally he
would slip back behind the front, where the horses were kept, to
stroke the beautiful jumper and admire the smoothness of its coat.

"Yes, Captain," Wainwright had said, "I knew that this was coming. We have a lot of men here who are also short of food and horse meat is not so bad." Pausing a moment and looking out toward the South China Sea, he had resumed, "Captain, you will begin killing the horses at once. Little Boy is the horse you will kill first." Wainwright had then turned around and slowly walked back to his trailer, his eyes filled with tears.[13]

Wainwright was born August 23, 1883, and was graduated from the U.S. Military Academy in 1906. He had served with the First Cavalry in Texas from 1906 to 1908, had participated in an expedition against the Moros in the Philippines from 1909 to 1910, and had served on the General Staff of the Eighty-second Division at Toul, St. Mihiel, and Meuse-Argonne during World War I. Commissioned a brigadier general in 1938, he was ordered to the Philippines in October 1940 to take command of the I Corps, Northern Luzon Force.

Wainwright was tall, with sloping shoulders and a very thin, almost gaunt, face. His eyes were "quick, piercing, and in moments of humor and gladness, there was an unmistakable twinkle in them." His movements were "slow but calculated." Calm and gentle in demeanor, fearless and skillful as a fighter, he was "much beloved by all his soldier and subordinates, who affectionately referred to him as 'Skinny.'"[14]

Under the mistaken impression that MacArthur had left Wainwright in command of all forces in the Philippines, on March 17 General Marshall had the following message dispatched to Wainwright on Corregidor:

General MacArthur has arrived in Australia and has been assigned to supreme command. The president and the War Department felt justified in agreeing to his new assignment because of confidence in your leadership and the demonstrated fighting morale of your army. The prestige of the white man in the Orient, particularly in China, has rested on the gallantry and determination of the fight in Bataan and the loyalty of the Filipino soldier and people. Your task is therefore one of vast importance and, we recognize, of exceeding difficulty. We hope to relieve pressure on you by a series of determined naval and air attacks against the Japanese left flank.

I assume that you are fully acquainted with the various measures that have been instituted for running the blockade and keeping our forces partially supplied with critical items. In an effort to provide you with some air assistance we are placing one or two crated P-40s on each blockade runner, including six converted destroyers of which the leading vessels are now enroute from the United States via Hawaii. Any questions on these and similar matters will be promptly answered.

The area of General MacArthur's responsibility extends northward to include the Philippines and consequently you remain under his supervisory control. Because of the isolation of your command you are instructed to maintain direct communication with the War Department and submit daily reports as has been the practice in the past. These instructions will not be construed as interference with your subordination to General MacArthur. A paraphrase copy of this radiogram is being repeated to him. Acknowledge.[15]

Wainwright was not on Corregidor to receive or to acknowledge the message, nor had he been left in complete command of all forces in the Philippines by MacArthur. It had been MacArthur's intention to exercise complete command from Australia over all forces in the Philippines through a deputy chief of staff, Brigadier General Lewis C. Beebe, on Corregidor. Wainwright's command was to include only the units on Luzon.

On March 19 Colonel Bunker wrote in his diary: "Heard yesterday that MacArthur had been placed in Supreme Command in the Far East: Army, Air Corps, even Navy! Three rousing cheers! Maybe we'll get somewhere now!"[16] The same day General Beebe received from the War Department several messages addressed to General Wainwright expressing confidence in his leadership and notifying him of a promotion to lieutenant general by the Senate. Anxious and perplexed, Beebe radioed MacArthur, informed him of the confused situation, and requested that he explain to the War Department the command structure that had been established in the Philippines prior to his departure.[17]

MacArthur promptly informed Marshall of the subdivided command. He justified it on "special problems involved with the intangible situation in the Philippines" and said he considered the command changes to be "most advantageous."[18] Marshall, however, considered a subdivided command to be controlled by MacArthur approximately four thousand miles away in Melbourne "an impractical proposition."

In a memorandum to Roosevelt, Marshall argued that the subdivided command would have "a very depressing effect on the morale of General Wainwright while he was waging the fight on Bataan." A further complication, Marshall pointed out, was that as supreme commander of forces in the Southwest Pacific, MacArthur did not have the authority, because of previous agreements entered into by the United States with the British and Dutch governments concerning the establishment of combined commands, to exercise direct command over a national force. He reminded Roosevelt that this proviso had originally been insisted upon by them to avoid the "national tendency" by which General Wavell might become too involved "personally in the affairs of Singapore and Burma, and [neglect] the problems of the Netherlands East Indies and the Philippines."

Roosevelt agreed with Marshall and authorized him to notify MacArthur that Wainwright would remain in command of all U.S. forces in the Philippines. MacArthur replied that he thoroughly understood the difficulties inherent in his subdivided command for the Philippines. He could accommodate himself to any command arrangement for the Philippines that the War Department desired, MacArthur said; he was heartily in accord with Wainwright's promotion to lieutenant general and his assignment to the Philippine command was "appropriate."[19]

In the meantime, Beebe on Corregidor had notified Wainwright that he had been promoted to lieutenant general and had been placed in command of all forces in the Philippines by the War Department. On the morning of March 21, Wainwright turned over to Major General Edward P. King his Bataan command, along with his battered trailer, and departed for Corregidor with his three aides. Earlier he had remarked to them, "Lee marched on Gettysburg with less men than I have here. We're not licked by a damn sight."[20]

About 8:00 A.M. on March 21 at the Mariveles pier, Wainwright and his three aides climbed aboard the cabin cruiser dispatch boat commanded by Lieutenant William H. Baldwin. Baldwin noticed that Wainwright was wearing his khaki uniform with two white stars embroidered on each shoulder along with a third star cut from tin and pinned on each shoulder. Baldwin congratulated him, but Wainwright "made same wry remark indicating that he felt it was a hollow promotion."[21]

General Beebe met Wainwright on Corregidor's North Dock. Escorting Wainwright into the headquarters lateral of Malinta Tunnel, Beebe showed him the War Department order placing him in command of all U.S. forces in the Philippines.[22]

The following morning Major General Moore took Wainwright on an inspection tour of Corregidor's defenses. They had reached Battery Monja, on the South Shore Road, when an air raid began. Wainwright was reluctant to use an available hillside shelter but a moment later bombs started exploding just outside, "causing a big landslide and wrecking the battery kitchen. It had been a narrow escape." During a lull in the bombing, the two generals were hurriedly driven back to Malinta Tunnel. Right after they left the car and entered the tunnel "another load of bombs came down, one which demolished the car they had vacated."

"My Gosh!" exclaimed Wainwright. "On Bataan you can move around a little, but here on Corregidor you're right on the bull's eye."[23]

On March 23 Secretary of War Stimson participated in a War Council Meeting and later entered in his diary:

> Marshall told us of his troubles in getting the southwestern Pacific command organized. MacArthur in a pretty complete disregard of everything except his own personal interests had taken his entire staff away with him from Bataan, leaving Wainwright with the job of building up a new staff. In addition to that, MacArthur had divided the Philippines into four separate departments, all of which were to report to him and were to be governed by him in Australia. This was in entire violation of all sensible policy and also in violation of the rules we had adopted when we set up the ABDA area. We discovered it from the fact that, although we last week had promoted Wainwright to be a lieutenant general, we could not hear from him and couldn't get in touch with him. During my absence in Highhold, however, Marshall received a report from MacArthur telling what he had done and he at once responded by notifying MacArthur of the

plan which we had laid out from Washington of having Wainwright command locally the American forces in the Philippines and thus assimilating Wainwright's command to the commands of the other nations such as Australia which would all act under the supreme strategic command of Mac-Arthur in the southwest Pacific.[24]

On Thursday, March 26, the U.S. minister to Australia, Nelson T. Johnson, presented the Congressional Medal of Honor to General MacArthur. The citation, written by General George C. Marshall, read:

> Douglas MacArthur, General, United States Army, commanding, United States Army forces in the Far East. For conspicuous leadership in preparing the Philippine Islands to resist conquest, for gallantry and intrepidity above and beyond the call of duty in action against invading Japanese forces, and for the heroic conduct of defensive and offensive operations on the Bataan Peninsula. He mobilized, trained, and led an army which has received world acclaim for its gallant defense against a tremendous superiority of enemy forces in men and arms. His utter disregard of personal danger under heavy fire and aerial bombardment, his calm judgment in each crisis, inspired his troops, galvanized the spirit of resistance of the Filipino people and confirmed the faith of the American people in their armed forces.

In reply to the Army chief of staff, MacArthur stated:

> Please express to the President and to the Secretary of War, and accept for yourself, my sincere thanks and appreciation for the Medal of Honor. I feel that this award is intended not so much for me personally as it is a recognition of the indomitable courage of the gallant army which it was my high honor to command. As a symbol of their heroism it fills me with gratification and solemn pride.[25]

Having received a paraphrased copy of the February 9 order Roosevelt had submitted to MacArthur (pp. 101–4), on March 26 Wainwright sent a reply to the president:

> I fully understand your instructions directing me to resist as long as it is humanly possible to do so and that our continued

resistance eclipses in importance all other obligations in the Philippines. I further understand the necessity of maintaining the unbroken line of opposition which has been cemented by the United States in resisting those nations which are attempting to destroy the liberty and freedom of governments and of peoples.

Your Excellency may rest assured that no weakness either in fact or in spirit will be shown here. The Filipino soldier has been and continues to be indoctrinated with American determination and the will to win.

While fully realizing the desperate conditions that are fast developing here because of shortage of supplies due to the effectiveness of the hostile blockade, I pledge myself to you to keep our flag flying in the Philippines as long as an American soldier or an ounce of food and a round of ammunition remains.[26]

On March 27 Wainwright reported to MacArthur:

Rations for troops on Bataan have been reduced to approximately one thousand calories which, according to the surgeon, is barely sufficient to sustain life without physical activity. I am holding a ration reserve for Fort Mills, as directed by you, to subsist troops there to June 1. This is of the utmost importance in view of the President's instructions to you of February ninth which have been repeated to me by Marshall. I am trying to run in some motor launches of about one hundred tons capacity each from Cebu but have no assurance that this venture will be successful. I am still hoping that you will be able to send two converted destroyers from Australia and that similar vessels from the states will arrive early in April.

However, I feel that further steps should be taken to move the large stocks of subsistence which are available in Cebu. . . . I urgently recommend that one squadron of B-17 bombers be dispatched to Del Monte at the earliest practicable date with a view to their employment against hostile destroyers in Visayan waters and against the hostile naval base in Subic Bay. These ships operating in conjunction with three new P-40s now being assembled in Mindanao, would probably result in breaking the blockade at least to the point where our supplies could be moved. As a last resort ten B-17 bombers could, by making a round trip each night, deliver a few days reduced ration for Bataan troops.

In the light of the obligation that the United States has assumed with reference to the Philippines, I deem it to be of paramount importance to save Filipino troops from starvation or surrender if humanly possible to do so. With ample food and ammunition we can hold the enemy, in his present position, I believe, indefinitely.[27]

The same day Wainwright received a radiogram from Marshall:

I am sending orders today to Australia to send quinine by plane to Mindanao in the hope that your new P-40 planes there, or your speedboats, can carry to Bataan a sufficient temporary supply. Plans are under way for later delivery by submarine of more substantial quantities of your critical medical requirements, directly to Corregidor. Do you think it possible for the converted sixteen knot cargo carrying destroyers now enroute across the Pacific to reach Manila Bay and unload there or should they aim at some other port in the Islands?

Naval offensives against the Japanese flank are being attempted to relieve pressure on you by inducing enemy to again withdraw his air and naval shipping from that region.

Senate and House military affairs committees have recommended a bill to raise Filipino pay to American rates.

The gallantry of your troops has become a national symbol of determination to destroy the enemy's military power. I want you to feel that the president, the secretary of war, and I understand the immense difficulties of your situation. We realize how increasingly difficult your task has become. With the renewed bombardments of Corregidor the eyes of the entire country have focused on the ordeal through which you and your men are passing. My hourly concern is what can we do to help you. Radio me with complete frankness your desires and any information or comments you wish me to have. Our great desire is to employ every possible means to assist and strengthen you.[28]

On March 28, Wainwright sent the following report to Marshall:

. . . Information received this morning indicates a shipment of quinine arrived in Mindanao by plane on March 26. The quantity received is not sufficient to warrant use in prophylactic doses.

I believe it is necessary for converted sixteen knot cargo carrying destroyers now enroute to come direct to Manila Bay rather than to some other port in the Philippines. It will probably be as easy for these destroyers to reach Manila Bay as any other port. We now have large quantities of supplies on Cebu but the enemy blockade is successfully preventing the movement of these supplies to Corregidor. Request has been made on Australia to send a squadron of bombers with a view to their operating versus hostile destroyers in Visayan waters as well as versus the Japanese naval base in Subic Bay. If the blockade could be broken for a day, we could move several thousand tons of badly needed subsistence from Cebu. Our most pressing need is subsistence as only a sufficient quantity remains on hand in Bataan to feed the troops there until April 15 at about ⅓ rations which is poorly balanced and very deficient in vitamins.

As conditions now exist we can continue to hold our position indefinitely if the necessary subsistence, ammo and other supplies can be provided. . . . To be utterly frank, if additional supplies are not received for Bataan by April 15 the troops there will be starved into submission. We are now slaughtering carabao and horses and will be forced to slaughter pack mules in ten days. Holding in reserve on Corregidor sufficient stocks of subsistence to supply the garrison of the Harbor Defense until June 1. All attempts to supply Bataan with subsistence from Cebu during last three weeks have failed.[29]

Marshall subsequently sent a paraphrased copy of Wainwright's report to MacArthur, commenting that the first cargo vessel en route to Manila Bay from the United States, even if it succeeded in breaking through the Japanese naval blockade, would not arrive there before April 15. He concluded by requesting MacArthur's recommendations.[30]

On March 29, Major General Sutherland, who considered himself an air tactician, walked into General Brett's office and informed him that General MacArthur wanted a bombing mission dispatched to the Philippines. Brett believed the Philippines were already lost and vehemently opposed sending a bombing mission there. He told Sutherland that his pilots, who were flying worn-out planes, were exhausted and had all they could do to prevent the Japanese from capturing Port Moresby.

"General MacArthur," Sutherland replied sharply, "promised the Filipino people he would be back. If we send a bombing mission it will prove they have not been forgotten." The mission would have doubtful results, Brett countered; the bombers would suffer heavy losses from Japanese fighters stationed throughout the islands.

"The air strips in Mindanao are perfectly camouflaged," Sutherland said impatiently. "They will never find our bombers." When Brett insisted that the Japanese fighters would gang up against the bombers like "flies around a fruit cake," MacArthur's exasperated chief of staff snapped, in a voice as tight as wire, "General Mac-

Arthur wants the mission accomplished!" Not wishing to push the issue any further, Brett told Sutherland he would authorize the bombing mission.[31]

On March 30, Wainwright sent another urgent message to Marshall:

> Manila Bay approaches effectively blockaded by enemy sur-face vessels preventing entrance of our supply vessels from Southern Islands. Food, anti-aircraft ammunition with mechanical fuse, fuel oil and gasoline situation requires emergency measures. Request assignment of at least two submarines adaptable to cargo carrying operations (Argonaut or Narwhal class) to bring the above supplies from Hawaii and remain in this area to bring in food and fuel from Southern Islands. I make this seemingly ex-travagant request in view of your invitation to tell you frankly what my requirements are.
>
> When may I expect the six converted destroyers carrying sup-plies from the States to arrive off the Northern Coast of Luzon? I will endeavor to provide aerial protection as far to sea as is possible.
>
> I urgently recommend that orders be sent from Washington diverting three submarines now operating in adjacent waters from present missions to the task of breaking blockade in Philippine waters and then to transport urgently needed supplies from Cebu. I have made this same request of MacArthur but do not know that he will feel that he can spare these submarines from their present missions, which seems to be the attack of enemy shipping in gen-eral, in view of pressure that will undoubtedly be brought on him by United Nations and navy representatives to use his available means for the good of the whole rather than for the Philippines in particular.[32]

The same day Wainwright received the following radiogram from MacArthur:

> I understand fully the complete and compelling necessity for airplane reinforcement. I have here, however, only a handful of planes. Twelve large bombers are all that are now operating. The pursuits are relatively almost as weak and there is no way at the moment that I can fly them to you. I intend to operate the bombers as far as possible in the Philippines with a view to re-lieving pressure on you. I will do everything possible to support arrival of blockade runners.[33]

On April 1, MacArthur radioed Marshall his views and recommendations with respect to the critical situation in the Philippines:

In order to relieve the blockade pressure in an endeavor to permit passage of supplies from Cebu to Corregidor, I prepared prior to my departure delayed plans for an air attack of B-17 bombers from here to Mindanao and thence to mission destination. I am now preparing its prompt execution. This effort is a critical one due to the lack of air force available here. I have only twelve serviceable B-17s, many of which are approaching exhaustion. I believe there is a fair hope for blockade runners from the United States to reach destination if they approach by the route north of Luzon. Their speed will give them an excellent chance to get through as the enemy is concentrating his patrols on the routes from Visayan waters and the entrance to Manila Bay is not yet mined by the enemy. I believe also that the supplies on Bataan will last beyond the date of April 15th. I am in addition diverting submarines sufficient for the purpose to ferry food supplies from the southern Philippine Islands to Corregidor. The supply should be ample for maintenance for an indefinite time. When I left on March 11th it was my estimate that serious shortage would not develop at the earliest before May 1st, allowing sufficient time for arrival of blockade runners from the United States. It is of course possible that with my departure the rigor of application of conservation may have relaxed.

I am utterly opposed, under any circumstances or conditions, to the ultimate capitulation of this command as visualized in General Wainwright's radio [of March 28]. If it is to be destroyed it should be upon the actual field of battle taking full toll from the enemy. To this end I had long ago prepared a comprehensive plan to endeavor to cut a way out if food or ammunition failed. This plan contemplated an ostentatious artillery preparation on the left by the I Corps as a feint and a sudden surprise attack on the right by the II Corps. This movement to be made in conjunction with the full tank strength and with the maximum artillery concentration with heavy guns run forward under cover of darkness the night before so that their fire would reach and cover an infantry advance as far as possible toward the Dinaluphan-Olongapo Road; this road to be seized and the II Corps to thrust with all speed and force due west taking the enemy's Subic Bay positions in reverse simultaneously with a frontal attack by the I Corps. If successful, the supplies seized at this base might well rectify the situation. This would permit them to operate in central Luzon where food supplies could be obtained and where they could still protect Bataan and the northern approaches to Corregidor. If the movement is not successful and our forces [are] defeated many increments thereof after inflicting important losses upon the enemy could escape through the Zambales Mountains and continue guerrilla warfare in conjunction with forces now operating in the north. Simultaneously aggressive action within their capabilities would be launched by both the Visayan force and the Mindanao force. I had not informed General Wainwright of this plan as I feared it might tend to shake his morale and determination. I shall however, in view of his radio to you, inform him thereof in the near future. I would be very glad if you believe it advisable to attempt myself to rejoin this command temporarily and take charge of this movement.

The pressure on this situation could be immeasurably relieved if a naval task force with its own air protection could make some kind of threat in that general direction. The long series of disasters in the Pacific theatre can be traced basically to one cause: the unopposed control of the sea lanes by the Japanese. Until this condition is remedied these disasters will continue. Line of communications control is fundamental either on land or sea. Enemy control has been complete up to the present time. I know how desperately you are pressed for reinforcements and supplies in all areas and I do not intend to harass you by requisitions that cannot be accomplished. It would, however, tend to relieve the dangers here if without delay a small force of say nine B-17 bombers could immediately be made available instead of awaiting the normal flow as now anticipated. . . .

I have complete and instantaneous communication with General Wainwright and all the forces in the Philippine Islands and I believe that greater rapidity of action and more complete coordination of command can be achieved if he routes his communications except for routine administration matters through my headquarters rather than direct to the War Department and essentially in his operations reports for he not only reports direct to you but also paraphrases them to me. I have no doubt that not only efficiency but speed will be accomplished if a clear channel of communications [can] be established from Wainwright to MacArthur to Washington.[34]

Marshall notified MacArthur on April 2 that he should not return to the Philippines; that all operations in the Philippines, although they would be under his strategic supervision, would be conducted by Wainwright; and that Wainwright would continue to dispatch all routine and daily operational reports direct to the War Department. Marshall also said that B-17 bombers would be dispatched to Australia immediately for the Philippine bombing mission.[35]

On April 4 MacArthur received Wainwright's plan for the bomber strike against Japanese blockade vessels and airfields in the Philippines. According to his plan, the bombers, based at Del Monte in Mindanao, would first attack Japanese airfields on Luzon, then return to Del Monte, refuel, and reload with bombs, and finally launch a second strike against Japanese blockade vessels in Visayan waters and at Subic Bay. Although Wainwright believed both missions could be accomplished in one day, he recommended to MacArthur that the bombers be allowed to remain in the Philippines for two more days in order to launch additional air strikes against the Japanese. Ships loaded with food, gasoline, and fuel oil would sail from Cebu and Iloilo for Bataan on the first day of the air strike, and would be given protection en route by three P-40s from Bataan. Wainwright believed the Japanese would be completely taken by surprise, the blockade would be temporarily interrupted, and sufficient substance would be moved from Cebu to supply the army on Bataan for another month. MacArthur reviewed Wainwright's plan and thought it was "excellent." He promptly notified Wainwright that bombers were being prepared for the mission, which would be executed the following week.[36]

The same day MacArthur dispatched a second radiogram to Wainwright explaining in detail the operational plan he had submitted to Marshall on April 1. This desperate, last-resort plan of attack was only to be implemented, MacArthur informed Wainwright, when the army's food supplies were completely exhausted. "Under no conditions," he stated emphatically, "should this command be surrendered." Earlier the War Department had answered MacArthur concerning his plan, "We fully concur that any action is preferable to capitulation. Should it become necessary for you to direct a last resort attack with the objectives you outlined, we feel sure that Wainwright and his forces will give a good account of themselves."[37]

It was April 5 on Corregidor when General Wainwright and his aide, Major Thomas Dooley, boarded a crash boat and returned to Cabcaben on the southeastern tip of Bataan. For several days the Japanese had been pounding and exerting heavy pressure against the left flank of General Parker's II Corps in an effort to break through their front. Having received MacArthur's "no surrender" order containing the counterattack operational plan, Wainwright wanted to make a firsthand assessment of the situation on both the I and II Corps fronts.

Wainwright went first to General King's headquarters. Although King wanted to accompany Wainwright to Parker's headquarters south of Limay, Wainwright thought King should remain at his command post and watch the developments affecting the I and II Corps.[38]

Leaving King, Wainwright was driven hurriedly in a jeep by Major Dooley to Parker's headquarters. Parker and his chief of staff, Colonel Charles L. Steel, had been so ill that Parker had been forced to request the services of Brigadier General Maxon S. Lough's chief of staff, Colonel Harrison C. Browne. Before conferring with Parker, Wainwright stopped to talk to Browne, who was leaving to return to Lough's headquarters. Wainwright told Browne that he planned to order the I Corps under General Jones to counterattack in order to relieve the enemy's pressure on the II Corps. Browne believed it was the "best solution to restore the situation."[39]

Parker talked to Wainwright about plans for a counterattack that would push back the Japanese and restore the ground that had been lost by Brigadier General Vincente Lim's Forty-first Division. Although Wainwright approved Parker's counterattack plans, he doubtedly seriously that they would be successful against the advancing Japanese.[40]

After returning to Corregidor, Wainwright radioed MacArthur:

> The operation suggested in your [radiogram of April 4] has been under consideration by me for some time and I had about decided to adopt it if and when supplies become exhausted. The troops have been on half rations for three months and are now on less than that amount which results in much loss of physical vigor and sickness. Nevertheless, before allowing a capitulation the operation you suggest will be adopted. I hope, however, that supplies will arrive in good time. Enemy has been very active on front of II Corps for the past two days with resultant loss of a little ground on our part. Situation still serious if not alarming. I counterattack tomorrow.[41]

The following day the II Corps launched a counterattack. It was quickly repulsed by the Japanese, who continued their offensive with greater intensity and fury against Parker's II Corps. Heavy

artillery fire was concentrated against the Corps' left flank while
enemy dive bombers bombed and strafed the front lines and rear
areas. Wainwright reported to MacArthur that between March 24
and April 5, the Japanese had launched "sixty-five separate and
distinct bombing attacks" against the area of the II Corps front. The
continued air attacks were damaging the morale of his troops,
Wainwright said, urging MacArthur to dispatch the bombers as
soon as possible from Australia.[42]

During the morning of April 7, Brigadier General Funk, General
King's chief of staff, walked into Malinta Tunnel and headed for
Wainwright's headquarters lateral. Previously Wainwright had
phoned King and told him to issue counterattack orders to General
Jones's I Corps. Because Funk was more familiar with the deteriorating frontline conditions caused by the Japanese breakthrough, he
was sent by King to see Wainwright and to "explain the military
situation without reservations."

With General Wainwright and his chief of staff, General Beebe,
Funk discussed the Japanese breakthrough in the II Corps front, and
stated that supplies were exhausted, including food and ammunition.
They talked particularly about the almost nonexistent medical sup-
lies, and the fact that the two hospital stations were overflowing with
sick and wounded men. Of the frontline troops approximately 80
percent had malaria, 35 percent beriberi, and 75 percent dysentry.
All were badly undernourished as a result of daily rations consisting
of between 3 and 5 ounces of rice and about 1½ ounces of meat.

On his desk, directly in front of Wainwright, was MacArthur's
operational plan for a counterattack and the "no surrender" order
of April 4. Wainwright had also received instructions from Roosevelt
late in March prohibiting surrender. Wainwright believed King had
sent Funk to obtain his approval for a capitulation, but he could
not give his consent. Instead he ordered Funk to tell King that
"surrender was out of the question," and that he should order Jones
to attack due east with his I Crops and outflank the advancing
Japanese forces on the east side of Bataan. After a moment, with
tears in his eyes, Funk replied, "General, you know, of course, what
the situation is over there. You know what the outcome will be."

"I do," Wainwright answered, shaking Funk's hand. "I understand the situation. God help you all over there. I have done all I
can." Tired, worried, and downcast, Funk turned and walked out
of the headquarters lateral.[43]

Returning to Bataan, Funk informed King of Wainwright's instructions. Both officers surmised "that General Wainwright's orders were from General MacArthur's headquarters in Australia." Although King discussed Wainwright's instructions with Jones, they were never implemented. As a result of the physical and logistical condition of the troops, a counterattack could not be tactically launched. Instead, Jones ordered a withdrawal southward to the Binuangan River.[44]

That night Wainwright informed MacArthur that fierce fighting had been going on throughout the day; that the Japanese, reinforced with fresh reserves, accompanied by heavy artillery fire, tanks, and dive bombers, had been able to drive a wedge approximately 7,000 yards deep into the main front line of the II Corps; that the Twenty-first, Thirty-first, and Forty-first divisions had been dispersed; that Mount Samat, which separated the I and II Corps and was heavily fortified with artillery, had been enveloped by the enemy; and that Base Hospital No. 1 had been bombed intentionally by the Japanese on three successive flights. Reporting that he had been forced to use all of the Philippine divisions and other available reserves in an attempt to halt the advance, Wainwright said that the I Corps would attack to the east in an effort to strike the Japanese right flank and restore the original front line.[45]

After reading Wainwright's report, MacArthur sent the following message to the War Department:

> It is apparent to me that the enemy has driven a wedge between the I and II Corps and is still advancing. In view of my intimate knowledge of the situation there I regard the situation as extremely critical and feel you should anticipate the possibility of disaster there very shortly.[46]

In Washington on the morning of April 7, Stimson reviewed with Major General Joseph T. McNarney the cables that had come into the War Department during the night. McNarney was acting chief of staff for General Marshall, who was on his way to London for a series of conferences with the British concerning the buildup of U.S. forces and supplies in England for a cross-channel attack in France. In his diary, Stimson wrote:

> The situation on Corregidor is getting desperate. We canvassed carefully every possible way that anyone could think of to get supplies there but we have been blocked. Appar-

ently the attack on the blockading fleet has not materialized
and the great majority of the vessels we have sent during the
past month or six weeks have been sunk. Some three submarines are on their way but each of them can carry only
about two days' provisions. A large ship is on its way from
Hawaii but chances of getting through are desperate. The
garrison is much larger than any of us had expected. We
had thought it was in the neighborhood of 40,000 men. Instead of that there are nearly 90,000 men there. That adds to
the difficulty and complexity. MacArthur kept his figures
secret from the very beginning and everyone was astonished
when Wainwright revealed the present roster.[47]

On April 8 the Japanese attack on Bataan continued, growing in
momentum and ferocity. The enemy poured through the gap in the
II Corps front like a spring flood. The II Corps was quickly dis-
integrating. During the day, General King informed Wainwright
that if he intended to withdraw any troops from Bataan, the withdrawal should take place that night or else it would be too late.
Wanting three battalions of the Forty-fifth Infantry Regiment (PS)
to strengthen the defense of Corregidor and the brave nurses on
Bataan, Wainwright sent his G-2, Colonel Nicoll F. Galbraith, and
G-3, Colonel Constant L. Irwin, to General King's headquarters to
make the arrangements. Although King said nothing to Galbraith
or Irwin about intending to capitulate, he did leave the two officers
with the impression that he believed a surrender decision "might be
forced upon him."[48]

During the day Wainwright sent the following recommendation to
MacArthur and asked that he transmit it to the War Department:

> I request that radio broadcasting stations and the press in the
> United States be urged unobtrusively to avoid inviting further
> Japanese action against the Philippines by inflammatory remarks
> directed against the failure of Japanese leaders to take the
> islands. We are doing our utmost to hold our own and we feel we
> are not in a position to urge the enemy to put more power against
> us by such misdirected publicity.[49]

At 4:00 P.M. on the eighth Wainwright sent for Colonel Carlos
Romulo. When Romulo walked into the hot, stuffy headquarters
lateral, the general was sitting at his table tieless and with his collar
open. As Romulo saluted, Wainwright stood up, pushed aside the

reports piled in front of him, and said, "Colonel Romulo, I'm ordering you out of Corregidor. Bataan is hopeless." When Romulo
started to protest, Wainwright raised his hand and went on, "You're
under orders. At seven tonight take the little launch to Bataan. Go
to the Bataan airfield. From there you will take off for Mindanao,
where you will report to General Roxas and General Sharp. Here
are your secret orders." Wainwright was abrupt and official as he
handed the envelope to Romulo.

"Goodbye, sir," Romulo said stiffly. He saluted. Then Wainwright,
walking around his table, shook his hand warmly and said, "God
bless you, my boy. . . . Tell President Quezon and General Mac-
Arthur I will do my best to the end."[50]

Late in the afternoon Wainwright also advised Captain Kenneth
Hoeffel, in command of all naval units on Corregidor and Bataan, to
order the destruction of all equipment of military value at Mariveles.
That night two immobilized vessels, U.S.S. *Canopus* and U.S.S.
Napa, were scuttled; the Dewey drydock was sunk, following the
explosion of six 155-mm. shells inside the drydock; and 80,000
gallons of fuel oil, 130 tons of diesel oil, more than one million
rounds of 30-mm. ammunition, and 45 tons of food were moved
to Corregidor.[51]

During the moonless night of April 8–9, the southern tip of Bataan
was the scene of violent, earth-shaking explosions. As demolition
squads detonated ammunition dumps, "white hot pieces of metal
from exploded shells and bombs shot skyward by the thousands in
every conceivable direction." Colored flares burst like skyrockets and
towering orange and yellow flames from burning oil stores illumi-
nated the sky. Like an erupting volcano, Bataan presented an awe-
inspiring spectacle of conflagration.

Around midnight a violent earthquake caused Malinta Tunnel to
"shake like a weaving snake." For a moment it seemed the entire
tunnel would collapse. Following the earthquake, about a hundred
Army nurses and one Navy nurse were evacuated to Corregidor.
General Wainwright had directed that no civilians or troops, except the nurses, two antiaircraft gun batteries, and the Forty-fifth
Infantry, should be evacuated to Corregidor. The two antiaircraft
batteries embarked for "the Rock," but the Forty-fifth Infantry, although it had been assembled, never reached Mariveles for em-
barkation. Despite Wainwright's prohibition, until the following
day an exodus of 1,600 Army, Navy, and Philippine Constabulary

personnel and 800 civilians poured across the narrow channel to Corregidor by boat, raft, and *banca*. Some of the refugees carried leaflets that had been dropped on Bataan by Japanese planes: "Your convoy is due in the Philippines on 15 April, but you won't be alive to see it. Ha! Ha!"[52]

Wainwright reported to the War Department:

> The situation in Bataan has become extremely critical during the past 24 hours. For several days an enemy attack has been in progress and it appeared that this attack would be similar to others which were launched previously against the I Corps front. In previous attacks a wedge was driven into our main line of resistance and enemy troops would attempt to filter through. In each case we were successful in blocking these attacks, closing the gap in the front line and mopping up hostile troops contained within the pocket thus formed. In the attack now in progress our troops have been subsisted on ½ to ⅓ rations for so long a period that they do not possess the physical strength to endure the strain placed upon the individual in an attack. In this attack, as in others preceding it, we were successful in blocking hostile progress. We placed our best troops in position to make an attack on both flanks with a view to closing the pocket. They were able to advance only a short distance before they were physically exhausted. Thereafter the enemy increased his strength in the pocket, continued the attack, and placed heavy artillery fire on our position. Hostile bombers continuously bombed and strafed our lines to assist the enemy in the attack. As days passed our troops began getting weaker from their continued exertions. Last night the Luzon force commander ordered a withdrawal of a portion of the line in order to rectify the position. A similar withdrawal was ordered in the I Corps to conform. Troops are now in position along the new line but their morale has been badly shaken by their experience of the past few days.[53]

At the War Department on April 8 Stimson had a long talk with Lieutenant Colonel Warren J. Clear, who had recently returned from the Philippines and Australia. Clear informed Stimson that, although the regular Philippine Army defending the beaches at Lingayan Gulf "broke every time it came in contact with the Japanese," later "it got its battle spirit" and fought very well during and after the retreat into Bataan. He reported that the Philippine Scouts at Lingayan Gulf, on the other hand, distinguished themselves by driving the first Japanese landing back into the water with bayonets and rifles, "causing a complete failure of the attack." Clear praised highly the fighting in January of all units on Bataan.[54]

Stimson's diary entry read:

> I was at the office until 6:30 P.M. considering the difficult situation which may lie before us—whether we shall order [the army on Bataan] to make a stand up to the bitter end, or permit them to make a surrender. Clear, who was here this morning and spoke as he admitted emotionally on account of his friends in Bataan, was urging that we should not order a fight to the bitter end because that would mean that the Japanese would massacre everyone there. McCloy, Eisenhower, and I in thinking it over agreed that he was exaggerating but that, even if such a bitter end had to be, it would probably be better for the cause of the country in the end than would surrender. The only doubt in my mind was the effect of starvation. That presents a different element in the problem than the one which Marshall and I had a couple of months ago when Quezon and MacArthur proposed a virtual settlement with the Japanese. But it is a sorely hard problem to be confronted with.[55]

On April 8 in the War Department, General McNarney read Wainwright's and MacArthur's recent radiograms. It was readily apparent to McNarney that the situation on Bataan had "deteriorated to a marked degree" and was quickly becoming desperate. He believed that the "mandatory character" of President Roosevelt's instructions prohibiting surrender, which had been issued to Mac-Arthur on February 9 and repeated to Wainwright on March 23, should be modified. In a memorandum to Roosevelt referring to this order, McNarney wrote: "These instructions were issued at a time when it appeared necessary to make very clear to the Commander in the Philippines the nature of the defense expected. It is possible that in the literal execution of these orders General Wainwright may be tempted to carry them through to an illogical extreme. I think there should be no doubt that his resolution and sense of duty will preclude any untoward or precipitous action, but on the other hand it is possible that greater latitude in a final decision would be allowed him."[56] McNarney attached to the memorandum the draft of a message that he thought should be dispatched to Wainwright, but Roosevelt decided that it should be dispatched only with Mac-

Arthur's acquiescence. Consequently the following message was sent to General MacArthur:

> The president has directed that the following message for Wainwright be dispatched to you. He further directs that you send this message to Wainwright only if you concur both as to substance and to timing.

>> I have read your message of April 8 and am keenly aware of the tremendous difficulties under which you are waging your great battle. The physical exhaustion of your troops obviously precludes the possibility of a major counter stroke unless our efforts to rush food to you should quickly prove successful. Because of the state to which your forces have been reduced by circumstances over which you have had no control I am modifying my orders to you as contained in my telegram to General MacArthur dated February 9 and repeated to you on March 23. My purpose is to leave to your best judgment any decision affecting the future of the Bataan garrison. I have nothing but admiration for your soldierly conduct and your performance of your most difficult mission and have every confidence that whatever decision you may sooner or later be forced to make will be dictated only by the best interests of the country and of your magnificent troops. I am still hopeful that the efforts of the navy to supply you by submarine will be effective and in time and that at least one or more of the surface vessels attempting to run the blockade will reach you shortly. Nevertheless I feel it proper and necessary that you should be assured of complete freedom of action and of my full confidence in the wisdom of whatever decision you may be forced to make. Please acknowledge receipt of this message. Franklin D. Roosevelt.

> Please report your decision as to the dispatch of this message to General Wainwright.[57]

Early in the morning of April 9, MacArthur received simultaneously Roosevelt's proposed message to Wainwright and the following report from Wainwright:

> At six o'clock this morning General King commanding Luzon force without my knowledge or approval sent a flag of truce to [the] Japanese commander. The minute I heard of it I disapproved of his action and directed that there would be no surrender. I was

informed it was too late to make any change that the action had already been taken. Enemy on east had enveloped both flanks of the small groups of what was left of the II Corps and was firing with artillery into the hospital area which undoubtedly prompted King's action. In order to relieve the pressure on the right, last night I ordered the I Corps to attack to the north with its ultimate objective Olongapo but the attack did not get off. Physical exhaustion and sickness due to a long period of insufficient food is the real cause of this terrible disaster. When I get word what terms have been arranged I will advise you. Fearing just what happened, I endeavored last night to withdraw some of the Philippine Division and other regular units but only succeeded in getting out some scattered mixtures of individuals. I will endeavor to hold Corregidor. Enemy yesterday landed on Guimaras Island so it is very possible that he will be in Iloilo today. Please send bombers as contemplated. We will still inflict as much damage as possible on the enemy and attempt to bring through ships from Visayan Islands.[58]

In a message relaying Wainwright's report to the War Department, MacArthur stated that he did not believe it was "advisable" to transmit the contents of Roosevelt's message to Wainwright since "the action taken on Bataan anticipated the authority conveyed in the message." He reported that bombers would be dispatched to the Philippines at the end of the week.[59]

That morning MacArthur called his naval aide, Captain H. James Ray, into his office and informed him of the surrender of the Bataan forces. "Pacing the floor with tears streaming down his face," MacArthur told Ray that he had asked General Marshall's permission to return to his forces in the Philippines, but had been turned down. Later, taking pen in hand, MacArthur wrote out his tribute to the defenders of Bataan:

> The Bataan force went out as it would have wished, fighting to the end its flickering forlorn hope. No army has ever done so much with so little and nothing became it more than its last hour of trial and agony. To the weeping Mothers of its dead, I can only say that the sacrifice and halo of Jesus of Nazareth has descended upon their sons, and that God will take them unto himself.[60]

From Corregidor, Wainwright reported to the War Department and MacArthur:

Hostilities in Bataan ended for the most part, soon after flag of truce passed through our front line this morning. General King was sent for about 10:00 A.M. today for a conference with the Japanese High Command. As of 7:00 P.M. General King had not returned to his headquarters and I have not yet learned the result of the conference. Southern end of Bataan now under control of hostile forces. Hostile batteries have already been placed on southern top of Bataan so as to bring fire on this island. A battery situated near Cabcaben and others are known to be west of that point. I cannot now fire at these batteries as our troops are located in the same general area. Enemy planes have renewed their attacks on island today. This afternoon several flights passed over Corregidor dropping their bombs, but damage was negligible.[61]

That night Lieutenant Colonel Pugh wrote in his diary:

We learned this morning at 6:00 A.M. that General King was attempting to negotiate a peace for Bataan with the Japanese High Command. His troops, primarily in the II Corps, are demoralized. They are coming to the rear uncontrolledly. The I Corps still holds the line at the Binuangan River in the West. General King's action is not in accordance with General Wainwright's instructions. The command given was: "Do not surrender."

I know, however, that General King had no choice. The enemy twice bombed our main Bataan hospital and was shelling into the area of the only other. Troops were no longer under control. This Philippine Army again in underwear, without weapons. What ever happens will soon be history. Many will criticize MacArthur, the Philippine Army, etc. I know too much for me to criticize. The number of clay footed individuals in this fracas is appalling.

However, I particularly regret one thing. MacArthur never told the real truth about this situation. All reports were glorified. The Philippine Army painted as magnificent and invincible. This report is not true. The Philippine Army was raw, green and untrained. It has been due to the work of the American officers that they have stood as they have. Now they are tired, hungry and disillusioned. Help promised them has never arrived, and never will arrive in time. For soon the Bataan defense will be no more.

I have had to closely guard General Wainwright in the past few days. He has taken this new blow very hard. He is thinking of it in the light of history. Never has a general officer been given a more difficult assignment. I have heard that General MacArthur by his own admission did not expect Bataan to hold through January.[62]

North on Bataan there was a strange silence while the remnants of a diseased, exhausted, and starved army rested in the darkness and waited for a terrible dawn.

Corregidor and Capitulation

April 10–May 8, 1942

"Never has so much been done with so little. The nation will be forever grateful."[1]

—General Marshall to Wainwright
May 6, 1942

On April 10 General Wainwright issued a proclamation to his besieged forces on Corregidor:

Corregidor can and will be held.

There can be no question of surrendering this mighty fortress to the enemy. It will be defended with all the resources at our command. Major General George F. Moore, commanding general of Fort Mills, is wholeheartedly with me in the unalterable decision to hold this island together with its auxiliary forts

I call upon every person in this fortress—officer, enlisted man, or civilian—to consider himself from this time onward as a member of a team which is resolved to meet the enemy's challenge each hour of every night and day.

All men who have served here before will remain at their posts, while those who have come from Bataan will be assigned to appropriate tasks and battle stations. It is essential above all that the men who have joined us from the mainland promptly rid themselves of any defeatist attitude which they may have and consider themselves as part of this fighting unit.

Bataan has fallen—but Corregidor will carry on! On this

mighty fortress—a pearl of great price on which the enemy has set his covetous eyes—the spirit of Bataan will continue to live![2]

The same day MacArthur read a message from General Mc-Narney:

> The message quoted to General Wainwright in our radiogram of April 8 to you has been sent directly to General Wainwright. At the conclusion of the message the president again expressed his satisfaction of Wainwright's conduct in the performance of his mission and stated that he understood that whatever decision Wainwright had been forced to make had been dictated by the best interests of the country. The president expressed his hope that Corregidor would be held, assured Wainwright of complete freedom of action and expressed confidence in the wisdom of his decisions.[3]

> Following is paraphrase of message sent to President Roosevelt this morning in reply to one received from him:

>> I have received no message from General MacArthur concerning your radio of April 9. The kindness of your message and the confidence Your Excellency places in my judgment in this desperate situation merits my heartfelt gratitude. I have left nothing undone in my efforts to hold Bataan but men who are starved, without air support and with inadequate field artillery, are ill prepared to endure punishment that was inflicted by terrific plane and artillery bombardment. Heavy artillery has now been emplaced by hostile forces on southern tip of Bataan peninsula and Corregidor is now under constant artillery fire as well as air attack. This morning I was advised that enemy troops in some force are now landing on Cebu. I can communicate with Cebu only by radio and have no additional information at present on progress being made by hostile forces. It will no longer be possible to ship subsistence and other supplies which have been accumulated at Cebu if the island is taken by hostile forces. Warships and Japanese transports in unusual number have been reported in waters of the southern islands recently. Enemy activity there indicates that there is at least the possibility of an attack on other islands of the Visayas. I have been unable to obtain information concerning terms arranged by General King as all communications with Bataan have been severed. However the flag of the United States is still flying on this isolated island.[4]

On April 13 General Wainwright received a personal message from General Marshall:

> Due to my being on [the] way to London during the tragic crisis of Bataan prevented me sending word to you. Your troops and you command my admiration for your fortitude and spirit. Prime Minister Churchill with whom I am at present speaks in superlative terms of admiration for the gallantry of your action. Data is now being secured for me of methods used by British in supplying Malta with submarines which may enable us to supply you more food. Good luck and may the Lord keep you.[5]

Wainwright replied:

> Your kind message . . . encourages me and will when published, be an inspiration to the gallant troops of my command. The constant and incessant air bombardment of major caliber artillery from Bataan and south shore of Manila Bay is answered round for round by the gallant harbor defense troops. The Fourth Marines and other troops that I succeeded in extracting from Bataan hold the beaches in a determined manner and I intend to keep the flag on this tiny rock as long as food and ammunition hold out. I am in constant touch with MacArthur on these matters and he is doing what he can to keep us supplied. However three inch anti-aircraft ammunition is now a critical item. Please express to Prime Minister Churchill my deep appreciation of his kind words.[6]

On April 13 Marshall radioed MacArthur to ask whether steps were still being taken to forward supplies via submarines, surface vessels, and airplanes from Australia to Corregidor. MacArthur sent the following answer:

> Food supplies on Corregidor should be sufficient to supply the garrison for six to eight weeks unless there has developed some new circumstance of which I know nothing. . . . Other supplies excepting anti-aircraft ammunition although naturally dependent upon degree of enemy pressure should last longer. As explained in previous radios this fortress was built before the full power of air attack had been developed and is vulnerable along many lines. Medium and heavy artillery mounted on the Bataan shore can without question destroy vital features of the defenses. With the premature fall of Bataan the enemy has probably captured numbers of 155 millimeter guns and ammunition which will unquestionably soon be put into action. The life of this fortress is therefore definitely limited and its destruction certain unless sea communications can be restored. I have the impression from your

previous radios that such a step in the immediate future is impracticable. Under these conditions you must be prepared for the fall of the Harbor Defenses. With both Cavite and Bataan shores occupied by the enemy it becomes practically impossible for shipping to reach the defenders. Moreover, with the enemy moving in strength into the Visayas, no supply help can be expected from that quarter. The small landing field on Corregidor is available only for light aircraft. Under these circumstances I regard it as useless to attempt further general supply by blockade running although an attempt will be made to provide additional anti-aircraft ammunition. I believe the only alternatives which present themselves are a major effort involving grand strategic considerations to be executed within the next two months or the acceptance of ultimate defeat in Manila Bay.[7]

On April 14 MacArthur received a radiogram from Wainwright asking about President Roosevelt's message of April 9. (This message had been sent to MacArthur on April 8 with instructions to forward it to Wainwright if MacArthur agreed with its substance and timing. MacArthur had not forwarded the message.)

[President Roosevelt] states only if you concur both as to substance and timing that you send this message to me. As I have had no reply I assume that you do not concur in one or the other. The above message was quoted to me in full and the following is a paraphrase of additional instructions to me direct contained in the same message:

Have read your message of April 9. . . . Have received no information yet of action taken by MacArthur. At this time I desire to repeat my appreciation of your soldierly conduct in performing a very difficult task and to express confidence that whatever decision you have made has been dictated by best interests of your troops and of the country. I hope that you will be able to maintain your position on Corregidor. You are assured however of complete freedom of action and you have my complete confidence in the wisdom of any decision you may be forced to make.
Franklin D. Roosevelt

That portion of his message to me direct appears to leave to my discretion that decision which I must ultimately make unless anti-aircraft ammunition in the near future and food in the more distant future are received. If I am not correct in this assumption I hope you will so advise me. The fall of Bataan was a most severe blow to me but it was inevitable sooner or later in view of the effectiveness of the blockade. With men in full health and vigor, we could have held the enemy as we have on many occasions. I managed to withdraw about 3,000 military personnel and am now determined to hold my present position with God's help until a major diversion by you in some other theatre releases the pressure on us here. While my morale and that of my troops is still high in spite of adversity, a word of cheer and encouragement from you would be welcomed by all. Have just had a radio from Marshall which I paraphrased to you in another message. . . .[8]

In his reply, MacArthur stated:

The message from Roosevelt to you transmitted here for delivery was not received until after the fall of Bataan and consequently was not forwarded as it referred entirely to the possibility of surrender in Bataan. Almost immediately thereafter the president's message came direct to you which has amplified the subject matter and now gives you complete authority to use your own judgment regarding the Harbor Defenses. I cannot tell you how anxious I have been to bring you relief. My resources however are practically negligible. I have not as yet been placed in command of the contemplated new area and am operating merely in my old capacity as commanding general of the USAFFE. The naval units are the remnants of the Asiatic Fleet, my air and ground forces little more than embraced in the original convoys destined for the Philippines which never arrived there. The Pacific Fleet is not under my control nor are the Australian forces. I have represented to the War Department that the only way in which you can be relieved is by the use of the Pacific Fleet. I have had no reply. If I had any real force at my disposal I think you know without my saying that no matter how desperate the chances of success I would move in an endeavor to reach you. I am trying to get you anti-aircraft ammunition by submarine.[9]

In the meantime, two B-17s from the Nineteenth Attack Group and ten B-25s from the Third Group, under the command of Brigadier General Ralph Royce, had completed during April 13 and 14 a series of bombing raids against the Japanese in the Philippines. Refueled and reloaded with bombs from air strips at Malaybalay, Butuan, and the Del Monte Pineapple Plantation in Mindanao, the bombers attacked Nichols Field, Batangas, Cebu, and Davao. At Nichols Field hangars were destroyed and runways damaged; at Davao one bomber was destroyed and several damaged, two transports hit and one probably sunk, two seaplanes damaged and one shot down, troop concentrations dispersed, and docks and warehouses damaged; at Cebu three transports were sunk and two hit, three planes shot down and several damaged on the ground, and some docks damaged; at Batangas one freighter was sunk.

According to the original plan for the bombing mission, the quartermaster at Cebu was to load with food about twenty small interisland boats, varying in size from a few tons to about 200 tons, and secretly assemble them just north of Panay. Since it would take the boats approximately forty-eight hours to make the run from Panay, through the Japanese naval blockade of Manila Bay to a point where Corregidor's guns could give them protection, they would need defense en route from Japanese ships and aircraft. Consequently the squadron of bombers operating from Mindanao was to make continuous nuisance raids against Japanese naval vessels in the blockade force and scatter them, while the last five P-40s in the Philippines, operating from San Bernardino airfield in Panay, were to harass and distract any hostile aircraft from Manila that tried to interfere with, or observe, the movement of the supply boats. The operation's success would have depended on the surprise and sheer audacity of the scheme. Because the forces on Bataan surrendered on April 9, it could not be implemented and an alternate plan was adopted.

The only major casualty of "Royce's raid" was one B-17. It had mechanical failure and was later burned when attacked at Del Monte by Japanese float planes, but its crew was saved. Although the Japanese were taken completely by surprise, only minor damage was inflicted "due to inadequate bombardier training, poor aircraft bomb systems, and poor target intelligence." Since only a few float planes interfered with the bombers, the raid revealed the fact that the Japanese had staged just about all of their available aircraft forward and were not prepared for incursions behind their invasion forces. Yet owing to the lack of fuel, bombs, and an adequate communication or warning system, continued air operations coordinated and planned from Mindanao were virtually impossible, and the bombers were forced to return to Australia.[10]

On April 15 Wainwright informed MacArthur that he planned to transfer surplus officers from Corregidor to Mindanao as soon as he could arrange plane transportation, a serious problem because of the limited number of planes. Two days later he urged MacArthur to consider the following plan:

> Assign a navy sea plane to the mission of ferrying personnel between here and Lake Lanao. On the trip north it might carry medicines or other necessary supplies and going south could I believe carry ten or fifteen people. Naval officers here believe that although not without risk one of these sea planes could land and take off between Corregidor and Fort Hughes but prefer to leave decision as to practicability to naval officers in close touch with sea planes. I request that this plan be studied and if it possesses any merit that it be given a trial.[11]

Wainwright also reported that Japanese forces had landed at Iloilo, Cebu, and were on the verge of capturing the island in spite of heavy resistance by Brigadier General Chynoweth's forces. Believing the enemy would soon make an effort to subdue all of the Visayan Islands and then concentrate on capturing Mindanao, Wainwright urged MacArthur to dispatch a second bombing mission consisting of six B-25s to Mindanao to attack enemy warships and transport in Visayan waters.[12]

On April 18 MacArthur received a radiogram from General McNarney concerning information about "Royce's raid" that had been released to the press by General Brett's headquarters:

> Press releases emanating from the United States forces in Australia concerning our air attack in the Philippines give numbers and types of planes involved, landings made, and many similar details of value to the enemy which will assist him in adopting immediate counter measures. Orders are being issued by the secretary of war today on the subject of release of military information.[13]

MacArthur replied:

> I deeply regret and have condemned most heartily the unsoldierly release here by General Brett's headquarters of the information referred to in your radio. Due to previous directions not to assume command of the United States Army forces in Australia and not to interfere with its interior administration I had not attempted to control contacts of that headquarters with the press. The information given out by the air force on the Philippine raid was, however, so damaging and irresponsible that even before receipt of your radio I issued orders insuring control of future releases and publicity from that headquarters. I shall at once take

steps to put into effect the orders issued by the secretary of war and request that I be advised promptly of any leakage that may occur in America so that I may insure an adequate execution of the order. I may add that the giving out of this information has seriously embarrassed future plans of air operations that I had contemplated.[14]

There had been tension between MacArthur and Brett even before MacArthur's arrival in Australia. Delayed in Mindanao during his evacuation from Corregidor, an exasperated MacArthur, after sending uncomplimentary messages to Brett, had waited impatiently for bombers from Brett's command to fly his party to Australia. Harsh words had been exchanged between General Royce, Brett's chief of staff, and MacArthur in arranging transportation from Batchelor Field to Melbourne. When MacArthur arrived in Melbourne he had greeted Brett coldly. MacArthur's irritation had grown when he learned that Brett had authorized General Royce to lease a large mansion with servants for himself and his family. MacArthur had remarked to one of his staff that Brett had the unique ability to surround himself with "deadheads" like Brigadier Generals Royce and Martin F. Scanlon. There had also been a definite personality conflict between Brett and General Sutherland with respect to air operations. During one heated argument Sutherland had exclaimed to Brett, "When have you ever heard a shot fired in anger!" Brett did not have MacArthur's confidence and his days as commander of the Allied air forces in Australia were numbered. In August he would be replaced by Major General George C. Kenney.[15]

On April 19 MacArthur informed Wainwright that plans were being perfected to dispatch two Navy PBYs to Corregidor in order to evacuate about fifty officers and nurses to Mindanao. The large seaplanes would be sent as soon as the moon's phase permitted a night landing.[16] MacArthur also dispatched a message to Marshall:

It is quite apparent that with the limited life of Corregidor and the initiation of the hostile movement into the Visayas our last remaining foothold in the Philippines will be Mindanao which will take on an added importance. The garrison there while adequate in numbers is only partially trained, poorly equipped and lacks the stiffening effect that was afforded in Luzon by white units and adequate numbers of American officers. It is capable, however, of withstanding anything short of a serious attack. The numerous

airfields that we have developed there, particularly on the Bukid-
non plateau, will be of the greatest value in our future operations.
Food is plentiful and the garrison is self supporting in that respect.
I am making every possible effort to remedy some of the most
acute of other deficiencies. Attempt is also being made to evacuate officers from Corregidor who can serve no useful purpose
there but who could be of the greatest value in Mindanao. I am
planning shipments of armaments, ammunition, aviation gasoline,
medical supplies and essential quartermaster items. The shipping
available to me here, however, lacks the speed which is essential
for the success of this undertaking if serious losses are to be
avoided. Would it be possible to send here for this use some of
the converted destroyers which were being prepared to run the
blockade into Corregidor? It is requested that the reply be expe-
dited giving the date of expected arrival of the ships in these
waters if they can be provided.[17]

On April 23 MacArthur received the following radiogram from
Wainwright:

In line with our radiogram of April 6 your attention is invited to
following: Press reports of April 4 quoted Resident Commissioner
Elizalde as saying during radio speech that unless the Japs take
Bataan within ten weeks they will have lost opportunity perhaps
forever due to rough seas, approaching typhoon season, etc. In
press release of April 23 Elizalde is reported to have stated that
unless Japs subdue Corregidor in next month, typhoon season
will endanger supply lines.

While we are eager to meet any Japanese threat, request that
some action be taken to prevent persons and agencies at home,
particularly prominent and influential personages, from inciting
Japs to take action by such utterances.[18]

On the twenty-fourth MacArthur forwarded to Wainwright instructions he had received from the War Department:

Desire that you direct Wainwright to evacuate as many officers
and men as possible for instructional duty in the United States.
Personnel evacuated for this purpose should have participated
actively in operations on Bataan and Corregidor. Infantry, field
artillery and anti-aircraft artillery should be represented. Personnel should be of highest type of instructor capable of describing
latest data on both own and Jap tactical weapons and equipment.
Individuals should be ordered to report to War Department G-2
Washington and should be instructed that their origin, destina-

tion, knowledge, and mission will be kept secret until otherwise authorized by War Department.[19]

MacArthur reported to General Marshall that his instructions had been transmitted to Wainwright, and that two PBYs would be dispatched early the following week with the capacity to evacuate fifty men to Mindanao. From Mindanao they would be transported to Australia in army and navy planes.[20] On April 25, Wainwright sent the following reply to MacArthur:

Due to the fact that the entire Luzon force has surrendered in terms arranged by General King, I have very few officers and men with the qualifications indicated in your radio. Such infantry and field artillery personnel that escaped from Bataan did so on their own initiative, and all such personnel have been incorporated into beach defenses. I have experienced anti-aircraft personnel but do not have the number of batteries required for the defense of the fortified islands as additional batteries were expected from Bataan but did not arrive. If any officers and men were sent with the qualifications as indicated, they would be the personnel which could be spared least, and the defenses of the fortified islands would correspondingly be weakened. Since my mission contemplates that I hold the fortified islands until relieved, I strongly recommend that no personnel be detailed from these defenses as indicated in the reference radio. Some surplus personnel are being evacuated at the first opportunity who have had experience in Bataan. For example, Colonel Thomas W. Doyle, who is familiar with Bataan methods of combat, could doubtless give valuable information to the War Department which could thereafter be disseminated throughout the service.[21]

Wainwright further reported to MacArthur that Corregidor was being subjected to continuous bombardment from different caliber shells fired from artillery emplacements on Bataan, and that all of the fortified islands were under steady bombing. Knocked out at Fort Mills were two 55-mm. guns, two three-inch guns, two six-inch guns, two ten-inch guns, one twelve-inch gun and two twelve-inch mortars, and two three-inch antiaircraft guns. Power and pumping plants and electric cables were severely damaged and constantly under repair. Communications between administration and tactical units were continually breaking down. A great deal of motor transportation had been destroyed. The roads on Corregidor were a maze of shell craters. Attrition was taking place not only on Corregidor but also on Forts Frank, Hughes, and Drum. Since April 9 there had been 300 casualties, including 123 killed, on the fortified islands in Manila Bay. "Regardless of these adverse conditions," Wainwright concluded his somber report, "our morale is high and we will hold Fortified Islands to the last."[22]

April 29 was Emperor Hirohito's birthday. That morning Corregidor was heavily bombed for the hundredth time since the fall of Bataan. Boats in South Harbor were also bombed and the fortified islands were heavily shelled for four continuous hours. Although batteries on Corregidor fired on critical roads, troop columns, and bridges in Bataan, they only silenced three enemy batteries, destroyed a truck column, and started three fires.[23]

During that day of incessant shelling and bombing, Wainwright was notified that two PBYs had arrived at Lake Lanao in Mindanao and would reach Corregidor that night. Wainwright conferred with Captain Kenneth M. Hoeffel, the senior naval authority on Corregidor, and it was decided to have the planes land between Corregidor and Caballo Island (Fort Hughes). As a result of orders emanating from Captain Hoeffel, two minesweepers, U.S.S. *Quail* and U.S.S. *Tangier*, removed mines in the area where the big seaplanes would land, and two lighted bouys were set out as guides.

Shortly after 11:00 P.M. two PBYs, carrying 600 pounds of medical supplies and 1,800 pounds of antiaircraft fuses, emerged low out of a clear night with a full moon and landed in the designated area. Thirty nurses, four civilian women, and sixteen officers quickly boarded small boats and were taken to the planes. After helping some of the women into the boats, Wainwright watched from South Dock as the two planes rose from the sea "with a roar that could be heard for miles around" and disappeared into the darkness.[24]

On April 30 Brigadier General Patrick J. Hurley wrote MacArthur:

> I know that you have noticed in the newspapers that Secretary Stimson stated that I was charged with the responsibility of getting supplies to you in the Philippines. I had thought that that was a deep secret. I think possibly it was announced by my friend Harry in defending himself against the criticism that was being leveled at the Department for not having fought through for the relief of yourself and your

garrison. His statement did silence a lot of the criticism. He did not give any details of our effort, but said that we lost nearly two ships for every one that got through. This latter statement gave rise to a number of other questions. The most pertinent one is why we used foreign ships instead of using our own with convoys and systematic defense. Neither you nor I have expressed any opinion publicly on that subject. I think it is best for us not to do so. I was disappointed as I said to you in the fact that we did not put on an act that would have struck terror to the Japanese and attracted the admiration of the free people. We are handicapped for even the poorest quality of transportation. While I was in Java I had thoughts of getting control of enough naval and air force to drive a destructive wedge through the Japanese blockade instead of slipping in and out of the different hiding places in the night. The Japanese were at that time so intensely committed elsewhere that I believe we could have fought our way through. The means were so limited and the time so short that I suppose we should feel grateful even for our limited accomplishments.

I had almost forgotten all my disappointments in the joy I felt that you and your family were out and your splendid skill and your unbreakable will are again available to our country in a large field.

But between ourselves, Douglas, I will always feel that our country missed an opportunity when it did not show the old spirit of the greatest Republic on earth, the Republic that has never lost a war, by going to your relief with the strength and valor worthy of our traditions.[25]

On May 2 Brigadier General Lewis C. Beebe, Wainwright's chief of staff, radioed General Sutherland:

> I am sending this unofficially to give you off the record information which I believe should be in your possession. From present indications it appears that Mindanao will soon be in the hands of the enemy. Hostile forces were in the vicinity of Lake Lanao this morning and it is likely that the entire western half of the island will be in the hands of the Japs within the next day or two. Thereafter it is merely a matter of time before the remaining coastal areas will be in possession of the enemy. Sharp will probably be able to continue operations in the mountains for some time to

come, but he will not be able to hold areas which can be used as a base for the operations of our forces. Cebu and Panay are now in the hands of the Japs and as there are very few troops on the remaining islands of the Visayan group it can be expected that the Japs will be able to take them at their leisure.

In my opinion, Corregidor will be able to hold out longer than any other place in the Philippines. As the situation is now developing, there remains very little that can be accomplished by the staff of the USFIP. General Moore will be in command of the fortified islands and there will be no duties for this staff to perform which could not be handled by other officers. It is therefore my considered opinion that General Wainwright, with as many of his staff as can be accommodated, should be evacuated to Australia where they can be of further service to the government. I am making this statement in the hope that you will not misunderstand my motives. If I could accomplish anything by remaining here, with the ultimate probability of becoming a Japanese prisoner of war, I can say in all sincerity that I would be only too glad to remain. I am certain that the other officers on the staff are not only willing to remain, but are anxious to as long as they feel that they are accomplishing something. However, since it is likely that American prisoners will be held for the duration of the war, I feel that the interests of the government would be served best if this staff were moved to Australia.

I am sending this because General Wainwright believes he should go down with the ship. However I do not believe that he should be permitted to fall into the hands of the Japs. His experience and knowledge of Jap tactics are too valuable to the government to be lost. I have not discussed this matter with him nor have I ever made any effort to get him to leave Corregidor. However, I do know from various conversations that he expects to remain here to the end, and surrender himself with the troops if the necessity arises. Since he is a soldier, he will move only if he is ordered to do so. It is my fixed belief that he should be ordered to move with such members of his staff as can be accommodated, in the near future.[26]

At a conference preceding the dispatch of this message, Generals Beebe and Moore and Lieutenant Colonel Pugh had urged General Wainwright to move his headquarters to Mindanao. Knowing that Corregidor's fall was imminent, the officers emphasized to Wainwright that the Japanese would not be content with the surrender of the forts in Manila Bay but would blackmail him into surrendering all American forces in the Philippines. Wainwright, believing it was his duty to remain on Corregidor, replied, "This was General MacArthur's headquarters, and this is where I will stay."[27]

On May 3 Wainwright had a message dispatched to MacArthur:

> Beebe's radio of May 2 to Sutherland was prepared without my knowledge or consent. It was shown to me prior to its dispatch but I neither authorized nor prohibited its dispatch. The conditions he predicts have actually occurred. Enemy is now in possession of most of western Mindanao and this morning landed at three o'clock near Bugo, about 20 miles from Del Monte which is probably in his hands now. The entire group of the Visayan Islands must now be considered to be in enemy hands. Situation here is fast becoming desperate. With artillery that outranges anything we have except two guns he keeps up a terrific bombardment as well as aerial bombing. Even when we can reach his batteries they are almost impossible to locate as he moves them around and we have no air to spot them while our batteries are fixed and he accurately adjusts his guns on them from the air. His two hundred forty millimeter cannon batter our fixed emplacements to pieces. Since April 9 of following major armament originally on Corregidor there remain useful the number indicated as left: twelve inch guns 8, left 4; twelve inch mortars 12, left 1; ten inch guns 2, left none; six inch guns 5, left none; 155 guns 20, left 16 of which only 9 bear on Bataan; three inch guns 10, left 7 of which only 4 bear on Bataan; one eight inch gun, left none. Serious losses in AA fire control equipment and searchlights renders AA ineffective except on battery. Great toll has been taken of machine guns both ground and AA as well as of automatic weapons of all types. The island is practically denuded of vegetation and trees leaving no cover and all structures are leveled to the ground. Communications and utilities are almost impossible of maintenance. Casualties since April 9 approximate 600. Again referring to Beebe's radio to Sutherland whatever your decision may be it will be fully and cheerfully carried out.[28]

The same day Beebe received a reply from Sutherland:

> General Wainwright was assigned to his command by the War Department and General MacArthur has no repeat no authority to relieve him therefrom. With reference to other officers see our radio of April 14 directing the evacuation of all who cannot assist materially in the defense of Corregidor. It was the hope of General MacArthur and myself that General Wainwright would apply this

specifically to you, other members of the staff and heads of departments whose functions have been contracted to such a point that the normal staff of the coast artillery garrison would meet all requirements. We still hope that such may be the case. Best regards.[29]

Submerged in the mouth of Manila Bay was the submarine *Spearfish,* commanded by Lieutenant James C. Dempsey. He was waiting for darkness in order to surface and evacuate twenty-five passengers along with personnel and official records and mail from Corregidor. In Malinta Tunnel, Wainwright informed Pugh that he intended to evacuate him that night aboard the *Spearfish.* Pugh was to be promoted to Assistant Chief of Staff, G-2, for Intelligence, and his rank advanced to full colonel. Wainwright wanted him to take certain headquarters records and explain them to officials in the War Department. Adamantly refusing to leave his chief, Pugh replied that he was too young to be promoted to full colonel, and that it was his duty as an army officer to remain on Corregidor. Deeply moved, Wainwright reluctantly acquiesced to his aide's desire to remain with him.

Among the nurses and army and naval officers that Wainwright had designated to leave the besieged fortress aboard the *Spearfish* were Lieutenant Commander Thomas C. Parker, who had been told by Wainwright, "They will have to come take us. They will never get this place any other way"; Colonel Royal G. Jenks, a finance offier who would carry with him financial records; Colonel Thomas W. Doyle, who had commanded the Forty-fifth Infantry (PS) on Bataan; and Colonel Constant L. Irwin, Wainwright's assistant chief of staff, G-3, for Operations, who was suffering from ulcers. Before leaving Malinta Tunnel with a complete roster of all army, navy, and marine personnel still alive, Irwin spoke with Wainwright. "Very much perturbed" about what the reaction of the American people and especially General MacArthur would be to the surrender of his command, Wainwright told Irwin to explain to General George C. Marshall the hopeless situation that existed in the Philippines, and the eventual necessity for surrendering American forces. Irwin tried to assure Wainwright "that everyone, both high and low in the armed forces and out, would understand the necessity of his actions." Leaving Corregidor's South Dock at 7:45 P.M., Irwin, Doyle, Jenks, Parker, and twenty-one other evacuees were taken to the *Spearfish* bound for Australia.[30]

The following day, May 4, MacArthur dispatched a message to Marshall:

> You must be prepared for the collapse shortly of the Harbor Defenses in Manila Bay. The generally optimistic tone of reports from there do not repeat not reflect an accurate military estimate of the situation. The occupation of Bataan definitely condemned these fortresses and enemy guns of large caliber located there are rapidly destroying our fixed fortifications. Personnel losses have not been great aggregating about six hundred since April ninth of which approximately two thirds are wounded. It is apparent to me however that morale is rapidly sinking and the end is clearly in sight. There will be a few scattered bands of desperate men left whose effectiveness will be practically negligible. The numerous secret air fields in Mindanao which I prepared with the hope of using them as a general base for a counterdrive will be in the enemy's hands very shortly and this strategic possibility can now definitely be discarded. The internal political repercussions in the Philippines which may follow the complete collapse of our military effort cannot be estimated at this time but the potentialities involved may prove to be of the gravest significance. A report just received from Wainwright states that ships can no longer reach Mindanao. I have recalled a blockade runner proceeding from here and have advised Emmons to that effect. I have not yet requested the recall of the converted destroyer en route to Corregidor but depending upon operations reports I anticipate the necessity for doing so very shortly. I believe it is useless to continue to load ships from the United States for this purpose.[31]

After reading MacArthur's message of impending doom, Marshall informed Wainwright that he wanted his "frank personal opinion of the situation." On May 5, Wainwright replied:

> Since 24 March, enemy air force has been bombing fortified islands continuously. . . . Immediately after Bataan was taken, hostile forces moved forward heavy artillery to south shore of Bataan and since that date has directed intense artillery bombardment on fortified islands. Since the Emperor's birthday on 29 April, artillery fire has increased in intensity and heavy volume of fire continues up to the present time. Fire from large caliber artillery batteries, including 240 mm guns, has been very effective and has destroyed a considerable number of harbor defense and beach defense weapons. Hostile bombing has been much less effective. There have been about 600 casualties in the fortified islands since the fall of Bataan.

Continued and intense bombing and artillery fire has lowered the morale of troops. Since these units have been operating under conditions which have made them subject to bombardment, either air or artillery, since 29 December, and have been issued only one-half of poorly balanced rations since 5 January, it is difficult to maintain morale. Nevertheless, morale continues at high level considering conditions which exist.

Intelligence information indicates that hostile force plans an attack against Corregidor. Motor boats on which weapons are mounted have been constructed or rebuilt for that purpose and many smaller boats have been prepared for use in ferrying troops. Since fall of Bataan, it has been difficult to estimate hostile troop strength on Luzon. Cebu and Panay have been seized in past few days by enemy forces and reports indicated that about 10,000 were employed in each of the two attacks. The enemy is now attacking the island of Mindanao and I believe that more than 10,000 troops are employed in this operation. I am of the opinion that there remains on Luzon a large enough force to undertake an attack against Corregidor, unless the enemy has withdrawn troops from the Philippines. Hostile troops will shortly be in control of all essential areas on or near the coast of Mindanao. Thereafter our forces on that island will be restricted to operations in the mountainous areas. The enemy can then clean up Mindanao and Visayan Islands at leisure.

It is my belief that the enemy has the means to assault Corregidor at any time. Whether or not such an assult is successful will depend upon the conduct of our troops in defense of the beaches. In my opinion, since morale undoubtedly has been lowered, the enemy has a good repeat good chance to make a successful assault. My opinion has been expressed very frankly of conditions here in accordance with request contained in your radio.[32]

On May 5 about 8:30 P.M. the Japanese, using more than 400 pieces of artillery on Bataan, opened up with a full barrage against Corregidor. Although they concentrated their fire against the north shore and the tail of Corregidor, the barrage completely covered the island. The furious shelling caused landslides on the slopes of the hills, severed communication lines, put numerous beach defense guns and searchlights out of action, activated a large number of land mines, and killed or wounded many of the troops manning the beach defenses. According to Lieutenant Commander John H. Morrill, who viewed the bombardment aboard the U.S.S. *Quail* in

South Harbor, "The entire island appeared as one vast sheet of flame. . . . Dust clouds arose which reached the proportions of heavy fog and island defense searchlights were rendered useless, appearing only as yellow spots in the dust fog." From a small observation post near the east entrance of Malinta Tunnel, for a short time, General Wainwright watched the deadly bombardment.[33]

Walking back into Malinta Tunnel, Wainwright knew that a Japanese landing was imminent. Earlier he had been informed by a Philippine army officer stationed in Manila with a clandestine radio that the "Japanese 4th Division had finished extensive landing maneuvers on the shores of Cavite," and that the Japanese had been busy constructing thousands of ladders for the purpose of scaling the precipitous heights of Corregidor. The beautiful full moon was another indication of a probable Japanese attack.[34]

At approximately 11:30 P.M. the first wave of Japanese troops landed near Corregidor's North Point. Shortly thereafter, a Marine Corps runner barged into Harbor Defense Headquarters and informed General Moore of the amphibious landing. He estimated enemy strength at about 600 men. Immediately, notification messages were dispatched to every control station. Phoning Wainwright, Moore stated: "The Nips are landing out near North Point!" Wainwright reported to General MacArthur:

> Landing attack on Corregidor in progress. Enemy landed North Point. Further details as the situation develops.

MacArthur had Wainwright's message relayed to the War Department.[35]

There were actually 2,000 Japanese troops in the first wave, but only 800 reached the shore. In the second wave, of 10,000 troops, about 6,000 made it to the beach. A continuous stream of tracer bullets from the guns of the Filipino and American soldiers defending the beaches provided sufficient illumination to permit hitting the Japanese in their landing barges. Every battery on Corregidor that could bear on the landing site, along with the batteries on Fort Hughes, began firing, and troops of the beach defense forces engaged the enemy on the beach with rifle and machine-gun fire and bayonets.[36]

During the night Wainwright alternated between General Moore's Harbor Defense Headquarters and Lieutenant Colonel Curtis L. Beecher's command post at the eastern entrance of Malinta Tunnel.

Beecher was in command of the beach defenses on the eastern sector of Corregidor. In a second report to MacArthur, Wainwright stated:

> Enemy landing made during hours of darkness on east end of island vicinity of Kindley Field. Some barges loaded with Japanese troops known to have been sunk but strength of force, losses, and number landed not yet determined. Action is confined at present to area east of Ninety-second Coast Artillery Barracks. Am developing situation with view to attack at daylight to eject hostile force.[37]

After learning of the Japanese landing on Corregidor from MacArthur, Marshall directed Eisenhower to write a final message to Wainwright. Marshall made several corrections and additions to Eisenhower's draft, then authorized the message to be dispatched in Roosevelt's name. The message was turned over to the War Department's message center at 12:37 P.M. and sent in the clear to Corregidor. Since the message center in Malinta Tunnel had completely depleted its supply of official message blanks, the radio operator wrote it out on rough ruled paper. At 2:30 A.M. on May 6 it was handed to General Wainwright:

> During recent weeks, we have been following with growing admiration the day by day accounts of your heroic stand against the mounting intensity of bombardment by enemy planes and heavy siege guns. In spite of all the handicaps of complete isolation, lack of food and ammunition, you have given the world a shining example of patriotic fortitude and self-sacrifice. The American people ask no finer example of tenacity, resourcefulness, and steadfast courage. The calm determination of your personal leadership in a desperate situation sets a standard of duty for our soldiers throughout the world. In every camp and on every naval vessel, soldiers, sailors, and marines are inspired by the gallant struggle of their comrades in the Philippines. The workmen in our shipyards and munition plants redouble their efforts because of your example. You and your devoted followers have become the living symbols of our war aims and the guarantee of victory.[38]

In his reply to President Roosevelt, Wainwright wrote:

> Your gracious and generous message . . . has just reached me. I am without words to express to you, Mr. President, my gratitude for, and deep appreciation of, your great kindness. We have all done our best to carry out your former instructions and

keep our flag flying here as long as humanly possibly to do so. At 10:30 P.M. May 5, the enemy effected a landing here following such terrific air and artillery bombardment of the beaches during the past seven days that the beach defense organization was completely obliterated and great many weapons were destroyed. As I write this at 3:30 A.M. our patrols are attempting to locate the enemy positions and flanks and I will counter attack at dawn to drive him into the sea or destroy him. Thank you again Mr. President for your wonderful message which I will publish to my entire command.[39]

As dawn came about 4:20 A.M., the Japanese were slowly approaching Denver Hill, between Malinta Tunnel and the Japanese landing site. They also made a landing near Infantry Point behind the American line of resistance, necessitating a withdrawal toward Malinta Hill. Although the Beach Defense Reserve Battalion and Batteries B and C of the Fifty-ninth Coast Artillery launched a counterattack and pushed the Japanese back some distance, the counterattack was bogged down and thwarted by effective artillery fire from Bataan and by continuous strafing. While most of the troops were pinned to the ground, some were driven back into Malinta Tunnel.[40]

At 10:00 A.M. Wainwright learned from Colonel Samuel L. Howard, whose Fourth Marine Regiment manned the beach defenses, that the Japanese had landed additional tanks and were assembling them in the vicinity of Kindley Field. Knowing that a tank attack against Malinta Tunnel would precipitate a bloody massacre, Wainwright called for Generals Moore and Beebe and informed them that "in order to prevent the further useless sacrifice of lives, he had decided to surrender the fortified islands to the Japanese."

"We can't hold out very much longer," he told the two generals. "Maybe we could last through the day, but the end certainly must come tonight. It would be better to clear up the situation now, in day light." All regimental and fort commanders should destroy their heavy armament and be prepared to lay down their arms at noon, Wainwright said; he was authorizing a radiobroadcast to the Japanese command, announcing an end to hostilities at 12:00 noon, at which time the American flag would be lowered on Corregidor and replaced with a white flag. Moore and Beebe agreed that, considering the circumstances, there was nothing else Wainwright could do.[41]

By telephone Wainwright informed Captain Hoeffel that he had decided to surrender. He asked Hoeffel "to approve of his contemplated action and support him later" if following the war the government should hold an inquiry into the surrender. Tanks would soon threaten the occupants of Malinta Tunnel, Wainwright told Hoeffel, and "I cannot permit the slaughter of thousands of our people." Shortly thereafer, Hoeffel had the following message dispatched to the Navy Department:

> Our few remaining ships being sunk. Now destroying all military equipment. 172 officers and 2126 men of the navy send last expression of loyalty and devotion to country, to families, and to friends. Going off the air. Captain Hoeffel.[42]

At 10:30 A.M. General Beebe started to broadcast a message for the commander in chief of the Imperial Japanese forces on Luzon. General Wainwright would surrender the four fortified islands in Manila Bay, Beebe announced. The white flag would be displayed, and all firing from the harbor forts would cease at noon. If there was a complete cessation of Japanese shelling and aerial bombing by noon, Wainwright would delegate two of his staff officers to proceed to Cabcaben in order to meet with a Japanese staff officer and arrange for a formal surrender.[43]

Although the surrender announcement was rebroadcast in Japanese, the shelling continued while Japanese troops moved closer and closer to the east entrance of Malinta Tunnel. At 11:00 A.M. and again at 11:45 A.M., Wainwright had General Beebe repeat the surrender message. The Japanese bombardment continued without respite.[44]

Before noon Wainwright wrote out final messages for Major General William F. Sharp, commander of the Visayan-Mindanao force, for President Roosevelt, and for General MacArthur. In the message to Sharp, Wainwright authorized him to assume command of all forces in the Philippines with the exception of the Filamerican forces on the fortified islands in Manila Bay. Ordering Sharp to report to General MacArthur for instructions, Wainwright said, "I believe you will understand the motive behind this order." Wainwright wanted to surrender as few troops as possible.[45]

To President Roosevelt, Wainwright stated:

> For the President of the United States: It is with broken heart and head bowed in sadness, but not in shame, that I report to

Your Excellency that I must go today to arrange terms for the surrender of the fortified islands of Manila Bay: Corregidor (Fort Mills), Caballo (Fort Hughes), El Fraile (Fort Drum), and Carabao (Fort Frank).

With anti-aircraft fire control equipment and many guns destroyed, we are no longer able to prevent accurate aerial bombardment. With numerous batteries of the heaviest caliber emplaced on the shores of Bataan and Cavite out ranging our remaining guns, the enemy now brings devastating cross fire to bear on us.

Most of my batteries, seacoast, anti-aircraft and field, have been put out of action by the enemy. I have ordered the others destroyed to prevent them from falling into enemy hands. In addition we are now overwhelmingly assaulted by Japanese troops on Corregidor.

There is a limit of human endurance and that limit has long since been past. Without prospect of relief I feel it is my duty to my country and to my gallant troops to end this useless effusion of blood and human sacrifice.

If you agree, Mr. President, please say to the nation that my troops and I have accomplished all that is humanly possible and that we have upheld the best traditions of the United States and its Army.

May God bless and preserve you and guide you and the nation in the effort to ultimate victory.

With profound regret and with continued pride in my gallant troops I go to meet the Japanese commander. Good-by, Mr. President.[46]

To MacArthur, Wainwright sent the following message:

. . . I feel it is my duty to the nation and my troops to end this useless slaughter. There is apparently no relief in sight. American and Filipino troops have engaged and held the enemy for nearly five months. . . .

We have done our full duty for you and for our country. We are sad but unashamed. I have fought for you to the best of my ability from Lingayan Gulf to Bataan to Corregidor, always hoping relief was on the way. . . .

Good-by, General, my regards to you and our comrades in Australia. May God strengthen your arm to insure ultimate success of the cause for which we have fought side by side.[47]

At noon General Wainwright ordered Colonel Paul D. Bunker, the Seaward Defense commander, whose command post was near the flagpole on Topside, to lower the Stars and Stripes and to raise a white flag. Accompanied by Lieutenant Colonel Dwight Edison of the Fifty-ninth Coast Artillery, Bunker carried out the order with profound sadness.[48]

Just before 1:00 P.M., with the bombardment continuing in full fury, Wainwright instructed a marine officer, Captain Golland L. Clark, to proceed eastward from Malinta Tunnel, contact the senior officer of the Japanese invasion force, and arrange a conference inside Malinta Tunnel in order to effect a cease-fire. Accompanied by First Lieutenant Allan S. Manning of the Marine Corps, Clark left Malinta Tunnel and headed for the Japanese front line. Although neither Clark nor Manning could speak Japanese, Lieutenant Manning and a Japanese officer managed to converse in French. About an hour later, Clark and Manning returned to Malinta Tunnel. "He won't come to see you, General," Clark told Wainwright. "He insists that you go and meet him."[49]

Removing his service automatic from its holster, Wainwright placed it on his headquarters desk. Accompanied by General Moore, his aide Major Robert Brown, and Lieutenant Colonel Pugh and Major Doolcy, Wainwright was driven in Moore's Chevrolet, under a white flag, to the bottom of Kindley Field Water Tank Hill. They left the car and climbed the hill. Near the top they were met by a Japanese lieutenant named Uemura and a Japanese private who roughly grabbed the field glasses hanging from Colonel Pugh's neck.

"We will not accept your surrender unless it includes all American and Filipino troops in the whole archipelago," Uemura shouted before Wainwright could speak.

"I do not choose to discuss surrender terms with you," Wainwright replied. "Take me to the senior officer present on Corregidor."[50]

Colonel Motoo Nakayama, General Homma's senior operations officer, joined the group. Uemura told Nakayama, who looked at Wainwright "sharply," that Wainwright desired to surrender the four fortified islands of Manila Bay. In an "angry torrent of Japanese," Nakayama told Uemura to inform General Wainwright that his surrender had to include all Filamerican forces in the Philippines. Wainwright answered, "In that case I will deal only with General Homma and with no one of less rank. I want an appointment with him. I have made repeated efforts to contact him by radio." Nakayama agreed to take Wainwright to Cabcaben to see Homma.[51]

Wainwright asked Nakayama to walk to North Dock with him

and wait for a boat to be brought around from South Dock, where it had been anchored for protection from the shelling. Wainwright then instructed Moore to return to Malinta Tunnel and wait for his return from Cabcaben. When Wainwright turned to ask Pugh to accompany them to North Dock, he discovered that Pugh had left. He was heading back to the east entrance of Malinta Tunnel. Intending to make sure that the boat was taken from South Dock to North Dock, and to pick up some of Wainwright's personal effects, Pugh managed "by crawling, crouching, and edging along with what little cover as he could find" to move through a terrible storm of exploding artillery shells. At one point he dove into a shell crater, looked around, and saw a Japanese soldier in the same crater. The two soldiers regarded one another speechlessly for a few seconds before Pugh crawled out and moved on. Reaching Malinta Tunnel, Pugh found Brigadier General Beebe, Major William Lawrence, and Sergeant Hubert Carroll. Together they went to South Dock, boarded Lieutenant Baldwin's cabin cruiser–dispatch boat, and shoved off for North Dock.[52]

Meanwhile, Wainwright, Nakayama, Uemura, and Dooley were stopped on their way to North Dock by intensive Japanese shelling. When Nakayama refused to proceed any further for fear of being killed, Wainwright shouted, "Why the hell don't you people stop shooting? I put up my white flag hours ago." Viewing the heavy shelling in a crouched position, Nakayama answered through Uemura, "We have not accepted any surrender from you as yet."[53]

Nakayama finally straightened up and led the officers to Kindley airfield, where he radioed an order to Bataan for a boat to be dispatched to Corregidor. At Cavalry Point the party waited until nearly 4:00 P.M. for the Japanese boat. Finally a 50-foot armored tank barge arrived. The party boarded from a rubber raft and headed for Cabcaben.[54]

In the meantime the dispatch boat carrying Pugh, Beebe, Lawrence, and Carroll had reached North Dock. General Wainwright was not there. Believing that Wainwright had already left for Bataan, the officers ordered Baldwin to set a course for Cabcaben. The dispatch boat, which had been damaged in the shelling of Corregidor, could proceed on only one engine, and its speed was greatly reduced. It leaked and the crew was kept busy pumping.

As the dispatch boat headed slowly across Manila Bay for Cabcaben, a Japanese fighter pilot sighted it. The pilot maneuvered his fighter into position to strafe and headed straight for the defenseless craft. One of the men in the boat saw the oncoming fighter and frantically waved a white flag. The pilot withheld his fire, dipped one wing, and flew off.

Upon reaching Cabcaben's small dock, Lieutenant Colonel Pugh, carrying a white flag, disembarked and walked to the head of the dock to confer with the Japanese. Soon some Japanese soldiers appeared on the pier and ordered the officers and crew out of the boat. In a short time Wainwright arrived at the pier in the armored tank barge. He was met on the dock by Major Lawrence. Helping Wainwright out of the barge, Lawrence said, "Hello, General. I came over with General Beebe and Colonel Pugh. They couldn't find you at the north dock on the Rock, so they came ahead. They and Sergeant Carroll just took a Jap truck and went off to look for you, figuring you might have landed someplace else."[55]

Colonel Nakayama learned from several Japanese officers at the Cabcaben dock that General Homma planned to meet with General Wainwright at a home on the main east-coast road of Bataan, about three-quarters of a mile northeast of Cabcaben. Nakayama procured a car and the officers were driven in silence to a battered white house encircled by a large porch. The officers sat down on the porch to wait for Homma. They were joined by Beebe, Pugh, and Carroll, who had driven up in a Japanese truck. A Japanese soldier brought them some cold drinking water, which they gratefully accepted. From the porch the American officers, looking to the south across Manila Bay, could see Japanese artillery shells exploding on Corregidor.[56]

While Wainwright and his officers were impatiently waiting on the veranda for Homma, Japanese newsmen and cameramen arrived. A newsreel cameraman hurriedly set into position his camera and sound-effects equipment, then started taking long-distance pictures of the American officers. When Wainwright noticed that the cameraman was focusing on him, he quickly turned away. In an effort to placate the cameraman, Colonel Katsuya, chief of the Japanese Army Propaganda Corps in the Philippines, stepped onto the porch, saluted Wainwright, and ordered him and his party to line up on the lawn for the benefit of the still photographers and newsreel cameramen. Reluctantly they complied.[57]

They had been posing for about thirty minutes and were still lined up in front of the veranda at 5:00 P.M. when a Cadillac, followed by two other cars, stopped before the house. Accompanied by three aides, Lieutenant General Masaharu Homma, commander of the Imperial Japanese Fourteenth Army, got out.

Homma was about 5 feet, 10 inches tall, barrel-chested and heavy-set, weighing close to 200 pounds. His size somewhat "astonished" Wainwright. He wore an olive drab tropical uniform, displaying several rows of bright decorations and campaign ribbons, and carried a sword at his side. The collar of his uniform was open and his white shirt collar was turned down over it. Followed by his aides, principal staff officers, and Japanese newsmen, who had been in the other two cars, Homma approached Wainwright. He gave the American general a contemptuous look and a sketchy salute, then brushed past the waiting group onto the veranda. Wainwright and his officers followed silently.[58]

Taking a center seat behind an oblong table that had been set up on the porch, Homma motioned for his staff officers to occupy the chairs on either side of him. Wainwright was motioned into the seat opposite Homma. Brigadier General Beebe took the seat at Wainwright's left and Lieutenant Colonel Pugh that at his right. Major Dooley sat next to Beebe and Major Lawrence sat next to Pugh. Standing behind the American officers was Sergeant Hubert Carroll.[59]

As soon as everyone was seated, Homma had his interpreter, Lieutenant Nakamura, read the following statement in English: "Welcome to Cabcaben. You must be very tired and weary."

"Thank you, General Homma. I have come to surrender my men unconditionally," Wainwright replied, taking a formally signed surrender statement from his pocket and handing it to Homma. Without glancing at the paper Homma handed it to Nakamura, who read it in Japanese.[60]

Glaring several times at Wainwright, Homma spoke sharply to Nakamura after the surrender statement had been read. "General Homma replies that no surrender will be considered unless it includes all United States and Philippine troops in the Philippines," Nakamura translated.

"Tell him I command no forces in the Philippines other than the harbor defense troops and small detachments in northern Luzon," Wainwright answered. "Tell him that the troops in the Visayan

Islands and on Mindanao are no longer under my command. They are commanded by General Sharp, who in turn is under General MacArthur's command."

Homma spoke again to Nakamura, who exclaimed, "General Homma says that he does not believe you. He says that it has been reported many times by the United States radio that you command all troops in the Philippines. He will not accept any surrender unless it includes all forces."[61]

When Wainwright repeated that he no longer was in command of Sharp's troops, Homma shrewdly asked him when he had released Sharp from his command. "Several days ago," Wainwright replied, even though it had been done that morning. "Besides, even if I did command General Sharp's troops, I have no means left for communicating with him. I destroyed my radio equipment."

"Send a staff officer," Homma retorted. "I will furnish a plane."[62]

The Japanese officers conversed emotionally among themselves, while General Wainwright and his officers looked worried. Suddenly, General Homma slammed his fist on the table and slowly and emphatically announced: "At the time of General King's surrender in Bataan, I did not see him. Neither have I any reason to see you if you are only the Commander of a unit of the American forces. I wish only to negotiate with my equal, the Commander in Chief of American forces in the Philippines. Since you are not in supreme command, I see no further necessity for my presence here."[63]

"Wait!" Colonel Pugh exclaimed, as Homma started to rise. Pugh, Wainwright, and Beebe held a murmured conference. Then Wainwright addressed Homma.

"In face of the fact that further bloodshed in the Philippines is unnecessary and futile, I will assume command of the entire American forces in the Philippines at the risk of serious reprimand by my government following the war."

"You have denied your authority," replied Homma, who had listened very intently, "and your momentary decision may be regretted by your men. I advise you to return to Corregidor and think this matter over. If you see fit to surrender, then surrender to the officer of the division on Corregidor. He in turn will bring you to me in Manila. I call this meeting over. Good day."[64]

As Homma rose he told Wainwright that the assault against the fortified islands would be continued. Followed by his staff officers and aides, he "strode haughtily off the porch." After Homma's party had left, the American officers stood up. Beebe was speechless. Wainwright leaned on his cane, his face lined, thinking of the helpless people on Corregidor.

"General," said Major Dooley, breaking the poignant silence, "you'll have to arrange something. At your command all troops on Corregidor and the other harbor islands disarmed this afternoon. The Japs will slaughter our unarmed people."[65]

"What do you want us to do now?" Wainwright asked Colonel Nakayama.

"We will take you and your party back to Corregidor, and then you can do what you damn please," Lieutenant Uemura snapped.

Completely exasperated, Wainwright walked away. When Pugh asked Uemura what was going to happen, he replied that Wainwright should return to Corregidor and surrender to the commander of the invasion force or resume fighting.[66]

Using Kazumaro Uno, a Japanese newsman who had been educated at the University of Utah, as an interpreter, Pugh and Beebe conversed with Colonel Nakayama. At one point in the conversation, Uno remarked, "General Wainwright was given his opportunity and he refused it. We will continue our offensive against Corregidor." Rushing over to Wainwright, Pugh and Beebe told him that "some kind of concession" would have to be made. Finally agreeing, Wainwright told Pugh that he would send him to Sharp's headquarters.

"General Wainwright will surrender the entire American forces in the Philippines to General Homma unconditionally," Pugh said, returning to Uno and Nakayama. "We have given orders for our men to lay down their arms. Take us to General Homma and General Wainwright will dispatch me to Mindanao to instruct General Sharp to comply with his demands."

"I am not authorized to accept your surrender," Nakayama replied through Uno. "Now that General Homma has gone you can surrender only to the commanding officer of the Imperial Japanese Forces on Corregidor." He added, "I shall go with you to Corregidor and safely turn you over to the commanding officer there. Stay for the night and first thing tomorrow go to General Homma with a new surrender and an understanding to contact other U.S. forces in the Philippines."[67]

It was growing dark as the officers returned to the dock at Cabcaben. General Wainwright's boat, which Pugh, Beebe, Lawrence, and Carroll had brought from Corregidor, had rammed the pier and sprung a leak. Their luggage had been removed from the sinking boat and was sitting on the dock. They loaded it onto the tank barge and started for Corregidor.

In virtual darkness the tank barge plowed through the rough waters of Manila Bay. A stillness filled the night. During the trip, Wainwright thought about General Sharp's command and whether he should order Sharp to surrender. He knew that MacArthur had envisioned Sharp breaking up his command into small units and initiating guerrilla warfare in Mindanao. But Wainwright also knew that the lives of the 11,000 men and women on Corregidor would be in jeopardy as long as fighting continued in the Philippines.

As the barge neared Corregidor, its passengers could see lights from American positions and numerous campfires indicating Japanese positions. Turning around, Uno saw an American soldier lying prostrate on top of the luggage. "What's the matter?" he asked with a slight shock. "I'm not feeling well," General Beebe said in a choked voice. He was seasick.

Taking a small paper bag from his pocket, Colonel Nakayama handed it to Uno to give to Wainwright. "This is what the Japanese soldier eats in place of candy," Nakayama explained. Wainwright took several of the small cookies it held and passed the bag to Pugh. Eating one, Pugh remarked, "Not bad."

About 50 feet from North Point, at the foot of a 60- to 70-foot bluff, the barge grounded on rocks. Attempts to free it were unsuccessful. "You walk—when you can!" Nakayama shouted, jumping over the side into the water. Although some of the men tried to carry Wainwright and Beebe through the chest-high water, they tripped and both generals were dunked. Beebe collapsed in the sand on reaching the shore. Seeing that everyone needed a breather, Nakayama ordered a rest and passed around the cookies again. For a few moments they shared the beach with the bodies of a large number of Japanese soldiers.[68]

Going on, the group, led by Colonel Nakayama, Lieutenant Uemura, and Uno, climbed a steep embankment for about a hundred yards and reached the main road to Malinta Tunnel's east entrance. As they approached the tunnel, Wainwright saw many enemy campfires. When he was near enough to see that the main Japanese line was only one hundred yards from the tunnel entrance, he turned to Uemura and said, "Take me to your commander."

Wainwright, Dooley, Pugh, and Lawrence were taken by Uemura

and Nakayama around Malinta Tunnel to the small *barrio* of San José. The others remained behind. In the destroyed market area of the *barrio*, Wainwright was introduced to Colonel Gempachi Sato, commander of the invasion force. Wainwright learned that the Japanese were in complete control of Malinta Tunnel and were planning to occupy Topside. An unconditional surrender document was drawn up and at midnight Wainwright signed it. In accordance with Homma's demands, he authorized the surrender of all Filamerican forces in the Philippines. Then, accompanied by several Japanese guards, Wainwright, Pugh, and Lawrence were escorted to Malinta Tunnel.[69]

When General Wainwright and his party had left Malinta Tunnel at about 1:00 that afternoon, Brigadier General Charles C. Drake, the chief quartermaster, had become the highest ranking officer in the tunnel. While the troops, nurses, and wounded men waited anxiously inside the tunnel for Wainwright's return, fighting continued outside Malinta Tunnel with machine-gun and rifle fire continually pouring into the east entrance. The Japanese were gradually approaching the tunnel, which had become a "virtual hell-hole."

By 2:30 P.M. there was still no sign of General Wainwright. Drake, who believed Wainwright and his party "had either been killed or muted into captivity," decided to take command. Drake's executive officer, Lieutenant Colonel Theodore Kalakuka, a West Point graduate who spoke five languages, requested permission to leave the tunnel in an effort to make contact with the Japanese and to bring about a cease-fire. Kalakuka reasoned that he could find a Japanese soldier who could speak one of his five languages. With Drake's okay, Kalakuka left the tunnel and returned in a short time with a Japanese major and a lieutenant who spoke Russian. The Russian-speaking officer demanded that everyone leave the tunnel via the west entrance within ten minutes. Knowing that the demand was an absurdity, Drake flared at Kalakuka: "You tell him there are 2,000 men in this tunnel alone. It will be impossible to get them out in that time. Also, there is firing going on outside that entrance and it must be stopped before the men will place themselves in a position to be shot down." Thinking he had been too abrupt, Drake added, "Give them my guarantee that I will get every man outside of the tunnel as quickly as I can." The Japanese officers gave their consent.

With the exception of the doctors, nurses, and wounded, who

remained behind in the hospital section, the tunnel's occupants emerged from the west entrance. Everyone was outside by 4:00 P.M. They remained in the vicinity of the west entrance until the following morning. Actually, then, General Wainwright did not formally surrender Corregidor; "it just fell," as a result of the actions taken by Kalakuka and Drake.[70]

Making his way to the west entrance of the tunnel, Wainwright passed through the rank and file of its former occupants. Some of the men shook his hand, others patted him on the back and said, "It's all right, General, you did your best." By the time he reached the west entrance his eyes were wet with tears.

Wainwright found the tunnel practically deserted. He walked past the silent wounded men on their hospital cots, to General Moore's headquarters lateral. There he told Moore that he had agreed to surrender all Filamerican forces in the Philippines—that failure to do so "would have caused the annihilation of the people of Corregidor, at no permanent advantage to the men left on the other islands." Moore agreed that there was no sense in further jeopardizing the lives of the people on the fortified islands. "But I feel I have taken a dreadful step," Wainwright concluded. Exhausted and humiliated, he and Pugh returned to their headquarters lateral, collapsed on their cots, and tried to sleep.[71]

The following morning, Wainwright was visited by Lieutenant Nakamura, who had been Homma's interpreter at Cabcaben, and Lieutenant Colonel Hikaru Haba, one of Homma's staff officers. Haba informed Wainwright that he was there to discuss the details of the surrender. Calling for his assistant chief of staff for operations, Colonel Jesse T. Traywick, Wainwright dictated to Traywick a memorandum of instructions ordering General Sharp to surrender. To Traywick was assigned the mission of flying to Mindanao in a Japanese plane for the purpose of delivering the memorandum personally to Sharp.

When Haba informed Wainwright that he was taking him to Manila to deliver a radiobroadcast that night ordering the surrender of all Filamerican forces in the Philippines, Wainwright at first refused. Then it occurred to him that the broadcast would give Sharp additional time to contact General MacArthur while his written orders were en route with Colonel Traywick.

At five o'clock in the afternoon, Haba returned to Malinta Tunnel for Wainwright. Escorted by Haba, Wainwright and five other officers were taken to Manila. Arriving at Manila's radio station KZRH around midnight, Wainwright delivered the following appeal:

This is Lieutenant General Jonathan M. Wainwright. I have a message for General William F. Sharp, commanding the Mindanao forces. For General Sharp, commanding in Mindanao. Anyone receiving this message please notify him.

By virtue of the authority vested in me by the President of the United States, I, as Commanding General of the United States forces in the Philippines hereby resume direct command of Major General Sharp, commander of Visayan and Mindanao forces, and all troops under his command. I will now give a direct order to General Sharp. I repeat, please notify him. The subject is surrender. To Major General William J. Sharp, Jr. This is the message: To put a stop to further useless sacrifice of life on the fortified islands, yesterday I tendered to Lieutenant General Homma, commander in the Philippines, the surrender of the four harbor defense posts in Manila Bay. General Homma declined to accept unless the surrender included places under your command. It became apparent that they would be destroyed by the airplanes and tanks which have overwhelmed Corregidor.

After leaving General Homma with no agreement, I decided to accept, in the name of humanity, his proposal and tendered at midnight to the senior Japanese officer on Corregidor the formal surrender of all American and Filipino troops on the Philippine Islands. You will, therefore, be guided accordingly and will, I repeat, will surrender all of your forces to the proper Japanese officer.

This position, you will realize, was forced on me by circumstances beyond my control. My assistant chief of staff will deliver this letter to you personally and is fully empowered to act for me. You are hereby ordered by me as senior officer in the Philippine Islands to scrupulously carry out the order in this letter and also whatever else this staff officer might give you. You will repeat this letter and other instructions by radio to General MacArthur.

However, let me emphasize that there must be no disregard of these instructions. If you do not obey them your actions will only have the most disastrous results.

Continued to Colonel Nakar and General Sharp, the following message:

For Lieutenant Colonel Horan, commanding American and Filipino forces in the mountainous provinces, and for Colonel Nakar, commanding American and Filipino forces in the Tayan Valley. I repeat, for Lieutenant Colonel Horan, and Colonel Nakar. To put a stop to further useless sacrifice of life. . . . [The above message was repeated][72]

Gradually, one by one, the commanders of the American army units on the other islands of the archipelago would follow General Wainwright's instructions to cease hostilities and to surrender. For Wainwright the war in the Philippines had finally come to an end.[73]

When MacArthur learned of Wainwright's surrender, he wrote out in longhand: "Corregidor needs no comment from me. It has sounded its own story at the mouth of its guns. It has scrolled its own epitaph on enemy tablets. But through the bloody haze of its last reverberating shot I shall always seem to see a vision of grim, gaunt, ghastly men, still unafraid."[74]

11

In Retrospect

"What a glorious thing must be a victory, Sir."
"The greatest tragedy in the world, Madam, except a defeat."[1]

—Duke of Wellington

Japan had conquered the Philippine Islands. A Filamerican force of 140,000 men had been defeated. More than seven million Filipinos had been enslaved by the invader. The United States had failed in its political and moral commitment to defend the Philippines, and more than 20,000 American officers and enlisted men had been either killed or captured. It was the worst military disaster in the history of the U.S. armed forces.[2]

As a result of her conquest, Japan eliminated the threat that the Philippines posed to her sea communications with the Netherlands East Indies and Southeast Asia, and also obtained the finest port of the Orient, Manila. Japan had swallowed Guam, Wake, Hong Kong, Singapore, the Netherlands East Indies, and finally the Philippines, to achieve hegemony in the South Pacific. Concerning this catastrophe, Brigadier General Bradford G. Chynoweth stated:

> The plain fact stands out that the greatest industrial power on earth, the United States, was impotent in the defense of the Philippines. . . . In full truth, it was an unsavory mess. It was a tragedy, a disgrace, a disaster. The American nation had done so much to help the Philippine Republic. This disaster wiped it all away, and left deep wounds that have never yet been healed.[3]

Was the Japanese conquest of the Philippines inevitable? Or, on

231

the other hand, were there political and military measures that could have been adopted by the U.S. government prior to Pearl Harbor which would have prevented the subjugation of the islands? What were the fundamental reasons for the fall of the Philippines?

In the years following World War I, seeds were sown which brought forth the bleak harvest of May 1942—seeds that were psychological, political, and military. Disillusioned with the results of World War I, the American people favored to a large degree an isolationist foreign policy, despite the fact that America was a world power with vital global interests.[4] America underestimated the political ambitions and military potential of Japan. Most Americans thought the Japanese were so ill equipped and so inefficient that they would not dare attack the great United States. While the American people were psychologically obsessed with the conviction of white supremacy, the American political leaders appeared weak and indecisive. They did not understand the nature of the potential enemy, failed to analyze his strategy, and failed to plan and act accordingly.[5]

The Armament Limitation Treaty of 1922 and the London Naval Reduction Treaty of 1930 tied the hands of the United States and played into the hands of Japan. In 1935, for example, the War Department purchased new searchlight equipment. Although new searchlights were needed in the Philippines, they were instead shipped to Panama because the treaties with Japan did not permit an "increase in defensive armament." While the U.S. government adhered to the treaties, neglecting the defenses of Wake, Guam, and the Philippines, the Japanese government fortified the mandated islands and prepared for war. Colonel Edward C. Englehart, who was a language student in Tokyo from 1927 to 1931, recalled a very popular book during his sojourn in Japan: *The Inevitability of War With the United States.*[6]

In the 1920s and 1930s Congress refused to appropriate funds for strengthening the defenses in the Philippines. Plans for strengthening the defenses of Manila and Subic bays and for constructing airfields, storage facilities, and roads on Bataan were not fulfilled, owing to a lack of funds. Former Assistant Secretary of War John J. McCloy wrote:

> A strong and flexible Air Force operating in the Philippines might have been a decisive deterrent, but this would have involved far greater expenditures of money than we

seemed to be prepared to spend at that time. Steps such as these could have been taken but we did not have the will to take them. There had been plans made up for the defense of the Philippines which would certainly have constituted a deterrent to the Japanese but none of them were even adopted, or, I believe, seriously considered.[7]

In the early 1930s Japan started her expansion in China. The Chinese mainland became the training ground for the Japanese armies which later overran Malaya, the Netherlands East Indies, and the Philippines. The U.S. government chose to ignore this muscle-flexing and aggrandizement just as the European powers were ignoring the rise of Hitler and Mussolini in the Western world. The lethargy and weakness on the part of the Western powers and the patent support of those powers by the United States led Japanese leaders to assume that the United States would not interfere with Japan's expansion in Southeast Asia.[8]

Shocked by the fall of France and the German threat to Great Britain, in the summer of 1940 the Roosevelt administration started to take seriously the Japanese military threat in Asia. Economic pressure was suddenly brought to bear on Japan. Japanese assets were frozen in the United States and Japan was denied oil and steel. But this pressure was applied too abruptly and too late. Instead of thwarting Japanese aggression, the economic pressure merely stimulated it.[9]

The Roosevelt administration had suddenly switched from an appeasement policy to a hard-line policy, concerning which John J. McCloy commented:

> I doubt whether any radically different policy in respect of Japan would have averted or deterred the Japanese military from their objectives, or, put another way, I cannot think of any United States policy which would have been successful in averting the then ambitions of Japan. We could have gone along with or encouraged their expansion in the South Pacific, i.e., we could have entered into a sort of Munich with them in respect of their ambitions in the Pacific, but I doubt whether in the long run it would have proven effective.[10]

The new U.S. policy, however, gave Japan no alternative but to draw back ignominiously or to attack. According to General Albert C. Wedemeyer, who served in the War Plans Division of the

War Department, "Every stratagem was being resorted to . . . but principally repressive and stringent economic measures against Japan in order to precipitate some deliberate act of war that would justify our entrance." Although the Roosevelt administration had finally decided to stand up, to speak loudly, to take a hard line, to court war with Japan, it lacked a "big stick."[11]

Roosevelt's administration attempted to create one overnight in the Philippines. Reinforcements in the form of B-17 bombers, P-40 fighters, radar, war material, officers, and enlisted men were hurriedly assembled and dispatched to the Philippines. The reinforcements were too little and too late. For instance, when the war started there were several Air Groups of fighter pilots in the Philippines without any fighter planes. According to Colonel E. C. Lentz, "We were one and a half to two years short of developing a capability of holding the Philippine Islands against a determined attack."[12]

When the Japanese struck on December 8, they were fully aware of the atrocious condition of the Filamerican forces in the Philippines. For years prior to the attack, Japanese agents had visited the islands, taking pictures of military sites, asking questions, and gathering information of a military nature. The weapons and equipment of the Filamerican forces were largely World War I vintage and in many cases defective. "We had obsolete ammunition and antiaircraft artillery. Three-quarters of my mortar shells were duds," said Colonel Donovan Swanton. According to Lieutenant Colonel William B. Reardon, who was a captain in command of antiaircraft battery E of the 200th Coast Artillery in the middle of Clark Field during the first Japanese attack, "My own experience was that I entered a shooting war with guns that would not fire. They had never been test fired. Ammunition had not been issued. All the ammunition my battery had was borrowed from the Air Corps or salvaged from wrecked B-17s on Clark Field." Colonel Edmund J. Lilly, who served in the 57th Infantry (PS), wrote, "Logistics planning reached an all time low. Here is one 'grass roots' example: my regiment had its complement of 60-mm mortars, but not *round one* of ammunition. There are literally hundreds of other examples."[13]

In the days immediately preceding Pearl Harbor there seems to have been a great deal of confusion among political leaders in the Philippines with respect to Japan's intentions. Some political officials believed that the Japanese would not attack the islands, but instead would bypass them in their southward advance. Brigadier General

Chynoweth, who arrived in Manila on the U.S.S. *Coolidge* just before the Japanese attack on Pearl Harbor, said that "Manila was in a state of political paralysis." Chynoweth recalled attending a dinner the night following his arrival in Manila at which Major Cyril Q. Marron, High Commissioner Sayre's military advisor, was completely in despair. "The Japs have already won!" Marron said bitterly. "The political situation is such that nobody can do anything."[14]

Apparently the Japanese attack on December 8 surprised even MacArthur. According to Major General Chih Wang, Generalissimo Chiang Kai-shek's liaison officer with General MacArthur:

> General MacArthur never did have a high opinion for Japanese military strategy; at least he was not fully aware of Japan's capacity of making a daring decision in the last days of 1941. In my first interview with him in May 1941, he told me that Japan would never dare to attack the Philippines. . . . I am certain that it was out of his expectations that Japanese troops landed for the conquest of the Philippines immediately after wiping out the little American air force on the ground.[15]

MacArthur made several other errors of judgment that hastened the fall of the Philippines. He completely overestimated the quality and capability of his Philippine Army. The Filipino soldiers were not adequately trained, organized, or equipped to seriously match, let alone destroy, Homma's Fourteenth Army. Colonel Ernest B. Miller, commander of the 194th Tank Battalion (National Guard), stated:

> The Philippine Army could not be depended upon. This should have occasioned little surprise. MacArthur had been told that before. These people had no chance for proper training and had not handled firearms before. The Filipino was no coward. He was untrained—a part of a mob. Americans have had ample experience to clearly show the folly of placing untrained personnel against a well-trained and well-equipped army. . . . Why should anyone have thought that the Filipino was any different?[16]

MacArthur should have compensated for the weaknesses inherent in the Philippine army by obtaining, prior to the war, additional troops from the United States which would have bolstered and strengthened his fledgling army. He failed to do so because he be-

lieved that when the Japanese struck his Philippine army would be
ready. He was naive and unrealistic in expecting that army to engage
successfully in large-scale offensive operations.

On December 22, when about 40,000 troops of Homma's Fourteenth Army came ashore in Lingayen Gulf, MacArthur elected to
oppose the landing at the beaches. Although two Philippine Army
divisions and the Twenty-sixth Cavalry of Philippine Scouts endeavored to resist the invasion, they could not stop the enemy on the
beaches and drive him back into the sea. Instead of opposing the
Japanese landing force, MacArthur should have ordered immediately the withdrawal into the Bataan peninsula, organized his defenses there, and concentrated on moving available supplies from
the Manila area into the peninsula.[17]

Further, MacArthur neglected the logistic requirements of the
Filamerican Army for withstanding a lengthy siege of Bataan. At
the start of hostilities the Manila docks were stacked high with
food and supplies. Only a small fraction of this precious logistic
material was transferred to Bataan. Most of it was burned on the
docks when Manila was declared an open city. Later, as a result, the
Filamerican Army slowly starved on the Bataan peninsula. "General MacArthur's weakness was his concentration on tactical versus
logistic considerations," said Lieutenant Colonel John R. Pray. One
general officer was even more emphatic: "The Philippine disaster
[stemmed from] a complete breakdown in logistics due to the gross
ineptitude of MacArthur's own headquarters." Colonel Achille C.
Tisdelle, who was Major General Edward P. King's aide-de-camp
and was with him when he surrendered Bataan, concluded, "Ours
was a logistics, not a military defeat."[18]

Two major factors ensured the eventual Japanese conquest of the
Philippines. The first was that "commitments had been made by
responsible American officials to enter the war against Germany
prior to Pearl Harbor." The second was the failure of the United
States Navy to keep open the sea communications between the
United States and the Philippines.[19]

Secretary of War Stimson had been profoundly concerned with
the timidity and inactivity of the United States Navy in the months
following the Japanese attack at Pearl Harbor. Brigadier General
Eugene L. Harrison, Stimson's military aide, wrote:

Mr. Stimson was greatly distressed over the loss of our troops and our inability to supply, reinforce, or remove them from the Islands. Our Navy . . . was in such a state of shock after Pearl Harbor that it did practically nothing for six months or more. I felt and I believe that Mr. Stimson agreed that some attempt should have been made to relieve Bataan and Corregidor. In fact I made a study for Mr. Stimson of the comparative strengths of the Allied and Japanese navies in the Pacific and Indian oceans shortly before the surrender of Corregidor. Using *Jane's Fighting Ships* as a source, and giving the Japanese credit for two super-battleships which they never had built, and de-militarized cruisers built in 1898, I found that the Allied navies—British and United States—had more ships of all types except aircraft carriers than the Japanese. Our carriers were larger and could put more planes in the air than the more numerous Japanese carriers. Our battleships and cruisers had larger guns and more armor. The Japanese cruisers and destroyers were about two knots faster. Taken all together, we were superior in every way except speed of the Japanese new cruisers and destroyers. Mr. Stimson took the study over to show Secretary of the Navy Knox. Nothing came of it. But it leads me to believe that Mr. Stimson felt as I did—that some attempt should have been made to relieve our forces at Bataan and Corregidor.

Incidentally, later I was called before the attorney conducting the Pearl Harbor Investigation for the Congress. An entry on the Navy Department log at about 8:00 P.M. December sixth stated, "Major Harrison, aide to the Secretary of War, requested the positions of all United States and British ships this date." I did not make such a call, although I did ask and get this information a few months later shortly before the surrender of Corregidor.

The attorney apparently doubted my denial of making the request on December sixth and intimated that I would be very much embarrassed trying to explain this to the Congressional Committee. When I told him that I would simply tell the Committee that my purpose in getting this information at a later date was to prove that the Navy was in such a state

of shock it would not fight, I was never called before the
Committee.[20]

During the winter of 1941, and even on previous occasions, American and British military authorities conferred secretly in Washington. It was decided that in the event the United States entered the war, the United States and Great Britain would concentrate their military forces and conduct offensive operations in the Atlantic theater with the objective of defeating Germany. It was also decided that if Japan entered the war, defensive operations of a holding nature would be conducted against her. The Pacific would be a secondary theater of operations and Allied forces would be concentrated against Japan only following the defeat of Nazi Germany.

The die was cast and a significant precedent, never reversed, was established. After the United States entered the war, American political and military leaders, knowing that Germany was the more powerful and dangerous of the two enemies, did not deviate from the "Europe first" principle of global war strategy. One idea behind this strategy was to sacrifice a few lives in the short run in order to save many lives in the long run. Another was to concentrate first on the stronger enemy, Hitler's Germany, which occupied most of Europe. For the Philippines, its ramifications meant defeat and conquest. In order to defeat Nazi Germany and thereby shorten the war, it was necessary to sacrifice the Philippines.[21]

Stimson's dilemma with respect to the Philippines and the "Europe first war strategy" is best explained by John McCloy:

> Stimson was deeply affected by the Japanese attack on the Philippines and the subsequent retreat down the peninsula. He used to say like Queen Mary in respect of Calais, his heart was involved in the plight of the Philippines.
>
> I do not believe that he disagreed with the fundamental decision to give priority to the European theatre. His military and political training was such as to convince him that this was the proper decision, but his sentiments were deeply imbedded in the Philippines and the Pacific. . . . Those who were closely associated with Stimson, I am sure, can well recall, as I do, the meetings that he had with his immediate staff at Woodley, which was his house in Washington, after the close of the day's work in the Department. The subject of the Philippines and the fate of the Army there was almost

invariably brought up in these evening discussions. [Robert A.] Lovett, Harvey Bundy, usually a General Staff Officer, frequently the head of the Operations Division, and myself were the usual group at those meetings. [Because] Stimson had known both MacArthur and Wainwright . . . their positions, as well as that of the Army on the peninsula, were never far from his mind. The speed [at which Stimson arrived at his decision that] the Army should stand and fight and not compromise over the Quezon proposals was an indication of Stimson's deep interest in the preservation of the integrity of the Philippines.[22]

The decision to give Wainwright complete command of all forces in the Philippines was one of the greatest errors that the War Department committed in its handling of the war in the Philippines. Although MacArthur had originally intended to exercise overall command in the Philippines from Australia, the War Department turned this command over to Wainwright. Since Wainwright was faced with a hopeless situation in March of 1942, "all that this action did was to add manifold to his responsibility without helping him in the slightest degree to carry out his hopeless task." Because Wainwright was left in legal command, the Japanese could rightly order him to surrender all forces in the Philippines. And in the end, this was what General Homma demanded.[23]

If the War Department had decentralized the Philippine command, the Filamerican forces on each island could have carried on guerrilla operations. "I believe," wrote Major General Chih Wang, "a well planned guerrilla based defense should have prolonged the guerrilla warfare after the conquest and should have made the comeback much easier and much earlier." If the various island commanders had been detached from Wainwright's command, said General Chynoweth:

> We could have organized guerrilla warfare. This was my intention and plan.
>
> In September 1942, I arrived in a prison camp at Karenko, Taiwan, with the other senior officers from the southern islands. The next morning when I went out to the washstands, I encountered General Wainwright. In utter abjection, he apologized to me for having ordered us all to surrender. The surrender was a bitter blow to me. But I

assured him, from the depth of my heart, that I did not blame him for his action.

The function of *command* is rightly considered a great honor. But *command,* without the *means,* or the *authority* to fulfill it, is a bitter cup. I think that our political leaders often fail to appreciate this.[24]

The cup of command had been passed from General MacArthur to General Wainwright. Each in his own way had drunk its bitter contents.

Essentially a tactician, General Wainwright was a flamboyant cavalryman, a great corps commander. In the mold of those officers of chivalry who fought for the South during the Civil War, Wainwright was a field soldier who enjoyed being with his officers, soldiers, and horses. A "soldier's soldier," easily approachable, Wainwright was greatly liked and admired by his men. He had the ability to arouse their personal affection. Denied generalship in the sense of strategy or grand tactics on Bataan and Corregidor, Wainwright "did well the only thing that he could do; he kept up the morale and spirit of his men admirably." Two great qualities enabled him to cope with the debacle and to surrender the Filamerican forces in the Philippines: humility and compassion. Wainwright coupled a modest sense of his own importance with a profound sense of sorrow for the sufferings of his brave but defeated soldiers.[25]

If General MacArthur had remained in command in the Philippines, it is doubtful that he would ever have surrendered to the Japanese. Death would have been preferable to surrender. Corregidor would have followed Thermopylae and the Alamo in the annals of military history. As Brigadier General Charles C. Drake, quartermaster general on Corregidor and the third-ranking officer behind Generals Wainwright and Moore, explained, "We knew how MacArthur felt about surrender. There would be no surrender of Bataan and/or Corregidor and the other fortified islands in Manila Bay. Always counterattack. That was his creed."[26]

Essentially a strategist, MacArthur was a brilliant and articulate planner of military campaigns. He was a staff officer who was not only a master of the military profession but also a student of oriental psychology, philosophy, political science, economics, and history. With a profound sense of history and his place in it, he was one of the greatest military captains of all time. He maintained cool, unruffled control of his emotions during critical periods. Greatly respected, MacArthur aroused professional admiration for his outstanding reputation and ability. His tremendous competence as a military leader instilled confidence in his men. According to Colonel Edmund J. Lilly, "There was little that man could not do." Not socially inclined, above the crowd, and slightly egotistical and pompous, MacArthur liked to refer to himself as "austere." "MacArthur was always on Mount Olympus, reserved, remote," said Colonel Donovan Swanton, "but a master in the art of projecting himself in a dramatic fashion."[27]

It is difficult to compare Generals MacArthur and Wainwright. "General MacArthur had the opportunity for his star to rise to the zenith," one officer observed, "and General Wainwright never had this opportunity." General Albert C. Wedemeyer, who knew both of them, wrote:

> General MacArthur was one of our greatest military leaders of all time. He not only was skilled in military art but also had a deep insight into historical developments—to the organization and functioning of governments, and to economic matters—to a degree seldom found among our military leaders. I would state without fear of refutation that he could rightfully be described as a military commander of outstanding ability, a shrewd statesman, and a sound economist.
>
> General Wainwright, on the other hand, was proficient as a military leader, but I am confident that his capacity in other fields was limited, at least was not above average. He did epitomize the finest traditions of the military profession and was fully capable of carrying out the responsibilities which were his in World War II.[28]

Both generals enjoyed prestige and esteem in the professional army. While MacArthur was primarily a strategist, Wainwright was a tactician. MacArthur aroused professional admiration; Wainwright aroused personal affection. Wainwright was basically on the corps level, but MacArthur was far above the corps level. To Colonel Paul H. Krause, "General MacArthur was Moses—commanding the waters to separate; General Wainwright was King Saul—fearlessly leading his people in battle." Lieutenant General Alva R. Fitch said, "Both were splendid leaders. . . . MacArthur shone justly as a theatre commander. Wainwright did an excellent job with his limited resources. Neither would have been satisfactory in the other's role." And in the words of Brigadier General Royal Reynolds, "Thank God we had both of them."[29]

MacArthur and Wainwright were giants of their time. During the fear-filled days that followed Pearl Harbor, they captured the imaginations of people longing to be free. They exhibited indomitable courage and perseverance in the face of overwhelming forces. Both graduates of the U.S. Military Academy, they personified the motto of West Point: "Duty, Honor, Country." As long as Bataan and Corregidor are remembered, so also will be remembered the gallant Filamerican army that fought there, and the names MacArthur and Wainwright.

Acknowledgments

Since the fall of 1966, when I started my research, I have been greatly helped by many individuals. Indeed, this history could never have been written without aid, encouragement, and cooperation from the following people.

Maj. Gen. John R. Pugh, USA (Ret.), Gen. Wainwright's senior aide-de-camp, graciously spent two weekends with me, discussing Gen. Wainwright and the war in the Philippines. Gen. Pugh generously permitted me to use excerpts from a diary that he kept in the Philippines for his wife. He also read the entire draft manuscript and pointed out several errors.

Maj. Gen. Hugh J. Casey, USA (Ret.), Gen. MacArthur's chief of engineers, patiently spent a weekend with me going over the draft manuscript page by page. Pointing out numerous factual and grammatical errors, Gen. Casey was by far my severest and most helpful critic. He also provided additional information.

Maj. Gen. Richard J. Marshall, USA (Ret.), MacArthur's deputy chief of Staff, took the time to answer in detail a number of questions concerning MacArthur and the war in the Philippines. He reviewed the entire draft manuscript and pointed out a number of errors.

Maj. Gen. Spencer B. Akin, USA (Ret.), chief of MacArthur's signal corps, read the first eight chapters of the draft manuscript and sent me an important memorandum concerning an incident that occurred aboard PT-32 during the early morning of March 12, 1942.

Brig. Gen. Arnold J. Funk, USA (Ret.), Maj. Gen. Edward P. King's chief of staff, reviewed the entire draft manuscript and supplied additional pertinent information.

Joseph R. McMicking, MacArthur's assistant chief of intelligence, answered a number of questions concerning MacArthur and the war in the Philippines, and later critically read the first eight chapters of the draft manuscript.

Brig. Gen. Charles H. Morhouse, USAF (Ret.), an Air Force physician who accompanied MacArthur to Australia, read the first eight

ACKNOWLEDGMENTS

chapters of the draft manuscript and provided me with additional pertinent information concerning MacArthur.

Col. Francis H. Wilson, USA (Ret.), aide-de-camp to Gens. Mac-Arthur and Sutherland, closely reviewed the first eight chapters of the draft manuscript and wrote out in longhand eight legal-size pages of comments and information.

Col. Charles E. N. Howard, USA (Ret.), who served with the U.S. Army on Bataan, reviewed the entire draft manuscript and supplied me with helpful additional information.

Brig. Gen. Bradford G. Chynoweth, USA (Ret.), who commanded American-Filipino forces in the Visayan Islands, contributed valuable first-hand information, reviewed the entire draft manuscript, and provided me with a nine-page letter of helpful and confidential observations.

Col. Achille C. Tisdelle, USA (Ret.), Gen. King's aide-de-camp, reviewed the entire draft manuscript, pointed out several errors, and contributed a number of fascinating annotations.

Rear Admiral John D. Bulkeley, USN, commander of MTB Squadron Three, read the draft of Chapter 7, pointed out several errors, and furnished maps and additional information.

Rear Admiral Herbert James Ray, USN (Ret.), Admiral Rockwell's chief of staff and later MacArthur's naval aide, read the draft of Chapter 7, made a number of helpful and informative comments, and answered in detail a list of questions.

Captain Robert B. Kelley, USN (Ret.), captain of PT-34, read the draft of Chapter 7 and wrote a seven-page memorandum concerning the PT-boat evacuation.

Captain Vincent E. Schumacher, USN (Ret.), captain of PT-32, read the draft of Chapter 7 and sent an informative letter concerning the PT-boat evacuation.

Commander Henry J. Brantingham, USN (Ret.), who served with MTB Squadron Three, read the draft of Chapter 7 and pointed out several errors.

Col. Thomas Dooley, USA (Ret.), Wainwright's junior aide-de-camp, read the draft of Chapters 9, 10, and 11 and pointed out several errors and omissions.

Col. Theodore J. Sledge, USA (Ret.), assistant to Brig. Gen. Lewis L. Beebe, read the entire draft manuscript.

John J. McCloy, former Assistant Secretary of War, answered in detail two questions concerning Secretary of War Stimson and the war in the Philippines.

Robert A. Lovett, former Assistant Secretary of War, sent a helpful letter concerning Stimson.

Brig. Gen. Eugene L. Harrison, USA (Ret.), sent a very informative letter concerning Secretary of War Stimson.

The late Adolf A. Berle, former Assistant Secretary of State, described a conversation that he had had with Secretary of State Cordell Hull following President Roosevelt's decision to order MacArthur to leave Corregidor and proceed to Australia.

Municipal Court Judge Malcolm M. Champlin, Wainwright's naval aide on Bataan, gave me a copy of his MS. narrative, "One Man's Version," of the Philippine campaign.

Maj. John K. Wallace, USA (Ret.), provided a copy of his MS., "Memoirs of a Convict," a fascinating account of his ordeal in the Philippines.

Martin Greif of Life and Time Publications helped by giving the first eight chapters of the draft manuscript a highly critical reading.

Lt. Gen. Stephen J. Chamberlin, USA (Ret.), wrote concerning MacArthur's arrival in Australia.

Charles I. Romanus of the Office of the Chief of Military History critically read the draft of the first eight chapters and made a number of suggestions for improvement.

Former Senators Stephen M. Young and Frank J. Lausche and Congressman Thomas Ludlow Ashley helped me to obtain a large number of essential documents.

The Adjutant General of the United States Army, Maj. Gen. Kenneth G. Wickham, helped me to obtain numerous documents concerning Generals MacArthur, Marshall, and Wainwright and the war in the Philippines.

James H. Baldwin furnished a helpful and informative letter concerning the war in the Philippines.

During the spring of 1969, Col. George F. Leist, USA (Ret.), a 1937 graduate of West Point who had served on Corregidor just prior to World War II, read the first eight chapters of the draft manuscript. Col. Leist, urging me to do additional research and to expand the story, permitted me to use his copy of "The Register of West Point Graduates" for the purpose of locating officers who had served in the Philippines. I prepared and mailed a large number of questionnaires. The following West Point graduates graciously took the time to reply and to supply a wealth of information concerning MacArthur and Wainwright and the war in the Philippines: Gen. Harold K. Johnson, USA (Ret.), Gen. Lauris Norstad, USAF (Ret.), Gen. Albert C. Wedemeyer, USA (Ret.), Lt. Gen. Joseph H. Moore, USAF, Lt. Gen. Gordon A. Blake, USAF, Lt. Gen. Alva R. Fitch, USA (Ret.), Lt. Gen. Francis D. Gideon, USAF, Maj. Gen. John M. Wright, USA, Maj. Gen. Chih Wang, Chinese Army (Ret.), Maj. Gen. Cecil E. Combs, USAF (Ret.), Maj. Gen. Richard H. Carmichael, USAF (Ret.), Maj. Gen. Harry C. Porter, USAF (Ret.), Brig. Gen. Elliott Vandevanter, Jr., USAF (Ret.), Brig. Gen. William G. Hipps, USAF (Ret.), Brig. Gen. Charles C. Drake, USA (Ret.), Brig. Gen. Royal Reynolds, Jr., USA (Ret.), Brig. Gen. Paul D. Phillips, USA (Ret.), Brig. Gen. John J. McGee, USA (Ret.), Col. Stuart C. MacDonald, USA (Ret.), Col. Armand Hopkins, USA (Ret.), Col. William Massello, Jr., USA (Ret.), Col. R. S. Kramer, USA (Ret.), Col. Clyde A. Selleck, USA (Ret.), Col. E. C. Engelhart, USA (Ret.), Col. Morris L. Shoss, USA (Ret.), Col. William E. Chandler, USA (Ret.), Col. Donovan Swanton, USA (Ret.), Col. Paul H. Krause, USA (Ret.), Col. Victor C. Huffsmith, USAF (Ret.), and Lt. Col. Stephen C. Farris, USA (Ret.).

Col. Ray M. O'Day, USA (Ret.), the editor of *Chit Chat* and a veteran of Bataan, generously supplied the names and addresses of a large number of Bataan and Corregidor veterans.

The following officers and enlisted men also answered the questionnaire and furnished helpful and informative material: Rear Admiral Denys W. Knoll, USN (Ret.), Rear Admiral Melvyn H. McCoy, USN (Ret.), Capt. Kenneth M. Hoeffel, USN (Ret.), Maj. Gen. Charles A. Willoughby, USA (Ret.), Brig. Gen. Constant L. Irwin, USA (Ret.), Col. Jesse A. Villamor, USA (Ret.), Col. Harrison C. Browne, USA (Ret.), Col. Lee C. Vance, USA (Ret.), Col. Frederick A. Ward, USA (Ret.), Col. E. C. Lentz, USA (Ret.), Col. Arnold D. Amoroso, USA (Ret.), Col. R. W. Bockmon, USA (Ret.), Col. Roscoe Bonham, USA (Ret.), Col. Roy D. Russell, USAF, Col. Edmund J. Lilly, Jr. USA (Ret.), Col. N. F. Galbraith, USA (Ret.), Lt. Col. James H. Clem, USA (Ret.), Lt. Col. John R. Pray, USA (Ret.), Lt. Col. William B. Reardon, USA (Ret.), Chief Petty Officer Forrest G. Hogg, USN (Ret.), Staff Sergeant Robert K. Branch, USA (Ret.), Edward C. Atkinson, Robert B. Lewis, M.D., J. H. Bahranburg, M.D., Arthur A. Bressi and Paul Wasson.

The authors of *Corregidor: Saga of a Fortress,* Dr. William M. Belote and Dr. James H. Belote, helped me to obtain additional information concerning MacArthur's visit to Battery "Chicago" on Corregidor.

Richard Pheatt read part of the draft manuscript and offered much encouragement.

Doris Taube typed parts of the draft manuscript and a large number of questionnaires.

Edwin D. Dodd, a former member of MacArthur's staff and now president of Owens-Illinois Corporation, kindly gave me an interview during the spring of 1967 and reminisced about General MacArthur.

Dr. Louis Morton's *The Fall of the Philippines* and John Toland's *But Not in Shame* were valuable sources.

Philip P. Brower, director of the MacArthur Memorial Bureau of Archives, was immensely helpful. He permitted an examination of the documents in his bureau, promptly photostated a number of important documents, and courteously supplied a number of illustrations.

Thomas E. Hohmann, Herman G. Goldbeck, Wilbur J. Nigh, and Joseph Avery of the Modern Military Records Division, National Archives, supplied many needed documents.

At the Office of the Chief of Military History I was aided by Col. H. A. Schmidt, Charles I. Romanus, Hannah M. Zeidlik, Detmar Finke, and William Tobin.

Captain F. Kent Loomis, assistant director of Naval History, granted me access to Rear Admiral Rockwell's report to Admiral King at the Naval History Division, along with other materials supplied by Mildrid D. Mayeux.

Dr. Elizabeth B. Drewry, Anne Morris, and Robert H. Parks facilitated my research at the Franklin D. Roosevelt Library.

Frank Lilly, chief of the Reference Service Branch of the Federal Records Center in Kansas City, Missouri, supplied pertinent documents from MacArthur's Southwest Pacific Files.

At the Sterling Memorial Library at Yale University, Miss Judith A. Schiff, head of the Historical Manuscripts and University Archives Department, allowed me on short notice to have access to Stimson's diaries and correspondence.

The staff at the Toledo Public Library was most helpful.

In a letter to me, the late Lt. Col. William B. Reardon, USA (Ret.), who served on Bataan in the 200th Coast Artillery, wrote that following the war he needed to write a thesis in order to complete a Master's degree in history at the University of New Mexico. He requested permission to do research and to write an account of the Philippine campaign. However, the head of the History Department at the University of New Mexico turned down his request, stating "it would not be history and it would not be research."

I was more fortunate than Col. Reardon. My thesis advisor, Dr. William H. Leckie, former dean of the Graduate School of the University of Toledo and now vice president in charge of academic affairs, enthusiastically gave me the green light to start research on MacArthur and the war in the Philippines. Dr. Leckie has been a continual source of encouragement and wise counsel. Moreover, I am exceedingly grateful to Dr. Noel L. Leathers, former dean of the College of Arts and Sciences at the University of Toledo and now vice president for academic affairs at the University of Akron, and to Dr. J. Carroll Moody, former assistant dean of the College of Arts and Sciences at the University of Toledo, who carefully read parts of the manuscript, pointed out its many errors and shortcomings, and offered helpful suggestions as to how it could be improved. I am, of course, responsible for any errors and defects that remain.

Notes

ABBREVIATIONS USED FOR SOURCES

FDRL	Franklin D. Roosevelt Library
FRC	Federal Records Center, Kansas City, Missouri
MMBA	MacArthur Memorial Bureau of Archives
MMRDNA	Modern Military Records Division, National Archives
OCMH	Office of the Chief of Military History
YUL	Yale University Library

CHAPTER 1

1. Louis Morton, *The Fall of the Philippines* (Washington, D.C.: U.S. Government Printing Office, 1953), p. 31.

2. Clare Boothe Luce, "General Douglas MacArthur," *Life*, 8 Dec. 1941, pp. 126–27.

3. Vorin E. Whan, Jr., ed., *A Soldier Speaks: Public Papers and Speeches of General of the Army Douglas MacArthur* (New York: Frederick A. Praeger, 1965), pp. 79–99.

4. Louis Morton, *Strategy And Command: The First Two Years* (Washington, D.C.: U.S. Government Printing Office, 1953), pp. 24–29, 45–50; Louis Morton, "Germany First: The Basic Concept of Allied Strategy in World War II," Kent Roberts Greenfield, ed., in *Command Decisions* (New York: Harcourt, Brace and Co., 1959), p. 5.

5. Douglas MacArthur, *Reminiscences* (New York: McGraw-Hill, 1964), p. 102; Manuel L. Quezon, *The Good Fight* (New York: D. Appleton-Century Co., 1946), pp. 153–55.

6. MacArthur, op. cit., pp. 9–67, et passim.

7. Whan, op. cit., pp. 92–93; MacArthur, op. cit., pp. 103–4; Morton, op. cit., pp. 8–13.

8. Joseph R. McMicking to author, 13 June 1967; Morton, op. cit., pp. 8–13; Luce, op. cit., pp. 123–26; MacArthur, op. cit., pp. 104–5.

9. Louis Morton, *Strategy and Command: The First Two Years* (Washington, D.C.: U.S. Government Printing Office, 1962), pp. 58–66; Morton, *The Fall of the Philippines,* op. cit., p. 15.

10. Morton, *The Fall of the Philippines,* op. cit., pp. 15–19; MacArthur, op. cit., p. 109.

11. Joseph R. McMicking to author, 13 June 1967; MacArthur, op cit., p. 112; Morton, *The Fall of the Philippines,* op. cit., pp. 61–64; Morton, *Strategy and Command,* op. cit., pp. 33–39.

12. Morton, *The Fall of the Philippines,* op. cit., p. 31.

13. Letter, MacArthur to Marshall, 28 Oct. 1941, MacArthur's Personal File, Nov. 25–Dec. 15, 1941, MMBA (see Abbreviations, p. 249).

14. Lewis H. Brereton, *The Brereton Diaries, 3 October 1941–8 May 1945* (New York: William Morrow & Co., 1946), p. 18; Henry L. Stimson and McGeorge Bundy, *On Active Service in Peace and War* (New York: Harper & Brothers, 1948), pp. 388–89.

15. Morton, *The Fall of the Philippines,* op. cit., pp. 48–50, 69–71; MacArthur, op. cit., p. 113.

16. Radiogram, Stark to Hart, 24 Nov. 1941, USAFFE, Chief of Staff, Radios and letters dealing with Plans and Policies, Dec. 1941–Feb. 1942, MMBA.

17. Conference in the Office of Chief of Staff, 26 Nov. 1941, WDCSA-381 Philippines (12-4-41), MMRDNA.

18. Radiogram, Marshall to MacArthur, 27 Nov. 1941, WPD 4544-13, MMRDNA.

19. Francis B. Sayre, *Glad Adventure* (New York: Macmillan Co., 1957), p. 221.

20. Radiogram, MacArthur to Marshall, No. 1004, 28 Nov. 1941, OCS 18136-118, MMRDNA.

21. Brereton, op. cit., pp. 36–37.

CHAPTER 2

1. Radiogram, Marshall to MacArthur, No. 762, 12 Dec. 1941, USAFFE, Chief of Staff, Radios and letters dealing with Plans and Policies, Dec. 1941–Feb. 1942, MMBA.

2. Interview with Maj. Gen. Hugh J. Casey, USA (Ret.), 3 Oct. 1970; Comments concerning Chapter 2 of draft MS., Maj. Gen. Hugh J. Casey, USA (Ret.), to author; Maj. Gen. Richard J. Marshall, USA (Ret.), to author, 16 Jan. 1969; MacArthur MS. Diary, 8 Dec. 1941 entry, pp. 32–33, MMBA; Frazier Hunt, *MacArthur and the War Against Japan* (New York: Charles Scribner's Sons, 1944), p. 27.

3. Radiogram, Marshall to MacArthur, No. 733, 7 Dec. 1941, USAFFE, Chief of Staff, Radios and letters dealing with Plans and Policies, Dec. 1941–Feb. 1942, MMBA.

4. MacArthur MS. Diary, 8 Dec. 1941 entry, pp. 32–33, MMBA.

5. Lewis H. Brereton, *The Brereton Diaries* (New York: William Morrow and Co., 1946), pp. 38–39.

6. Radiogram, Marshall to MacArthur, No. 736, 7 Dec. 1941, 4544-20 WPD, MMRDNA.

7. Interview with Maj. Gen. Hugh J. Casey, USA (Ret.), 3 Oct. 1970.

8. Record of telephone conversation between Gen. Gerow, WPD, and Gen. MacArthur in Manila, P.I., 7 Dec. 1941, 4622 WPD, MMRDNA. Col. Achille C. Tisdelle thought that MacArthur probably said, "Our tails are over the dashboard," an allusion to a frisky horse carrying his tail over the dashboard of a runabout or escort wagon. According to Tisdelle, the saying was a "favorite expression" of MacArthur's. Comments concerning Chapter 2 of draft MS., Col. Achille C. Tisdelle, USA (Ret.), to author, 30 Dec. 1972.

9. MacArthur MS. Diary, 8 Dec. 1941 entry, pp. 32–33, MMBA.

10. Ibid; Brereton, op. cit., pp. 39–40.

11. USAFFE, Chief of Staff, "Brief Summary of Action in the Office of Chief of Staff," Dec. 8, 1941–Feb. 22, 1942, p. 1, MMBA.

12. Ibid.

13. Brereton, op. cit., p. 40.

14. Ibid.

15. Brereton, op. cit., p. 41.

16. USAFFE, Chief of Staff, "Brief Summary of Action in the Office of Chief of Staff," Dec. 8, 1941–Feb. 22, 1942, p. 1, MMBA.

17. Ibid.

18. Louis Morton, *The Fall of the Philippines* (Washington, D.C.: U.S. Government Printing Office, 1953), p. 88.

19. Interview with Maj. Gen. Hugh J. Casey, USA (Ret.), 3 Oct. 1970; Comments concerning Chapter 2 of draft MS., Maj. Gen. Hugh J. Casey, USA (Ret.), to author; Morton, op. cit., p. 67. The following officers commented on the Clark Field disaster.

Maj. Gen. Richard J. Marshall, MacArthur's deputy chief of staff: "I remember that we talked about reconnaissance missions planned to go to Formosa. It was an extension of discussions of reconnaissance before the 8th, which we were very cautious about due to War Department restrictions on committing the first act of war. I don't believe that a bombing attack could have been launched with the information available to the Air Force that morning." Maj. Gen. Richard J. Marshall to author, 16 Jan. 1969.

Col. Francis H. Wilson, an aide-de-camp to Sutherland and MacArthur: "The doubt existing in General MacArthur's mind as to the intent of the directive from Washington, and the tactical situation, were reasons for his not ordering an immediate, and probably disastrous, raid against well-defended Formosa." Col. Francis W. Wilson, USA (Ret.), to author, 20 Feb. 1969.

Col. Victor C. Huffsmith: "My boss and very close friend, Colonel Eugene L. Eubank, commanded the 19th Bombardment Group. On the day of the Clark Field attack I was en route to Mindanao. As I understand, General Brereton ordered the 19th to be bombed up and ready for action as soon as he learned of Pearl Harbor. When he reported his action to General MacArthur the General reminded him that war had not been declared and that the 19th should be unloaded and then moved out. As a result of this order the Japanese caught the 19th on the ground and caused great loss. I personally believe that General Brereton was correct and MacArthur completely wrong." Col. Victor C. Huffsmith, USA (Ret.), to author, 7 July 1969.

Brig. Gen. William G. Hipps, who served on Brereton's staff: "It would be difficult to assess either Brereton or MacArthur with responsibility in the Clark Field disaster. When the decision was made, misjudging Japanese offensive capability, to build up United States air strength in the Far East prior to building the basic requirements for air power, we were committed. Inadequate provisions for logistics support, communications, aircraft control and warning doomed our forces to destruction.

"Lack of good intelligence on enemy order of battle or intentions, coupled with MacArthur and Sutherland's wishful thinking that the Japanese would bypass the Philippines—even after word of Pearl Harbor had filtered through—contributed. No clear-cut answer on the Brereton-Eubank decision for strike commitment of our B-17s at Clark Field was given as a consequence. Fortunately, 17 of the 35 B-17s of the 19th had been dispersed to Del Monte and were not attacked.

"Brereton was more realistic and had explored courses of action to more safely exploit the small potential. Sutherland who fancied himself as an air tactician was a major factor in MacArthur's decisions." Brig. Gen. William G. Hipps, USAF (Ret.), to author, 25 July 1969.

Maj. Gen. Cecil E. Combs: "When the attack on Clark Field occurred, there were two squadrons of B-17s on the ground there. The other two, one commanded by Rosie O'Donnell, and the other, the 93rd which I commanded, were at Del Monte in Mindanao. I was told that General Brereton had asked for permission to attack Japanese airfields in Formosa as soon as he heard of the attack on Pearl Harbor. I was also told that General MacArthur would only authorize reconnaissance flights. MacArthur may have been under instructions not to attack unless the Philippine Islands were attacked first. I have not seen anything in MacArthur's writings, or in Brereton's, that says anything definitive on the subject." Major Gen. Cecil E. Combs, USAF (Ret.), to author, 27 June 1969.

Brig. Gen. Charles H. Morhouse, MacArthur's personal physician: "As to the attack on Formosa, MacArthur called it off because war had not been declared and subsequent information indicated he had been right. The Japanese had 1,300 fighters on Formosa, so instead of losing half our B-17s we would have lost them all. He told Sutherland to tell Brereton . . . to protect his bombers any way he could and that is as much as he ever said about the screw-up at Clark." Brig. Gen Charles H. Morhouse, USAF (Ret.), to author, April 1969.

Col. E. C. Lentz, flight surgeon at Clark Field at the time of the Japanese attack: "No one has fully answered why our loaded B-17 squadron was still sitting on Clark Field when the Japs hit. Scuttlebutt at Clark was that permission could not be procured from MacArthur's headquarters because President Quezon felt that since no attack had been made on the Philippine Islands, the Philippine Islands should not be a base for launching an attack against Japan." Col. E. C. Lentz, MC, USAF (Ret.), to author, 17 Oct. 1969.

Col. Achille C. Tisdelle: "The fact is that the junior commands, division, regimental, etc., of the army saw clearly that this was *war* and the bombing of Pearl Harbor could not be brushed off as a new 'Panay gunboat sinking' incident which could be reconciled with a 'So Sorry' diplomatic note. It was war and MacArthur should have recognized it the way his juniors did. MacArthur, however, hesitated at his high level waiting for further instructions . . . and got caught." Comments concerning Chapter 2 of draft MS., Col. Achille C. Tisdelle to author, 30 Dec. 1972.

20. MacArthur MS. Diary, 8 Dec. 1941 entry, p. 33, MMBA; Radiogram, Stimson to Hart, 8 Dec. 1941, USAFFE, Chief of Staff, Radios and letters dealing with Plans and Policies, Dec. 1941–Feb. 1942, MMBA.

21. USAFFE, Chief of Staff, "Brief Summary of Action in the Office of Chief of Staff," Dec. 8, 1941–Feb. 22, 1942, MMBA; MacArthur MS. Diary, 8 Dec. 1941 entry, p. 33, MMBA.

22. Francis Bowes Sayre, *Glad Adventure* (New York: Macmillan Co., 1957), p. 223.

23. MacArthur MS. Diary, 8 Dec. 1941 entry, p. 33, MMBA.

24. Radiogram, MacArthur to AGWAR, No. 1133, 8 Dec. 1941, AG 381 (11-27-41 Gen) Far East, MMRDNA.

25. Radiogram, MacArthur to AGWAR, No. 1135, 9 Dec. 1941, AG 381 (11-27-41 Gen) Far East, MMRDNA.

26. Stimson MSS. Diary, 10 Dec. 1941, Historical Manuscripts & University Archives Department, YUL.

27. Comments concerning Chapter 2 of draft MS., Maj. Gen. Hugh J. Casey, USA (Ret.), to author.

28. Memorandum, MacArthur to Hart, 19 Dec. 1941, Personal File of General MacArthur, MMBA.

29. Radiogram, MacArthur to Marshall, 10 Dec. 1941, WPD 4544-26, MMRDNA.

30. Ibid; Stimson MSS. Diary, 10 Dec. 1941, YUL.

31. John J. McCloy to author, 16 Sept. 1969; Letter, Robert A. Lovett to author, 8 Sept. 1969.

32. Stimson MSS. Diary, 10 Dec. 1941, YUL.

33. Ibid.

34. Ibid.

35. Brereton, op. cit., p. 50. Brereton's statement concerning the "strictly defensive attitude" is quite true, according to Col. Achille C. Tisdelle: "I know personally for a fact as I knew him well through Gen. King that he phoned 1 Calle Victoria over and

over and could never get through to MacArthur. Sutherland refused to authorize the mission to Formosa." Comments concerning Chapter 2 of draft MS., Col. Tisdelle, USA (Ret.), to author, 30 Dec. 1972.

36. Brereton, op. cit., p. 50: Radiogram, Arnold to MacArthur, No. 749, 8 Dec. 1941, AG 381 (11-27-41 Gen) Far East, MMRDNA; Radiogram, MacArthur to Arnold, 10 Dec. 1941, AG 381 (11-27-41 Gen) Far East, MMRDNA.

37. Radiogram, MacArthur to Marshall, 12 Dec. 1941, AG 381 (11-27-41 Gen) Far East, MMRDNA.

38. Radiogram, MacArthur to Marshall, 12 Dec. 1941, AG 381 (11-27-41 Gen) Far East, MMRDNA.

39. Radiogram, Marshall to MacArthur, No. 776, 12 Dec. 1941, WPD 4628, MMRDNA; Radiogram, MacArthur to Marshall, 13 Dec. 1941, OPD Exec O, MMRDNA.

40. Radiogram, MacArthur to Marshall, 14 Dec. 1941, OPD "Messages From General MacArthur" (Exec. File 20, No. 7), MMRDNA.

41. Dwight D. Eisenhower, *Crusade in Europe* (Garden City, N.Y.: Doubleday & Co., 1948), pp. 17–19.

42. Ibid, pp. 19–23.

43. Stimson MSS. Diary, 14 Dec. 1941, YUL.

44. Ibid.

45. Radiogram, Marshall to MacArthur, No. 787, 15 Dec. 1941, WPD 4544-31, MMRDNA.

46. Stimson MSS. Diary, 16 Dec. 1941, YUL.

47. Manuel L. Quezon, *The Good Fight* (New York: D. Appleton-Century Co., 1946), pp. 195–98; Sidney L. Huff, *My Fifteen Years with General MacArthur* (New York: Paperback Library, 1964), pp. 35–37.

48. Radiogram, Stark to Hart, No. 170105, 17 Dec. 1941, Hart Radio File, OCMH.

49. Radiogram, MacArthur and Hart to Brink, No. 171335, 17 Dec. 1941, Hart Radio File, OCMH.

50. Stimson MSS. Diary, 17 Dec. 1941, YUL.

51. Stimson MSS. Diary, 18 Dec. 1941, YUL.

52. Ibid.

53. Radiogram, Marshall to MacArthur, No. 824, 18 Dec. 1941, WPD 4622-38, MMRDNA.

54. Radiogram, MacArthur to Marshall, No. 790, 18 Dec. 1941, Gen. Gerow's File, MMRDNA.

55. Ibid.

56. Memorandum, MacArthur to Hart, 19 Dec. 1941, Personal File of General MacArthur, Dec. 12–21, 1941, MMBA.

57. Stimson MSS. Diary, 19 Dec. 1941, YUL.

58. Stimson MSS. Diary, 20 Dec. 1941, YUL. Stimson gave a copy of the memorandum to Grenville Clark for comment. In reply to Stimson, concerning the Southwestern Pacific Area, Clark wrote: "It is, of course, foolish to depreciate the importance of this. [The fact that the United States had a moral and a political obligation to defend the Philippines.] *And yet*, the war will be won or lost in the North Atlantic, Europe, Africa and the Near East. We must do what we reasonably can against the Japanese in the Pacific; *but* we must not waste or diffuse our efforts *too much* against the Japanese. If we really beat Hitler (in the North Atlantic, Europe, Africa and the Near East) Japan can be taken care of later. There is a great temptation emotionally and sentimentally to concentrate against Japan. We must resist this realistically and firmly."

Memorandum, Clark to Stimson, 23 Dec. 1941, Stimson Correspondence, Dec. 1 to 31, Box 391, Folder Dec. 23–26, YUL.

59. Concerning this strategic decision, Robert E. Sherwood later wrote: "The principle of Germany first was based on strictly military reasoning: it was assumed—and, it would seem from the results, correctly—that Germany had far greater potential than Japan in productive power and scientific genius and, if given time to develop this during years of stalemate in Europe, would prove all the more difficult if not impossible to defeat." Robert E. Sherwood, *Roosevelt and Hopkins: An Intimate History* (New York: Harper & Brothers, 1948), p. 446.

CHAPTER 3

1. Homer Lea, *The Valor of Ignorance* (New York: Harper & Brothers, 1942), p. 135.

2. Radiogram, MacArthur to Marshall, No. 22, 21 Dec. 1941, AG 381 (11-27-41 Gen) Far East, MMRDNA.

3. Stimson MSS. Diary, 21 Dec. 1941, Historical Manuscripts & University Archives Department, YUL.

4. Radiogram, MacArthur to Marshall, No. 3, 22 Dec. 1941, AG 381 (11-27-41 Gen) Far East, MMRDNA.

5. MacArthur MS. Diary, July 27, 1941 to February 23, 1942, 22 Dec. 1941 entry, p. 40, MMBA; Courtney Whitney, *MacArthur: His Rendezvous with History* (New York: Alfred A. Knopf, 1964), p. 15; Comments concerning Chapter 3 of draft MS., Maj. Gen. Hugh J. Casey, USA (Ret.), to author. According to Achille C. Tisdelle, "The Navy had about 14 submarines, some S-type and some K-type. They fired torpedoes at the Japanese ships outside the gulf on their way in. The torpedoes, however, did not explode underneath the enemy ships nor did those set on contact, they just bounced off. Only one ship was sunk by one action and that by a two-gun battery of 155-mm G.P.F. 'Long Tom' guns from the shore. The battery was commanded by Lt. Col. Alexander Quintard." Comments concerning Chapter 3 of draft MS., Col. Achille C. Tisdelle, USA (Ret.), to author, 30 Dec. 1972.

6. Royal Arch Gunnison, *So Sorry, No Peace* (New York: Viking Press, 1944), pp. 27–28.

7. MacArthur MS. Diary, 22 Dec. 1941, p. 40, MMBA; Allison Ind, *Bataan: The Judgment Seat* (New York: Macmillan Co., 1944), pp. 151–52.

8. Stimson MSS. Diary, 22 Dec. 1941, YUL.

9. Ibid.

10. Radiogram, Marshall to MacArthur, No. 855, 22 Dec. 1941, AG 381 (11-27-41 Gen) Far East, MMRDNA.

11. Radiogram, MacArthur to Marshall, No. 40, 22 Dec. 1941, AG 381 (11-27-41 Gen) Far East, MMRDNA.

12. Memorandum, Stark for Marshall, 23 Dec. 1941, Subject: Transportation of short range aircraft to the Philippines, AG 381 (11-27-41 Gen) Far East, MMRDNA.

13. Radiogram, Marshall to MacArthur, 23 Dec. 1941, OPD Exec O, MMRDNA.

14. Stimson MSS. Diary, 23 Dec. 1941, YUL.

15. Memorandum, Casey to Roosevelt, 23 Dec. 1941, Australia File, 1939–41, FDRL.

16. Radiogram, MacArthur to Marshall, 24 Dec. 1941, AG 381 (11-27-41 Gen) Far East, MMRDNA.

17. Memorandum, Maj. Gen. Richard J. Marshall, USA (Ret.), to author, 13 July 1967; Comments concerning Chapter 3 of draft MS., Maj. Gen. Hugh J. Casey, USA (Ret.), to author; Louis Morton, *The Fall of the Philippines* (Washington, D.C.: U.S. Government Printing Office, 1953), p. 162.

18. Lewis H. Brereton, *The Brereton Diaries, 3 October 1941–May 1945* (New York: William Morrow & Co., 1946), p. 62.

19. Memorandum, Maj. Gen. Richard J. Marshall, USA (Ret.), to author, 13 July 1967.

20. Carlos P. Romulo, *I Saw the Fall of the Philippines* (New York: Doubleday, Doran & Co., 1942), pp. 61–62.

21. MacArthur MS. Diary, 24 Dec. 1941, p. 41, MMBA; Morton, op. cit., p. 164; Charles A. Willoughby and John Chamberlain, *MacArthur 1941–1951* (New York: McGraw-Hill, 1954), p. 34; Comments concerning Chapter 3 of draft MS., Brig. Gen. Arnold J. Funk, USA (Ret.), to author; Lt. Cdr. Thomas C. Parker, USN, "The Epic of Corregidor-Bataan December 24, 1941–May 4, 1942," *United States Naval Institute Proceedings,* Vol. 69, No. 1 (Jan. 1943), p. 11; John Toland, *But Not In Shame* (New York: Random House, 1961), p. 118. Remembering this Christmas Eve, Col. Achille C. Tisdelle, who was aboard the *Don Esteban,* wrote, "Capt. Kircher of the Engineers, Col. Funk, Gen. King and some others and I would never forget the receding lights of the Army & Navy Club and Manila Hotel, back on again after a blackout since 8 December. We started to sing *Silent Night* and shortly were joined by others including Jean MacArthur and little Arthur and then the General himself. We were all up on the Boat Deck. Tom Parker had the best voice, as I recall. It was pitch dark when the *Don Esteban* came in to the long concrete Navy dock at 'Bottomside' on Corregidor." Comments concerning Chapter 3 of draft MS., Col. Achille C. Tisdelle, USA (Ret.), to author, 30 Dec. 1972.

22. Morton, op. cit., pp. 472–78.

23. Ibid.

24. Sidney L. Huff, *My Fifteen Years with General MacArthur* (New York: Paperback Library, 1964), pp. 39–40.

25. Stimson MSS. Diary, 24 Dec. 1941, YUL.

26. Ibid.

27. Radiogram, Marshall to MacArthur, No. 879, 24 Dec. 1941, AG 381 (11-27-41) Far East, MMRDNA.

28. MacArthur MS. Diary, 25 Dec. 1941, p. 41, MMBA.

29. Radiograms, MacArthur to Marshall, 25 Dec. 1941, AG 381 (11-27-41 Gen) Far East, MMRDNA.

30. Stimson MSS. Diary, 25 Dec. 1941, YUL. Stimson further wrote, "This incident shows the danger of talking too freely in international matters of such keen importance without the President carefully having his military and naval advisors present. This paper, which was a record made by one of Churchill's assistants, would have raised any amount of trouble for the President if it had gotten into the hands of an unfriendly press. I think he felt that he had pretty nearly burned his fingers and had called this subsequent meeting to make up for it. Hopkins told me at the time I talked with him over the telephone that he had told the President that he should be more careful about the formality of his discussions with Churchill."

31. Memorandum, Hart to MacArthur, 25 Dec. 1941, Subject: Move of Command Post of the Commander in Chief, U.S. Asiatic Fleet, USAFFE, Personal File of General MacArthur, Dec. 21–29, 1941, MMBA; Radiogram, MacArthur to Marshall, 26 Dec. 1941, AG 381 (11-27-41 Gen) Far East, MMRDNA.

32. Radiogram, MacArthur to Marshall, 26 Dec. 1941, AG 381 (11-27-41 Gen) Far East. According to Col. Charles E. N. Howard, USA (Ret.), "There was no artillery duel at the Agno River. The Philippine Army artillery was never capable . . . of sustained or indirect artillery fire. The Philippine Army divisions were in mad retreat." Comments concerning Chapter 3 of draft MS., Col. Charles E. N. Howard, USA (Ret.), to author.

33. Huff, op. cit., p. 42.

34. Stimson MSS. Diary, 26 Dec. 1941, YUL.

35. Ibid.

36. Radiogram, Marshall to MacArthur, No. 885, 27 Dec. 1941, USAFFE, Personal File of General MacArthur, Dec. 30, 1941–Feb. 19, 1942, MMBA.

37. Radiogram, MacArthur to Marshall, 27 Dec. 1941, AG 381 (11-27-41 Gen) Far East, MMRDNA.

38. Radiogram, MacArthur to Marshall, 28 Dec. 1941, AG 381 (11-27-41 Gen) Far East, MMRDNA.

39. Radiogram, MacArthur to Marshall, 28 Dec. 1941, AG 381 (11-27-41 Gen) Far East, MMRDNA.

40. Press Release, Roosevelt, 28 Dec. 1941, Box 40 Philippines, July to Dec. 1941, Franklin D. Roosevelt Library; *New York Times,* 29 Dec. 1941. Commenting on Roosevelt's speech, Col. Paul D. Bunker, USA, who commanded the Seaward Defenses on Corregidor, wrote in his diary: "Note that Pres. Roosevelt's latest speech guarantees that we will redeem Philippines' INDEPENDENCE! Gratuitous, unnecessary and damn bad strategy." Bunker MS. Diary, OCMH.

41. MacArthur MS. Diary, 29 Dec. 1941, p. 42, MMBA; Col. William C. Braly, "Corregidor—A Name, A Symbol, A Tradition," *Coast Artillery Journal,* LXXX, No. 4 (July–August 1947), p. 6; Lt. Col. Warren J. Clear, "The Heroic Defense of the Philippines," *Reader's Digest,* Vol. 41, No. 243 (July 1942), p. 164.

42. MacArthur MS. Diary, 29 Dec. 1941, p. 42, MMBA; Huff, op. cit., pp. 43–44; Romulo, op. cit., p. 101.

43. Major John K. Wallace, "Memoirs of a Convict" (MS.), pp. 8–9. Wallace also wrote: "I feel that General MacArthur may be criticized for a lot of things, but he can never be criticized for cowardice or of the appellation of 'Dugout Doug.' If General MacArthur is to be criticized I think he should be criticized for exposing himself too much because if he was a big enough man to be in charge of the entire show in the Far East, then he was too big a man to be exposing himself to bombing and strafing. However, all during the raid he remained in the Top Side barracks or around it but sent all of his staff and the enlisted personnel of his headquarters down to Malinta Tunnel as soon as the raid started but he himself remained there all during the raid."

44. MacArthur MS. Diary, 29 Dec. 1941, p. 42, MMBA; Braly, op. cit., p. 6.

45. Manuel L. Quezon, *The Good Fight* (New York: D. Appleton-Century Co., 1946), pp. 226–27.

46. MacArthur MS. Diary, 30 Dec. 1941, p. 42, MMBA. Huff, op. cit., p. 44.

47. MacArthur MS. Diary, 30 Dec. 1941, pp. 42–43, MMBA; Quezon, op. cit., pp. 227–35; Huff, op. cit., p. 48; Frazier Hunt, *MacArthur and the War Against Japan* (New York: Charles Scribner's Sons, 1944), pp. 48–49; Maj. Gen. George F. Moore, USA, Report of Operations—USAFFE & USFIP in the Philippine Islands, 14 Feb. 1941 to 6 May 1942, MMRDNA.

48. Moore, op. cit.

49. MacArthur MS. Diary, 30 Dec. 1941, pp. 42–43, MMBA.

50. Radiogram, MacArthur to Marshall, 30 Dec. 1941, USAFFE, Personal File of General MacArthur, Dec. 16, 1941–Jan. 18, 1942, MMBA.

51. Radiogram, Marshall to MacArthur, No. 909, 30 Dec. 1941, USAFFE, Personal File of General MacArthur, Dec. 16, 1941–Jan. 18, 1942, MMBA.

52. Stimson MSS. Diary, 27 Dec. 1941, YUL; Maurice Matloff and Edwin M. Snell, *Strategic Planning For Coalition Warfare 1941–1942* (Washington, D.C.: U.S. Government Printing Office, 1953), pp. 120–26.

53. Memorandum, Roosevelt to Stimson and Knox, 30 Dec. 1941, Philippines File

1938–39, 1941–43, p. 45, Franklin D. Roosevelt Library; Stimson MSS. Diary, 28 Dec. 1941, YUL.

54. MacArthur MS. Diary, 31 Dec. 1941, MMBA. Morton, op. cit., p. 200.

55. MacArthur MS. Diary, 31 Dec. 1941, p. 43, MMBA.

56. Stimson MSS. Diary, 31 Dec. 1941, YUL.

57. Winston S. Churchill, *The Grand Alliance*, Vol. III (Boston: Houghton Mifflin Co., 1950), pp. 680–81.

CHAPTER 4

1. Charles Eade, ed., *The War Speeches of Winston S. Churchill*, Vol. II (Boston: Houghton Mifflin Co., 1953), p. 179.

2. Radiogram, MacArthur to Marshall, 1 Jan. 1942, AG 381 (11-27-41 Sec 1) Far East, MMRDNA.

3. Comments concerning Chapter 4 of draft MS., Maj. Gen. Hugh J. Casey, USA (Ret.), to author; Interview with Maj. Gen. Hugh J. Casey, USA (Ret.), 3 Oct. 1970, Van Landingham, "I Saw Manila Die," *Saturday Evening Post*, 26 Sept. 1942, p. 70: "To the native population of Manila, encircled by fires, bewildered, panic-stricken and not comprehending the reason for this destruction, it seemed like the end of the world"; Hugh J. Casey, ed., *Engineers of the Southwest Pacific 1941–1945*, Vol I: *Engineers in Theater Operations* (Washington, D.C.: U.S. Government Printing Office, 1947), p. 16.

4. Maj. Gen. Richard J. Marshall, USA (Ret.), to author, 13 July 1967.

5. Joseph R. Micking to author, 13 June 1967; Maj. Gen. Richard J. Marshall, USA (Ret.), to author, 13 July 1967.

6. Maj. Gen. Richard J. Marshall, USA (Ret.), to author, 13 July 1967.

7. Carlos P. Romulo, *I Saw The Fall of the Philippines* (New York: Doubleday, Doran & Co., 1942), p. 100.

8. MacArthur MS. Diary, July 27, 1941 to February 23, 1942, 1 Jan. 1942 entry, p. 44, MMBA. According to Maj. Gen. Casey, "more likely 50 million" dollars' worth of property was destroyed. Comments concerning Chapter 4 of draft MS., Maj. Gen. Hugh J. Casey, USA (Ret.), to author.

9. MacArthur MS. Diary, 1 Jan. 1942 entry, p. 44, MMBA; Manuel L. Quezon, *The Good Fight* (New York: D. Appleton-Century Co., 1946), pp. 236–41; Radiogram, MacArthur to Marshall, No. 2 & 3, 1 Jan. 1942, AG 381 (21 Dec. 1941) Far East Situation, MMRDNA.

10. Stimson MSS. Diary, 2 Jan. 1942, Historical Manuscripts & University Archives Department, YUL.

11. Ibid.

12. Radiogram, Marshall to MacArthur, No. 913, 3 Jan. 1942, 4639-2 WPD, MMRDNA.

13. Memorandum, Brig. Gen. L. T. Gerow for Marshall, 3 Jan. 1942, Subject: Relief of the Philippines, 4639-3, MMRDNA.

14. Ibid.

15. Col. Paul D. Bunker MS. Diary, 4 Jan. 1942, OCMH.

16. Brig. Gen. Charles C. Drake, USA (Ret.), to author, 26 June 1969.

17. Stimson MSS. Diary, 5 Jan. 1942, YUL.

18. Dr. James H. Belote to author, 8 Sept. 1971; Arthur Bressi to author, 28 October

1971; Paul W. Wasson to author, 31 October 1971; James H. and William M. Belote, *Corregidor: The Saga of a Fortress* (New York: Harper & Row, 1967), p. 54.

19. Radiogram, MacArthur to Marshall, No. 9, 4 Jan. 1942, AG 381 (11-27-41 Sec 1) Far East, MMRDNA.

20. Radiogram, MacArthur to Marshall, No. 20, 7 Jan. 1942, Philippine Islands, Jan.–May 42, PSF Safe File FDRL.

21. Brig. Gen. Dwight D. Eisenhower, Personal Notebook, 8 Jan. 1942, OPD History Unit File, Item 3, OCMH.

22. Radiogram, MacArthur to Marshall, No. 26, 9 Jan. 1942, AG 381 (21 Dec. 1941) Far East Situation, MMRDNA.

23. MacArthur MS. Diary, 10 Jan. 1942, p. 47, MMBA; Comments concerning Chapter 4 of draft MS., Maj. Gen. Hugh J. Casey, USA (Ret.), to author.

24. Brig. Gen. Arnold J. Funk, USA (Ret.), to author, 31 July 1969; Jonathan M. Wainwright, *General Wainwright's Story* (Garden City, N.Y.: Doubleday & Co., 1946), p. 49.

25. Col. Harrison C. Browne, USA (Ret.), to author, Sept. 1969.

26. Brig. Gen. Arnold J. Funk, USA (Ret.), to author, 31 July 1969; Comments concerning Chapter 4 of draft MS., Brig. Gen. Arnold J. Funk, USA (Ret.), to author.

27. Comments concerning Chapter 4 of draft MS., Brig. Gen. Arnold J. Funk, USA (Ret.), to author; Brig. Gen. Royal Reynolds to author, 21 June 1969.

28. Brig. Gen. Arnold J. Funk, USA (Ret.), to author, 31 July 1969; Comments concerning Chapter 4 of draft MS., Brig. Gen. Arnold J. Funk, USA (Ret.), to author.

29. Wainwright, op. cit., pp. 49–50.

30. Diary of Lieutenant Colonel (later Major General) John R. Pugh, 10 Jan. 1942. Pugh kept the diary for his wife. On 3 May 1942 he placed it in the possession of Colonel Savage, an air force officer who was about to leave Corregidor aboard a submarine. On 5 July 1969, General Pugh read excerpts from his diary to the author.

31. Maj. Gen. Richard J. Marshall, USA (Ret.), to author, 25 April 1968.

32. Brig. Gen. Arnold J. Funk, USA (Ret.), to author, 31 July 1969; MacArthur MS. Diary, Jan. 10, 1942 entry, p. 47, MMBA.

33. Radiogram, Marshall to MacArthur, No. 930, 12 Jan. 1942, 4639–14 WPD, MMRDNA.

34. Col. Paul D. Bunker MS. Diary, 15 Jan. 1942, OCMH. Regarding Bunker's diary entry, Maj. Gen. Casey wrote: "We gathered *all* of this and shipped it to Bataan for *all*, not just for Bunker." Comments concerning Chapter 4 of draft MS., Maj. Gen. Hugh J. Casey, USA (Ret.), to author. On December 29 when the Japanese bombed Corregidor, they hit and sank President Quezon's beautiful 260-foot yacht, the Steam Yacht *Casiana*, at her anchorage just off Corregidor. The yacht's large liquor supply attracted a number of salvagers from Bunker's command. According to Col. Tisdelle, "The *Casiana* was originally built for Henry L. Doheny, the oil miltimillionaire of 'Teapot Dome' repute." Comments concerning Chapter 4 of draft MS., Col. Achille C. Tisdelle USA (Ret.), to author, 30 Dec. 1972.

35. Lt. Cdr. Thomas C. Parker, USN, "The Epic of Corregidor-Bataan, December 24, 1941–May 4, 1942," *United States Naval Institute Proceedings,* Vol. 69, No. 1 (Jan. 1943), p. 13. Maj. Gen. Casey wrote that MacArthur's message was "based on my memorandum to him urging his visit to Bataan with draft of similar message I suggested he issue if he could not leave his GHQ nerve center to see and be seen by troops on Bataan." Comments concerning Chapter 4 of draft MS., Maj. Gen. Hugh J. Casey, USA (Ret.), to author.

36. Col. Paul D. Bunker MS. Diary, 16 Jan. 1942, OCMH.

37. Radiogram, MacArthur to Marshall, No. 72, 17 Jan. 1942, AG 381 (11-27-41 Sec 1) Far East, MMRDNA.

38. Forrest C. Pogue, *George C. Marshall: Ordeal and Hope* (New York: Viking Press, 1966), pp. 244–45; Dwight D. Eisenhower, *Crusade in Europe* (Garden City, N.Y.: Doubleday & Co., 1949), p. 25; Don Lohbeck, *Patrick J. Hurley* (Chicago: Henry Regnery Co., 1956), pp. 159–60.

39. Stimson MSS. Diary, 17 Jan. 1942, YUL.

40. Eisenhower, op. cit., p. 25; Brig. Gen. Dwight D. Eisenhower, Personal Notebook, 17 Jan. 1942; OPD History Unit File, Item 3, OCMH.

41. Radiogram, Marshall to MacArthur, No. 949, 17 Jan. 1942, 4560-9 WPD, MMRDNA.

42. Radiogram, MacArthur to Marshall, No. 78, 18 Jan. 1942, AG 381 (21 Dec. 1941) Far East Situation, MMRDNA.

43. Letter, Quezon to Roosevelt, 19 Jan. 1942, USAFFE, General MacArthur's Personal File, July 26, 1941–April 13, 1942, Folder Jan. 19 to April 17, 1942, MMBA.

44. Radiogram, MacArthur to Marshall, No. 108, 23 Jan. 1942, AG 381 (11-27-41 Sec 1) Far Eastern Situation, MMRDNA. Concerning the decision to withdraw, Maj. Gen. Casey wrote: "I strongly opposed [it] and sent a memorandum analyzing estimate of sitution on which this decision was based and urging review. These positions were well prepared. I had been going to each front almost daily. We had excellent forward observation [for] artillery coverage of Orani-Olongapo Road. Wire [was] in position." Comments concerning Chapter 4 of draft MS., Maj. Gen. Hugh J. Casey, USA (Ret.), to author. Louis Morton, *The Fall of the Philippines* (Washington, D.C.: U.S. Government Printing Office, 1953), pp 290–95.

45. Radiogram, MacArthur to Marshall, No. 134, 27 Jan. 1942, AG 381 (11-27-41 Sec 1) Far East, MMRDNA.

46. Letter, Sayre to Roosevelt, 26 Jan. 1942, Philippines 1938–39, 1941–43, p. 45, FDRL.

47. Radiogram, Roosevelt to MacArthur, 26 Jan. 1942, PPF—4914 Douglas MacArthur, FDRL. On January 27, MacArthur sent Roosevelt the following reply: "Grateful indeed to you for your inspiring message." Radiogram, MacArthur to Roosevelt, 27 Jan. 1942, PPF—4914 Douglas MacArthur, FDRL.

48. Memorandum, Wainwright to MacArthur, 27 Jan. 1942, Chief of Staff, Radios and letters dealing with Plans and Policies, MMBA.

49. Memorandum, MacArthur to Wainwright, 28 Jan. 1942, Chief of Staff, Radios and letters dealing with Plans and Policies, MMBA.

50. USAFFE, Chief of Staff, "Brief Summary of Action in the Office of Chief of Staff," Dec. 8, 1941 to Feb. 22, 1942, MMBA.

51. Radiogram, Quezon to Roosevelt, No. 1445, 28 Jan. 1942, Quezon File, MMRDNA.

52. Stimson MSS. Diary, 29 Jan. 1942, YUL.

53. Radiogram, Roosevelt to Quezon, 29 Jan. 1942, Philippines 1938–39, 1941, pp. 43, 45, FDRL.

54. Maj. Gen. George F. Moore, USA, Report of Operations—USAFFE & USFIP in the Philippine Islands, 14 Feb. 1941 to 6 May 1942, MMRDNA.

55. Radiogram, MacArthur to Marshall, No. 148, 29 Jan. 1942, AG 381 (11-27-41 Sec 1) Far East, MMRDNA.

56. Radiogram, Marshall to MacArthur, 30 Jan. 1942, AG 381 (11-27-41 Sec 1) Far East, MMRDNA.

57. Radiogram, MacArthur to Roosevelt, 29 Jan. 1942, PPF—4914 Douglas MacArthur, FDRL.

58. Telegram, O'Daniel to Roosevelt, 30 Jan. 1942; Letter, Watson to O'Daniel, 6 Feb. 1942, FDRL.

59. Radiogram, MacArthur to Marshall, No. 166, 31 Jan. 1942, AG 381 (21 Dec. 1941) Far East Situation, MMRDNA.

CHAPTER 5

1. Elting E. Morison, *Turmoil and Tradition: A Study of the Life and Times of Henry L. Stimson* (Boston: Houghton Mifflin Co., 1960), p. 550.

2. Radiogram, MacArthur to Marshall, No. 178, 1 Feb. 1942, AG 381 (21 Dec. 1941) Far East Situation, MMRDNA.

3. Radiogram, Marshall to MacArthur, No. 994, 31 Jan. 1942, WPD 3251-76, MMRDNA.

4. Radiogram, MacArthur to Marshall, No. 180, 1 Feb. 1942, AG 381 (21 Dec. 1941), Far East Situation, MMRDNA.

5. Allison Ind, *Bataan: The Judgment Seat* (New York: Macmillan Co., 1944),

6. Radiogram, MacArthur to Marshall, No. 187, 2 Feb. 1942, Quezon File, MMRDNA.

7. Radiogram, Marshall to MacArthur, 2 Feb. 1942, Quezon File, MMRDNA.

8. Maj. Gen. George F. Moore, USA, Report of Operations—USAFFE & USFIP in the Philippine Islands, 14 Feb. 1941 to 6 May 1942, MMRDNA.

9. Colonel William C. Braly, USA, "Corregidor—A Name, A Symbol, A Tradition," *Coast Artillery Journal*, LXXX, No. 4 (July-August 1947), p. 9; Letters, Colonel Warren J. Clear, USA (Ret.), to author, 8 July 1968 and 10 Sept. 1968.

10. Radiogram, Marshall to MacArthur, 4 Feb. 1942, Quezon File, MMRDNA.

11. Radiogram, MacArthur to Marshall, No. 201, 4 Feb. 1942, WDCSA 381 (2-17-42) Philippines, MMRDNA.

12. Manuel L. Quezon, *The Good Fight* (New York: D. Appleton-Century Co., 1946), pp. 266–67; Douglas MacArthur, *Reminiscences* (New York: McGraw-Hill, 1964), p. 134.

13. Charles A. Willoughby and John Chamberlain, *MacArthur 1941–1951* (New York: McGraw-Hill, 1954), pp. 55–56.

14. Quezon, op. cit., pp. 266–68.

15. James K. Eyre, Jr., *The Roosevelt-MacArthur Conflict* (Chambersburg, Pennsylvania: Craft Press, 1950), p. 39. Concerning President Quezon's neutralization proposal, Eyre wrote: "By early February, 1942, MacArthur had decided to throw aside all pretense. His own demands for assistance having produced few tangible results, he decided to use to the fullest the one weapon which seemed to be left to him—Manuel Quezon, and through him, the Filipino people. Having resolved upon this course, he not only encouraged but actually assisted the Filipino leader to prepare his ultimatum to the occupant of the White House." Eyre, op. cit., p. 53. Maj. Gen. Richard J. Marshall, USA (Ret.), disagreed with Eyre's assertion: "Of course I was on Bataan at the time these messages were being sent back and forth but believe the assistance given Quezon was technical—helping him to communicate. Quezon was a positive individual." Maj. General Richard J. Marshall, USA (Ret.), to author, 16 Jan. 1969. Col. Francis H. Wilson also disagreed with Eyre: "I do not feel that the assumption that MacArthur encouraged or assisted Quezon is warranted. On several occasions he had asserted, 'I will fight this command to destruction.' His plan further envisaged a desperate breakthrough on Bataan and a continuation of guerrilla warfare. That he sympathized with the sick and unhappy President is probable, that as a soldier he considered the surrender of American troops is unthinkable." Col. Francis W. Wilson, USA (Ret.), to author, 20 Feb. 1969.

16. Radiogram, Marshall to MacArthur, 8 Feb. 1942, WDCSA 381 (2-17-42), MMRDNA.

17. Stimson MSS. Diary, 8 Feb. 1942, Historical Manuscripts & University Archives Department, YUL; Radiogram, MacArthur to Marshall, No. 2265, 8 Feb. 1942, Quezon File, MMRDNA.

18. Stimson MSS. Diary, 8 Feb. 1942, YUL.

19. Stimson MSS. Diary, 9 Feb. 1942, YUL; Radiogram, MacArthur to Marshall, No. 2275, 8 Feb. 1942, MMRDNA.

20. Stimson MSS. Diary, 9 Feb. 1942, YUL: Morison, op. cit., p. 550. The first draft of the message that Stimson prepared for President Roosevelt for reply to Quezon's message is found in the Safe File PSF, Philippine Islands, Jan. to May 1942, FDRL. This draft has the corrections that Roosevelt made.

21. Radiogram, Roosevelt to MacArthur, No. 1029, 9 Feb. 1942, Item #8, Exec. #10, Quezon File, MMRDNA.

22. Radiogram, Signal Corps of Fort Mills to Eisenhower, 10 Feb. 1942, Item #8, Exec. #10, Quezon File, MMRDNA; Comments, Col. Francis W. Wilson, USA (Ret.), to author, 20 Feb. 1969.

23. Eyre, op. cit., pp. 40–41.

24. USAFFE, Chief of Staff, "Brief Summary of Action in the Office of Chief of Staff," Dec. 8, 1941 to February 22, 1942, MMBA; Radiogram, MacArthur to Marshall, No. 3, 10 Feb. 1942, Item #8, Exec. #10, Quezon File, MMRDNA.

25. Eyre, op. cit., pp. 42–43.

26. Radiogram, MacArthur to Roosevelt, No. 252, 11 Feb. 1942, AG 381 (2-11-42), MMRDNA.

27. Radiogram, MacArthur to Roosevelt, No. 162, 11 Feb. 1942, PSF Safe File, Philippine Islands, Jan. to May 1942, FDRL.

28. Radiogram, Marshall to MacArthur, No. 1031, 10 Feb. 1942, Item #8, Exec. #10, Quezon File, MMRDNA.

29. Stimson MSS. Diary, 11 Feb. 1942, YUL; Radiogram, Roosevelt to MacArthur, 11 Feb. 1942, Item #8, Exec. #10, Quezon File, MMRDNA.

30. Radiogram, MacArthur to Marshall, No. 259, 12 Feb. 1942, Item #8, Exec. #10, Quezon File, MMRDNA.

31. USAFFE, Chief of Staff, "Brief Summary of Action in the Office of Chief of Staff," Dec. 8, 1941 to February 22, 1942, MMBA; Eyre, op. cit., p. 42; Radiogram, Quezon to Roosevelt, No. 262, 12 Feb. 1942, AG 381 (21 Dec. 1941) Far East Situation, MMRDNA.

32. Stimson MSS. Diary, 12 Feb. 1942, YUL.

33. *New York Times*, 12 Feb. 1942.

34. Ibid.

35. Stimson MSS. Diary, 13 Feb. 1942, YUL.

36. Ibid.

37. Bunker MS. Diary, 13 Feb. 1942, OCMH.

38. Stimson MSS. Diary, 14 Feb. 1942, YUL.

39. Ibid.

CHAPTER 6

1. Radiogram, Marshall to MacArthur, No. 1087, 25 Feb. 1942, Chief of Staff Super Secret File: MacArthur's Move to Australia, MMRDNA.

2. Radiogram, Marshall to MacArthur, 14 Feb. 1942, WDCSA 370.05 (3-17-42) Philippines, MMRDNA.

3. *New York Times*, 14 Feb. 1942.

4. Radiogram, MacArthur to Marshall, 15 Feb. 1942, Chief of Staff Super Secret File: MacArthur's Move to Australia, MMRDNA.

5. Radiogram, MacArthur to Marshall, No. 296, 16 Feb. 1942, AG 381 (21 Dec. 1941) Far East Situation, MMRNDA.

6. Radiogram, MacArthur to Marshall, No. 297, 16 Feb. 1942, PSF Safe File, Philippine Islands, January to May 1942, FDRL.

7. Memorandum, Marshall to Roosevelt, 26 Feb. 1942, AG 381 (11-27-41, Sec. 2B), MMRDNA.

8. Carlos P. Romulo, *I Saw the Fall of the Philippines* (New York: Doubleday, Doran & Co., 1942), p. 186; Rear Admiral Francis W. Rockwell, USN, to the Commander-in-Chief, U.S. Fleet, Admiral Ernest J. King, Narrative of Naval Activities in Luzon Area, Dec. 1, 1941 to March 19, 1942, Submitted 1 Aug. 1942, p. 18, Naval History Division (hereinafter cited as Rockwell Report); Douglas MacArthur, *Reminiscences* (New York: McGraw-Hill, 1964), p. 140; Douglas MacArthur, "They Died Hard—Those Savage Men." *Life,* 10 July 1964, p. 73.

9. Stimson MSS. Diary, 20 Feb. 1942, Historical Manuscripts & University Archives Department, YUL.

10. Stimson MSS. Diary, 21 Feb. 1942, YUL. Col. Paul D. Bunker on February 21 wrote in his diary: "A good word for Walter Winchell. At last I approve of him:—he recently said 'To hell with this talk about MacArthur's *heroes*—Let's send them some help!' Just what we've been thinking!" Bunker MS. Diary, OCMH.

11. Stimson MSS. Diary, 21 Feb. 1942, YUL.

12. Radiogram, Marshall to MacArthur, 21 Feb. 1942, Chief of Staff Super Secret File: MacArthur's Move to Australia, MMRDNA.

13. Radiogram, MacArthur to Marshall, No. 341, 22 Feb. 1942, PSF Safe File, Philippine Islands, January to May 1942, FDRL.

14. Radiogram, MacArthur to Marshall, No. 344, 22 Feb. 1942, AG 381 (21 Dec. 1941) Far East Situation, MMRDNA.

15. Clark Lee, *They Call It Pacific: An Eye-Witness Story of Our War against Japan from Bataan to the Solomons* (New York: Viking Press, 1943), pp. 248–52; Clark Lee and Richard Henschel, *Douglas MacArthur* (New York: Henry Holt & Co. 1952), p. 157. Lee, Jacoby, and Jacoby's wife, Annalee, reached Cebu safely. On March 8 they boarded the *Dona Nati,* a blockade runner, which took them from Cebu to Brisbane. On April 30, 1942, Melville Jacoby was killed along with Brig. Gen. Harold H. George when a P-40 fighter crashed into their transport plane.

16. Memorandum, Maj. Gen. Richard J. Marshall, USA (Ret.), to author, 13 July 1967, USAFFE, Chief of Staff, "Brief Summary of Action in the Office of Chief of Staff," Dec. 8, 1941 to Feb. 22, 1942, MMBA.

17. Memorandum, Hurley to Marshall, 21 Feb. 1942, OPD 381 SWPA, Sec. 1, Case 21, MMRDNA.

18. Robert E. Sherwood, *Roosevelt & Hopkins* (New York: Harper & Brothers, 1948), pp. 505, 509; Letter, Adolf A. Berle to author, 1 June 1967; Stimson MSS. Diary, 17 March 1942, YUL; Louis Morton, *Strategy And Command: The First Two Years* (Washington, D.C.: U.S. Government Printing Office, 1962), p. 193. Letters urging the recall of MacArthur from Corregidor can be found in: Correspondence concerning MacArthur, Box 40, from July to December 1941, and Box 42, from January to June 1942, FDRL. Claiming that "practical military considerations" called for General MacArthur's recall from Corregidor to Australia, former Assistant Secretary of State Adolf A. Berle wrote: "The human mind likes devious or romantic explanations better and frequently manufactures them, refusing the simpler, more straightforward ones. In the MacArthur situation, I think romance can be discarded."

19. Radiogram, Marshall to MacArthur, No. 1078, 22 Feb. 1942, Memorandum, W.F.D. to Marshall, 23 Feb. 1942, both documents in Chief of Staff Super Secret File: MacArthur's Move to Australia, MMRDNA.

20. Sidney L. Huff, *My Fifteen Years with General MacArthur* (New York: Paperback Library, 1964), p. 50.

21. Francis B. Sayre, *Glad Adventure* (New York: Macmillan Co., 1957), p. 241; Elizabeth E. Sayre, "Submarine From Corregidor: Manila Goes Under," *The Atlantic Monthly*, Vol. 170 (August 1942), p. 40; Romulo, op. cit., p. 188; Francis B. Sayre, "War Days on Corregidor," *Life*, Vol. XII (April 20, 1942), p. 103. After a seventeen-day voyage aboard the *Swordfish*, Sayre and his family reached Australia. On March 24, Secretary of War Stimson wrote in his diary: "Francis Sayre, the High Commissioner of the Philippines who has just arrived from the Islands, came in to see me and I had a good talk with him. He gave a pessimistic picture of the progress of the Philippine Commonwealth during his, Sayre's, residence out there; also of Quezon. The government had deteriorated, had become more expensive and less efficient. I was not surprised because Sayre has not gotten on well with them; in fact he has been the least successful Commissioner or Governor we have had there for some time. He quite lacks sympatico with the Filipinos and I cannot imagine him and Quezon getting on well together." Stimson MSS. Diary, 24 March 1942, YUL.

22. MacArthur, op. cit., p. 140; Courtney Whitney, *MacArthur: His Rendezvous With History* (New York: Alfred A. Knopf, 1964), pp. 45–47; Frazier Hunt, *The Untold Story of Douglas MacArthur* (New York: New American Library, 1964), pp. 234–35. Concerning the staff meeting, Joseph R. McMicking wrote: "I had no knowledge of the staff meeting that persuaded General MacArthur not to disobey President Roosevelt's orders, but from my knowledge of the General and his closest advisers in 1942, the only two persons the General would have consulted were Major General Richard K. Sutherland and Brigadier General Richard J. Marshall." Joseph R. McMicking to author, 13 June 1967.

The author queried Maj. Gen. Richard J. Marshall about the staff meeting and MacArthur's reaction to President Roosevelt's order to leave Corregidor for Australia. Marshall wrote that Sutherland informed him that the radiogram "had only been seen by himself and one or two others. I believe Akin and Willoughby. They had taken the same stand as Sutherland that General MacArthur would have to comply with orders. USAFFE had been made a part of Wavell's Command and the move was really within that Allied Force. I don't believe that the decision was made as a result of any one meeting. I don't know where General MacArthur was when he finally decided to carry out orders as given, but it was probably at the house where General MacArthur and family slept. It was off limits for everyone else and he and Sutherland could talk privately there." Maj. Gen. Richard J. Marshall, USA (Ret.), to author, 13 July 1967.

On October 3, 1970, Maj. Gen. Hugh J. Casey went over the draft manuscript with the author page by page. When General Casey came to the section about MacArthur resigning his commission and disobeying Roosevelt's order, Casey suddenly exclaimed, "Where in the hell did you get this! I don't believe it!" Somewhat startled, the author replied, "From General MacArthur's *Reminiscences*." Casey quickly retorted, "I still don't believe it. He never would have resigned his commission."

On February 8, 1969, the author asked Maj. Gen. Charles A. Willoughby, USA (Ret.), who was MacArthur's Chief of Intelligence during this period of time, the following question: "On February 23, General MacArthur received the order from President Roosevelt ordering him to leave Corregidor and to proceed to Australia. General MacArthur in his *Reminiscences* claimed that at first he thought of disregarding the order and joining his army on Bataan. In fact, he stated that he even wrote out a refusal to the presidential order. But at a meeting, his staff, led by General Sutherland, talked him out of disobeying the order and convinced him that he should go to Australia. Could you describe and relate what transpired at this meeting? Where was it held? Who was present? Did you read General MacArthur's written refusal?"

In his reply, Willoughby stated: "If you are *trained in methodology* (as I was in post-graduate work in history, under the late Dr. Hudder of the University of Kansas) you will differentiate between primary evidence, or documentation. The phraseology "claim to" have done this or that does not require confirmation from an outside source, anymore than Grant's Memoirs require apologies. *They are primary sources.* You accept them—because there is nothing more valid." Memorandum, Maj. Gen. Charles A. Willoughby to author, 11 Feb. 1969.

23. Radiogram, MacArthur to Marshall, No. 358, 24 Feb. 1942, Chief of Staff Super Secret File: MacArthur's Move to Australia, MMRDNA.

24. Memorandum, Marshall to Roosevelt, 24 Feb. 1942, Chief of Staff Super Secret File: MacArthur's Move to Australia, MMRDNA.

25. Press Conferences, #807, 24 Feb. 1942, and #806, 17 Feb. 1942, Press Conferences, Vol. 19, Jan. 1, 1942 to June 30, 1942, FDRL.

26. Stimson MSS. Diary, 23 Feb. 1942, YUL.

27. Stimson MSS. Diary, 25 Feb. 1942, YUL.

28. Radiogram, Marshall to MacArthur, No. 1087, 25 Feb. 1942, Chief of Staff Super Secret File: MacArthur's Move to Australia, MMRDNA.

29. Radiogram, MacArthur to Marshall, No. 373, 26 Feb. 1942, Chief of Staff Super Secret File: MacArthur's Move to Australia, MMRDNA.

30. Memorandum, Marshall to Roosevelt, 26 Feb. 1942, PSF Safe File, Philippine Islands, January to May 1942, FDRL.

31. Radiogram, Marshall to Brett, No. 439, 26 Feb. 1942, 384-1 GHQ SWPA, Federal Records Center.

32. Lt. Gen. George H. Brett, USAF (Ret.), with Jack Kofoed, "The MacArthur I Knew," *True* (New York: Fawcett Publications, Oct. 1947), p. 139.

33. Memorandum, Libby to Marshall, 26 Feb. 1942, Chief of Staff Super Secret File: MacArthur's Move to Australia, MMRDNA.

34. *Toledo Blade,* 26 Feb. 1942.

35. Radiogram, Marshall to MacArthur, No. 1107, 28 Feb. 1942, Super Secret Messages to Gen. MacArthur, OPD Exec O, MMRDNA.

36. Radiogram, MacArthur to Marshall, No. 383, 28 Feb. 1942, PSF Safe File, Philippine Islands, January to May 1942, FDRL.

CHAPTER 7

1. Radiogram, MacArthur to Marshall, No. 5, 21 March 1942, Msgs from Gen. MacArthur, OPD Exec O, MMRDNA. In this radiogram, MacArthur also stated: "I wish to commend the courage and aloofness of the officers and men of this headquarters who were engaged in this hazardous enterprise. It was due entirely to their invincible resolution and determination that the mission was successfully accomplished."

2. James H. Baldwin to author, 17 Feb. 1970; Sidney L. Huff, *My Fifteen Years with General MacArthur* (New York: Paperback Library, 1964), pp. 52–53; Rear Admiral H. James Ray, USN (Ret.), to author, 24 April 1969; W. L. White, *They Were Expendable* (New York: Harcourt, Brace & Co., 1942), pp. 102–4.

3. Joseph R. McMicking to author, 13 June 1967, 20 March 1969.

4. Radiogram, MacArthur to Brett, 1 March 1942, Records of USAFPAC, Series entitled: Correspondence with USAFFE, MMBA.

5. Radiogram, Marshall to MacArthur, No. 1078, 22 Feb. 1942, Chief of Staff Super Secret File: MacArthur's Move to Australia, MMRDNA; Douglas MacArthur, *Reminiscences* (New York: McGraw Hill, 1964), p. 141; Louis Morton, *The Fall of the Philippines* (Washington, D.C.: U.S. Government Printing Office, 1953), p. 359; Col. Francis W. Wilson, USA (Ret.), to author, 20 Feb. 1969. According to Col. F. W.

Wilson, Master Sergeant Paul P. Rogers was selected by Maj. Gen. Sutherland to make the trip because of his speed and accuracy as a stenographer-typist. On March 11, 1942, he was promoted in rank to Master Sergeant. Before the war ended, he attained the rank of Second Lieutenant.

6. Rear Admiral Francis W. Rockwell, USN, to the Commander-in-Chief, U.S. Fleet, Admiral E. J. King, *Narrative of Naval Activities in Luzon Area,* Dec. 1, 1941 to March 19, 1942, 1 August 1942, p. 20, Naval History Division (hereinafter cited as Rockwell Report).

7. Rear Admiral H. James Ray, USN (Ret.), to author, 24 April 1969; Maj. Gen. Chih Wang, Chinese Army, (Ret.), to author, 22 July 1969.

8. Rockwell Report, p. 20.

9. A short biography on Rear Admiral John D. Bulkeley, USN, 7 Dec. 1965, Navy Department, Office of Information, Internal Relations Division, Naval History Division; Lieutenant Commander Malcolm M. Champlin, USN, "One Man's Version," MS. pp. 70–71. "One Man's Version" is an unpublished account of Champlin's experiences in the Philippines. On March 14, 1942, Champlin departed from Corregidor aboard the submarine *Permit* bound for Australia.

10. Radiogram, Marshall to MacArthur, No. 1125, 6 March 1942, Chief of Staff Super Secret File: MacArthur's Move to Australia, MMRDNA.

11. Radiogram, MacArthur to Marshall, No. 434, 7 March 1942, Chief of Staff Super Secret File: MacArthur's Move to Australia, MMRDNA.

12. Radiogram, MacArthur to Marshall, No. 449, 8 March 1942, Chief of Staff Super Secret File: MacArthur's Move to Australia, MMRDNA.

13. Allison Ind, *Bataan: The Judgment Seat* (New York: Macmillan Co., 1944), p. 331.

14. Rockwell Report, p. 20.

15. Operation Order, The Commandant, Sixteenth Naval District, to The Commander, Motor Torpedo Boat Squadron Three, 10 March 1942, Naval History Division. The operation order was drawn up mainly by Rockwell, Ray, Bulkeley, and Huff. Most of the navigational data was obtained from the *Sailing Directions for the Philippine Islands.*

16. Ibid. Rear Admiral H. James Ray, USN (Ret.), to author, 24 April 1969. Huff, op. cit., p. 53.

17. Rockwell Report, p. 20.

18. Maj. Gen. Richard J. Marshall, USA (Ret.), to author, 13 July 1967.

19. James H. Baldwin to author, 17 Feb. 1970; Jonathan M. Wainwright, *General Wainwright's Story* (New York: Doubleday & Co., 1946), pp. 1–2.

20. Wainwright, op. cit., pp. 2–5.

21. Ind, op. cit., p. 333.

22. Brigadier General Charles H. Morhouse, USAF, to author, April 1969.

23. Radiogram, Marshall to Brett, No. 613, 10 March 1942, Marshall Folder, PSF, Safe File, Franklin D. Roosevelt Library.

24. Brig. Gen. Charles H. Morhouse, USAF, to author, April 1969.

25. Maj. Gen. Richard J. Marshall, USA (Ret.), to author, 13 July 1967.

26. Carlos P. Romulo, *I Saw the Fall of the Philippines* (New York: Doubleday, Doran & Co., 1943), pp. 218–26.

27. William E. Dyess, *The Dyess Story* (New York: G. P. Putnam's Sons, 1944), p. 61. Regarding General George, Dyess wrote, "He was one of the grandest officers I ever have known. We always thought of him as a genius who was human." General George was killed on April 30, 1942 in Australia when a P-40 fighter crashed into his transport plane. Dyess was later captured by the Japanese on Bataan. He managed to

escape from a Japanese prisoner of war camp in Mindanao and was evacuated to Australia on a submarine. Dyess was killed late in 1943 when a P-38 fighter he was flying burst into flames and crashed against a church steeple in California. Ind, op. cit., pp. 339–40, 379–89.

28. MacArthur, op. cit., p. 142; Huff, op. cit., pp. 55–56.

29. Brig. Gen. Charles H. Morhouse, USAF, to author, April 1969; James H. Baldwin to author, 17 Feb. 1970; John Toland, *But Not In Shame* (New York: Random House, 1961), p. 270; Clark Lee and Richard Henschel, *Douglas MacArthur* (New York: Henry Holt & Co., 1952), p. 83.

30. Maj. Gen. George F. Moore, USA, Report of Operations—USAFFE & USFIP in the Philippine Islands, 14 Feb. 1941 to 6 May 1942, MMRDNA; Toland, op cit., p. 270.

31. Toland, op. cit.; Rear Admiral Melvyn H. McCoy, USN (Ret.), to author, 23 Feb. 1970.

32. MacArthur, op. cit., p. 143; Charles A. Willoughby and John Chamberlain, *MacArthur 1941–1951* (New York: McGraw-Hill, 1954), pp. 48–49.

33. Rockwell Report, p. 21; Rear Admiral H. James Ray, USN (Ret.), to author, 24 April 1969.

34. Ray, op. cit.

35. Ibid.

36. Comments concerning Chapter 7 of draft MS., Captain Robert B. Kelly, USN (Ret.), to author, 11 April 1969; Huff, op. cit., 56.

37. MacArthur, op. cit., p. 144; Comments concerning Chapter 7 of draft MS., Captain Robert B. Kelly, USN (Ret.), to author, 11 April 1969. Captain Kelly stated: "The four PT-boats became separated during the first night not because of the rough seas but rather because of the problems they had with their engines. These were caused by carbon build-up and contaminated fuel systems. During the period from December 1941 to March 1942 most of the PT-boat patrols had been conducted at low speed in order to conserve on fuel. Its effect was to markedly decrease the maximum speed of which each boat was capable until the carbon burned off with full power operation. Contaminated fuel—the high test gasoline which the boats used had been stored in a barge which had formerly been used to transport coconut oil—caused the strainers on the engines' fuel intakes to become clogged. When this occurred, the engines sputtered and stopped. The boat then had to lie to for about 20–30 minutes until the strainers could be disconnected and cleaned. In the meanwhile, the other boats continued on. This happened to all of the boats, including the PT-34 which I commanded."

38. Interview with Maj. Gen. Hugh J. Casey, USA (Ret.), 3 Oct. 1970; Comments concerning Chapter 7 of draft MS., Maj. Gen. Hugh J. Casey, USA (Ret.), to author; Maj. Gen. Spencer B. Akin, USA (Ret.), to author, 5 March 1969; Captain Vincent E. Schumacher to author, 2 May 1969; Huff, op. cit., p. 59.

39. Captain Vincent E. Schumacher, USN (Ret.), to author, 2 May 1969.

40. Comments concerning Chapter 7 of draft MS., Maj. Gen. Hugh J. Casey, USA (Ret.), to author; Toland, op. cit., p. 272. Huff, op. cit., p. 60; Rear Admiral H. James Ray, USN (Ret.), to author, 24 April 1969.

41. Ray, op. cit.

42. Rockwell Report, p. 21; Comments concerning Chapter 7 of draft MS., Captain Robert B. Kelly, USN (Ret.), to author, 11 April 1969. Captain Kelly stated: "Only one boat arrived at its destination the first morning. That was the PT-34 and this was accomplished without benefit of charts. All we had was a rough pencil sketch of the island."

43. Rockwell Report, p. 21; Comments concerning Chapter 7 of draft MS., Maj. Gen.

Hugh J. Casey, USA (Ret.), to author; Maj. Gen. Spencer B. Akin, USA (Ret.), to author, 5 March 1969.

44. Huff, op. cit., p. 61; Toland, op. cit., p. 272.

45. Rockwell Report, p. 21. PT-32 was destroyed by gunfire from the submarine *Permit* at 6:30 A.M. on March 13, 1942. In his report to the secretary of the navy, Schumacher stated: "When the vessel was abandoned and destroyed two engines were out of commission and the third unreliable due to sea-water leakage into the engine room. The previously patched deck over the engine room was cracked and leaking badly from damage caused by a deck load of one thousand gallons of fuel in drums. The bolts holding the center shaft tail strut were sheared off, rendering the shaft out of commission and causing a leak into the after compartment. The only spare magneto available (an old one) had been used with unsatisfactory results. The quantity of fresh water on hand was twenty gallons. There remained on hand approximately one thousand gallons of fuel.

"Because of the unsafe condition of the vessel, the prevailing easterly wind, and the rough sea, and the probability of the third engine being flooded and put out of commission, the possibility of making a safe landing on the island of Panay was considered remote. Therefore, in order to safeguard the lives of the crew, assistance was requested from the U.S.S. *Permit* and the U.S.S. PT-32 was destroyed." Report of destruction of U.S.S. PT-32, From The Commanding Officer, U.S.S. PT-32, To The Secretary of the Navy, 15 March 1942.

Later, Lieutenant John D. Bulkeley disagreed with Schumacher's decision to destroy PT-32. On April 23, 1942, in a letter to the Commander Allied Naval Forces Southwest Pacific, Bulkeley stated: "The conditions of the engines and hull of the U.S.S. PT-32 at 6:00 P.M., 12 March 1942 were good. The studs of the center strut were loose and the strut was vibrating. This condition should have been remedied at the time as replacement studs and shallow water diving equipment were left with the PT-32. Even if repairs were not effected this boat was able to make 20 knots when it parted company.

"The PT-32 had about 1,900 gallons of gas aboard, enough for 300 miles at 20 knots, and the nearest island (Panay) was approximately 60 miles distant where gas could be obtained. Lt. (jg) Schumacher's orders were to proceed to Iloilo City, Negros, approximately 120 miles distant, refuel and then proceed to Cagayan, Mindanao. He had sufficient gas to accomplish this mission." Letter, Bulkeley to Commander Allied Naval Forces Southwest Pacific, 23 April 1942.

46. Comments concerning Chapter 7 of draft MS., Captain Robert B. Kelly, USN (Ret.), to author, 11 April 1969; Huff, op. cit., p. 61.

47. Interview with Maj. Gen. Hugh J. Casey, USA (Ret.), 3 Oct. 1970; Comments concerning Chapter 7 of draft MS., Maj. Gen. Hugh J. Casey, USA (Ret.); Huff, op. cit., p. 62; Rockwell Report, p. 21; Brig. Gen. Charles H. Morhouse, USAF, to author, April 1969.

48. Rockwell Report, p. 21.

49. Ibid; Comments concerning Chapter 7 of draft MS., Captain Robert B. Kelly, USN (Ret.), to author, 11 April 1969; Rear Admiral H. James Ray, USN (Ret.), to author, 24 April 1969; Radiogram, MacArthur to Marshall, No. 5, 21 March 1942, Msgs from Gen. MacArthur, OPD Exec O, MMRDNA.

50. Huff, op. cit., pp. 63–64.

51. Rockwell Report, p. 21; Comments concerning Chapter 7 of draft MS., Captain Robert B. Kelly, USN (Ret.), to author, 11 April 1969. Captain Kelly stated: "For one not versed in the ways of the seas who had not made this voyage it would be difficult to visualize the rigors of that night or odds against success of the mission. Two small boats (77 feet long) in very questionable state of repair had evaded the enemy,

bested the elements and reached their destination–precisely on time! . . . The fact that the destination was reached on time was the result of damn fine seaman's intuition."

52. Edward Haggerty, *Guerrilla Padre In Mindanao* (New York: Longmans, Green & Co., 1946), p. 7.

53. Rockwell Report, p. 21; Rear Admiral John D. Bulkeley, USN, to author, 9 April 1969; MacArthur, op. cit., pp. 144–45; Toland, op. cit., p. 273.

54. Col. Francis W. Wilson, USA (Ret.), to author, 20 Feb. 1969.

55. Comments concerning Chapter 7 of draft MS., Captain Robert B. Kelly, USN (Ret.), to author, 11 April 1969.

56. Haggerty, op. cit., pp. 7–9.

57. Ind, op. cit., pp. 346–47.

58. Lt. Gen. George H. Brett, USAF (Ret.), with Jack Kofoed, "The MacArthur I Knew," *True* (New York: Fawcett Publications, Oct. 1947), p. 140. Capt. Henry ("Hank") C. Godman was the pilot of the B-17 that crashed in Cagayan Bay. Both Godman and his copilot were saved. Later, while serving in the Headquarters Flight of GHQ in Australia, Godman became MacArthur's pilot. Joseph R. McMicking to author, 13 June 1967.

59. Brett with Kofoed, op. cit., p. 140. The B-17s that Brett dispatched to Del Monte were from the Nineteenth Bomb Group. Having Survived the Philippine-Java period, they suffered from inadequate maintenance, overcommitment, and battle fatigue. Brig. Gen. William G. Hipps, USAF (Ret.), to author, 25 July 1969. According to Brig. Gen Hipps, "The aircraft sent were the best available."

60. Radiogram, MacArthur to Brett, No. 58, 13 March 1942, 384-1, MacArthur File, G 3 Files, GHQ SWPA, Federal Records Center, GSA. Due to the possibility of an air attack, Pease felt he could not leave his plane on the ground during daylight and, after refuelling, left immediately for Australia with sixteen passengers. According to Brig. Gen. Hipps, there was a question of whether the B-17 would make it back to Darwin. However, Pease was able to fly his passengers to Melbourne. Joseph R. McMicking to author, 13 June 1967.

Brett disagreed with MacArthur's claim that Lt. Pease was an "inexperienced" pilot. Brett stated that Pease "had conducted himself with the greatest courage and skill in combat, and he had seen plenty of combat. Later, Pease was killed in action and posthumously awarded the Congressional Medal of Honor."

Regarding the difficulty in arranging plane transportation for the MacArthur party, Brig. Gen. Hipps, who was the Assistant Officer for Operations & Plans in Brett's Allied Air Force Headquarters in Melbourne, recalled that "MacArthur was exercised to say the least and sent some uncomplimentary messages." For instance, on March 15 MacArthur received a message from Brett via Fort Mills that was incoherent. In his reply to Brett, MacArthur was abrupt: "Verify, clarify and repeat your message [of March 14], signed Brett addressed Fort Mills part one contradicts part four. Absolutely essential this be clarified before midnight March 15. This is urgent." Radiograms, Bett to MacArthur, No. 79, 15 March 1942, and MacArthur to Brett No. 61, 15 March 1942, 384–1, MacArthur File, G-3 Files, GHQ SWPA, Federal Records Center, GSA; Brig. Gen. William G. Hipps, USAF (Ret.), to author, 25 July 1969; Brett with Kofoed, op. cit., p. 140.

61. Radiogram, MacArthur to Marshall, No. 482, 14 March 1942, Chief of Staff Super Secret File: MacArthur's Move to Australia, MMRDNA.

62. Brett with Kofoed, op. cit., p. 140.

63. This message was not dispatched to MacArthur by Brett. A draft of the message was found in 384-1, MacArthur File, G-3 Files, GHQ SWPA, Federal Records Center, GSA.

64. Radiogram, Brett to MacArthur, No. 77, 14 March 1942, 384-1, MacArthur File, G-3 Files, GHQ SWPA, Federal Records Center, GSA.

65. Radiogram, Marshall to MacArthur, No. 1172, 14 March 1942, AG 311.23 (4 Feb. 1942), GHQ SWPA, MMRDNA.

66. Radiogram, Brett to MacArthur, No. 81, 15 March 1942, MacArthur File, G-3 Files, GHQ SWPA, Federal Records Center, GSA. On March 15 in Washington, Secretary of War Stimson told Roosevelt about the recent messages the War Department had received from MacArthur in Mindanao "and his rather imperative demand for the three best planes [the War Department] had to take him down to Australia." Stimson MSS. Diary, 15 March 1942.

67. Maj. Gen. Richard J. Marshall, USA (Ret.), to author, 13 July 1967; Rockwell Report, p. 22; Maj. Gen. Richard H. Carmichael, USAF (Ret.), to author, 17 July 1969.

Col. Francis H. Wilson stated: "Each passenger, with the possible exception of General and Mrs. MacArthur, was directed to leave his one piece of hand luggage on the field, [so] that it might be sent to Australia later. No one objected. We would gladly have removed our clothes if that had been ordered. Our baggage did arrive later on another plane." Col. Francis W. Wilson, USA (Ret.), to author, 20 Feb. 1969.

Col. Victor C. Huffsmith recalled that while MacArthur stayed at the Del Monte Plantation numerous meetings were held "with regard to making a holding action on Mindanao." Col. Victor C. Huffsmith, USA (Ret.), to author, 7 July 1969.

Brig. Gens. George and Casey during their stay at Del Monte spent three days conducting reconnaissance flights over Mindanao. They were looking for potential airfields for aircraft which they hoped to send from Australia to Mindanao. The first reconnaissance flight was made toward Davao, the second to the northwest, and the third to the northeast toward Surigao. As a result of the information obtained on these reconnaissance flights, Casey, following his arrival in Australia, arranged with MacArthur for the transfer of Col. Wendell W. Fertig from Bataan to supervise the construction of airfields in Mindanao. Interview with Maj. Gen. Hugh J. Casey, USA (Ret.), 3 Oct. 1970; Comments concerning Chapter 7 of draft MS., Maj. Gen. Hugh J. Casey, USA (Ret.), to author.

68. Maj. Gen. Richard J. Marshall, USA (Ret.), to author, 13 July 1967; Huff, op. cit., pp. 66–67; Rockwell Report, p. 22.

69. Rockwell Report, p. 22.

70. Huff, op. cit., p. 67; Frazier Hunt, The Untold Story of Douglas MacArthur (New York: New American Library, 1964), pp. 246–47; Joseph R. McMicking to author, 13 June 1967.

71. Rockwell Report, p. 22; Brett with Kofoed, op. cit., p. 141.

72. Brig. Gen. Charles H. Morhouse, USAF, to author, April 1969; Toland, op. cit., p. 276. Brig. Gen. Hipps stated: "I was at Batchelor Field along with Brig. Gen. Royce to meet MacArthur's plane. He landed and asked about his train to continue to Melbourne. He agreed to fly on to Alice Springs when he learned there was no rail line south of Birdum. He was not happy during the period at Batchelor Field." Brig. Gen. William G. Hipps, USAF (Ret.), to author, 25 July 1969.

73. Huff, op. cit., p. 68; Maj. Gen. Richard H. Carmichael, USAF (Ret.), to author, 17 July 1969.

74. Brig. Gen. Charles H. Morhouse, USAF, to author, April 1969; Maj. Gen. Richard H. Carmichael, USAF (Ret.), to author, 17 July 1969.

75. Rockwell Report, p. 22; MacArthur, op. cit., p. 145.

76. Brett with Kofoed, op. cit., p. 141.

77. Telephone message, Brett to Curtin, 17 March 1942, 384-1, MacArthur File, G-3 Files, GHQ SWPA, Federal Records Center, GSA.

78. Radiogram, Brett to Marshall, No. 736, 17 March 1942, 384-1, MacArthur File, G-3 Files, GHQ SWPA, Federal Records Center, GSA.

79. Memorandum, Brig. Gen. Stephen J. Chamberlin, USA, 18 March 1942, 384-1, MacArthur File, G-3 Files, GHQ SWPA, Federal Records Center, GSA.

80. Ibid.

81. Ibid. Joseph R. McMicking to author, 13 June 1967 and 26 Feb. 1969; Rockwell Report, p. 22; Maj. Gen. Richard J. Marshall, USA (Ret.), to author, 13 July 1967.

82. Radiogram, Roosevelt to Churchill, 17 March 1942, Item No. 10, Exec. No. 10, Col. Gailey's File, OPD Exec File, MMRDNA.

83. Press Conference #812, President Franklin D. Roosevelt, Executive Office of the President, 17 March 1942, FDRL.

84. Stimson MSS. Diary, 17 March 1942. On March 19 Frederic Condert sent Stimson a letter in which he congratulated Stimson for having MacArthur transferred to Australia. In his reply of March 25, Stimson stated: "The MacArthur problem was a difficult one and, if I say it myself, was handled with skill and success, chiefly by General Marshall." Stimson Correspondence, 1942 Feb. 17 to March 31, Box 393, March 19–20 Folder, Historical Manuscripts and University Archives, YUL.

CHAPTER 8

1. Winston S. Churchill, *Their Finest Hour* (Boston: Houghton Mifflin Company, 1949), p. 115. Although Churchill was commenting on the British evacuation at Dunkirk from May 29 to June 4, 1940, the quote has a bearing on General MacArthur's evacuation from Corregidor to Australia.

2. *New York Times,* 18 March 1942.

3. Telegram, Spyros P. Skouras to Roosevelt, 18 March 1942; Telegram, Frank T. Priest to Roosevelt, 18 March 1942; Telegram, Mrs. H. M. Jarvis to Roosevelt, 21 March 1942. These telegrams and other telegrams and letters of a similar nature can be found in Official File No. 4771, MacArthur, FDRL.

4. *New York Times,* 18 March 1942.

5. Press Conference #813, President Franklin D. Roosevelt, Executive Office of the President, 20 March 1942, Franklin D. Roosevelt Library. *New York Times,* 21 March 1942.

6. Telegram, Mr. and Mrs. A. M. James to Roosevelt, 17 March 1942, Official File No. 4771, MacArthur, FDRL.

7. Sidney L. Huff, *My Fifteen Years with General MacArthur* (New York: Paperback Library, 1964), pp. 70–73.

8. Lt. Gen. George H. Brett, USAF (Ret.), with Jack Kofoed, "The MacArthur I Knew," *True* (New York: Fawcett Publications, Inc., Oct. 1947), p. 141. Joseph R. McMicking stated: "Hurley did not talk to the staff, he only spoke to Sutherland. This attitude was frequently expressed by Sutherland. . . . this was not the feeling of MacArthur's staff, who were pretty much down-to-earth individuals and quite sober after their experience." Comments concerning Chapter 8 of draft MS., Joseph R. McMicking to author; Joseph R. McMicking to author, 26 Feb. 1969.

Maj. Gen. Hugh J. Casey wrote: "I can't conceive of *any* of the group giving *any* such impression. As a matter of fact, only a few of us on that staff were actually *in combat.*" Comments concerning Chapter 8 of draft MS., Maj. Gen. Hugh J. Casey, USA (Ret.), to author.

Concerning Maj. Gen. Richard K. Sutherland, McMicking stated: "Sutherland was an ambitious person with a drive to make a name for himself. Hardboiled and ruthless. For instance, Eisenhower left MacArthur's Hq. in 1939 because while MacArthur was away in Washington, Sutherland pulled the rug from under him in Manila. If this politicking had not taken place by Sutherland, Eisenhower might have remained as MacArthur's Chief of Staff and continued in that position throughout World War II." Joseph R. McMicking to author, 26 Feb. 1969.

McMicking's opinion of Sutherland was also shared by Brig. Gen. Charles H. Morhouse, who wrote: "I distrusted him and disliked him." Brig. Gen. Charles H. Morhouse, USAF, to author, April 1969. Brig. Gen. William G. Hipps remembered, "Sutherland was difficult to work with." Brig. Gen. William G. Hipps, USAF (Ret.), to author, 25 July 1969. However, Rear Admiral H. James Ray, who served as MacArthur's naval adviser from March 1942 to April 1943, stated, "General Sutherland appeared to be the work horse of the staff; capable, not particularly warm in his relationships with his juniors but efficient as the General's 'Man Friday.' I liked him." Rear Admiral H. James Ray, USN (Ret.), to author, 24 April 1969.

9. Maj. Gen. Richard J. Marshall, USA (Ret.), to author, 13 July 1967; Radiogram, Marshall to MacArthur, No. 7939, 18 March 1942, OPD Exec Office File, Book 4, MMRDNA; Frazier Hunt, *The Untold Story of Douglas MacArthur* (New York: New American Library, 1964), p. 247; Huff, op. cit., pp. 73–75. Marshall related that "the whole purpose in going to Australia" was to prepare an offensive that would liberate the Philippines. "We had talked about it, the magnitude of the task, what we needed [in the way of forces and supplies] to do it, what we could expect to find in Australia, and when we could get started back. General MacArthur was constantly talking about these details to Sutherland and me. . . . It was only after I had gone to Melbourne and gotten information on the American and Australian forces available and given [this information] to the General that we could see the long delay that would ensue before we could retake the Islands." Maj. Gen. Richard J. Marshall, USA (Ret.), to author, 13 July 1967.

10. *New York Times*, 21 March 1942. It was stated on the front page of the March 21, 1942 edition of the *New York Times* that General MacArthur "issued the statement at Adelaide before boarding a train for Melbourne." However, General MacArthur in his *Reminiscences*, p. 145, said that he made the statement at Batchelor Field. Maj. Gen. Charles A. Willoughby in *MacArthur 1941–1951*, p. 64, also said that MacArthur made the statement at Batchelor Field.

On the other hand, Maj. Gen. Courtney Whitney in *MacArthur: His Rendezvous With History*, p. 52, wrote that MacArthur made the pledge at "Alice Springs" where he "changed trains." MacArthur did not change trains at Alice Springs, but he did change trains at Adelaide. The author believes that Maj. Gen. Whitney confused Alice Springs with Adelaide. It is doubtful that any reporters were present at the remote airfields at Batchelor Field or Alice Springs, especially since MacArthur's specific whereabouts in Australia was secret. Therefore, it is the author's opinion that MacArthur's famous "I shall return" pledge was made at Adelaide, not at Batchelor Field or Alice Springs.

11. *New York Times*, 21 March 1942 and 22 March 1942; *Toledo Blade*, 21 March 1942.

12. *Toledo Blade*, 21 March 1942.

13. Vorin E. Whan, Jr., ed., *A Soldier Speaks: Public Papers and Speeches of General of the Army Douglas MacArthur* (New York: Frederick A. Praeger, 1965), p. 115; *New York Times*, 22 March 1942.

14. Brett with Kofoed, op. cit., p. 141. The author asked Lt. Gen. Stephen J. Chamberlin if Brett had ever mentioned anything to him about this incident. Chamberlin answered, "Gen. Brett told me to conduct Gen. MacArthur to the hotel which I did. Although it is my recollection that Gen. Brett's instructions to me were given prior to Gen. MacArthur's arrival, it could have been later. Gen. Brett at no time told

me of his question [to MacArthur] nor of [MacArthur's negative reply]. I can see no reason for Gen. Brett to make such a statement unless it was true." Lt. Gen. Stephen J. Chamberlin, USA (Ret.), to author, 23 March 1969.

15. Lt. Gen. Stephen J. Chamberlin, USA (Ret.), to author, 23 March 1969.

16. Brett with Kofoed, op. cit., p. 141. Maj. Gen. Hugh J. Casey wrote: "This to me seems unbelievable. Is source from Generals Brett or Royce?" Comments concerning Chapter 8 of draft·MS., Maj. Gen. Hugh J. Casey, USA (Ret.), to author.

17. Radiogram, MacArthur to Marshall, No. 21, 21 March 1942, AG 381 (21 Dec. 1941) Far Eastern Situation, MMRDNA. Joseph R. McMicking wrote: "To me, the most interesting historical item of that period was the fact that when Gen. MacArthur landed in Australia on the 17th of March 1942, he did not have written orders or Letters of Instructions appointing him Commander-in-Chief. Until the 18th of April he was an important guest of the Australian Government, but without authority from the Allied Powers, or an appointment from the President of the United States." Joseph R. McMicking to author, 13 June 1967.

CHAPTER 9

1. Radiogram, Stimson to Wainwright, 8 April 1942, Messages to Wainwright, Item #9 Exec #10, MMRDNA.

2. Col. Arnold D. Amoroso, USA (Ret.), to author, 24 Sept. 1969.

3. Robert K. Branch to author, 17 Sept. 1969.

4. Diary of Lt. Col. John R. Pugh, USA, 11 March 1942.

5. Brig. Gen. Bradford G. Chynoweth, USA (Ret.), to author, 17 June 1969.

6. Diary of Lt. Col. John R. Pugh, USA, 13 March 1942; Jonathan M. Wainwright, General Wainwright's Story (New York: Doubleday & Co., 1946), p. 67; Col. Stuart C. MacDonald, USA (Ret.), to author, 24 July 1969.

7. Diary of Col. Paul D. Bunker, USA, 12 March 1942, OCMH.

8. Col. Clyde A. Selleck, USA (Ret.), to author, 21 July 1969.

9. Forrest G. Hogg to author, 22 Sept. 1969; Col. Roscoe Bonham, USA (Ret.), to author, 28 Sept. 1969.

10. Brig. Gen. Arnold J. Funk, USA (Ret.), to author, 31 July 1969; Col. Charles E. N. Howard, USA (Ret.), to author 11 July 1969.

11. Brig. Gen. Charles C. Drake, USA (Ret.), "No Uncle Sam: The Story of a Hopeless Effort to Supply the Starving Army of Bataan and Corregidor," 29 March 1946 (a copy of Drake's report is in OCMH). In his report, Drake stated: "It is an interesting study in mental psychology that we in the Philippines came to believe more and more as the war went on and no help came from the United States that we had been abandoned to our fate and the business of war was being carried on elsewhere, and even today I still believe that we were not far wrong. Our country had bigger troubles to solve than getting us out of the Philippines. When I reached the States last September after living in a Japanese prison camp for forty-four months, I found that here in the states we had been nicknamed 'The Expendables.' A very apt name I would say in view of what happened."

12. Lt. Cdr. Malcolm M. Champlin, USN, "One Man's Version," MS., pp. 113–14.

13. Ibid., pp. 95–96; Interview, Maj. Gen. John R. Pugh, USA (Ret.), with author, 24 April 1970.

14. Champlin, op. cit., p. 72; Memorandum, Col. Arthur F. Fischer, USA, to Col. Charles K. Gailey, USA, 16 July 1942; Memorandum, Col. Thomas W. Doyle, USA, to

Col. Charles K. Gailey, USA, 15 July 1942; Memorandum, Col. Milton A. Hill, USA, to Chief of Staff, 20 Sept. 1942. These memoranda are in 201 Wainwright, Gen. J.M., MMRDNA. Col. Hill wrote: "Upon General MacArthur's departure from Corregidor, there was considerable apprehension, lest his departure might adversely affect the high morale of the troops defending Bataan and Corregidor. To my surprise and satisfaction, the high morale continued, due to General Wainwright's influence and outstanding leadership."

15. Radiogram, Marshall to Wainwright, No. 1191, 17 March 1942, Messages to Wainwright, Item #9 Exec #10, MMRDNA.

16. Diary of Col. Paul D. Bunker, USA, 19 March 1942, OCMH.

17. Radiogram, Marshall to Wainwright, No. 1203, 20 March 1942, AG381 (11-27-41 Sec 3) Far East, MMRDNA; Radiogram, Marshall to Wainwright, 19 March 1942, OPD Phil Island (3-1-42), MMRDNA.

18. Radiogram, MacArthur to Marshall, No. 3, 21 March 1942, AG 381 (21 Dec. 1941) Far Eastern Situation, MMRDNA.

19. Memorandum, Marshall to Roosevelt, 22 March 1942, Philippine Islands, Jan.-May 1942, PSF Safe File, FDRL; Radiogram, Marshall to MacArthur, No. 810, 22 March 1942; Messages from Gen. MacArthur, OPD Exec O, MMRDNA; Radiogram, MacArthur to Marshall, No. 19, 24 March 1942, AG 381 (21 Dec. 1941) Far Eastern Situation, MMRDNA.

20. Diary of Lt. Col. John R. Pugh, USA, 15 March 1942; Wainwright, op. cit., pp. 68–69.

21. William H. Baldwin to author, 17 Feb. 1970.

22. Wainwright, op. cit., p. 69.

23. Col. William C. Braly, USA (Ret.), "Corregidor—A Name, A Symbol, A Tradition," *Coast Artillery Journal*, LXXX, No. 4 (July-August 1947), p. 38.

24. Stimson MSS. Diary, 23 March 1942.

25. Citation that accompanied the award of the Medal of Honor to General MacArthur, 25 March 1942, Douglas MacArthur File 1944–45, FDRL; *New York Times*, 29 March 1942. In response to a request from Secretary of War Henry L. Stimson, MacArthur's Chief of Staff, Maj. Gen. Sutherland, recommended the award and suggested that it be issued to MacArthur in Australia. Sutherland stated that the citation should be based upon MacArthur's "utter contempt of danger under terrific aerial bombardments during one of which a two hundred kilogram bomb exploded within thirty feet of him in the open except for momentary shelter taken in a shallow drain beside a sidewalk. His refusal to take cover and his complete calm on this and many other occasions had a tremendous effect upon the morale of his troops among whom his personal valor was the subject of constant comment; and upon the magnificent leadership and vision that enabled the General to conduct a defense with a partially mobilized and equipped citizen Army that has merited the acclaim of the world and that enabled him to galvanize the spirit of resistance of sixteen million Filipinos." Radiogram, Sutherland to Stimson, 16 March 1942, Douglas MacArthur File 1944–45, FDRL.

On August 21, 1944 President Roosevelt was asked to sign a copy of the citation for General MacArthur personally. Before signing it Roosevelt asked General Marshall what the wording was based on. Along with explaining that the wording was based on Sutherland's radiogram, Marshall stated, "the citation was drafted by me personally and publicized at the time he came out of the Philippines. This action was taken, among other things, to offset any propaganda by the enemy directed against his leaving his command and proceeding to Australia in compliance with your orders. I cleared it with the Secretary of War and then with you at the time." Memorandum, Roosevelt to

Marshall, 21 August 1944; Memorandum, Marshall to Roosevelt, 22 August 1944. Both memoranda are in Gen. Douglas MacArthur File 1944–45, FDRL.

26. Radiogram, Wainwright to Marshall, No. 598, 26 March 1942, AG 381 (21 Dec. 1941) Far East Situation, MMRDNA.

27. Radiogram, Wainwright to MacArthur, 27 March 1942, AG 311.23 (4 Feb. 1942), CHQ SWPA, FRC.

28. Radiogram, Marshall to Wainwright, 27 March 1942, AG 381 (11-27-41 Sec. 3) Far East, MMRDNA.

29. Radiogram, Wainwright to Marshall, No. 625, 28 March 1942, OPD Exec Official Misc. File "Messages from Wainwright," MMRDNA.

30. Radiogram, Marshall to MacArthur, No. 966, 29 March 1942, 384.3, GHQ SWPA, FRC.

31. Lt. Gen. George H. Brett, USAF (Ret.), with Jack Kofoed, "The MacArthur I Knew," *True* (New York: Fawcett Publications, Oct. 1947), pp. 144–45.

32. Radiogram, Wainwright to Marshall through COMINCH, 30 March 1942, Messages to MacArthur, OPD Exec O, MMRDNA.

33. Radiogram, MacArthur to Wainwright, 30 March 1942, 384.3, GHQ SWPA, FRC.

34. Radiogram, MacArthur to Marshall, No. 56, 1 April 1942, Messages from Gen. MacArthur, OPD Exec O, MMRDNA. Col. Charles E. N. Howard, who served in the Eighty-eighth Field Artillery on Bataan, wrote: "This counterattack plan shows MacArthur knew little of the terrain, transport requirement, intelligence on Jap forces, highway net and strength of units. It would have been asinine and a dismal failure. What tank forces?" Comments concerning Chapter 9 of draft MS., Col. Charles E. N. Howard to author. Col. Achille C. Tisdelle, USA (Ret.), Maj. Gen. Edward P. King's aide-de-camp, took exception with several of MacArthur's statements in this radiogram. If MacArthur "had long ago prepared a comprehensive plan to endeavor to cut a way out if food or ammunition failed," Tisdelle asked, "then why didn't he carry it out before we were exhausted by malaria and starvation?" Regarding MacArthur's statement that he had not informed Wainwright of the plan because he "feared it might tend to shake his morale and determination," Tisdelle exploded, "What the g—— d—— hell did he think 'Skinny' was . . . a tenderfoot boy scout?"

Tisdelle called MacArthur's offer to return to Bataan "the action of someone immature and boyish or of a super egotist living in a dream world. To offer to return prematurely from his responsibility in Australia was to grossly insult the training and wisdom of both Gen. Wainwright and Gen. King, which he did with a puerile naiveté apparently unaware of the enormity of his affront to these two splendid soldiers." Comments concerning Chapter 9 of draft MS., Col. Achille C. Tisdelle to author. Letter, Col. Tisdelle, USA (Ret.), to author, 30 Dec. 1972.

35. Radiogram, Marshall to MacArthur, No. 1031, 2 April 1942, OPD 381, Philippine Islands, MMRDNA.

36. Radiogram, Wainwright to MacArthur, No. 154, 4 April 1942, 384.3, GHQ SWPA, FRC; Radiogram, MacArthur to Wainwright, No. 25, 4 April 1942, SWPA Correspondence with USFIP, MMBA.

37. Radiogram, MacArthur to Wainwright, No. 68, 4 April 1942, SWPA Correspondence with USFIP, MMBA.

38. Wainwright, op. cit., p. 77.

39. Ibid., pp. 77–78; Col. Harrison C. Browne, USA (Ret.), to author, 8 Sept. 1969; Col. Harrison D. Browne, USA (Ret.), to author, 14 Oct. 1969.

40. Wainwright, op. cit., p. 78.

41. Radiogram, Wainwright to MacArthur, No. 177, 6 April 1942, 384.3, GHQ SWPA, FRC.

42. Radiogram, Wainwright to MacArthur, No. 187, 7 April 1942, SWPA Correspondence with USFIP, MMBA.

43. Brig. Gen. Arnold J. Funk, USA (Ret.), to author, 31 July 1969; Wainwright, op. cit., p. 79; Memorandum for Chief, Far Eastern Branch, Col. J. K. Evans, Southeast Asia Section, 4 July 1942, Subject: Interview with Col. Milton A. Hill, IGD (Inf) OPD 381, Philippine Islands, Sec. 1 Case 50, MMRDNA.

44. Brig. Gen. Arnold J. Funk, USA (Ret.), to author, 31 July 1969.

45. Radiogram, Wainwright to MacArthur, No. 192, 7 April 1942, SWPA Correspondence with USFIP, MMBA.

46. Radiogram, MacArthur to Marshall, No. 116, 8 April 1942, SWPA Correspondence with War Dept., MMBA.

47. Stimson MSS. Diary, 7 April 1942.

48. Wainwright, op. cit., p. 80; Radiogram, Wainwright to MacArthur, No. 398, 4 May 1942, SWPA Correspondence with USFIP, MMBA.

49. Radiogram, MacArthur to Marshall, No. 91, 8 April 1942, MacArthur Radio File, OCMH.

50. Carlos P. Romulo, I Saw the Fall of the Philippines (New York: Doubleday, Doran & Co., 1942), pp. 272–73.

51. Radiogram, COM 16 to COMINCH, Messages from Gen. Wainwright, MMRDNA.

52. Lt. Cdr. Thomas C. Parker, USN, "The Epic of Corregidor-Bataan, December 24, 1941–May 4, 1942," United States Naval Institute Proceedings, Vol. 69, No. 1 (Jan. 1943), p. 18; Braly, op. cit., p. 40.

53. Radiogram, Wainwright to Marshall, No. 734, 8 April 1942, Messages from Wainwright, MMRDNA.

54. Stimson MSS. Diary, 8 April 1942.

55. Ibid.

56. Memorandum, McNarney to Roosevelt, 8 April 1942, Subject: Bataan Situation, Chief of Staff Bataan-Corregidor File, MMRDNA.

57. Radiogram, Marshall to MacArthur, No. 1158, 8 April 1942, AG 384.1, GHQ SWPA.

58. Radiogram, MacArthur to Marshall, No. 83, 9 April 1942, Messages from Gen. MacArthur, OPD Exec O, MMRDNA. Concerning Maj. Gen. Edward P. King's decision to surrender his forces on Bataan, Brig. Gen. Arnold J. Funk, who served as King's Chief of Staff, later wrote: "The evening of the 8th of April Gen. King called a conference of his staff and after a lengthy discussion it was decided that a party would proceed the next morning to contact the Japanese and secure terms of capitulation, that all troops would cease fire and all artillery, small arms and ammunition would be destroyed, and all commanding officers to be notified to comply at once.

"Gen. King, his two aides, Majors Wade Cothern and Achille C. Tisdelle, Col. Everett C. Williams, his chief of artillery, and Maj. Marshall H. Hurt, the assistant operations officer, proceeded early April 9th and contacted the Japanese. The Japanese held the party except for Maj. Hurt who returned and informed me that all would proceed as planned. My duty as directed by Gen. King was to carry out the details of capitulation as directed by him.

"The evening before as the conference mentioned above broke up a severe earthquake shook Bataan. One officer remarked: 'Even the earth is shaken by our decision.' " Comments concerning Chapter 9 of draft MS., Brig. Gen. Arnold J. Funk, USA, to author.

59. Radiogram, MacArthur to Marshall, No. 83, 9 April 1942, Messages from Gen. MacArthur, OPD Exec O, MMRDNA.

60. Rear Admiral H. James Ray, USN (Ret.), to author, April 1969; Vorin E. Whan,

Jr., ed., *A Soldier Speaks: Public Papers and Speeches of General of the Army Douglas MacArthur* (New York: Frederick A. Praeger, 1965), p. 119.

61. Radiogram, Wainwright to MacArthur, No. 202, 9 April 1942, 384.3, GHQ SWPA, FRC.

62. Diary of Lt. Col. John R. Pugh, USA, 9 April 1942. Later, Lt. Col. Pugh wrote: "The fall of Bataan has saddened me more than I can say. But no end of work was done there. For months we continued to improve our positions. Every inch of the front line was walked by General Wainwright and it is pathetic that when the break came it was in General Parker's II Corps. The right flank of General Wainwright's old Corps was first struck just West of the Pantingan River. Failing there they moved the force of their attack to the East, folding up in order the 41st, 21st and 51st Divisions. The Philippine Division moving up to fill the gap found so much chaos that the avalanche could not be stopped as the line folded from West to East. Panic reigned until the whole II Corps line was gone, enabling tanks to drive into our rear areas. Actually there was little infantry action except by elements of the Philippine Division. Front lines had been so bombed, strafed and shelled that the lines gave way on first contact. It was inevitable, however, that these lines should go, and it is a tribute to General Wainwright that the lines of his old Corps held, in spite of the debacle on the East Side. However, they were unable to attack as ordered by General Wainwright and found themselves pocketed. No doubt in spite of General King's capitulation, many preferred to fight guerrilla warfare in the mountains." Diary of Lt. Col. John R. Pugh, USA, 3 May 1942.

Rear Admiral Melvyn H. McCoy, who served as a Lieutenant Commander on Corregidor as the Communication Officer for the Naval Forces in the Philippines, later wrote that starvation was one of the basic reasons for the fall of Bataan: "It was well known that Bataan was to be the last stand; I mean prior to the war. Hence, the peninsula should have been well stocked with food. This had not been done. . . . After the surrender, I was on a working party which went to Rizal Stadium in Manila to load supplies onto trains and trucks for Japanese troops. We had been told we were to load milk for other prison camps. This stadium, circular, and holding about 30,000 [people], had every tier, for 3,600 around, jammed with U.S. Army Quartermaster supplies, almost all food. A good question is: 'What were they doing in Rizal Stadium, instead of in Bataan?' " Rear Admiral Melvyn H. McCoy, USN (Ret.), to author, 23 Feb. 1970.

CHAPTER 10

1. Radiogram, Marshall to Wainwright, 6 May 1942, Secret Messages to Gen. Wainwright, Item #9 Exec #10, MMRDNA.

2. Diary of Lieutenant Colonel John R. Pugh, USA, 10 April 1942.

3. Radiogram, McNarney to MacArthur, No. 1173, 8 April 1942, AG 384.3, GHQ SWPA, FRC.

4. Radiogram, Wainwright to MacArthur, No. 204, 10 April 1942, AG 384.3, GHQ SWPA, FRC.

5. Radiogram, Wainwright to MacArthur, No. 219, 13 April 1942, AG 384.3, GHQ SWPA, FRC.

6. Radiogram, Wainwright to Marshall, 13 April 1942, C/S Mgs. from Wainwright, Item #9 Exec #10, MMRDNA.

7. Radiogram, Marshall to MacArthur, No. 1241, 12 April 1942, 384.3, GHQ SWPA, FRC; Radiogram, MacArthur to Marshall, No. 228, 13 April 1942, SWPA Correspondence with War Department, MMBA.

8. Radiogram, Wainwright to MacArthur, No. 218, 13 April 1942, AG 384.3, GHQ SWPA, FRC.

9. Radiogram, MacArthur to Wainwright, No. 241, 14 April 1942, SWPA Correspondence with USFIP, FRC.

10. Radiogram, MacArthur to Marshall, No. 277, 15 April 1942, CM-IN-4509 (4-17-42), ABC 381 SWPA, OPD Registered Documents, MMRDNA; Brig. Gen. William G. Hipps, USAF (Ret.), to author, 25 July 1969; Lt. Gen. Joseph H. Moore, USAF to author, 12 June 1969. Gen. Moore, who commanded the Twentieth Pursuit Squadron at Clark Field when the war began and later at Mariveles on Bataan until the fall of Bataan, stated: "The Japanese bypassed the southern islands of the Philippines after taking Luzon and the principal middle islands in their push southward. Cebu and Mindanao were in our hands and had plenty of food stocks available. I used to fly an old salvaged U.S. Navy amphibian down to Cebu and Mindanao at night bringing food back to my squadron at Mariveles. Food was in pretty short supply on Bataan.

"On the night of 8 April I was ordered to fly the last P-40 on Bataan down to Mindanao to join the four P-40s there and to prepare for this operation. I departed Bataan about 2130 hours and reached Cebu where I spent the rest of the night and proceeded to Mindanao the next day.

"Bataan surrendered on 9 April after the front line defenses collapsed under a sustained major assault. Brigadier General Ralph Royce arrived in Mindanao late one afternoon about three or four days later, with three [sic] B-17s and ten B-25s. It was too late to attempt the plan so General Royce spent two days bombing targets of opportunity then returned to Australia. I was fortunate to make the trip back to Australia in one of the B-25s."

Col. Victor C. Huffsmith, the Base Ordnance Officer at Del Monte in Mindanao, wrote: "We refueled and provided ammunition for General Royce and Colonel Davies . . . on their strike in the Manila Area. I believe the strike was designed to help relieve the Bataan situation and when it could not be made in time became a token strike at shipping. Targets were at extreme range and were not previously reconnoitered. I would believe this strike was a token effort similar in nature to the first bombing of Tokyo." Col. Victor C. Huffsmith, USA (Ret.), to author, 7 July 1969; Lt. Gen. George H. Brett, USAF (Ret.), with Jack Kofoed, "The MacArthur I Knew," *True* (New York: Fawcett Publications, Oct. 1947), p. 145.

11. Radiograms, Wainwright to MacArthur, No. 230, 15 April 1942, and No. 232, 16 April 1942, SWPA Correspondence with USFIP, MMBA.

12. Radiograms, Wainwright to MacArthur, No. 234, 16 April 1942, No. 231, 15 April 1942, and No. 233, 16 April, SWPA Correspondence with USFIP, MMBA.

13. Radiogram, McNarney to MacArthur, No. 1319, 18 April 1942, AG 000.17, GHQ SWPA, FRC.

14. Radiogram, MacArthur to Marshall, 18 April 1942, AG 000.17, GHQ SWPA, FRC.

15. Brig. Gen. Charles H. Morhouse, USAF (Ret.), to author, April 1969. Concerning the MacArthur-Brett relationship, Brig. Gen. Morhouse wrote: "The final blow came early one morning when he called me and sent me for Gen. Brett and in my presence told Brett that two-thirds of the Japanese bomber force was wing tip to wing tip on Kendara airstrip [and waiting] for Brett to wipe them out. Brett sent three bombers for the job which were never even fired on. . . . Later, I was instrumental in getting Gen. Kenney assigned for I had lived next to him at Mitchell Field years before and knew him to be a scrapper. Gen. MacArthur used to call him his right arm!" Comments concerning Chapter 8 of draft MS., Joseph R. McMicking to author, 26 Feb. 1969. Concerning the MacArthur-Brett relationship, Col. Victor C. Huffsmith wrote: "It

278 NOTES TO PP. 205–12, CHAP. 10

is my understanding that General MacArthur would not speak to General Brett [at the Melbourne railroad station]. . . . . I personally admired General Brett very much. I believe that General Brett suffered because of the difficulties of organization in the early phases of World War II and because General MacArthur did not believe in the abilities of the Air Corps." Commenting on the relationship between Brett and Mac-Arthur, Brig. Gen. William G. Hipps, who served on Brett's staff, wrote: "A distinct Philippine group spirit existed for a period in Australia. . . . Gen. Brett did not establish effective communications with MacArthur's headquarters. Air Corps/Allied Air Planning was based on a defensive philosophy. General Kenney arrived and used a salesman technique to establish a better rapport. To what extent personal rivalries, prejudices or jealousies might have contributed, I'm not prepared to say. Such problems as the B-17 evacuation problem of MacArthur's party from Mindanao undoubtedly contributed to the feeling. MacArthur's group had no air power/air corps representation and little or no understanding of air power application." Brig. Gen. William G. Hipps, USAF (Ret.), to author, 25 July 1969.

16. Radiogram, MacArthur to Wainwright, No. 350, 19 April 1942, SWPA Correspondence with USFIP, MMBA.

17. Radiogram, MacArthur to Marshall, No. 365, 19 April 1942, SWPA Correspondence with War Department, MMBA.

18. Radiogram, Wainwright to MacArthur, No. 279, 23 April 1942, AG 000.71, GHQ SWPA, FRC. MacArthur wrote on the radiogram, "File—no action necessary—MacA."

19. Radiogram, MacArthur to Wainwright, No. 444, 24 April 1942, SWPA Correspondence with USFIP, MMBA.

20. Radiogram, MacArthur to Marshall, No. 443, 24 April 1942, SWPA Correspondence with War Department, MMBA.

21. Radiogram, Wainwright to MacArthur, No. 299, 25 April 1942, SWPA Correspondence with USFIP, MMBA.

22. Radiogram, Wainwright to MacArthur, No. 302, 25 April 1942, SWPA Correspondence with USFIP, MMBA.

23. Radiogram, Wainwright to MacArthur, No. 349, 29 April 1942, SWPA Correspondence with USFIP, MMBA.

24. Jonathan M. Wainwright, *General Wainwright's Story* (New York: Doubleday & Co., 1946), pp. 101–2; Lt. Cdr. Thomas C. Parker, USN, "The Epic of Corregidor-Bataan, December 24, 1941–May 4, 1942," *United States Naval Institute Proceedings,* Vol. 69, No. 1 (Jan. 1943), pp. 20–21.

25. Letter, Hurley to MacArthur, 30 April 1942, SWPA Correspondence, 1942–45, MMBA.

26. Radiogram, Beebe to Sutherland, No. 381, 2 May 1942, SWPA Correspondence with USFIP, MMBA. Col Charles E. N. Howard wrote that Brig. Gen. Beebe "was MacArthur's ablest staff officer on Corregidor and probably the only one that would stand up to him. The Bataan people had confidence and respect in him. . . ." Comments concerning Chapter 7 of draft MS., Col. Charles E. N. Howard, USA (Ret.), to author.

27. Interview with Maj. Gen. John R. Pugh, USA (Ret.), 5 July 1969.

28. Radiogram, Wainwright to MacArthur, No. 392, 3 May 1942, SWPA Correspondence with USFIP, MMBA.

29. Radiogram, Sutherland to Beebe, No. 153, 3 May 1942, Correspondence with USFIP, MMBA.

30. Interview with Maj. Gen. John R. Pugh, USA (Ret.), 5 July 1969; Lt. Cdr. Thomas C. Parker, USN. op. cit., p. 21; Morton, op. cit., p. 548; Brig. Gen. Constant L. Irwin, USA (Ret.), to author, 22 Oct. 1969; 4 Dec. 1969. Before leaving Corregidor,

Gen. Wainwright gave Irwin a specific message which he wanted delivered orally to the Army Chief of Staff, Gen. George C. Marshall. Irwin wrote: "[When] I gave his message orally [to] Gen. Marshall, [he] assured me he understood that the forces had to be surrendered and that there was no stigma or discredit to Gen. Wainwright [who] had to do the job." Wainwright, op. cit., pp. 108–9.

31. Radiogram, MacArthur to Marshall, 4 May 1942, SWPA Correspondence with War Department, MMBA.

32. Radiogram, Wainwright to MacArthur, No. 411, 5 May 1942, SWPA Correspondence with War Department, MMBA.

33. Col. William C. Braly, "Corregidor—A Name, A Symbol, A Tradition," *Coast Artillery Journal*, LXXX, No. 4 (July–August 1947), p. 43; Col. William C. Braly, *The Hard Way Home* (Washington, D.C.: Infantry Journal Press, 1947), p. 2; Memorandum, Lt. Cdr. John H. Morrill to C-in Chief U.S. Fleet, 16 June 1942, C/S Philippines (Bataan April 8th, Corregidor), MMRDNA; Wainwright, op. cit., p. 115.

34. Wainwright, op. cit., p. 114. Concerning the bombardment of Corregidor, James H. Baldwin, who was on Corregidor at the time, later wrote: "The 4th Marine regiment manning the beach defenses on the north side of Corregidor had been taking a terrible beating from artillery shells and finally, according to information, had requested an audience with Gen. Wainwright requesting that something be done about their situation. Presumably this was to surrender. . . . These marines *were* taking a beating. . . . At any rate Gen. Wainwright told them to hold on for 48 hours. Our understanding was that he felt Corregidor had to fall but wanted the Japanese to make an attack in order to strike as much of a blow as possible while going down. At the end of the 48 hours he was reported to have asked for another 48 hours. Our surmise was that he had intelligence that the Japanese were massing and he was waiting for them to come." William H. Baldwin to author, 17 Feb. 1970.

35. Wainwright, op. cit., p. 115; Braly, "Corregidor—A Name, A Symbol, A Tradition," op. cit., p. 43; Radiogram, MacArthur to Marshall, No. 161, 5 May 1942, (CM-IN-1670, 5-6-42) Exec. File 20, No. 7, OPD "Messages from Gen. MacArthur," MMRDNA.

36. Braly, "Corregidor—A Name, A Symbol, A Tradition," op. cit., p. 43.

37. Radiogram, MacArthur to Marshall, 6 May 1942, SWPA Correspondence with War Department, MMBA; Wainwright, op. cit., p. 115.

38. Radiogram, Roosevelt to Wainwright, 5 May 1942, Secret Messages to Gen. Wainwright, Item #9 Exec #10, MMRDNA.

39. Radiogram, Wainwright to Marshall, 6 May 1942, SWPA Correspondence with USFIP, MMBA.

40. Braly, "Corregidor—A Name, A Symbol, A Tradition," op. cit., p. 43.

41. Ibid; Wainwright, op. cit., p. 119.

42. Rear Admiral Kenneth M. Hoeffel, USN (Ret.), to author, 5 Sept. 1969; Radiogram, Hoeffel to COMINCH, 6 May 1942, C/S Mgs. from General Wainwright, MMRDNA.

43. Wainwright, op. cit., pp. 119–21.

44. Ibid., pp. 121–22.

45. Ibid., pp. 120–23.

46. Ibid., pp. 122–23.

47. Ibid., p. 123.

48. Braly, op. cit., p. 44.

49. Ibid; Wainwright, op. cit., p. 124.

50. Interview with Maj. Gen. John R. Pugh, USA (Ret.), 5 July 1969; Wainwright, op. cit., p. 124; Braly, op. cit., p. 44.

51. Wainwright, op. cit., p. 125.

52. Ibid., p. 126; Interview with Maj. Gen. John R. Pugh, USA (Ret.), 5 July 1969.

53. Wainwright, op. cit., p. 126.

54. Ibid.

55. James H. Baldwin to author, 17 Feb. 1970; Interview with Maj. Gen. John R. Pugh, USA (Ret.), May 1970; Wainwright, op. cit., p. 128.

56. Wainwright, op. cit., pp. 128–29.

57. Kazumaro Uno, *Corregidor: Isle of Delusion* (Shanghai, China: Mercury Press, Sept. 1942), pp. 23–24.

58. Wainwright, op. cit., pp. 129–30.

59. Uno, op. cit., p. 24; Wainwright, op. cit., p. 130.

60. Wainwright, op. cit., pp. 130–31.

61. Ibid., p. 131.

62. Ibid., p. 131; Uno, op. cit., p. 25.

63. Uno, op. cit., pp. 25–26.

64. Wainwright, op. cit., pp. 131–32.

65. Ibid., p. 132; Uno, op. cit., p. 26.

66. Uno, op. cit., p. 26.

67. Wainwright, op. cit., pp. 133–34; Uno, op. cit., pp. 27–29; James H. Baldwin to author, 17 Feb. 1970.

68. Wainwright, op. cit., p. 134; Uno, op. cit., p. 30.

69. Wainwright, op. cit., pp. 134–37; Letter, Col. Thomas Dooley, USA (Ret.), to author, 18 March 1970.

70. Brig. Gen. Charles C. Drake to author, 26 June 1969; Brig. Gen. Charles C. Drake, USA, "I Surrendered Corregidor," *Collier's*, 8 Jan. 1949, p. 12.

71. Wainwright, op. cit., pp. 137–38.

72. Ibid., pp. 138–40; Transcript of a radiobroadcast by Gen. Wainwright, 7 May 1942, C/S Mgs. from Wainwright, Item #9, Exec #10, MMRDNA. At the time General MacArthur did not understand why General Wainwright ordered the surrender of all American-Filipino troops in the Philippines. Concerning Wainwright's action, MacArthur had dispatched to General George C. Marshall the following radiogram: "I have just received word from General Sharp that General Wainwright in two broadcasts on the nights of the 7th and 8th announced he was reassuming the command of all forces in the Philippines and directed their surrender giving in detail the method of accomplishment. Sharp asked for instructions. I have informed him that General Wainwright's orders since his surrender have no validity; that if overcome by superior forces he will attempt to divide into small irregular bands and continue such resistance as may be possible. I believe General Wainwright has temporarily become unbalanced and his condition renders him susceptible to enemy use." Radiogram, MacArthur to Marshall, No. 677, 9 May 1942, SWPA Correspondence with War Department, MMBA.

Later, Brig. Gen. William F. Sharp, who commanded the Visayan-Mindanao Force, had the following radiogram dispatched to MacArthur: "I have seen Wainwright's staff officer [Col. Jesse T. Traywick] and have withdrawn my order releasing commanders of other islands and directed complete surrender. Dire necessity alone has prompted this action." Radiogram, Sharp to MacArthur, 11 May 1942, SWPA Correspondence with War Department, MMBA.

73. John Toland, *But Not In Shame* (New York: Random House, 1961), pp. 356–66.

74. Vorin E. Whan, Jr., ed., *A Soldier Speaks: Public Papers and Speeches of General of the Army Douglas MacArthur* (New York: Frederick A. Praeger, 1965), p. 119. In his *Reminiscences*, MacArthur wrote, "The bitter memories and heartaches will

never leave me." Douglas MacArthur, *Reminiscences* (New York: McGraw-Hill, 1964), p. 146.

CHAPTER 11

1. A quote attributed to the Duke of Wellington.
2. Louis Morton, *The Fall of the Philippines* (Washington, D.C.: U.S. Government Printing Office, 1953), pp. 31–50.
3. Brig. Gen. Bradford G. Chynoweth, USA (Ret.), to author, 17 June 1969.
4. Brig. Gen. Royal Reynolds, Jr., USA (Ret.), to author, 21 June 1969.
5. Lt. Col. Stephen C. Farris, USA (Ret.), to author, 4 July 1969; Brig. Gen. William G. Hipps, USAF (Ret.), to author, 25 July 1969; letter, R. K. Branch to author, 17 Sept. 1969.
6. Col. Roscoe Bonham, USA (Ret.), to author, 28 Sept. 1969; Col. E. C. Engelhart, USA (Ret.), to author, 22 June 1969.
7. Brig. Gen. Royal Reynolds, Jr., USA (Ret.), to author, 21 June 1969; John J. McCloy to author, 16 Sept. 1969.
8. Letter, Maj. Gen. Harry C. Porter, USAF (Ret.), to author, 9 July 1969.
9. Morton, op. cit., pp. 14, 51.
10. John J. McCloy to author, 16 Sept. 69.
11. Gen. Albert C. Wedemeyer, USA (Ret.), to author, 19 June 1969. Gen. Wedemeyer further stated: "I do not carry the torch for the Nazi officials in Germany or the military Jingoists in Japan, however I have always felt that we could and should have avoided involvement–resorting to political, psychological, and realistic economic measures. I feel that in our contacts today with other nations that those are the three principal weapons or instruments of national policy which should be used to accomplish our own aims." Col. Roy D. Russell, USAF, to author, 23 Sept. 1969.
12. Henry L. Stimson and McGeorge Bundy, *On Active Service in Peace and War* (New York: Harper & Brothers, 1948), p. 388; Col. E. C. Lentz, USAF (Ret.), to author, 30 Sept. 1969.
13. Lt. Col. Stephen C. Farris, USA (Ret.), to author, 4 July 1969; Col. Donovan Swanton, USA (Ret.), to author, 5 July 1969; Col. Edmund J. Lilly, Jr., USA (Ret.), to author, 16 August 1969; Lt. Col. William B. Reardon, USA (Ret.), to author, 16 Sept. 1969; Brig. Gen. Royal Reynolds, Jr., USA (Ret.), to author, 21 June 1969.
14. Brig. Gen. Bradford G. Chynoweth, USA (Ret.), to author, 17 June 1969.
15. Maj. Gen. Chih Wang, Chinese Army (Ret.), to author, 22 July 1969.
16. Col. Ernest B. Miller, *Bataan Uncensored* (Long Prairie, Minn.: Hart Publications, 1949), pp. 104–5. "MacArthur's Philippine Army was a paper army wholly untrained," according to Colonel Swanton. Actually, MacArthur had planned to have it trained and properly equipped by 1946. The Philippine Scouts, an elite corps of Filipinos trained over the years by the United States Army stationed in the Philippines, were well-trained soldiers and later had a first-class combat record; their number, however, was very small. Col. Donovan Swanton, USA (Ret.), to author, 5 July 1969; Col. E. C. Lentz, USAF (Ret.), to author, 30 Sept. 1969.
17. Lt. Cdr. Malcolm M. Champlin, USN, "One Man's Version," MS., p. 84; Louis Morton, *The Fall of the Philippines* (Washington, D.C.: U.S. Government Printing Office, 1953), pp. 161–90; Kent Roberts Greenfield, ed., *Command Decisions* (New York: Harcourt, Brace and Co., 1959), pp. 117–18.
18. Lt. Col. John R. Pray, USA (Ret.), to author, 18 Sept. 1969; Brig. Gen. Bradford C. Chynoweth to author, 1 August 1972 and 17 Jan. 1973; Col. Achille C. Tisdelle,

USA (Ret.), to author, 1 August 1972. Col. Tisdelle also stated: "MacArthur should have started moving foodstuffs and supplies by December 17 or earlier to Bataan and Corregidor. However, Col. Charles Lawrence, Quartermaster of Wainwright's staff, did. While MacArthur did not move food as early as possible neither was such movement forbidden. Far-sighted supply officers started the move by truck and barge. However, there were still large amounts of food in Manila—milk, grain, rice—in July 1943 when I sailed for Japan with a work detail of 500 prisoners." Comments concerning Chapter 2 of draft MS., Col. Achille C. Tisdelle, USA (Ret.), to author, 30 Dec. 1972.

19. Gen. Albert C. Wedemeyer, USA (Ret.), to author, 19 June 1969; Comments concerning Chapter II of draft MS., Maj. Gen. Hugh J. Casey to author; Col. Edmund J. Lilly, Jr., USA (Ret.), to author, 16 August 1969.

20. Brig. Gen. Eugene L. Harrison, USA (Ret.), to author, 18 August 1969. Concerning the Secretary of War, Brig. Gen. Harrison stated: "Henry L. Stimson was one of the greatest Americans of his time. He was Secretary of War in 1911, Secretary of State under President Hoover and again Secretary of War under President Roosevelt during the greatest war in our history. He was an extremely able, far-sighted man, devoted to his country and to his duty in serving it. Perhaps his most outstanding characteristic was his incredibly great degree of integrity and his high sense of honor. When he concluded a course of action to be correct, no one could change him, even under the greatest pressure—neither the President nor all the generals of the army. This was illustrated in his battle to keep the President from adopting the absurd Morganthau Plan for a pastoral Germany after the war.

"[Stimson] was a very kind man with great consideration and respect for his subordinates as well as his superiors. One illustration—Mr. Stimson, Secretary of the Treasury Morganthau and I were riding back from the capitol. Secretary of the Treasury Morganthau asked Mr. Stimson to have lunch with him, ignoring me, the aide, sitting on the jump seat. Mr. Stimson replied, '*My aide* and I will be glad to have lunch with you, Henry.'

"Mr. Stimson disliked bureaucracy, and unlike his successors, who have established the largest civilian bureaucracy in history in the Pentagon, had only four or five civilian consultants on his staff.

"I believe he will go down in history as the greatest and most respected civilian head of our military forces."

21. Maurice Matloff and Edwin M. Snell, *Strategic Planning For Coalition Warfare, 1941–1942* (Washington, D.C.: U.S. Government Printing Office, 1953), pp. 28–173; Louis Morton, "Germany First: The Basic Concept of Allied Strategy in World War II," in Kent Roberts Greenfield, ed., *Command Decisions* (New York, Harcourt, Brace and Co., 1959), pp. 3–38; Louis Morton, *The Fall of the Philippines* (Washington, D.C.: U.S. Government Printing Office, 1953), pp. 145–57, 239–42; Richard M. Leighton and Robert W. Coakley, *Global Logistics and Strategy, 1940–1943* (Washington, D.C.: U.S. Government Printing Office, 1955), pp. 52–57. Even President Quezon at the time he formulated his neutralization plan knew the Philippines were being sacrificed. "Our country is being destroyed," he told Carlos Romulo. "Do you expect me to continue this sacrifice?" Carlos P. Romulo, *I Walked with Heroes* (New York: Holt, Rinehart and Winston, 1961), p. 220.

22. John J. McCloy to author, 16 Sept. 1969.

23. Brig. Gen. Bradford G. Chynoweth, USA (Ret.), to author, 17 June 1969.

24. Brig. Gen. Bradford G. Chynoweth, USA (Ret.), to author, 17 June 1969 and 7 July 1969; Maj. Gen. Chih Wang, Chinese Army (Ret.), to author, 22 July 1969.

25. Brig. Gen. Paul D. Phillips, USA (Ret.), to author, 15 July 1969; Lt. Col. Stephen C. Farris, USA (Ret.), to author, 4 July 1969; Col. Roscoe Bonham, USA

(Ret.), to author, 28 Sept. 1969; Col. Edmund J. Lilly, USA (Ret.), to author, 16 August 1969; Col. William Massello, Jr., USA (Ret.), to author, 28 June 1969; Interview with Maj. Gen. John R. Pugh, USA (Ret.), 5 July 1969.

26. Brig. Gen. Charles C. Drake, USA (Ret.), to author, 26 June 1969.

27. Maj. Gen. John M. Wright, Jr., USA (Ret.), to author, 30 July 1969; Col. Edmund J. Lilly, Jr., USA (Ret.), to author, 16 August 1969; Maj. Gen. Chih Wang, Chinese Army (Ret.), to author, 22 July 1969; Col. Armand Hopkins, USA (Ret.), to author, 22 July 1969; Col. Donovan Swanton, USA (Ret.), to author, 5 July 1969; Lt. Col. Stephen C. Farris, USA (Ret.), to author, 4 July 1969; Col. Roscoe Bonham, USA (Ret.), to author, 28 Sept. 1969; Col. Morris L. Shoss, USA (Ret.), to author, 28 Sept. 1969. Concerning General MacArthur, Col. Shoss wrote: "I recognize a universal resentment against MacArthur by those he left behind in the Philippines. I translate this now as resentment against the American leadership of the times that created the setting of this shameful debasement of the American image in the Orient. As former Chief of Staff of the Army and later the influential advisor to the fledgling Filipino Army, [MacArthur] should have been more resourceful in assessing the relative capabilities and limitations of opposing forces. But to rise from this and return victorious is miraculous. In essence I see two MacArthurs, the bumbling, senile, pompous egotist of Bataan and Corregidor, and the brilliant strategist who left his stroke of genius in military history."

28. Col. R. S. Kramer, USA, to author, 25 June 1969; Gen. Albert C. Wedemeyer, USA (Ret.), to author, 19 June 1969.

29. Gen. Harold K. Johnson, USA (Ret.), to author, 8 July 1969; Col. William E. Chandler, USA (Ret.), to author, 13 July 1969; Col. Paul H. Krause, USA (Ret.), to author, 7 July 1969; Lt. Gen. Alva R. Fitch, USA (Ret.), to author, 16 June 1969; Brig. Gen. Royal Reynolds, Jr. USA (Ret.), to author, 21 June 1969.

Bibliography

Arnold, Henry H. *Global Mission*. New York: Harper & Brothers, 1949.
   Contains Arnold's reaction to Brereton's and MacArthur's explanations of what happened at Clark Field on December 8, 1941.

Baldwin, Hanson W. *Great Mistakes of the War*. New York: Harper & Brothers, 1949.
   A short, critical, and analytical study concentrating on the mistakes that were made by American political and military leaders during World War II. Highly critical of MacArthur, Baldwin briefly discusses (pp. 62–77) the Clark Field disaster, Quezon's neutralization proposal, and Army-Navy difficulties concerning the Philippines.

————. *Battles Lost and Won: Great Campaigns of World World II*. New York: Harper and Row, 1966.
   Writing about eleven of the greatest battles of World War II, Baldwin devotes a chapter (pp. 114–55) to " 'The Rock,' The Fall of Corregidor." Although he stresses the battle for Corregidor, Baldwin includes a brief but far-sighted narrative of the Philippine campaign. Along with explaining why the Philippines were ultimately doomed, the author exposes several "myths of history" concerning MacArthur, Corregidor, and Bataan.

Belote, James H., and William M. Belote. *Corregidor: The Saga of a Fortress*. New York: Harper and Row, 1967.
   The Belote brothers have written a historical narrative of what transpired on Corregidor, covering not only the December 1941–May 1942 siege, but also the Rock's recapture in February 1945. Relating the exploits of Maj. Gen. George F. Moore, Col. Paul D. Bunker, Captain Richard G. Ivey, and many others, the authors focus on the officers and enlisted men who defended Corregidor. Fast-moving, fascinating, and readable, their detailed history is based on extensive research.

Braly, William C. *The Hard Way Home*. Washington, D.C.: Infantry Journal Press, 1947.
   The author, who was Maj. Gen. Moore's operation officer on Corregidor, writes mainly about his experiences as a prisoner of war. At times, however, Braly mentions aspects of the Philippine defeat.

Brereton, Lewis H. *The Brereton Diaries, 3 October 1941–8 May 1945*. New York: William Morrow & Company, Inc., 1946.
   Even though several authorities believe that parts of the diary were deleted

285

and altered, the diary is still valuable because it sheds light on the Clark Field disaster. It presents Brereton's version of the events of December 8, 1941. Brereton also wrote about air operations in the Philippines until December 24 when he departed for Australia.

Bulkeley, Robert J., Jr. *At Close Quarters: PT Boats in the United States Navy.* Washington, D.C.: Naval Historical Division, 1962.
A comprehensive history of U.S. Navy PT-boat operations during World War II. It contains a factual account (pp. 3–28) of the achievements of Lt. John D. Bulkeley's PT-boat Squadron Three in the Philippines. The author covers PT-boat attacks against Japanese shipping, MacArthur's evacuation to Mindanao, and the fate of the six boats that made up the squadron at the start of the war.

Casey, Hugh J. (ed.). *Engineers of the Southwest Pacific 1941–1945.* Vol. I: *Engineers in Theater Operation.* Washington, D.C.: U.S. Government Printing Office, 1947.
A historical narrative revolving around and emphasizing the accomplishments of the U.S. Army Engineers. The first chapter (pp. 1–30) covers the defense of Luzon.

Chandler, Alfred D., Jr. (ed.). *The Papers of Dwight David Eisenhower.* Vol. I: *The War Years.* Baltimore: The Johns Hopkins Press, 1970.
Most of the radiograms that were drafted by Eisenhower for Marshall and then dispatched to MacArthur under Marshall's name can be found in this volume. It contains a wealth of information concerning Eisenhower, Marshall, MacArthur, the War Department, and the war in the Philippines in the form of complete radiograms and memoranda with helpful explanatory annotations.

Churchill, Winston S. *Their Finest Hour.* Vol. II. Boston: Houghton Mifflin Company, 1949.
Contains a recollection (p. 108) regarding the possible origin of the decision to order MacArthur out of the Philippines.

Craven, Wesley F., and James L. Cate (eds.). *Plans and Early Operations, January 1939 to August 1942.* Vol I: *The Army Air Forces in World War II.* Chicago: University of Chicago Press, 1948.
A comprehensive and scholarly history of the U.S. Air Force covering in detail (pp. 201–11) the series of events which led to the Clark Field disaster, subsequent air operations in the Philippines (pp. 211–20), attempts to aid the Philippines from Australia, and Brig. Gen. Ralph Royce's bomber raid (pp. 417–18) against Japanese-held facilities in the Philippines.

Dissette, Edward, and H. C. Adamson. *Guerrilla Submarines.* New York: Ballantine Books, 1972.
A story of the guerrilla movement in the Philippines and the U.S. Navy submarines which supported it. The author concentrated on the exploits of Commander Charles E. Parsons who was instrumental in organizing the Philippine guerrillas.

Dyess, William E. *The Dyess Story: The Eye-Witness Account of the Death*

March and the Narrative of Experiences in Japanese Prison Camps and of Eventual Escape. Edited by Charles Leavelle. New York: G. P. Putnam's Sons, 1944.

A first-person account by a fighter pilot who fought over Luzon, and who later survived the Bataan Death March. Describing air operations over Bataan, Dyess mentions continually the leadership and contributions of his commander, Brig. Gen. Harold H. George. The author also vividly depicts the horrors of the Bataan Death March.

Edmonds, Walter D. *They Fought With What They Had.* Boston: Little, Brown and Company, 1951.

A detailed narrative of the Nineteenth Bombardment Group in the Philippines and later in the Netherlands East Indies. Based on extensive interviews and correspondence with officers who served in the Nineteenth Bombardment Group, Edmonds's account focused on the exploits of the individual pilots.

Eisenhower, Dwight D. *Crusade in Europe.* Garden City, New York: Doubleday & Company, Inc., 1948.

Eisenhower's interesting memoir is valuable and revealing because he served in the War Plans Division and largely handled the Philippine situation for Gen. Marshall. He describes his first interview with Marshall at the War Department, discusses the dilemma the Philippines presented, and explains his attempts to send supplies to the Islands.

Eyre, James K., Jr. *The Roosevelt-MacArthur Conflict.* Chambersburg, Pennsylvania: The Craft Press, Inc., 1950.

A historical account that deals with the personalities of MacArthur, Quezon, Osmena, Sayre, and Roosevelt and with their relationships. It sheds important light on Quezon's neutralization proposal. The author, who served as an aide to Sergio Osmena in the Philippines, undoubtedly obtained most of his material directly from Osmena and other Filipino officials.

Falk, Stanley L. *Bataan: The March of Death.* New York: W. W. Norton, 1962.

A comprehensive, historical study and narrative of the Bataan Death March. Having interviewed and corresponded with a number of the survivors, both Filipino and American, Falk creates a vivid and fast-moving account of their terrible experiences following the Japanese capture of Bataan. He also explains the causes of the infamous march of death.

Greenfield, Kent Roberts (ed.). *Command Decisions.* New York: Harcourt, Brace and Company, 1959.

Contains two important informative monographs by Louis Morton concerning the "Europe first" war strategy and MacArthur's decision to withdraw his Luzon forces in the Bataan peninsula.

————. *The Historian and the Army.* New Brunswick, New Jersey: Rutgers University Press, 1954.

The author, who was Chief Historian of the Department of Army, discusses briefly the planning and writing of the official histories of the United States Army in World War II.

————. *American Strategy in World War II: A Reconsideration.* Baltimore: The Johns Hopkins Press, 1963.
    A short, perceptive monograph dealing with the formation and execution of British-American grand strategy. It contains an informative chapter on President Roosevelt as commander-in-chief.

Gunnison, Royal Arch. *So Sorry, No Peace.* New York: The Viking Press, 1944.
    A first-person account of the experiences of a newspaper correspondent in Manila at the start of the war. After Manila was declared an open city, the author and his wife lived for twenty-two months in Japanese internment camps. The author stresses how they were treated by the Japanese. Besides containing the gist of an interview with MacArthur (pp. 27–28), the author relates an interview with Kazumaro Uno, who told him the story (pp. 113–16) of the unsuccessful conference between Homma and Wainwright at Cabcaben on May 6. The story that Uno told Gunnison closely parallels Uno's account in his book, *Corregidor: Isle of Delusion.*

Gunther, John. *The Riddle of MacArthur.* New York: Harper and Row, 1950.
    Although Gunther's readable biography contains little information about MacArthur and the Philippines, it presents a colorful and chatty portrait of MacArthur and the occupation of Japan.

Haggerty, Edward. *Guerrilla Padre in Mindanao.* New York: Longmans Green and Company, 1946.
    The story of a Jesuit priest who aided the American and Filipino guerrillas on Mindanao. The author tells about meeting MacArthur at the Del Monte Pineapple Planation, working with guerrilla leaders Col. Wendell W. Fertig, Lt. Col. Robert V. Bowler, and Lt. Cdr. Parsons, and staying one jump ahead of the Japanese. It is a tale of Japanese atrocities and Filipino patriotism and courage.

Hersey, John. *Men on Bataan.* New York: Alfred A. Knopf, 1942.
    The main theme is the war in the Philippines. Brief biographical sketches of a number of officers who fought on Bataan are interspersed throughout the book. Basically Hersey has focused on the life of MacArthur and just about every other chapter consists of flashbacks of biographical material about the general. Although Hersey's account is not an in-depth study, it is interesting, informative, and readable.

Huff, Sidney, with Joe Alex Morris. *My Fifteen Years With General MacArthur.* New York: Paperback Library, Inc., 1964.
    The author, who served as MacArthur's aide during the war, presents an intimate and very informal biography of the general. Containing a number of anecdotes and amusing incidents involving MacArthur, Huff's account also contains useful information regarding the general's relationship with Quezon and the evacuation from Corregidor to Australia.

Hunt, Frazier. *MacArthur and the War Against Japan.* New York: Charles Scribner's Sons, 1944.

The author visited MacArthur's Southwest Pacific headquarters and conversed with the general and many of his staff officers. He based his biography on these conversations as well as on some documentary material. Although the biography is short, incomplete, and highly laudatory of MacArthur, it does contain firsthand information on the general and the war in the Philippines.

————. *The Untold Story of Douglas MacArthur*. New York: The Devin-Adair Company, 1954.
A full-length, pro-MacArthur biography which has over forty pages dealing with the December 1941–May 1942 period. The treatment, however, lacks organization and balance.

Ind, Allison W. *Bataan: The Judgment Seat*. New York: The Macmillan Company, 1944.
The author, who served on the staff of Brig. Gen. Harold H. George, writes about his experiences on Bataan and the air operations conducted by the remnants of the Twenty-fourth Pursuit Group on the Peninsula. The story stresses Gen. George and the many problems he had to deal with—dwindling, irreplaceable fighter planes, inadequate, poorly equipped airfields, and diminishing supplies.

James, D. Clayton. *The Years of MacArthur 1880–1941*. Vol. I. Boston: Houghton Mifflin Company, 1970.
A solid, balanced, and scholarly biography of MacArthur that combines praise and restrained criticism. The author devotes the last 136 pages of his biography to MacArthur's role in preparing for the defense of the Philippines, concluding with MacArthur learning of the Japanese attack on Pearl Harbor. It is by far the best biography to date on General MacArthur.

———— (ed.). *South to Bataan-North to Mukden: The Prison Diary of Brigadier General William E. Brougher*. Athens, Georgia: University of Georgia Press, 1971.
As editor, D. Clayton James did an admirable job. Based on the diaries and papers of Brig. Gen. Brougher, who commanded the Eleventh Division on Luzon, most of the book consists of diary entries mainly dealing with Brougher's life as a prisoner of war, although the first two chapters are a narrative revolving around Brougher and the fighting on Luzon. On page 32 is a bitter castigation of General MacArthur. Blaming MacArthur for the debacle in the Philippines, Brougher wrote: "A foul trick of deception has been played on a large group of Americans by a Commander in Chief and small staff who are now eating steak and eggs in Australia. God damn them!"

Lea, Homer. *The Valor of Ignorance*. New York: Harper & Brothers, 1942.
The book was first published in 1909. The author, a student of military tactics and strategy who was a hunchbacked soldier of fortune in China, foresaw a major war in the Pacific between Japan and the United States. He predicted a Japanese attack on the Philippines with the Japanese landing at Lingayen Gulf and then marching on Manila. Focusing on strategy, Lea's account is highly speculative but thought-provoking. It contains an interesting foreword by Clare Boothe Luce.

Lee, Clark. *They Call It Pacific: An Eye-Witness Story of Our War Against Japan From Bataan to the Solomons*. New York: The Viking Press, 1943.

An interesting and informative first-person account of the author's experiences in Manila and on Corregidor and Bataan as a correspondent for the Associated Press. Describing the war in the Philippines, Lee wrote briefly about MacArthur, Hart, Wainwright, Bulkeley, and many other officers.

————, and Richard Henschel. *Douglas MacArthur*. New York: Henry Holt and Company, 1952.

This chatty account contains interesting information about MacArthur, the alleged MacArthur-Marshall feud, MacArthur's first marriage, and the war in the Philippines. It also contains a large number of photographs of MacArthur and his family. According to Lee, MacArthur asserted (p. 166) that "Wainwright made an error in judgment in placing King, an artillery man, in command of infantry on Bataan."

Lee, Henry G. *Nothing But Praise*. Culver City, California: Murry and Gee, Inc., 1948.

A small collection of poignant poems and letters containing thoughtful and seasoned reflections on the war in the Philippines and its aftermath. The author, a first lieutenant in the infantry, survived the Bataan campaign and the Death March, but died on January 9, 1945 aboard a Japanese ship that was bombed in Takao Bay, Formosa. This rare book is a passionate and deeply moving collection emphasizing the horrors of war.

Leighton, Richard M., and Robert W. Coakley. *Global Logistics and Strategy 1940–1943*. Washington, D.C.: U.S. Government Printing Office, 1955.

An official army history dealing with logistics and strategy which contains some useful material on the "Europe first" strategy and the difficulties involved in supplying the army in the Philippines. Written more for the specialist and military historian than for the general reader.

Lohbeck, Don. *Patrick J. Hurley*. Chicago: Henry Regnery Company, 1956.

A full-length biography of the colorful and controversial lawyer, millionaire, secretary of war, army officer, and diplomat. The author describes Hurley's being commissioned as an army officer, his mission to the South Pacific, and his largely unsuccessful efforts to send supplies to the Philippines via blockade runners from Australia and the Netherlands East Indies.

MacArthur, Douglas. *Reminiscences*. New York: McGraw-Hill Book Company, 1964.

It has been said that a man is revealed by his writing. *Reminiscences* clearly reveals MacArthur's great egotism, his inability to accept criticism, his conviction that he was always right and anyone who opposed his views was wrong, his constant doting on praise (he mentions virtually every honor and decoration he received during his military career). MacArthur borrows heavily, sometimes almost verbatim, from biographers Hunt, Whitney, and Willoughby. Excellent reviews of MacArthur's *Reminiscences* have been written by Louis Morton ("Egotist in Uniform," *Harper's*, November 1964) and Arthur Schlesinger, Jr. (*The MacArthur Controversy* [New York: Farrar, Straus and Giroux, 1965], pp. 265–73).

Matloff, Maurice, and Edwin M. Snell. *Strategic Planning For Coalition Warfare 1941–1942*. Washington, D.C.: U.S. Government Printing Office, 1953.

An official army history containing a detailed account of the steps that were taken by the American and British military leaders in formulating the "Europe first" war strategy. The authors have explained the creation and development of the military alliance between the United States and Great Britain. They have also emphasized and explained the strategic concepts of Stark, Marshall, Gerow, and Eisenhower.

Mellnik, Steve. *Philippine Diary 1939–1945*. New York: Van Nostrand Reinhold Company, 1969.

A first-person account by a coast artillery officer who survived the siege of Corregidor, who later escaped from a prisoner of war camp in Mindanao, and who was taken on a submarine to Australia. Writing in a chatty and shallow manner, the author exonerates Brereton and MacArthur and blames the Clark Field disaster on the Japanese. He criticized Wainwright for failing to order the shelling of Japanese positions on Bataan following the surrender of the Bataan force in spite of the fact that such a bombardment from Corregidor would have killed a number of Filipino and American prisoners of war. The book contains several factual errors.

Miller, Ernest B. *Bataan Uncensored*. Long Prairie, Minn.: The Hart Publications, Inc., 1949.

The author, who was commander of the 194th Tank Battalion, vividly describes the fighting that he participated in on Luzon, the Death March, and his experiences as a prisoner of war. The author is critical of Generals MacArthur, Wainwright, and Weaver. It is the best first-person account of the Luzon campaign that has been published to date.

Morison, Elting E. *Turmoil and Tradition: A Study of the Life and Times of Henry L. Stimson*. Boston: Houghton Mifflin Company, 1960.

An interesting, scholarly, and well-written biography of Stimson. It does not, however, cover in detail Stimson's role in dealing with Quezon's neutralization proposal, and the overall Philippine dilemma.

Morison, Samuel Eliot. *Strategy and Compromise*. Boston: Little, Brown and Company, 1958.

A short, readable monograph emphasizing British and American strategic differences during World War II. It sheds some light on the "Europe first" strategy. The author, however, neglects the Pacific Theater to a large extent.

———. *The Rising Sun in the Pacific 1931–April 1942*. Vol. III. Boston: Little, Brown and Company, 1963.

A naval history covering the events leading to the Japanese attack on Pearl Harbor, and describing the attack in detail and its aftermath. Along with covering the Japanese attacks on Wake, Malaya, and the Netherlands East Indies, the author devotes three chapters to American plans for defending the Philippines, the Japanese invasion, and the loss of the islands. In a sketchy manner, Morison describes the limited naval operations of the Philippine campaign.

Morton, Louis. *The Fall of the Philippines.* Washington, D.C.: U.S. Government Printing Office, 1953.

The most detailed, informative, and scholarly history of the war in the Philippines that has been and probably ever will be written. Stressing strategy and tactics, Morton focuses on the conflict between Japanese and Filamerican forces in the Philippines from December 8, 1941 to May 6, 1942. He explains not only the measures taken prior to the war to prepare for the defense of the Philippines but also the events following Wainwright's surrender of Corregidor. The book is thoroughly researched, meticulously organized, and skillfully written.

Morton's history, however, would have been more complete if he had had access to MacArthur's personal files and Stimson's manuscript diary. His account contains several factual errors. For example, he says that MacArthur and his staff left Corregidor for Australia on March 12, 1942; actually, it was March 11. His conclusions concerning the Clark Field disaster and Quezon's neutralization proposal are incomplete and misleading. Furthermore, Morton tends to shy away from controversy and human blunders, reluctant to criticize or point out errors of judgment. Fundamentally, however, this is an outstanding military history.

————. *Strategy and Command: The First Two Years.* Washington, D.C.: U.S. Government Printing Office, 1962.

This is an in-depth study of Allied and Japanese engagements in the Pacific and the strategic concepts of the senior commanders. Morton stresses high-level strategic decisions and the reasons behind them. His study contains an informative chapter summarizing the war in the Philippines. In a misleading statement (p. 710), however, he wrote, "Henry L. Stimson did not figure prominently in the shaping of U.S. strategy."

Pogue, Forrest C. *George C. Marshall: Ordeal and Hope.* Vol. II. New York: The Viking Press, 1966.

A well-researched but poorly distilled biography of General Marshall. Instead of placing the main emphasis on Marshall, the author tends to focus on the events and individuals around Marshall, so that no distinct portrait of Marshall emerges. Actually, it is more an informative history of American leadership during World War II than a biography of Marshall.

In the chapter "Pacific Ordeal," which deals with the war in the Philippines, Pogue made several errors. Concerning Quezon's neutralization proposal, he wrote (p. 247), "A few days after President Quezon and Vice President Osmena were sworn in for a second term in a simple moving ceremony at Corregidor, Quezon decided on a policy of shock action." Quezon was inaugurated on December 30, 1941, and sent his neutralization proposal to Roosevelt on February 8, 1942, so that more than "a few days" elapsed between the two. The author wrote (p. 249) that Brig. Gen. Patrick J. Hurley "cabled" Marshall that Roosevelt should order MacArthur to leave the Philippines for Australia. Actually there was no radiogram. Hurley's recommendation was contained in a memorandum submitted to Marshall by Lt. Col. Warren J. Clear following MacArthur's arrival in Australia, and thus could not have influenced Marshall or Roosevelt. Regarding the Hollis memorandum controversy of December 25, 1941, Pogue's account of what happened (pp. 265–66) is slightly different from that in Stimson's diary.

Quezon, Manuel L. *The Good Fight*. New York: D. Appleton-Century Company, 1946.
An autobiography that contains important information concerning President Quezon and the Japanese attack on the Philippines. Quezon's story, however, is naturally not unbiased, especially concerning his neutralization plan and his disagreements with MacArthur and Roosevelt.

Romulo, Carlos P. *I Saw the Fall of the Philippines*. New York: Doubleday, Doran and Company, Inc., 1943.
An eye-witness account of the war in the Philippines. The author, who joined MacArthur's staff at the start of the war, describes wartime conditions in Manila and on Corregidor and Bataan. His account contains some interesting recollections of MacArthur and his staff.

————. *I Walked with Heroes*. New York: Holt, Rinehart and Winston, 1961.
An autobiography containing some informative recollections of MacArthur and Quezon. Especially interesting are pages 218–24, where Romulo writes about Quezon and his neutralization proposal and the crisis it created.

Rovere, Richard H., and Arthur Schlesinger, Jr. *The MacArthur Controversy and American Foreign Policy*. New York: Farrar, Straus and Giroux, 1965.
An anti-MacArthur account dealing mainly with MacArthur's recall during the Korean War and the investigation conducted by the Senate Armed Services and Foreign Relations committees. The authors briefly mention MacArthur's role in preparing for the defense of the Philippines, the Clark Field attack, and Quezon's neutralization proposal. MacArthur's negative aspects are clearly depicted and magnified. The book seems to have been hastily assembled and it lacks objectivity.

Sayre, Francis B. *Glad Adventure*. New York: The Macmillan Company, 1957.
An interesting autobiography; several chapters deal with the war in the Philippines. The author, who was high commissioner to the Philippines, wrote about his tenure of office and his life in Manila and later on Corregidor. His account contains interesting observations of MacArthur and Quezon and their relationship. Regarding the Clark Field attack, Sayre says (p. 223), "Through the tragic blunder of failure to attack we were ignominiously stripped of the planes on which our defense heavily rested, and consequently were at the mercy of the Japanese." Missing, however, is any mention of the crisis created by Quezon's neutralization scheme.

Sherwood, Robert E. *Roosevelt and Hopkins: An Intimate History*. New York: Harper and Brothers, 1948.
Contains a wealth of information on the Roosevelt-Hopkins relationship and their contribution to the winning of the war. Also contains important material concerning the "Europe first" strategy and Roosevelt's decision to order Mac-

Arthur from the Philippines to Australia. Although it is not a well-organized account, it is highly informative and extremely valuable from a historical standpoint.

Stimson, Henry L., and McGeorge Bundy. *On Active Service in Peace and War.* New York: Harper and Brothers, 1948.
  A revealing self-portrait of Stimson. Largely based on Stimson's extensive diaries, the autobiography includes many of the diary excerpts dealing with Stimson's handling of the Philippine situation and his interest in the fate of the Philippines. The authors did not, however, include all of the pertinent diary excerpts. Significant material has been left out, especially if it concerned criticism of another individual.

Thorpe, Elliott R. *East Wind, Rain.* Boston: Gambit Inc., 1969.
  An informative and readable memoir by a retired army officer who served on MacArthur's staff as an intelligence officer. Although the author joined MacArthur's staff in Australia and his account does not contain any material concerning the war in the Philippines, it does contain interesting recollections of MacArthur, Sutherland, and Willoughby.

Toland, John. *But Not in Shame.* New York: Random House, 1961.
  An intriguing and fluent narrative covering the highlights of the war in the Pacific from December 1941 to May 1942. It contains important material on MacArthur and Wainwright as well as the Japanese invaders. Although the author concentrates on the invasion of the Philippines, he also covers the Japanese conquests of Hong Kong, Malaya, and the Netherlands East Indies. Toland bases his account to a large extent on interviews and correspondence with many of the key participants.

————. *The Rising Sun: The Decline and Fall of the Japanese Empire 1936–1945.* New York: Random House, 1970.
  A fascinating and readable history, comprehensive in scope. Focusing on Japan and her military operations, as well as the military operations of her adversaries, the author covered the entire Pacific war from its origin to its culmination. He based his history on published and unpublished Japanese and American sources as well as extensive interviews with countless Japanese participants.

Underbrink, Robert L. *Destination Corregidor.* Annapolis, Maryland: Naval Institute Press, 1971.
  An interesting narrative of the futile efforts to send supplies from Australia and the Netherlands East Indies to the beleaguered Philippines.

Uno, Kazumaro. *Corregidor: Isle of Delusion.* Shanghai, China: The Mercury Press, 1942.
  A propaganda book issued by the Press Bureau of the Imperial Japanese Army General Headquarters in China and written in English by a Japanese press correspondent. The bilingual author had studied at the University of Utah and spoke Japanese with an American accent. He observed the unsuccessful

centrated on the difficulties he had to overcome: lack of medicine, lack of sur-
1942, and then returned to Corregidor with Wainwright. He wrote an objective
account of the conference and its aftermath. The book is very rare, but the
Newberry Library in Chicago does have a copy.

Wainwright, Jonathan M. and Robert Considine (ed.). *General Wainwright's
Story: The Account of Four Years of Humiliating Defeat, Surrender, and
Captivity.* Garden City, New York: Doubleday and Company, Inc., 1946.
Covers not only Wainwright's experiences on Bataan and Corregidor, but
also what he underwent as a prisoner of war. Contains Wainwright's recollections of what he saw and thought, whom he talked with, and what he did. Sad,
poignant and moving, his story is valuable from a historical standpoint although
it is sketchy in places.

Weinstein, Alfred A. *Barbed-Wire Surgeon.* New York: The Macmillan Company, 1948.
A surgeon's eye-witness account, gruesome at times, of his experiences in the
army medical corps on Bataan and later as a prisoner of war. The author concentrated on the difficulties he had to overcome: lack of medicine, lack of sur-
gical equipment, and the lack of food.

Whan, Vorin E., Jr. (ed.). *A Soldier Speaks: Public Papers and Speeches of
General of the Army Douglas MacArthur.* New York: Frederick A. Praeger,
1965.
A collection of MacArthur's most important speeches, reports, and public
announcements.

White, H. L. *They Were Expendable.* New York: Harcourt, Brace and Company, 1942.
A dramatic, detailed account of the exploits of Motor Torpedo Boat Squadron Three in the Philippines. The author wrote about PT-boat commanders
Lt. Robert B. Kelly and Lt. John D. Bulkeley, their precarious experiences, and
the difficulties they had to cope with following the Japanese attack.

————. *Queens Die Proudly.* New York: Harcourt, Brace and Company, 1943.
The material for the author's account was obtained from Lt. Frank A. Kurtz,
a Flying Fortress pilot, and four of his crew members. The story covers their
experiences in the Philippines, and later in the Netherlands East Indies.

Whitney, Courtney. *MacArthur: His Rendezvous with History.* New York: Alfred A. Knopf, 1964.
A distorted, subjective, and laudatory biography of General MacArthur. The
author, who joined MacArthur's staff in 1943 for the purpose of directing guerrilla forces in the Philippines, devotes the first 63 pages to MacArthur and the
war in the Philippines. MacArthur, according to him, was omniscient and in-
capable of making mistakes.
One of Whitney's false claims is that Roosevelt and Marshall deceived Mac-
Arthur into believing that large-scale reinforcements would be sent to the Philippines. Whitney attempted to prove his case by slanting or omitting pertinent
documentation.

Willoughby, Charles A., and John Chamberlain. *MacArthur 1941–1951*. New
    York: McGraw-Hill Book Company, Inc., 1954.
    A shallow, disorganized, unbalanced pro-MacArthur biography. The author,
who served as MacArthur's chief of intelligence from 1941 to 1951, has put together a jumble of excerpts from reports, letters, memoranda, radiograms,
and newspaper and magazine articles. However, Willoughby's account does
contain some useful raw material concerning MacArthur and the war in
Philippines.

———— (ed.) and others. *Reports of General MacArthur: The Campaigns of
    MacArthur in the Pacific*. Vol. I. Washington, D.C.: U.S. Government
    Printing Office, 1966.
    Contains excellent maps in color of the Philippines, Luzon, and Bataan show-
ing the main Japanese offensive movements and Filipino-American withdraw-
als and defenses. Unfortunately the written material sheds little light on
MacArthur and the Japanese invasion of the Philippines.

Index

Nimitz, Chester W., 27
Nine Power Treaty, 54
North American Newspaper Alliance, 32
North Luzon Force, 6, 25, 32, 38, 43, 45,
  56, 175
Norway, 103

Oahu, 15
O'Daniel, Lee, 84–85
Olongapo, 19, 56, 195
Orani-Olangapo Road, 259
Osmena, Sergio, 48, 49, 59, 88, 94, 105,
  106–7

Palmyra Island, 95
Pampanga, 136
Panama, 23
Panay, 115, 116, 120, 140, 148, 149, 172,
  203, 210, 214
Pandacan oil installations, 56
Pantingan River, 276
Parananique line, 51
Parker, George M., Jr., 6, 66, 67, 75, 186,
  187
Parker, Thomas C., 39, 212, 255
Paysawan, 56
Pearl Harbor, 11–12, 15, 236–37
Pease, Harl, Jr., 154, 268
Pensacola convoy, 18, 20, 26, 27, 28, 33
Permit, 136, 137, 148, 151, 265, 267
Perry, 116
Pilar-Bagac Road, 56, 67, 75
Poland, 103
Porac-Guagua line, 56
Portal, Sir Charles, 35
Pound, Sir Dudley, 35
Pray, John R., 236
Princesa de Cebu, 119
propaganda: American, 46–47, 58, 87;
  Japanese, 45–46, 79, 87
PT-boats, 132, 136, 144–51, 151–52,
  266, 267–68
Pugh, John R., 138, 172, 196–97, 210,
  212, 220–27 *passim*, 276

Quezon, Doña Aurora (Mrs. Manuel), 93
Quezon, Manuel L., 2, 3–4, 17–18,
  24–25, 38, 40, 43, 48–50, 54–55,
  58–60, 64, 74–75, 79–82, 84, 85,
  88–89, 111–12, 114–17 *passim*, 120,
  124, 130–31, 163, 191, 193, 258, 260,
  263, 282
Quintard, Alexander, 254

Rabaul, 156
Rainbow-5, Operations Plan, 5, 6, 9, 12
Ray, H. James, 132, 134–35, 137, 144,
  147, 148, 161, 174, 271
Reardon, William B., 234

Reminiscences (MacArthur), 263, 271
Reynolds, Royal, 242
Rockwell, Francis W., 42, 125, 132,
  133–34, 148, 154, 155, 156, 157, 174
Rogers, Paul P., 57, 133, 150, 265
Romulo, Carlos P., 38–39, 58, 116,
  142–44, 190–91, 282
Roosevelt, Franklin D., 4, 18, 23–29
  passim, 31–36 *passim*, 42, 46–50
  passim, 61, 74–85 *passim*, 90, 100–112
  passim, 115, 116, 117, 122-23, 127,
  128, 129, 140, 153, 161–62, 164–68
  passim, 171, 177, 179, 188, 193, 194,
  195, 199, 201, 202, 216–17, 218,
  233-34, 255, 256, 263, 269, 273, 282
Roosevelt, Theodore (son of president),
  87
Roxas, Manuel, 59, 94, 105, 116, 191
Royce, Ralph, 157, 161, 202–3, 204, 205,
  269, 277
Royle, Sir Guy C., 168, 169
Russell, Roy D., 281
Russia, 17, 23, 24, 27, 30, 90, 116

Samoa, 95
San Bernardino, 203
San Bernardino Strait, 26
San Fabian, 32
San Fernando, 45, 51, 56
San José, 39, 227
Sandakan, 134
Santos, José Abad, 48, 49, 59
Sato, Gempachi, 227
Sayre, Francis B., 9, 15, 38, 48, 59, 61,
  76, 88, 98, 99, 102, 107, 114–15, 116,
  120, 125, 235, 263
Scanlon, Martin F., 205
Schumacher, Vincent E., 146–47, 148,
  267
Seals, Carl H., 79
Seawolf, 76, 151
Selleck, Clyde A., 173
Sharp, William F., 6, 37, 138, 150,
  152–53, 154, 191, 218, 224, 225, 226,
  228, 229, 230, 280
Sherr, Joseph R., 133
Sherry, Harry A., 57
Sherwood, Robert E., 254
Shoss, Morris L., 283
Siberia, 96
Signal Hill, 58, 68
Silino Island, 149, 150
Singapore, 17, 20, 21, 23, 24, 26, 27, 30,
  36, 60, 61, 62, 120, 177, 231
South Luzon Force, 6, 25, 38, 43, 45, 51,
  56, 57, 67
Spearfish, 212
Stalin, Joseph, 96

2011 cire

AD	FF	MU
AV	GR	NC
BO	HI	SJ
CL	HO	CN L 12-13-76
DS	LS	

THIS BOOK IS RENEWABLE BY PHONE OR IN PERSON IF THERE IS NO RESERVE
WAITING OR FINE DUE.

LCP #0390